WORLD HISTORY IN BRIEF

WORLD HISTORY IN BRIEF

Major Patterns of Change and Continuity

Volume One: To 1450

SIXTH EDITION

PETER N. STEARNS

George Mason University

PEARSON

Longman

New York   San Francisco   Boston
London   Toronto   Sydney   Tokyo   Singapore   Madrid
Mexico City   Munich   Paris   Cape Town   Hong Kong   Montreal

Senior Acquisitions Editor: Janet Lanphier
Development Editor: Stephanie Ricotta
Executive Marketing Manager: Sue Westmoreland
Production Manager: Eric Jorgensen
Project Coordination, Text Design, and Electronic Page Makeup: Electronic Publishing Services Inc., NYC
Cover Design Manager: Wendy Ann Fredericks
Cover Designer: Maria Ilardi
Cover Art: Detail of Coffin of Djedhoriiufankh © The Trustees of the British Museum
Photo Researcher: Linda Sykes
Senior Manufacturing Buyer: Alfred C. Dorsey
Printer and Binder: Courier-Westford
Cover Printer: Coral Graphic Services

For permission to use copyrighted material, grateful acknowledgment is made to the copyright holders on p. 267, which is hereby made part of this copyright page.

Library of Congress Cataloging-in-Publication Data
Stearns, Peter N.
  World history in brief : major patterns of change and continuity / Peter N. Stearns. — 6th ed.
     p. cm.
  Includes bibliographical references and index.
  ISBN 0-321-48832-6 (v. 1) — ISBN 0-321-48668-4 (v. 2) — ISBN 0-321-48831-8 (SVE version) 1. World history. I. Title.
  D21.3.S77 2006
  909—dc22
                             2006024218

Please visit us at http://www.ablongman.com

ISBN
0-321-48831-8 (Single Volume Edition)
0-321-48832-6 (Volume One)
0-321-48668-4 (Volume Two)

3 4 5 6 7 8 9 10——CRW——09 08 07

Detailed Contents

List of Maps

List of Features

Preface

World history courses are steadily gaining ground at the college level for several reasons. Global issues dominate our newspapers, television screens, and computer monitors daily. Americans must gain a perspective on the dynamics of these issues and understand the diverse societies around the globe that help shape them and our future. History—even history that might seem rather remote—explains how the world became what it is now, including why global influences loom larger than ever before. Global issues are at work even within the United States, because the United States is increasingly a nation of people of different heritages from around the world. Finally, world history raises some classic issues of historical interpretation, allowing its students to sharpen their understanding of how to interpret change and historical causation and providing a rich field for comparative analysis. Some educators still prefer to concentrate on Western civilization, arguing that it lies at our origins and, sometimes, that it is measurably superior. Although Western heritage must be included in any study of world history, it is clear that a purely Western interpretation cannot describe the world as we need to know it.

APPROACH

World History in Brief, now entering its sixth edition, has always had two goals. The first is to present a truly global approach to world history. This is accomplished through the focus on *forces that cut across individual societies,* through a *balanced treatment* of major societies themselves, and through *invitations to comparisons on a global scale.* The second goal is brevity and manageability. It is no secret that many world history texts are large and demand a major commitment from instructors and students. *World History in Brief* offers an alternative. Its length is compatible with a serious treatment of the major issues in world history, but it is concise enough to set aside time for careful analysis and to use with other types of materials beyond the textbook. The purpose here is to allow instructors and students to have some cake while eating it: to have the advantages of a coherent textbook overview, but the opportunity also to spend serious time with documents and with other kinds of historical scholarship.

World history demands a commitment to a *global* rather than a Western-centered approach. *World History in Brief* shows how different civilizations have encountered the various forces of life—for example, population growth, economic changes, and international currents in diplomacy and art—over the centuries. Western civilization is included as one of the major world societies, but east Asian, Indian, Middle-Eastern, east European, African, and Latin American civilizations are all subjects of study in order to achieve a genuine worldwide perspective. World history also demands a balance between the examination of individual societies, within which the lives of most people are played out, and attention to the larger interactions across regional boundaries. These global interactions include trade, cultural contact, migrations, and disease. *World History in Brief* presents the major civilizations through a narrative overview combined with emphasis on regional and global political, cultural, social, and economic characteristics and trends. A grasp of these characteristics, in turn, facilitates comparisons and assessments of change.

World History in Brief is also designed to inspire additional readings and analytical exercises. World history teaching must follow the precedent of other survey history courses in reducing the emphasis on coverage and sheer memorization in favor of materials that provide facts that can be used to build larger understandings. Overwhelming detail, therefore, is not the chief goal of this book. Instead, *World History in Brief* presents enough data to facilitate comparison and assessment of changes and to highlight major developments in the world's history. Students can readily refer to large reference works if they wish to follow up on themes of special interest with greater factual detail. For this purpose, a list of suggested readings and Web sites follows each chapter.

PERIODIZATION

Chronological divisions—the basic periods of world history—reflect successive stages of international contact, from relative isolation to regional integration to the formation of global systems. This periodization is not conveniently tidy for the whole of world history, but it captures the leading dynamics of change at the global level. *World History in Brief* focuses on six major periods. The first involves the early features of human development, particularly the emergence of agriculture and civilization as a form of organization. The second examines the great classical societies from 1000 B.C.E. to 500 C.E. and their relationships with surrounding regions. The third, the postclassical period, from 500 to 1450 C.E., highlights the emergence of new contacts in trade and culture, the spread of world religions, and the development of civilizations in new as well as established centers. The fourth, the early modern period, from 1450 to 1750 C.E., treats the new world role of Europe, but also the diverse and often quite independent developments in many other societies. The fifth period emphasizes the age of European industrialization and imperialism in the "long" 19th century and again the opportunity for varied reactions. The emergence of a new period in world history during the 20th–21st centuries draws the text to a close. In all these periods, major themes are carefully defined, both as a springboard for assessing the interactions of individual societies with more global forces and as a basis for comparison and discussion of change and continuity over time.

THEMES

Using the global focus plus international periodization, students can follow the themes of change and continuity across time and comparative analysis. For example, we can track and compare the juxtaposition of the traditions and novel forces that have shaped the modern world; the response of China or Latin America to the issues of the modern state; or the conditions of women in developing and industrial economies. How different societies respond to common issues and contacts, and how these issues and contacts change over time—this is the framework for examining world history. By focusing on these problems of comparison and assessment of change, the text uses the leading patterns of world history to provide experience in analysis that will apply to other historical studies beyond a survey.

FEATURES

World History in Brief is the most accessible world history text available in the market. Its brevity allows instructors and students flexibility about what additional readings will be included in their study of world history. The text focuses only on substantive topics, so students understand major themes and developments in world history rather than memorizing an array of unconnected facts. The text is organized chronologically by civilizations, allowing for easy and orderly understanding by students. A number of features distinguish *World History in Brief,* and they have been carefully constructed over six editions.

- *History Debates,* included in every chapter, offer students a brief synopsis (usually two paragraphs long) of some topic over which historical debate currently rages. Among the many topics explored are the causes of the abolition of slavery in the European colonies; women in patriarchal societies; the contributions of nomads; the political implications of Islam; how Western is Latin America; and consumerism and industrialization. Students are given an opportunity to see that the discipline of world history is focused on actively debating the past.

- The *World Profiles* provide additional emphasis on the human component of world history through biographies. These profiles explore the history of an individual and how his or her story illuminates aspects of his or her society or a particular cultural interaction.

- The *Understanding Cultures* boxes help students explore specific cultural issues in world history, such as the role of cultures in causing historical changes, the nature of cultural contact, the unique cultural features of particular societies, and the interaction of social and economic forces.

- *Key Questions,* which appear after each chapter's introduction, help students focus on the major issues they will grapple with as they read the chapter.

NEW TO THIS EDITION

- *Part Openers.* A brief Part Opener highlights the major themes of each major period in world history. These are themes most major societies had to grapple with during the period—such as new trading patterns or new technologies—though various societies often reacted in different ways. The Part Openers have been a feature of this book before, but they have been overhauled and emphasized for this edition.

- *Global Connections.* At the end of each Part Opener, this section briefly explores the major types of contact among societies in the period. Understanding the unfolding and impact of the different patterns of contact, over time, is a crucial aspect of world history.

- *Part Retrospectives.* Following the final chapter in each part is a retrospective essay that recaps the dominant cross-civilizational (or cross-regional) contacts and divisions that occurred during the era under examination.

- *Rewritten "Contacts and Identities"* sections at the end of each chronological part highlight the inter-regional contacts occurring during each historical period and the defining issues that helped shape or influence the developing identity of individual civilizations. In this edition, these sections focus more directly on the relative importance of interaction and imitation in shaping societies' identities.

- *Newly revised and expanded Part II* offers increased coverage of the classical period, including new material on Persia.

- New coverage is included in the areas of social history, including *gender history, childhood,* and *consumerism.*

- *Chapter 35,* the last chapter in the text, brings the book up to date on recent developments, including terrorism, and gives much more attention to *globalization,* including resistance to it, and globalization's meaning in the perspective of world history.

- *Paths to the Present* chapter closers briefly suggest how the developments discussed in the chapter help explain our world today. Using the past to understand the present is not the only use of history, but it is a crucial one.

The revisions in this edition also take into account new knowledge about particular societies and periods, which is reflected in revisions to individual chapters. Chapters on the contempo-rary world incorporate recent developments but also the wider perspectives provided by ongoing trends such as globalization.

SUPPLEMENTS

The following supplements are available to qualified college adopters for use in conjunction with *World History in Brief.*

Instructor's Manual and Test Bank Written by Peter N. Stearns, this tool provides guidance in using the textbook and suggestions for structuring the syllabus for a world history course complete with assignment ideas; chapter summaries; multiple-choice, short-answer, and essay questions; and map exercises.

Test Gen-EQ Computerized Testing System This easy-to-customize test-generation software package presents a wealth of multiple-choice, true-false, short-answer, and essay questions. Allows users to add, delete, and print test items.

MyHistoryLab is available for use with *World History in Brief* and includes many features for students and instructors conveniently located online. Numerous documents and maps with gradable assignments, over 50 of the most commonly assigned history texts, an electronic version of the comprehensive textbook, co-authored by Peter Stearns, and much more, are all available to MyHistoryLab users. MyHistoryLab is available with course management—Course Compass, Blackboard, and WebCT—as well as in a non–course management Web site with Grade Tracker. Ask your Longman representative for details.

Discovering World History Through Maps and Views, Updated Second Edition, by Gerald A. Danzer, University of Illinois, Chicago, winner of the American History Association's James Harvey Robinson Award for his work in developing map transparencies. This set of more than 100 four-color transparency acetates is an unparalleled supplement that contains historical reference maps, source maps, views and photos, urban plans, building diagrams, and works of art. Available to qualified college adopters on Longman's Instructor Resource Center (IRC) at www.ablongman.com/irc.

For the Student

Longman-Penguin Putnam Inc. Value Packages Students and professors alike will love the value and quality of the Penguin books offered at a deep discount when bundled with *World History in Brief.*

Longman Atlas of World History Featuring 52 carefully selected historical maps, this atlas provides comprehensive global coverage for the major historical periods, ranging from the earliest of civilizations to the present and including such maps as the Conflict in Afghanistan 2001, Palestine and Israel from Biblical Times to Present, and World Religions. Each map has been designed to be colorful, easy to read, and informative, without sacrificing detail or accuracy.

World History Map Workbook *Volume I (to 1600)* and *Volume II (from 1600),* both prepared by Glee Wilson of Kent State University. Each volume includes more than 40 maps accompanied by more than 120 pages of exercises and is designed to teach the location of various countries and their relationship to one another. Also included are numerous exercises aimed at enhancing students' critical thinking capabilities.

Documents in World History *Volume I (The Great Traditions: From Ancient Times to 1500)* and *Volume II (The Modern Centuries: From 1500 to the Present),* both edited by Peter N. Stearns, Stephen S. Gosch, and Erwin P. Grieshaber. A collection of primary source documents that illustrate the human characteristics of key civilizations during major stages of world history.

Mapping Civilizations: Student Activities This student workbook, compiled by Gerald Danzer, University of Illinois, Chicago, features numerous map skill exercises written to enhance students' basic geographical literacy. The exercises provide ample opportunities for interpreting maps and analyzing cartographic materials as historical documents.

Study Card for World Civilization Colorful, affordable, and packed with useful information, Study Cards make studying easier, more efficient, and more enjoyable. Course information is distilled to the basics, helping students quickly master the fundamentals, review a subject for understanding, or prepare for an exam. Because they are laminated for durability, they will keep for years and can be referred to for quick review.

World History Study Site

www.longmanworldhistory.com
Students can take advantage of this online resource that supports the world history curriculum. The site includes practice tests, Web links,

and flash cards that cover the scope of topics discussed in a typical world history classroom.

Research Navigator and Research Navigator Guide Research Navigator is a comprehensive Web site comprising three exclusive databases of credible and reliable source material for research and for student assignments: (1) EBSCO's ContentSelect Academic Journal Database, (2) the *New York Times* Search by Subject Archive, and (3) "Best of the Web" Link Library. The site also includes an extensive help section. The *Research Navigator Guide* provides students with access to the Research Navigator Web site and includes reference material and hints about conducting online research. Available to qualified college customers when packaged.

ACKNOWLEDGMENTS

Many people helped shape this book. I am grateful to Barry Beyer, Donald Schwartz, William McNeill, Andrew Barnes, Donald Sutton, Erick Langer, Jayashiri Rangan, Paul Adams, Merry Wiesner-Hanks, and Michael Adas, who aided my understanding of world history in various ways. Comments by Steven Gosch and Donald Sutton, and editorial assistance by Clio Stearns, greatly aided in the preparation of this revised edition. Other colleagues who have furthered my education in world history include Ross Dunn, Judith Zinsser, Richard Bulliet, Jerry Bentley, and Stuart Schwartz. I also thank the various readers of earlier drafts of this manuscript, whose comments and encouragement improved the end result: Jay P. Anglin; Richard D. Lewis; Kirk Willis; Arden Bucholz; Richard Gere; Robert Roeder; Stephen Englehart; Marc Gilbert; John Voll; Erwin Grieshaber; Yong-ho Choe; V. Dixon Morris; Elton L. Daniel; Thomas Knapp; Edward Homze; Albert Mann; J. Malcom Thompson; Peter Freeman; Patrick Smith; David McComb; Charles Evans; Jerry Bentley; John Powell; B. B. Wellmon; Penelope Ann Adair; Linda Alkana; Samuel Brunk; Alexander S. Dawson; Lydia Garner; Surendra Gupta; Craig Hendricks; Susan Hult; Christina Michelmore; Lynn Moore; Joseph Norton; Elsa Nystrom; Diane Pearson; Louis Roper; Thomas O'Toole; John D. Boswell; Connie Brand; Robert Cassanello; John K. Hayden; Ben Lowe; Kenneth Wilburn; Dennis A. Frey Jr.; Matthew Maher; Kenneth J. Orosz; Warren Rosenblum; Brian Williams; and Robert H. Welborn. J. Michael Farmer's assistance has been invaluable.

My gratitude extends also to Janet Lanphier and Alicia Smallbrock, whose editorial assistance has been vital. Sincere thanks to Debbie Williams for help with the manuscript. I have been taught and stimulated as well by my students in world history courses at George Mason University. And thanks, finally, to my family, who have put up with my excited babble about distant places for some time now.

PETER N. STEARNS

WORLD HISTORY IN BRIEF

PART I

Early World History: From Origins to Agriculture and New Forms of Human Organization

INTRODUCTION: BEGINNING WORLD HISTORY

World historians are discussing when the effective history of the human experience began. A strong impulse has emerged to push treatment earlier, to take fuller account of the origins and evolution of the human species and the many migrations that brought humans from their starting point, in East Africa, to almost every habitable part of the world by about 27,000 years ago.

This very early history is fascinating and important. Scientific work has steadily expanded what we know about early humans. Discoveries multiply about previously unknown species that served as intermediaries between apes and early semi-humans, or about the startling amount of genetic material humans share with species such as chimpanzees. There's every reason to explore these diverse and complex beginnings.

At the same time, however, it's important to keep sight of main points. Without slighting far more detailed inquiry, or the possibilities of lifetimes of fruitful new research, the long early

In 1940 in Lascaux, France, four boys playing together discovered a long-hidden cave filled with thousands of complex and beautiful Stone Age paintings like this one. Most of the paintings are of animals, some of which were extinct by the time they were painted. No one knows for sure why Stone Age artists painted these pictures, but they remain a powerful reminder of the sophistication of so-called primitive peoples.

stages of the human journey highlight three points, which are covered in Chapter 1. First, evolution gradually improved human capacities—adding, for example, unprecedented facility in speech—yet with the arrival of the current species the evolutionary process halted at least for a time. There have been no fundamental changes in the species for about 120,000 years. Second, humans were tool-using animals and gradually improved their abilities, moving from picking up potential tools to shaping them deliberately. And third, humans were often on the move. Their hunting and gathering economy dictated recurrent migration in search of additional space. The wide dispersion of people was a fundamental feature of early history and a precondition of much that would follow.

After early history comes the first great transformation of the human economy, from hunting and gathering to agriculture or herding. This transformation, one of the great systems changes in the human experience, added to the framework for world history. This change is covered in Chapter 1 also.

Fundamental transformation is easy to say, but it is also abstract. Childhood provides a concrete example. In hunting and gathering societies, children were important but they could not be handled in large numbers. Families could not support many children, who were not very useful; and trying to travel with many young children during migrations to new hunting spots was impractical. But with agriculture, children gained new utility—they could do useful work, and indeed provided families with a vital labor force. So their number increased greatly, and human groups began approaching childhood in terms of labor expectations. This was one reason agricultural people normally placed such emphasis on obedience, to try to shape children into useful workers. Another huge transformation for all concerned.

Many agricultural societies ultimately created new organizational forms that we call civilizations. This subsequent change and the four specific centers of the earliest civilizations are discussed in Chapter 2. Chapter 3 turns to peoples who made a different transition, to nomadic herding, avoiding both agriculture and civilization. These peoples too played a vital role in world history for many centuries.

Chapters in this section thus deal with crucial building blocks of the human experience: evolution and migration; tool use that ultimately helped lead to agriculture and the domestication of animals; and new organizational forms for many human societies. The stretch of time involved is massive, but primarily emphasizes changes that took shape between 10,000 and 4000 years ago. The result was a set of practices and institutions that have not required reinvention in human history since that point.

GLOBAL CONNECTIONS

One of the key points of the early human experience involves the separateness that could come from dispersion. As people fanned out in search of space—each hunter-gatherer required an average of 2.5 square miles to operate, so even small population bumps could create big pressures—they normally lost contact with their points of origin.

Two obvious examples of this, late in the dispersion process, involve Australia and the Americas. People reached Australia about 60,000 years ago. At this point, because of the ice age, the Indian Ocean was smaller than it now is, so land extended south from Asia; the distance across water was not too great. But then the waters expanded, and the people who had reached Australia were cut off from further contacts. Only 300 years ago were new forms of contact developed, to the great disadvantage of the native Australians who simply lacked the experience, including disease immunities, to beneficially handle the new interactions.

On the other end of the planet, people reached the Americas about 25,000 years ago, crossing what was then a land bridge from northeast Asia to Alaska. Several surges of migration may have occurred before the land bridge was flooded and the process halted. It would be many millennia before peoples in the Americas had any

contact, or at least meaningful contact, with other humans in other regions.

These are two dramatic examples, but even migrants to Asia or Europe or other parts of Africa might easily lose connection with their relatives and ancestors. The emergence of different physical characteristics was a sign of this process. So was the welter of separate languages that emerged—more than 6000 at a high point (the number is smaller today). To be sure, basic language groups were far less numerous—many separate tongues sprang from common cores such as the Semitic or Indo-European or Bantu stems. Still, the process of diffusion and separation was both illustrated and encouraged when groups of people, even in the same linguistic family, lost the capacity to talk with each other in case of encounter.

Yet too much emphasis on separation misses the mark, even in these very early parts of the human experience, because connections of several sorts developed as well.

Migration and invasion, for example, proved to be recurrent processes. The Middle East, the

Prehistoric art in Los Toldos, Argentina, includes representations of deer and hands. Archeologists have dated the art to around 15,000 B.C.E.

cradle of civilization, was frequently overrun by new peoples, often coming in from central Asia. Egypt, though invaded less often, saw attacks from the Middle East and from farther south in Africa. These processes mixed peoples. Stone tablets have been found in the Middle East with inscriptions both in the local language and in ancient Egyptian, showing the need and ability to translate. Egyptian pictures show people from Africa along with Semitic peoples from the Middle East—as well as local Egyptians.

Mixing of this sort also brought knowledge of new technologies. Several of the technological changes vital to extend agriculture, such as knowledge of the wheel, came into the Middle East from peoples migrating or attacking from central Asia.

Beyond outright invasion, contacts also developed by a vaguer process often called diffusion, in which people in one region learned from their neighbors. Occasional travelers or traders might also bring new ideas. Thus we will see that agriculture, though separately invented in several places, gradually spread through diffusion. It took centuries for knowledge of this new system to reach southern Europe from the Middle East, for contacts were doubtless limited and there was outright resistance to change. But same diffusion process occurred, bringing knowledge of how to work metals and introducing foodstuffs from one region to another, where they might be adopted as basic crops.

And, of course, there was trade. We know that earlier agricultural communities often traded with nearby hunting and gathering groups, if only to provide symbolic exchanges that helped keep the peace. By the time of the early civilizations there was a certain amount of interregional trade—linking, for example, parts of the Middle East to northwestern India.

Separateness, in sum, was not an absolute. A few peoples truly became isolated, at least from population centers in other parts of the world. Contacts were sporadic for many groups. But the advantages of exchanges, in terms of trade and new knowledge, made contact an important part of the early human experience. And advantage or not, the force of migration and invasion made interaction inescapable for many of the world's peoples, at least recurrently.

SUGGESTED READINGS

Important explorations of world history that provide greater detail or a somewhat different vantage point from this study include: W. McNeill, *Rise of the West: A History of the Human Community* (1970) and *A History of the Human Community* (1996); J. M. Roberts, *The Pelican History of the World* (1984); Peter N. Stearns, Michael Adas, and Stuart B. Schwartz, *World Civilizations: The Global Experience* (2003); Richard Bulliet et al., *The Earth and Its Peoples* (1997); Jerry Bentley, *Traditions and Encounters: A Global Perspective on the Past* (2000). Also useful for background on the geographic distribution of the world's people is Gerald Danzer, *Atlas of World History* (2000); see also Peter N. Stearns, *Childhood in World History* (2005).

1 From Human Prehistory to the Rise of Agriculture

GETTING STARTED IS ALWAYS HARD

The human species has accomplished a great deal in a relatively short period of time. There are significant disagreements over how long an essentially human species, as distinct from other primates, has existed. However, a figure of about 2.5 million years seems acceptable. This is approximately 1/4000 of the time the earth has existed. If one thinks of the whole history of the earth to date as a 24-hour day, the human species began at about five minutes until midnight. Human beings have existed for less than 5 percent of the time mammals of any sort have lived. Yet in this brief span of time—by earth-history standards—humankind has spread to every landmass (with the exception of the polar regions) and, for better or worse, has taken control of the destinies of countless other species.

To be sure, human beings have some drawbacks as a species, compared to other existing models. They are unusually aggressive against their own kind: while some of the great apes, notably chimpanzees, engage in periodic wars, these conflicts can hardly rival human violence. Human babies are dependent for a long period, which requires some special family or child-care arrangements and often has limited the activities of many adult women. Certain ailments, such as back problems resulting from an upright stature, also burden the species. And, insofar as we know, the human species is alone in its awareness of the inevitability of death—a knowledge that imparts some unique fears and tensions.

Distinctive features of the human species account for considerable achievement as well. Like other primates, but unlike most other mammals, people can manipulate objects fairly readily because of the grip provided by an opposable thumb on each hand. Compared to other primates, human beings have a relatively high and regular sexual drive, which aids reproduction; being omnivores, they are not dependent exclusively on plants or animals for food, which helps explain why they can live in so many different climates and settings; the unusual variety of their facial expressions aids communication and enhances social life. The distinctive human brain and a facility for elaborate speech are even more important: much of human history depends on the knowledge, inventions, and social contracts that resulted from these assets. Features of this sort explain why many human cultures, including the Western culture that many Americans share, promote a firm separation between human and animal, seeing in our own species a power and rationality, and possibly a spark of the divine, that "lower" creatures lack.

Although the rise of humankind has been impressively rapid, its early stages can also be viewed as painfully long and slow. Most of the 2 million plus years during which our species has existed are described by the term *Paleolithic*, or *Old Stone Age*. Throughout this long time span, which runs until about 14,000 years ago, human beings learned only simple tool use, mainly through employing suitably shaped rocks and sticks for hunting and warfare. Fire was tamed about 750,000 years ago. The nature of the species also gradually changed during the Paleolithic, with emphasis on more erect stature and growing brain capacity. Archeological evidence also indicates some increases in average size. A less apelike species, whose larger brain and erect stance allowed better tool use, emerged between 500,000 and 750,000 years ago; it is called, appropriately enough, *Homo erectus*. Several species of *Homo erectus* developed and spread in Africa, then to Asia and Europe, reaching a population size of perhaps 1.5 million 100,000 years ago.

Considerable evidence suggests that more advanced types of humans killed off or displaced many competitors over time. Intermarrying also occurred. And even *Homo sapiens sapiens* coexisted with other human species in several regions for considerable periods, as recent archeological and genetic evidence suggests. Ultimately, however, the single species predominated throughout the world, rather than a number of rather similar human species, as among monkeys and apes. The newest human breed, *Homo sapiens sapiens,* of which all humans in the world today are descendants, originated about 120,000 years ago, also in Africa. The success of this subspecies means that there have been no major changes in the basic human physique or brain size since its advent.

Part of human evolution in this decisive later phase involved a probably modest genetic modification in the brain that allowed much more elaborate patterns of speech. A number of animals and birds have some power of speech, in terms of varied sounds that communicate. But with the advent of this "language gene," people became capable of a much wider variety of sounds. From this, it was possible to invent languages. Scientists have wondered what the first people who had this gene must have thought, surrounded by other people who were still confined to a series of grunts plus elaborate facial expressions.

■ KEY QUESTIONS   *What were the most significant human achievements before the rise of agriculture? How did agriculture change human life?*

HUMAN DEVELOPMENT AND CHANGE

Even after the appearance of *Homo sapiens sapiens,* human life faced important constraints. People who hunted food and gathered nuts and berries could not support large numbers or elaborate societies. Most hunting groups were small, and they had to roam widely for food. Two people required at least one square mile for survival. Population growth was slow, partly because women breast-fed infants for several years to limit their own fertility. On the other hand, people did not have to work very hard—hunting took about seven hours every three days on average. Women, who gathered fruits and vegetables, worked harder, but there was significant equality between the sexes based on common economic contributions.

TIMELINE Prehistoric Landmarks

Beginnings	Paleolithic Age	Mesolithic Age	Neolithic Age	Bronze Age
About 4 million years ago Beginnings of separation between humanlike apes (hominids) and other apes.	**About 2–2.5 million years ago** More humanlike species, larger brain size; initially in eastern Africa.	**12,000–8000 B.C.E.** Great improvements in stone tools; use of bone; development of more ships; domestication of some animals.	**8000–5000 B.C.E.** Further improvements in tool making; first development of agriculture; great expansion in human population.	**4000 B.C.E.** Early use of bronze and copper tools.
	750,000–1 million years ago Further development of the species into *Homo erectus*, a tool-using human; upright stance, close to modern human brain size. Growth of infant brain and head size, leading to more complicated child care; more division of labor between males as hunters and females as seed gatherers, child caretakers.	**10,000 B.C.E.** End of ice age.		**3500 B.C.E.** First civilization, in Middle East; end of "prehistoric" ages of humankind.
	600,000–700,000 years ago Spread of species, although in small numbers, across Asia, Europe, and Africa; signs of fire use (in China); improved human hunting abilities; more big game, diet less vegetarian.			**1500 B.C.E.** Early use of iron tools and weapons.
	200,000 years ago Development of Neanderthal species across Europe and Asia; burial rituals and monuments, suggesting knowledge of death.			
	250,000–100,000 years ago Arrival of *Homo sapiens sapiens;* displacement of Neanderthals and other species across Asia and Europe from initial center in Africa.			
	25,000 B.C.E. Passage of people to the Americas, via land link from Asia.			
	20,000 B.C.E. Deepest ice age.			

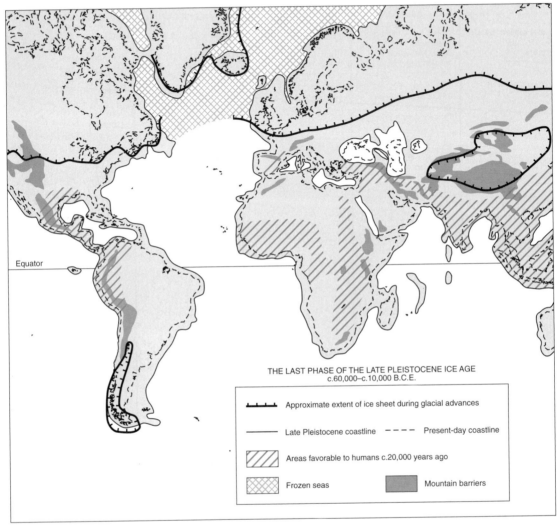

THE LAST PHASE OF THE LATE PLEISTOCENE ICE AGE
c.60,000–c.10,000 B.C.E.

- ▲▲▲ Approximate extent of ice sheet during glacial advances
- —— Late Pleistocene coastline   - - - - Present-day coastline
- ▨ Areas favorable to humans c.20,000 years ago
- ▧ Frozen seas   ▨ Mountain barriers

Equator

Human Development

Paleolithic people gradually improved their tool use, beginning with the crude shaping of stone and wooden implements. The development of speech allowed more group cooperation and the transmission of technical knowledge. By the later Paleolithic period, people had developed rituals to lessen the fear of death and created cave paintings to express a sense of nature's beauty and power. Goddesses often played a prominent role in the religious pantheon. Thus, the human species came to develop cultures—that is, systems of belief that helped explain the environment and set up rules for various kinds of social behavior. The development of speech provided rich language and symbols for the transmission of culture and its growing sophistication. At the same time, different groups of humans, in different locations, developed quite varied belief systems and corresponding languages.

The greatest achievement of Paleolithic people was the sheer spread of the human species over much of the earth's surface. The species originated in eastern Africa; most of the earliest types of human remains come from this region, in the present-day countries of Tanzania, Kenya, and Uganda. But gradual migration, doubtless caused by the need to find scarce food, steadily pushed the human reach to other areas. Key discoveries, notably fire and the use of animal skins for clothing—both of which enabled people to live in colder climates—facilitated the spread of Paleolithic groups. The first people moved out of Africa about 750,000 years ago. Human remains (Peking man, Java man) have been found in China and southeast Asia dating from 600,000 and 350,000 years ago, respectively. Humans inhabited Britain 250,000 years ago. They first crossed to Australia 60,000 years ago, followed by another group 20,000 years later; these combined to form the continent's aboriginal population. Dates of the migration from Asia to the Americas are under debate. Most scholars believe that humans crossed what was then a land bridge from Siberia to Alaska about 25,000 years ago and quickly began to spread out, reaching the tip of the South American continent possibly within a mere thousand years. Settlers from China reached Taiwan, the Philippines, and Indonesia 4500 to 3500 years ago.

In addition, soon after this time—roughly 14,000 years ago—the last great ice age ended, which did wonders for living conditions over much of the Northern Hemisphere. Human development began to accelerate. A new term, *Mesolithic,* or *Middle Stone Age,* designates a span of several thousand years, from about 12,000 to 8000 B.C.E.,* in which human ability to fashion

*In Christian societies, historical dating divides between years "before the birth of Christ" (B.C.) and after (A.D., *anno Domini,* or "year of our Lord"). This system came into wide acceptance in Europe in the 18th century as formal historical consciousness increased (although ironically, 1 A.D. is a few years late for Jesus' actual birth). China, Islam, Judaism, and many other societies use different dating systems, referring to their own history. This text, like many recent world history materials, uses the Christian chronology (one has to choose some system) but changes the terms to B.C.E. ("before the common era") and C.E. ("of the common era") as a gesture to less Christian-centric labeling.

stone tools and other implements improved greatly. People learned to sharpen and shape stone, to make better weapons and cutting edges. Animal bones were used to make needles and other precise tools. From the Mesolithic also date the increased numbers of log rafts and dugouts, which improved fishing, and the manufacture of pots and baskets for food storage. Mesolithic people domesticated more animals, such as cows, which again improved food supply. Population growth accelerated, which also resulted in more conflicts and wars. Skeletons from this period show frequent bone breaks and skull fractures caused by weapons.

In time, better tool use, somewhat more elaborate social organization, and still more

Stone tools.

HISTORY DEBATE

PEOPLE IN THE AMERICAS

As early as the 17th century, a Catholic scholar suggested that American Indians had come from Asia. But it was only in the late 19th century that speculation about where the Indians had come from turned into scientific inquiry. Then, using carbon dating techniques from Indian cities and artifacts, it was generally agreed that immigrants from Siberia poured across the land bridge that then connected to Alaska around 12,000–15,000 years ago. They moved very fast, reaching South America within a few hundred years. Archeological finds seemed to support this view. So did the belief that people would not have moved in this fashion, in the far north, before the end of the ice age.

More recently, new techniques—including better carbon dating but, above all, genetic analysis—have called this long-established view into question. Among other things, we realize that it would be very unlikely for migrants to develop such sophisticated settlements in South America so quickly. Now it is widely agreed that migrations began about 25,000 years ago. The migrants knew how to make boats, which allowed them to move down the Pacific Coast, bypassing ice-age glaciers. (Boats, after all, had allowed humans to reach Australia even before this.) There is still debate over the best scientific techniques to use, and over whether there was one migration or several. Some authors, though now a declining number, also long defended the older migration model. Is a debate of this sort significant? How does it affect judgments about human experience and capacity before the rise of agriculture?

---

population pressure led people in many parts of the world to the final Stone Age—the *Neolithic,* or *New Stone Age.* And from Neolithic people, in turn, came several more dramatic developments that changed the nature of human existence—the invention of agriculture, the creation of cities, and other foreshadowings of civilization, which ended the Stone Age altogether throughout much of the world.

THE NEOLITHIC REVOLUTION

Human achievements during the various ages of stone are both fascinating and fundamental, and some points are hotly debated. Our knowledge of Stone Age society is of course limited, although archeologists have been creative in their interpre-

tations of tool remains and other evidence, such as cave paintings and burial sites, that Stone Age people produced in various parts of the world. What people accomplished during this long period of prehistory remains essential to human life today; our ability to make and manipulate tools thus depends directly on what our Stone Age ancestors learned about physical matter.

However, it was the invention of agriculture that most clearly moved the human species toward more elaborate social and cultural patterns that people today would recognize. With agriculture, human beings were able to settle in one spot and focus on particular economic, political, and religious goals and activities. Agriculture also spawned a great increase in the sheer number of people in the world—from about 6 to 8 million across the earth's surface during early Neolithic times, to about 100 million some 3000 years later.

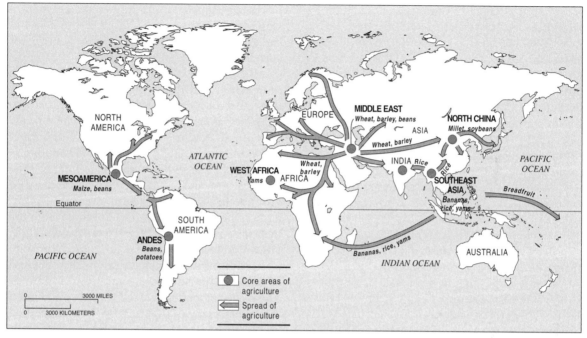

The Spread of Agriculture

The initial development of agriculture—that is, the deliberate planting of grains for later harvest—was probably triggered by two results of the ice age's end. First, population increases, stemming from improved climate, prompted people to search for new and more reliable sources of food. Second, the end of the ice age saw the retreat of certain big game animals, such as mastodons. Human hunters had to turn to smaller game, such as deer and wild boar, in many forested areas. Hunting's overall yield declined. Here was the basis for new interest in other sources of food. There is evidence that by 9000 B.C.E., in certain parts of the world, people were becoming increasingly dependent on regular harvests of wild grains, berries, and nuts. This undoubtedly set the stage for the deliberate planting of seeds (probably accidental to begin with) and the improvement of key grains through the selection of seeds from the best plants.

As farming evolved, new animals were also domesticated. Particularly in the Middle East and parts of Asia, by 9000 B.C.E. pigs, sheep, goats, and cattle were being raised. Farmers used these animals for meat and skins and soon discovered dairying as well. These results not only contributed to the development of agriculture; they also served as the basis for nomadic herding societies.

Farming was initially developed in the Middle East, in an arc of territory running from present-day Turkey to Iraq and Israel. This was a very fertile area, more fertile in those days than at present. Grains such as barley and wild wheat were abundant. At the same time, this area was not heavily forested, and animals were in short supply, presenting a challenge to hunters. In the Middle East, the development of agriculture may have begun as early as 10,000 B.C.E., and it gained ground rapidly after 8000 B.C.E. Gradually during the Neolithic centuries, knowledge of agriculture spread to other centers, including parts of India, North Africa, and Europe. Agriculture, including rice cultivation, soon developed independently in China. Thus, within a few thousand years agriculture had spread to the parts of the world that produced the first human civilizations. We will see that agriculture spread later to much of Africa south of the Mediterranean coast, reaching west Africa by 2000 B.C.E., although here too there were additional developments with an emphasis on local grains and also root crops such as yams. Agriculture had to be invented separately in the Americas, based on corn cultivation, where it was also a slightly later development (about 5000 B.C.E.).

Many scholars have termed the development of agriculture a "Neolithic revolution." The term is obviously misleading in one sense: agriculture was no sudden transformation, even in the Middle East, where the new system had its roots. Learning the new agricultural methods was difficult, and many peoples long combined a bit of agriculture with considerable reliance on the older systems of hunting and gathering. A "revolution" that took more than a thousand years, and then several thousand more to spread to key population centers in Asia, Europe, and Africa, is hardly dramatic by modern standards.

The concept of revolution is, however, appropriate in demonstrating the magnitude of change involved. Early agriculture could support far more people per square mile than hunting ever could; it also allowed people to settle more permanently in one area. The system was nonetheless not easy. Agriculture required more regular work, at least of men, than hunting did. Hunting-and-gathering groups today, such as the Kung or Khoisan peoples of the Kalihari Desert in southwest Africa, work an average of 2.5 hours a day, alternating long, intense hunts with periods devoted to such pursuits as music, dance, and decorative art. Settled agriculture concentrated populations and encouraged the spread of disease. As much as agriculture was demanding, it was also rewarding: agriculture supported larger populations, and with

better food supplies and a more settled existence, agricultural peoples could afford to build houses and villages. Animals provided not only hides but also wool for more varied clothing.

We know next to nothing of the debates that must have raged when people were first confronted with agriculture, but it is not hard to imagine that many would have found the new life too complicated, too difficult, or too unexciting. Most evidence suggests that gathering and hunting peoples resisted agriculture as long as they could. Gradually, of course, agriculture did gain ground. Its success was hard to deny. And as farmers cleared new land from forests, they automatically drove out or converted many hunters. Disease played a role: settled agricultural societies suffered from more contagious diseases because of denser population concentrations. Hunting-and-gathering peoples lacked resistance and often died when agriculturists who had developed immunity to these diseases carried them into their areas.

Not all the peoples of the world came to embrace the slowly spreading wave of agriculture, at least not until very recently. Important small societies in southern Africa, Australia, the islands of southeast Asia, and even northern Japan were isolated for so long that news of this economic system simply did not reach them. The white-skinned hunting tribes of northern Japan disappeared only about a hundred years ago. Northern Europeans and southern Africans converted to agriculture earlier, about 2000 years ago, but well after the Neolithic revolution had transformed other parts of their continents. Agriculture was initiated in the Americas as early as 5000 B.C.E. and developed vigorously in Central America and the northern part of South America. However, most Indian tribes in North America continued hunting-and-gathering existence, sometimes combined with limited agriculture, until recent centuries. Finally, the peoples of the vast plains of central Asia long resisted a complete conversion to agriculture, in part because of a harsh climate; herding, rather than grain growing, became the basic socioeconomic system of this part of the world. From this area came waves of tough, nomadic invaders and migrants whose role in linking major civilizations was a vital force in world history until a few centuries ago.

Development possibilities among people who became agriculturists were more obvious than those among smaller populations who resisted or simply did not know of the system: agriculture set the basis for more rapid change in human societies. Greater wealth and larger populations freed some people for other specializations, from which new ideas or techniques might spring. Agriculture itself depended on control over nature that could be facilitated by newly developed techniques and objects. For example, during the Neolithic period itself, the needs of farming people for storage facilities, for grains and seeds, promoted the development of basket-making and pottery. The first potter's wheel came into existence around 6000 B.C.E., and this, in turn, encouraged faster and higher-quality pottery production. Agricultural needs also encouraged certain kinds of science, supporting the human inclination to learn more about weather or flooding.

THE NATURE OF AGRICULTURAL SOCIETIES

Much of what we think of as human history involves the doings of agricultural societies—societies, that is, in which most people are farmers and in which the production of food is the central economic activity. Nonagricultural groups, such as the nomadic herders in central Asia, made their own mark, but their greatest influence usually occurred in interactions with agricultural peoples. Many societies remain largely agricultural today. The huge time span we have thus far considered, including the Neolithic revolution itself, is all technically "prehistorical"—involved with human patterns before the invention of writing allowed the kinds of recordkeeping historians prefer. In

fact, because we now know how to use surviving tools and burial sites as records, the prehistoric–historic distinction means less than it once did. The preagricultural–agricultural distinction is more central. Fairly soon after the development of agriculture—although not, admittedly, right away—significant human change began to occur in decades and centuries, rather than in the sizable blocks of time, several thousand years or more, that describe preagricultural peoples.

From their origins until about 200 years ago, and in some cases more recently, agricultural societies had a number of features in common. They varied, of course, depending on what kinds of crops they grew and a host of other factors. But it is vital to consider the shared characteristics.

All agricultural societies, for example, invented some kind of week. This is the only division of time that is entirely human-constructed, with no relationship to phenomena in nature. Agricultural weeks varied, from four days to nine, and this is a big difference. But all agricultural societies had something that marked an interruption in normal work. Usually, this interruption had or developed religious significance, seen as a special day of prayer or observance. Even more often, weeks were ended (or begun) by market days, and this need to exchange certain goods, even in villages where families produced most of their own requirements, may help explain why weeks were invented. It is also true that agricultural work was hard, so some interruption may have been essential in order to motivate people to resume their work when the next week began.

In agricultural societies, not surprisingly, most people farmed, at least part of the time. Agricultural societies often produced some surplus, but never enough to allow more than 20–25 percent of the population to specialize in something other than agriculture, or to live away from the land (in cities). Often, the agricultural percentage of the population was even higher. Agricultural societies also always developed certain rituals around planting and harvesting, often

UNDERSTANDING CULTURES

THE NATURE OF CULTURE

All human societies develop cultures—that is, patterns of beliefs, values, and assumptions that help them explain the world around them, define mutual obligations, and serve as a shared identity. Humans are not the only species that have cultures; several primates and a few bird species do. But human culture is unusually elaborate and important. With the power of speech, *Homo sapiens sapiens* had opportunities to construct more culture than other species. Also, spreading to very diverse environments, humans were able to use culture as part of basic adaptation. Compared with many other species, humans had fewer pure instincts but had more learned or partially learned behavior. This helped them cope. It also helps explain why it takes so long to train a human into what we regard as full adulthood.

Cultures provoke two kinds of discussion. First, and most fundamental, is discussion over how much of human behavior is explained by culture, how much by innate characteristics. This distinction is often called nature versus nurture. Cultural analysts note what a wide variety of ideas and practices can develop even around seemingly basic natural phenomena—such as whether urine is disgusting or useful, or how

to regard homosexuality. The nature versus nurture discussions are still valid, even for scholars not terribly interested in human history per se, because they condition how people react to diversities (are they innate or human caused) and how they seek to change behaviors that they find damaging—by education, for example, or by genetic manipulation.

A second culture discussion involves the two edges of diversity itself. Human societies generated very pronounced and different cultures. These different characteristics or strategies helped members of a society cope with their particular circumstances, but these differences could also greatly complicate relationships with other cultural groups. They could provide identity, and also a wondrous array of possibilities, and they could cause conflict or complicate the resolution of conflict. Different cultures can disagree fiercely over how children should be raised, or how to understand disease, or whether tolerance is a good quality or a dangerous distraction from the truth. Some cultural variance is simply interesting, but some can generate misunderstandings and clashes. We live with this dilemma of culture today, with a vengeance.

including special festivals. Here too, religion usually picked up some of the tasks of seeking a good season or giving thanks when the harvest was in, though there was great variety among the religions that arose among agricultural peoples. Agricultural societies always emphasized certain kinds of science and mathematics, in order for example to calculate seasons and permit the development of calendars. Sometimes, science became far more elaborate than this, but agricultural needs always figured in intellectual life.

Agricultural societies always emphasized the superiority of men over women, in what is called

the patriarchal system. The exact form and extent of male and fatherly power varied, but it was always there. Some historians have argued that, because agriculture encouraged the emergence of ideas of property, men tended to think of women as part of the property package. Trying to control women's sexual activity, so a father could be sure that his children were his, and so feel comfortable in passing on his land to them, may have been part of the arrangement as well. Certainly, patriarchal societies place a high premium on women's sexual faithfulness. Agricultural societies also encouraged higher birth rates than hunting-and-gathering societies had done, because a number of children were useful as labor on the land. This meant that more of women's time was taken up with bearing and caring for young children, which reduced their ability to match men's economic activities. Growing the staple grain crop was almost always seen as a male activity, which meant that men were more important economically.

Agriculture brought many disadvantages to many people involved, including greater liability to disease and an increase in human inequality. But it did allow societies to support a larger number of people than hunting and gathering had done, because the food supply became more reliable despite frequent bad harvests and famines. Before agriculture, and for many thousands of years, the global human population had fluctuated between 5 and 8 million. By 4000 B.C.E. the global population stood at 60 to 70 million. And this proved to be only the beginning.

AGRICULTURE AND CHANGE

Agriculture encouraged the formation of larger as well as more stable human communities than had existed before Neolithic times. A few Mesolithic groups had formed villages, particularly where opportunities for fishing were good, as around some of the lakes in Switzerland. However, most hunting peoples moved in relatively small groups, or tribes, each containing anywhere from 40 to 60 individuals, and they could not settle in a single spot without the game running out. With agriculture, these constraints changed. To be sure, some agricultural peoples did move around. A system called *slash and burn* agriculture existed in a few parts of the world, including portions of the American South, until about 150 years ago. Here, people burned off trees in an area, farmed intensively for a few years until the soil was depleted, and then moved on. Herding peoples also moved in tribal bands, with strong kinship ties. But most agricultural peoples did not have new lands close

by to which they could move after a short time. And there were advantages to staying put: houses could be built to last, wells built to bring up water, and other "expensive" improvements afforded because they served many generations. In the Middle East, China, and parts of Africa and India, a key incentive to stability was the need for irrigation devices to channel river water to the fields. This same need helps explain why agriculture generated communities and not a series of isolated farms. Small groups simply could not regulate a river's flow or build and maintain irrigation ditches and sluices. Irrigation and defense encouraged villages—groupings of several hundred people—as the characteristic pattern of residence in almost all agricultural societies from Neolithic days until our own century.

One Neolithic village, Çatal Hüyük in southern Turkey, has been elaborately studied by archeologists. It was founded about 7000 B.C.E. and was unusually large, covering about 32 acres. Houses were made of mud bricks set in timber frameworks, crowded together, with few windows. People seem to have spent a good bit of time on their rooftops in order to experience daylight and make social contacts—many broken bones attest to frequent falls. Some houses were lavishly decorated, mainly with hunting scenes. Religious images, both of powerful male hunters and "mother goddesses" devoted to agricultural fertility, were common, and some people in the village seem to have had special religious responsibilities. The village produced almost all the goods it consumed. Some trade was conducted with hunting peoples who lived in the hills surrounding the village, but apparently it was initiated more to keep the peace than to produce economic gain. By 5500 B.C.E., important production activities developed in the village, including those of skilled toolmakers and jewelers. With time also came links with other communities. Large villages such as Çatal Hüyük ruled over smaller communities. This meant that some families began to specialize in politics, and military forces were organized. Some villages became small cities, ruled by kings who were typically given divine status. Here were developments that led to bigger changes in the organization of some agricultural societies.

The discovery of metal tools dates back to about 4000 B.C.E. Copper was the first metal with which people learned how to work, although the more resilient metal, bronze, soon entered the picture. In fact, the next basic age of human existence was the Bronze Age. By about 3000 B.C.E., metalworking had become so commonplace in the Middle East that the use of stone tools dissipated, and the long stone ages were over at last—although, of course, an essentially Neolithic technology persisted in many parts of the world, even among some agricultural peoples.

Metalworking was extremely useful to agricultural or herding societies. Metal hoes and other tools allowed farmers to work the ground more efficiently. Metal weapons were obviously superior to those made from stone and wood. Agricultural peoples now supported the small number of individuals such as toolmakers, who specialized in this activity and exchanged their products with farmers for food. Specialization of this sort did not, however, guarantee rapid rates of invention; indeed, many specialized artisans seemed very conservative, eager to preserve methods that had been inherited. But specialization did improve the conditions or climate for discovery, and the invention of metalworking was a key result. Like agriculture, knowledge of metals gradually fanned out to other parts of Asia and to Africa and Europe.

Gradually, the knowledge of metal tools created further change, for not only farmers but also manufacturing artisans benefited from better tools. Woodworking, for example, became steadily more elaborate as metal replaced stone, bone, and fire in the cutting and connecting of wood. We are, of course, still living in the metal ages today, although we rely primarily on iron—whose working was introduced around 1500 B.C.E. by herding peoples who invaded the Middle East—rather than copper and bronze.

By about 4000 B.C.E., other changes began to accumulate in several agricultural centers, particularly in the Middle East. These changes depended on the extent to which agricultural production could free up a few people to specialize in craft manufacturing, initially on products used in the agriculture process, such as the manufacture of pots. Gradually, certain other inventions cropped up that could benefit agricultural production, while also spilling over into other human activities such as warfare. Around 4000 B.C.E., for example, the wheel was introduced, probably by peoples who migrated into the Middle East. Here was a vital contribution

Houses in early agricultural settlements, such as this one reconstructed at Skara Brae, usually included special storage areas for grain, water, and other essentials. Most were centered on clay or stone hearths that were ventilated by a hole in the roof or built into the walls. There were also clearly demarcated and slightly raised sleeping areas, and benches along the walls. More dependable and varied food supplies and sturdy houses greatly enhanced the security and comfort of human groups. These conditions spurred higher birth rates and lowered mortality rates, at least in times when crop yields were high.

to the movement of goods and, soon, to certain kinds of fighting.

PATHS
TO THE PRESENT

By definition, the initial human experiences were in many ways remote from what we do and how we live today. They do, however, illustrate human capacities that we see around us—including adaptability to many different situations and geographies. A basic feature of today's world—that people exist in virtually every place that can support human life—occurred quite early. To be sure, the number of people was miniscule by contemporary standards, but humans had moved to all the inhabitable continents and most of the island groups where we find people today.

Agriculture's arrival is more obviously relevant to how we live now. Just recently, in the early 21st century, the majority of humans began to live in cities, rather than the countryside, for the first time. But many agricultural societies still exist, societies in which characteristics that emerged several millennia ago still apply.

Even in societies no longer dominated by agriculture, such as our own, questions derived from agriculture have not disappeared. We know, in industrial society, that the patriarchal gender relations generated by agriculture need to be rethought. But no society has yet fully resolved the question of what new gender model should replace patriarchy; traces of the older system, and groups committed to its values, still exist almost everywhere.

Early human activities and changes thus established key aspects of the framework in which global societies still function—including wide geographic distribution and the capacity to increase food supply through agriculture. They also set up issues that have survived a long time as well, because of the force and durability of agricultural forms. As world society debates gender rights or even appropriate roles for children, it must take this agricultural legacy into account.

SUGGESTED WEB SITES

For more information on the Stone Age, see www.stoneageinstitute.org/; on archeology, see www.ucl.ac.uk/archaeology/; on the Field Museum, see www.fieldmuseum.org/.

SUGGESTED READINGS

David Christen's *Maps of Time: An Introduction to Big History* (Berkeley, 2005) provides insight into perspectives on early human history and on; another rich account of human prehistory is Brian Fagan's *Peoples of the Earth* (1998 ed.). See also John Mears, *Agricultural Origins in Global Perspective* (2000); Donald R. Kelley, "The Rise of Prehistory," *Journal of World History* (2003); www.historycooperative.org/jounals/jwh/14.1/kelley.html (2006); Raymond Corbey and Wil Roebrocks, eds., *Studying Human Origins: Disciplinary History and Epistemology* (2001); Joy Hakim, *The First Americas* (1999); David Tandy, ed., *Prehistory and History: Ethnicity, Class and Political Economy* (2001); Chris Gosden, *Prehistory: A Very Short Introduction* (2003); John F. Hoffecker, *A Prehistory of the North* [electronic resource]: *Human Settlement of the Higher Latitude* (2005); Steven Mithen, *After the Ice: A Global Human History, 20,000–5000 B.C.* (2004); and Barbara Sher Tinsley, *Reconstructing Western Civilization: Irreverent Essays on Antiquity* (2006).

On specific regions, see Douglas Price, *Europe's First Farmers* (2000); Ian Kuijt, *Life in Neolithic Farming Communities* (2000); P. D. Hunt, *Indian Agriculture in America* (1985); James Mellaart, *The Neolithic of the Near East* (1975); Chris Scarre, ed., *Monuments and Landscape in Atlantic Europe* (2002). Jared Diamond's *Guns, Germs and Steel: The Fate of Human Societies* (1997) deals powerfully with agriculture. On debates over human nature (culture and genetics), see Matt Ridley's *Nature Via Nurture* (2003). For a splendid guide to world history, from beginnings on, see Patrick Manning's *Navigating World History* (2003).

2

Early Civilization

By 3000 B.C.E., Çatal Hüyük, the agricultural city discussed in Chapter 1, had become part of a civilization. Although many of the characteristics of civilization had existed by 6000 or 5000 B.C.E. in this Middle Eastern region, the origins of civilization, strictly speaking, approximately date to only 3500 B.C.E. The first civilization arose in the Middle East along the banks of the Tigris and Euphrates rivers. Another center of civilization started soon thereafter in northeast Africa (Egypt), and a third by around 2500 B.C.E. along the banks of the Indus River in northwestern India. These three early centers of civilization had some interaction. The fourth early civilization center arose in China, although a bit later and considerably more separate.

■ KEY QUESTIONS *What did the river valley civilizations have in common? What were the main differences among them?*

CIVILIZATION

After the rise of agriculture, the introduction of civilization as a form of human organization was a crucial step for many people. Civilization first developed in Mesopotamia, after about 3500 B.C.E., on the heels of several changes in technology and communication. The form was copied in several other places, and separately developed in China and Central America. Human organization along civilization lines did not emerge everywhere at the same time, and many regions—even some successful agricultural economies—avoided it altogether, at least until much more recently. Hunting and gathering and nomadic societies lacked the economic surplus necessary to develop civilization, and often actively disliked the constraints they saw in civilization as well.

TIMELINE River Valley Civilizations (All dates B.C.E., or Before the Common Era)

Mesopotamia	Coast Cultures	Egypt	Indus River	Huanghe
3500–2600 Sumerian kingdom, development of cuneiform writing. **2600–2420** Akkadian invasions and empire. **2050–1750** Kingdom of Babylon. **2000** Writing of the *Gilgamesh*, world's first-known heroic epic. **1700** Hammurabi and his code. **1500** Spread of use of iron.		**3200–2780** Unification of regional kingdoms under one pharaoh. **2100–1788** Expansion to Sudan, Palestine.	**3000–1300** Indus River cities.	**2000? ff.** Xia dynasty, heroic myths of golden age. **1500–1000** Shang dynasty, use of iron.
1200–900 Particularly intense invasions. **933–605** Assyrian Empire.	**1400–774** Rise of Phoenician cities, colonies **1300** Alphabet. **1225–1200** Moses: spread of Jewish tribes in Israel. **1150–130** Writing of books of Old Testament. **933–722** Kingdom of Israel.	**1090 ff.** Decline of pharaohs, loss of territory. **800** Kushites rule Egypt.	**1300 ff.** Aryan (Indo-European) migration and invasions.	**1100–1000** Zhou dynasty begins.

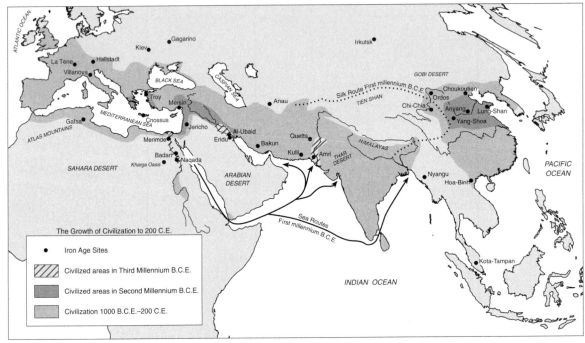

The Growth of Civilization to 200 C.E.

- Iron Age Sites
- Civilized areas in Third Millennium B.C.E.
- Civilized areas in Second Millennium B.C.E.
- Civilization 1000 B.C.E.–200 C.E.

Afro-Eurasia: The Growth of Civilization to 200 C.E.

Civilizations normally demonstrated four distinctive features, operating powerfully in combination. First, they developed greater amounts of economic surplus, beyond subsistence needs, and they distributed this surplus unequally. This provided funds for new kinds of monuments. It also heightened social inequalities, compared to other, "non-civilized" kinds of societies. Second, civilizations developed formal governments, with at least small bureaucracies. Leadership thus became more specialized than in simpler agricultural or nomadic societies. Third, almost all civilizations, including all the early ones, had writing. This facilitated trade over long distances, by facilitating standardized communication; it enhanced recordkeeping, which aided both commerce and bureaucracy. And fourth, while civilizations did not invent cities, they developed larger and more important urban centers.

In agricultural civilizations, most people lived in the countryside, and most people remained illiterate. But cities and writing were nonetheless influential in shaping societies with different characteristics from those of the earliest agricultural settlements.

There are problems with the definition of civilization. Some scholars prefer to use a smaller number of criteria, which would allow other societies—those that had surpluses and some formal leadership, for example, but not cities and writing—to be included as civilizations.

More serious is the common connotation of civilization as being more refined and restrained. Leaders of early civilizations often argued that their way of life was more cultivated than that of non-civilized peoples—barbarians—around them. But people in civilizations could be cruel and rude. To groups such as American Indians, their behavior—including drinking, violence to children, and the like—seemed far cruder than that of non-civilized peoples, whose habits and capacities for emotional control were often quite refined. Civilization as meaning greater impulse control should not be included in the definition of civilization as a form of human organization. The two meanings might, but also might very well not, overlap.

Civilizations also increased human impact on the environment. For example, the first center of copper production in Europe, along the Danube valley, led to such deforestation that the fuel supply was destroyed, and the industry collapsed after about 3000 B.C.E. The extensive agriculture needed to support Indus river cities opened the land to erosion and flooding because of overuse of the soil and removal of trees.

Having started in 3500 B.C.E., civilization developed in its four initial centers—the Middle East, Egypt, northwestern India, and northern China—over the following 2500 years. These areas covered only a tiny portion of the inhabited parts of the world, although they were the most densely populated. Such early civilizations, all clustered in key river valleys, were in a way pilot tests of the new form of social organization. Only after about 1000 B.C.E. did a more consistent process of development and spread of civilization begin—and with it came the main threads of world history. However, the great civilizations unquestionably built on the achievements of the river valley pioneers, so some understanding of this contribution to the list of early human accomplishments is essential.

Tigris-Euphrates Civilization

The most noteworthy achievements of the earliest civilizations were early versions of organizational and cultural forms that most of us now take for granted—writing itself, formal codes of law, city planning and architecture, and institutions for trade, including the use of money. Once developed, most of these building blocks of human organization did not have to be reinvented, although in some cases they spread only slowly to other parts of the world.

It is not surprising then, given its lead in agriculture, metalworking, and village structure, that the Middle East generated the first example of human civilization. Indeed, the first civilization, founded in the valley of the Tigris and Euphrates rivers in a part of the Middle East long called Mesopotamia, forms one of only a few cases of a civilization developed absolutely from scratch—and with no examples from any place else to imitate. (Chinese civilization and civilization in Central America also developed independently.) By 4000 B.C.E., the farmers of Mesopotamia were familiar with bronze and copper and had already invented the wheel for transportation. They had a well-established pottery industry and interesting artistic forms. Farming in this area, because of the need for irrigation, required considerable coordination among communities, and this in turn served as the basis for complex political structures.

By about 3500 B.C.E., a people who had recently invaded this region, the Sumerians, developed a cuneiform alphabet, the first known case of human writing. Their alphabet at first used different pictures to represent various objects but soon shifted to the use of geometric shapes to symbolize spoken sounds. The early Sumerian alphabet may have had as many as 2000 such symbols, but this number was later reduced to about 300. Even so, writing and reading remained complex skills, which only a few had time to master. Scribes wrote on clay tablets, using styluses shaped quite like the modern ballpoint pen.

Sumerian art developed steadily, as statues and painted frescoes were used to adorn the temples of the gods. Statues of the gods also decorated individual homes. Sumerian science aided a complex agricultural society, as people sought to learn more about the movement of the sun and stars—thus founding the science of astronomy—and improved their mathematical knowledge. (Astronomy defined the calendar and provided the astrological forecasts widely used in politics and religion.) The Sumerians employed a system of numbers based on units of 10, 60, and 360 that we still use in calculating circles and hours. In other words, Sumerians and their successors in Mesopotamia created patterns of observation and

Oracle bone.

Cuneiform and Chinese lettering. *Left*: Cuneiform tablet from the Middle East. *Right*: A Shang dynasty oracle bone with ideographs.

abstract thought about nature that a number of civilizations, including our own, still rely on, and they also introduced specific systems, such as charts of major constellations, that have been current at least among educated people for 5000 years, not only in the Middle East but, by later imitation, in India and Europe as well.

Sumerians developed complex religious rituals. Each city had a patron god and erected impressive shrines to please and honor this and other deities. Massive towers, called ziggurats, formed the first monumental architecture in this civilization. Professional priests operated these temples and conducted the rituals within. Sumerians believed in many powerful gods, for the nature on which their agriculture depended often seemed swift and unpredictable. Prayers and offerings to prevent floods as well as to protect good health were a vital part of Sumerian life. Sumerian ideas about the divine force in natural objects—in rivers, trees, and mountains—were common among early agricultural peoples; a religion of this sort, which sees gods in many aspects of nature, is known as *polytheism*. More specifically, Sumerian religious notions, notably their ideas about the gods' creation of the earth from water and about the divine punishment of humans through floods,

later influenced the writers of the Old Testament and thus continue to play a role in Jewish, Christian, and Muslim cultures. Sumerian religious ideas also included a belief in an afterlife of punishment—an original version of the concept of hell.

Sumerian political structures stressed tightly organized city-states, ruled by a king who claimed divine authority. The Sumerian state had carefully defined boundaries, unlike the less formal territories of precivilized villages in the region. Here is a key early example of how civilization and a more formal political structure came together. The government helped regulate religion and enforce its duties; it also provided a court system in the interests of justice. Kings were originally military leaders during times of war, and the function of defense and war, including leadership of a trained army, remained vital in Sumerian politics. Kings and the noble class, along with the priesthood, controlled considerable land, which was worked by slaves. Thus began a tradition of slavery that long marked Middle Eastern societies. Warfare remained vital to ensure supplies of slaves taken as prisoners during combat. At the same time, slavery was a variable state of existence, and many slaves were able to earn money and even buy their freedom.

Mesopotamian civilization developed a strongly patriarchal family structure. By 3000, only men were pictured as wielding a plow in Middle-Eastern art. Laws insisted that women remain sexually faithful, but they granted greater latitude to men. Women had a few legal protections, at least in principle: husbands were supposed to support their wives, and wives could legitimately leave if this support failed. Outside the law, customs developed, particularly in the cities, that further marked off women. By 2000 B.C.E., veiling of respectable women became common, in order to shield them from the eyes of men outside their family.

The Sumerians added to their region's agricultural prosperity not only by using wheeled carts but also by learning about fertilizers and by adopting silver as a means of exchange for buying and selling—an early form of money. However, the region was also hard to defend and proved a constant temptation to outside invaders from Sumerian times to the present. The Sumerians themselves fell to a people called the Akkadians, around 2400 B.C.E. The Akkadians continued much of Sumerian culture. It was an Akkadian king, Sargon, who is the first identifiable figure in world history, in terms of surviving records. He unified the empire and added to Sumerian art the theme of royal victory. Sargon maintained 5400 troops, a larger professional army than had existed before. Akkadians sent troops as far as Egypt and Ethiopia.

After about 200 years, another period of decline was followed by conquest by the Babylonians, who extended their own empire and thus helped bring civilization to other parts of the Middle East. It was under Babylonian rule that the king Hammurabi introduced the most famous early code of law, boasting of his purpose:

> to promote the welfare of the people, me Hammurabi, the devout, god-fearing prince, to cause justice to prevail in the land, to destroy the wicked and the evil, that the strong might not oppress the weak.

Bronze head of Sargon.

Hammurabi's code established rules of procedure for courts of law and regulated property rights and the duties of family members, setting harsh punishments for crimes.

For many centuries during and after the heyday of Babylon, peace and civilization in the Middle East were troubled by the invasions of hunting and herding groups. Indo-European

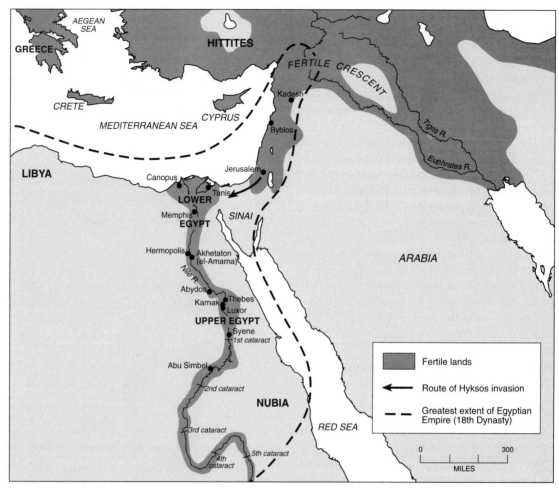

Ancient Egypt and Mesopotamia

peoples pressed in from the north, starting about 2100 B.C.E. In the Middle East itself, invasions by Semitic peoples from the south were more important, and Semitic peoples and languages increasingly dominated the region. The new arrivals adopted the culture of the conquered peoples as their own, so the key features of the civilization persisted. But large political units declined in favor of smaller city-states or regional kingdoms, particularly during the centuries of greatest turmoil, between 1200 and 900 B.C.E. Thereafter, new invaders, first the Assyrians and

then the Persians, created large new empires in the Middle East.

Egyptian Civilization

A second center of civilization sprang up in northern Africa, along the Nile River. Egyptian civilization, formed by 3000 B.C.E., benefited from the trade and technological influence of Mesopotamia, but it produced a quite different society and culture. Less open to invasion, Egypt retained a unified state throughout most of its history. With some fluctuations, the kingdom lasted almost 3000 years,

The sphinx of Giza.

though its greatest vitality had passed by 1000 B.C.E. Farming had developed along the Nile by about 5000 B.C.E., but economic activity increased before 3200, in part because of greater trade with Mesopotamia. This acceleration provided the basis for the formation of regional kingdoms and soon a unified empire along the great river.

Because of its early unity and its cohesion along the banks of the Nile, Egypt had fewer problems with political unity than Mesopotamia did. The king, or pharaoh, possessed immense power. The Egyptian economy was more fully government-directed than its Mesopotamian counterpart, which had a more independent business class. Government control may have been necessary because of the complexity of coordinating irrigation along the Nile. It nonetheless resulted in godlike status for the pharaohs, who built splendid tombs for themselves—the pyramids—from

2700 B.C.E. on. During periods of weak rule and occasional invasions, Egyptian society suffered a decline, but revivals kept the framework of Egyptian civilization intact until after 1000 B.C.E. At key points, Egyptian influence spread up the Nile to the area now known as the Sudan, with an impact on the later development of African culture. The kingdom of Kush interacted with Egypt and invaded it at some points.

Neither Egyptian science nor the Egyptian alphabet was as elaborate as its Mesopotamian equal, although mathematics was more advanced in this civilization. Egyptian art was exceptionally lively; cheerful and colorful pictures decorated not only the tombs—where the belief in an afterlife made people want to be surrounded by objects of beauty—but also palaces and furnishings. Egyptian architectural forms were also quite influential, not only in Egypt but in other parts of the Mediterranean as well. Egyptian mathematics produced the idea of a day divided into 24 hours, and here too Egypt influenced the development of later Mediterranean cultures.

The most famous Egyptian art form was of course the pyramid, which the pharaohs built to house themselves and their families after death. The largest pyramids required labor forces of up to 100,000 people, and they were amazing achievements given the state of Egyptian technology. Workers rolled the huge stones, weighing more than 5 tons, over logs and onto Nile barges. The pyramids attested to royal power. They also illustrated Egypt's ability to generate agricultural surpluses and to command a labor force.

Egypt interacted periodically with the Middle East, but the contacts were not terribly influential in either direction. Egypt's interactions with the upper reaches of the Nile, deeper into Africa, were more significant. After about 1570 B.C.E., in the final main phase of the great kingdoms, Egypt also expanded trade with the islands of the eastern Mediterranean, which extended the empire's influence to southern Europe, particularly in terms of monumental art but also in the area of mathematics.

EGYPT AND MESOPOTAMIA COMPARED

Comparisons in politics, culture, economics, and society suggest that the two civilizations varied substantially because of largely separate origins and environments. The distinction in overall tone was striking, with Egypt more stable and optimistic than Mesopotamia not only in its beliefs about gods and the afterlife but also in the colorful and lively pictures the Egyptians emphasized in their decorative art. The distinction in internal history was also striking: Egyptian civilization was far less marked by disruption than its Mesopotamian counterpart.

Egypt and Mesopotamia differed in many ways thanks to variations in geography, exposure to outside invasion and influence, and different beliefs. Despite trade and war, they did not imitate each other much. Egypt emphasized strong central authority, whereas Mesopotamian politics shifted more often over a substructure of regional city-states. Mesopotamian art focused on less monumental structures and embraced a literary element that Egyptian art lacked. Mesopotamians did not share the Egyptian concern for preparations for the afterlife, which motivated the great tombs and pyramids through which ancient Egypt and some of the pharaohs live on in human memory.

The economies differed as well. Mesopotamia generated more technological improvements because the environment was more difficult to manage than the Nile valley. Trade contacts were more wide-ranging, and the Mesopotamians gave considerable attention to a merchant class and commercial law.

Social differences between the two civilizations are less obvious because we have less information on daily life for this early period. It is probable, though, that the status of women was higher in Egypt than in Mesopotamia (where women's position seems to have deteriorated after Sumer). Egyptians paid great respect to women, at least in the upper classes, in part because marriage

Relief from the temple of Aten at Tel el-Amarna.

alliances were vital to the preservation and stability of the monarchy. Vivid love poetry indicated a high regard for emotional relations between men and women. Also, Egyptian religion included more pronounced deference to goddesses as sources of creativity. Egyptians did not practice female infanticide—the killing of baby girls—which most societies used for population control.

Differences were not the whole story, for as river valley civilizations, Egypt and Mesopotamia shared important features. Both emphasized social stratification, with a noble, landowning class on top and masses of peasants and slaves at the bottom. A powerful priestly group also figured in the elite. Although specific achievements in science differed, both civilizations emphasized astronomy and related mathematics and produced durable findings about units of time and measurement. Both Mesopotamia and Egypt changed slowly by more modern standards. Having developed successful political and economic systems, both societies tended strongly toward conservation. Change, when it came, usually was brought by outside forces (natural disasters or invasions).

Finally, both civilizations left important heritages in their regions and adjacent territories. Several smaller civilization centers were launched under the impetus of Mesopotamia and Egypt, and some produced important innovations of their own by about 1000 B.C.E.

INDIAN AND CHINESE RIVER VALLEY CIVILIZATIONS

River valley civilizations developed in two other centers. A prosperous urban civilization emerged along the Indus River by 2500 B.C.E., supporting several large cities, including Harappa, whose houses even had running water. Toilets, in fact, connected to citywide drainage systems, were perhaps the first that humans ever invented. Indus River peoples had trading contacts with Mesopotamia, but they developed their own distinctive alphabet and artistic forms. The large cities, including Harappa itself, contained buildings that were probably palaces, with audience rooms for people to appeal to the rulers for assistance. Public baths were also available. Governments stored grain for times of shortage and for festival days. Trade was extensive, and precious stones from China and southeast Asia have been found. Priests had great power in this civilization, servings as intermediaries between the people and the gods and goddesses who were believed to control fertility.

For all their achievements, the Harappan people seem to have become somewhat conservative.

Though they used bronze, they did not keep up with the tools available in Mesopotamia, though they had contact with this area. Notably, they did not manufacture swords, relying on bronze-tipped arrows instead. They became vulnerable to attack.

Harappa remains something of a mystery. Its ruins began to be discovered only in the mid-19th century, when it began to become clear that this had been a major center of ancient civilization but also rather unlike what later developed in India, for example in terms of the styles of writing. We also do not fully know what caused the civilization to decline after about 1500 B.C.E. The decline was gradual and probably resulted from several factors, including massive flooding. Invasions and, even more, migrations by a cattle-herding people,

Statuette of a mother goddess from Harappa, Indus River.

WOMEN IN PATRIARCHAL SOCIETIES

Most agricultural civilizations downgraded the status and potential of women, compared to the standards of hunting-and-gathering societies. Agricultural civilizations generally were *patriarchal;* that is, they were run by men and based on the assumption that men directed political, economic, and cultural life. Furthermore, as agricultural civilizations developed and became more prosperous and more elaborately organized, the status of women often deteriorated.

Individual families normally were patriarchal. The husband and father made the key decisions, and the wife gave humble obedience to this male authority. Patriarchal family structure rested on men's control of most or all property, starting with land. Marriage was based on property relationships, and it was assumed that marriage, and therefore subordination to men, was the normal condition for women. A revealing symptom of patriarchy in families was the fact that after marrying, a woman usually moved to the orbit (and often the residence) of her husband's family.

Characteristic patriarchal conditions developed in Mesopotamian civilization. Marriages were arranged for women by their parents, and a formal contract was drawn up. Early Sumerians may have given women greater latitude than they enjoyed later on: their religion attributed considerable power to female sexuality, and their law gave women important rights so that they could not be treated as outright property. Still, in Sumerian law, the adultery of a wife was punishable by death, whereas a husband's adultery was treated far more lightly—a double standard characteristic of patriarchalism. Mesopotamian societies after Sumerian times began to emphasize the importance of a woman's virginity at marriage and to require women to wear veils in public to emphasize their modesty. A good portion of Mesopotamian law (such as the Hammurabic code) was devoted to prescriptions for women, ensuring certain basic protections but clearly emphasizing limits and inferiority.

Patriarchal conditions varied from one agricultural civilization to another. Egyptian civilization gave women, at least in the upper classes, considerable credit and witnessed several powerful queens. Nefertiti, wife of Akhenaton, seems to have been influential in the religious disputes in this reign; artistic works suggest her religious role. Some agricultural societies traced descendants from mothers rather than from fathers. This was true of Jewish law, for example. But even these matrilineal societies held women to be inferior to men; for example, Jewish law insisted that men and women worship separately, with men occupying the central temple space. These variations are important, but they usually operated within a basic framework of patriarchalism. Egyptian art thus routinely conveyed women's supplementary role. It was around 2000 B.C.E. that an Egyptian writer, Ptah Hotep, put patriarchal beliefs as clearly as anyone in the early civilizations: "If you are a man of note, found for yourself a household, and love your wife at home, as it beseems. Fill her belly, clothe her back. . . . But hold her back from getting the mastery."

Why was patriarchalism so pervasive? As agriculture improved with the use of better techniques, women's labor, though still vital, became less important than it had been in hunting-and-gathering or early agricultural societies. This was particularly true in the upper classes and in cities, where men often took over the most productive work (craft production or political leadership, for example). The inferior position of women in the upper classes, relative to men, usually was more marked than in peasant villages, where women's labor remained essential. The higher birth rates of agricultural societies also deeply affected women's role, as did the emphasis on property rights and inheritance (see Chapter 1).

Patriarchalism raises important questions about women themselves: Why did they put up with it? Many women internalized the culture of patriarchalism, holding that it was their job to obey and to serve men and accepting arguments that their aptitudes were inferior to those of men. But patriarchalism did not preclude some important options for women. In many societies, a minority of women could gain expression through religious tasks, such as prayer or service in ceremonies. These could allow them to act independently of family structures. Patriarchal laws defined some rights for women even within marriage, protecting them in theory from the worst abuses. Babylonian law, for example, gave women as well as men the right to divorce under certain conditions when the spouse had not lived up to obligations. Women could also wield informal power in patriarchal societies by their emotional hold over husbands or sons. Such power was indirect, behind the scenes, but a forceful woman might use these means to figure prominently in a society's history. Women also could form networks, if only within a large household. Older women, who commanded the obedience of many daughters-in-law and unmarried daughters, could shape the activities of the family.

Patriarchalism was a commanding theme in most agricultural civilizations from the early centuries on. Its enforcement, through law and culture, was one means by which societies tried to achieve order. In many agricultural civilizations, patriarchalism dictated that boys, because of their importance in carrying on the family name and the chief economic activities, were more likely to survive: when population excess threatened a family or a community, female infants sometimes were killed as a means of population control.

the Indo-Europeans, probably challenged the control of the priestly group. Some violence was probably involved, and skeletons with crushed skulls and in postures of flight, either from invaders or from floods, have been found. The Harappan decline resulted in such complete destruction of this culture that we know little about its nature or its subsequent influence on India. Harappan writing, for example, has yet to be deciphered. It remains true that civilization never had to be fully reinvented in India. The Indo-European migrants combined their religious and political ideas with those that had taken root in the early cities. In recent times, Indians' pride in their early civilized history has become an important part of their national identity.

Civilization along the Huanghe (Yellow River) in China developed in considerable isolation, although some overland trading contact with India and the Middle East did develop. Huanghe civilization was the subject of much later Chinese legend, which praised the godlike kings of early civilization, starting with the

mythic ancestor of the Chinese, Pan Gu. The Chinese had an unusually elaborate concept of their remote origins, and they began early to record a part-fact, part-fiction history of their early kings. What is clear is the following: first, a well-organized state developed that carefully regulated irrigation in the fertile but flood-prone river valley. Early kings sponsored a considerable network of dikes and canals. Second, by about 2000 B.C.E., the Chinese had produced an advanced technology and developed an elaborate intellectual life. They had learned how to ride horses and were skilled in pottery; they used bronze well and by 1000 B.C.E. had introduced iron, which they soon learned to work with coal. Their writing progressed from knotted ropes to scratches of lines on bone to the invention of ideographic symbols. By 1500 B.C.E., at least 3000 pictographic characters had been devised. This standardized writing began to provide some unity to the very diverse peoples assembled in this river valley kingdom, who originally spoke a wide array of languages. Science, particularly

Early Chinese art. An elaborate clay vase, imitating bronze, from the Shang dynasty.

astronomy, also arose early. Chinese art emphasized delicate designs, and the Chinese claim an early interest in music. Because of limits on building materials in the region, the Chinese did not construct many massive monuments, choosing to live in simple houses built of mud. By about 1500 B.C.E., a line of kings called the Shang ruled over the Huanghe valley, and these rulers did construct some impressive tombs and palaces. Invasions disrupted the Shang dynasty and caused a temporary decline in civilization. However, there was less of a break between the river valley society and the later, fuller development of civilization in China than occurred in other centers.

River valley civilization in China generated a number of features of importance for later periods. Silk manufacturing developed. Some form of ancestor worship began. Emphasis on a strong, expansionist state, particularly under the Shang, set the basis for later Chinese politics. The Shang fought on horseback and from chariots, using conquered peoples as foot soldiers. They maintained fuller control over their armies than was characteristic of many other early societies. Shang rulers also directed important rituals, devoted to fertility. In times of famine or drought, the state provided dancers to woo the gods with their performance, and the dancers were later buried alive to calm the spirits who had caused the natural disaster. The state, in other words, took on cultural responsibilities, and this too characterized the Chinese political tradition.

TRANSITIONS: THE END OF THE RIVER VALLEY PERIOD

The river valley societies were widely separated, though they had trading contacts with their neighbors and, in the case of the Middle East and north Africa, an occasional military encounter. With this separation, it is not surprising that there was no single development, or even a single century, to signal the transition away from the river valley period. Several developments did, however, roughly coincide.

In China, the control of the Shang had loosened, and then a central Asian people, the Zhou, probably of Turkic origin, began to migrate into Shang territory. They initially recognized Shang rule but then seized power themselves, by about 1100 B.C.E. The Zhou set up a strong government based on feudalism. The rulers used Zhou kinsmen to rule particular regions, granting them land and insisting on elaborate oaths of mutual loyalty. The vassals passed on some of the local tax revenues to the central government. This system worked effectively for a while. It bore heavily on the peasants, who were taxed extensively. Ulti-

UNDERSTANDING CULTURES

USES AND VARIETIES

A society's culture involves its basic beliefs and values, and the styles it uses to express these values. All societies, whether civilizations or not, have cultures. Cultures profoundly shape the way people behave. For example, a recent study showed that when a French person becomes jealous, he or she gets angry. In a similar situation, a Dutch person grows sad, whereas the typical American consults with others to determine if he or she seems to be acting strangely. All responses involve the same emotion, but different cultures inspire vastly different reactions. Another recent study showed that Americans and Jamaicans try hard to conceal jealousy, whereas the Chinese feel that jealousy can be usefully expressed.

Cultures obviously vary from one place to the next. Sometimes, they respond to different geographical environments. Always, they reflect different past traditions, although we do not always fully understand why the traditions differed initially. Sumerian culture, for example, was much gloomier than Egyptian, with more of a focus on punishments after death and on the tragic potential of human life. Egyptians were more optimistic, their art more colorful and cheerful. Was this because the Nile River provided more predictable prosperity? Did Egypt's orderly government and freedom from frequent invasion encourage more orderly thinking, or was it the other way around? Whatever the case, Sumerian pessimism ultimately had greater influence. It was the story of a Sumerian flood that ultimately entered the Jewish Bible as a sign of divine punishment. Cultural differences can have surprisingly durable results.

mately, the political system broke down. But it was under the Zhou that improvements in agriculture, extensive cultural changes, and the sheer expansion of Chinese territory began to mark a new stage in Chinese history. Important ties to the river valley period remained, but changes were accumulating.

The end of the river valley period in northwestern India was of course far more decisive, given the gradual but conclusive decline of Harappan society. Migrating and invading Indo-European peoples even ignored agriculture for many centuries, relying on animal herding. The Indo-Europeans were more warlike than the Harappans, with far less emphasis on orderly government. They brought in different ideas about gods and goddesses, though some emphasis on the power of goddesses may have been borrowed from Harappan religion. The Indo-Europeans also fanned out over a wider area of India than the Harappans had controlled. Gradually, they

began to settle down, adopting agriculture and expanding trade. But in the process, most traces of Harappan civilization became a dim memory. A few symbols remained, including the mother goddess and yoga positions. So did certain artistic images, including a swastika that became prominent in later Indian religious art. Public bathing facilities, another Harappan legacy, persisted in some Indian cities, particularly in the south. Agricultural techniques, including the growing of cotton, were not abandoned, and the Indo-Europeans ultimately took them over. But with the passing of Harappa, a decisive new period in Indian history clearly began.

A different set of developments took place in the Middle East and north Africa. In Egypt, we have seen that the power of the pharaohs began to weaken by around 1000 B.C.E. Invasions, including from other African peoples in the south, became more common. At times, the kingdom was divided in half. After 500 B.C.E.

Persian, then Greek, then Roman invasions effectively brought an end to Egypt's independence.

In the Middle East, the pattern of outside invasion and formation of empires continued to 1000 B.C.E. and even beyond. As before, the new empires tended to adopt Mesopotamian culture and legal forms. Around 1100 invasions by an Assyrian ruler were marked by unusual cruelty, including mass execution and the deporting of civilian populations. But the Assyrians did not maintain consistent control, though parts of their empire revived periodically. This inconsistency, and the decline of Egypt, allowed the formation of a number of smaller states for several centuries around 1000 B.C.E.

THE HERITAGE OF THE RIVER VALLEY CIVILIZATIONS

Many accomplishments of the river valley civilizations had a lasting impact. Monuments such as the Egyptian pyramids have long been regarded as one of the wonders of the world. Other achievements, although more prosaic, are fundamental to world history even today: the invention of the wheel, the taming of the horse, the creation of usable alphabets and writing implements, the production of key mathematical concepts such as square roots, the development of well-organized monarchies and bureaucracies, and the invention of functional calendars and other divisions of time. These basic achievements, along with the awe that the early civilizations continue to inspire, are vital legacies to the whole of human history. Almost all the major alphabets in the world today are derived from the writing forms pioneered in the river valleys, apart from the even more durable concept of writing itself. Almost all later civilizations, then, built on the massive foundations first constructed in the river valleys.

Despite these accomplishments, we have seen that most of the river valley civilizations were in decline by 1000 B.C.E. The civilizations had flourished for as many as 2500 years, although of course with periodic disruptions and revivals.

But, particularly in India, the new waves of invasion did produce something of a break in the history of civilization, a dividing line between the river valley pioneers and later cultures.

This break raises one final question: besides the vital achievements—the fascinating monuments and the indispensable advances in technology, science, and art—what legacies did the river valley civilizations impart for later ages? The question is particularly important for the Middle East and Egypt. In India, we must frankly admit much ignorance about possible links between Indus River accomplishments and what came later; in China, there is a definite connection between the first civilization and subsequent forms. Indeed, the new dynasty in China, the Zhou, took over from the Shang about 1100 B.C.E., ruling a loose coalition of regional lords; recorded Chinese history flowed smoothly at this point. But what was the legacy of Mesopotamia and Egypt for later civilizations in or near their centers?

Europeans, even North Americans, are sometimes prone to claim these cultures as the "origins" of the Western civilization in which we live. These claims should not be taken too literally. It is not altogether clear that either Egypt or Mesopotamia contributed much to later political traditions, although the Roman Empire emulated the concept of a godlike king, as evidenced in the trappings of the office, and the existence of strong city-state governments in the Middle East continued to be significant. Ideas about slavery may also have been passed on from these early civilizations. Specific scientific achievements are vital, but scholars argue over how much of a connection exists between Mesopotamian and Egyptian science and later Greek thinking, aside from certain techniques of measuring time or charting the stars. Some historians of philosophy have asserted a basic division between a Mesopotamian and Chinese understanding of nature, which they claim affected later civilizations around the Mediterranean in contrast to China. Mesopotamians were prone to stress a gap between humankind and nature, whereas Chinese thinking developed along ideas of basic harmony. It is possible, then, that some fundamental thinking helped shape later outlooks, but the continuities here are not easy to assess. Mesopotamian art and Egyptian architecture had a more measurable influence on Greek styles, and through these, in turn, later European and Islamic cultures. The Greeks thus learned much about temple building from the Egyptians, whose culture had influenced island civilizations, such as Crete, which then affected later Greek styles.

NEW STATES AND PEOPLES AROUND 1000 B.C.E.

There was a final connection between early and later civilizations in the form of regional cultures that sprang up under the influence of Mesopotamia and Egypt, along the eastern shores of the Mediterranean and in northeastern Africa mainly after 1200 B.C.E. Although the great empires from Sumer through Babylon were disrupted and the Egyptian state finally declined, civilization in the Middle East and north Africa had spread widely enough to encourage a set of smaller cultures capable of surviving and even flourishing after the great empires became weak. These cultures produced important innovations that affected later civilizations in the Middle East and throughout the Mediterranean. They also created a diverse array of regional identities that continued to mark the Middle East even as other forces, such as the Roman Empire or the later religion of Islam, took center stage. Several of these small cultures proved immensely durable, and in their complexity and capacity to survive, they influenced other parts of the world as well.

Kingdoms began to develop south of Egypt, for example. A kingdom in Kush emerged about 2000 B.C.E., under strong Egyptian influence. Egypt conquered the area after 1500, setting up an elaborate bureaucracy and building large temples. At this point the population of Kush was about 100,000. Trade with southern Arabia expanded. In the 8th century, Kushites conquered Egypt,

though they were driven out by Assyrians. Kingdoms in northeastern Africa continued to flourish, with a growing population. Local artistic styles combined with the use of Egyptian forms such as pyramids and obelisks. Much of this tradition continued in the later kingdom of Ethiopia.

Along the Mediterranean cost of the Middle East, another mixture of societies emerged. A people called the Phoenicians, for example, devised a greatly simplified alphabet with 22 letters around 1300 B.C.E.; this alphabet, in turn, became the predecessor of Greek and Latin alphabets. The Phoenicians also improved the Egyptian numbering system. Great traders, they set up colony cities in north Africa and on the coasts of Europe. Phoenicians traded as far away as England, where they purchased tin to make bronze. Another regional group, the Lydians, first introduced coined money.

The most influential of the smaller Middle Eastern groups, however, were the Jews, who gave the world the first clearly developed monotheistic religion. We have seen that early religions, both before and after the beginnings of civilization, were polytheistic, claiming that many gods and goddesses worked to control nature and human destiny. The Jews, a Semitic people influenced by Babylonian civilization, settled near the Mediterranean around 1200 B.C.E. The Jewish state was small and relatively weak, retaining independence only when other parts of the Middle East were in political turmoil. What was distinctive about this culture was its firm belief that a single God, Jehovah, guided the destinies of the Jewish people. Priests and prophets defined and emphasized this belief, and their history of God's guidance of the Jews formed the basis for the Hebrew Bible. The Jewish religion and moral code persisted even as the Jewish state suffered domination by a series of foreign rulers, from 772 B.C.E. until the Romans seized the state outright in 63 B.C.E. Jewish monotheism has sustained a distinctive Jewish culture to our own day; it also served as a basis for the development of both Christianity and Islam as major world religions.

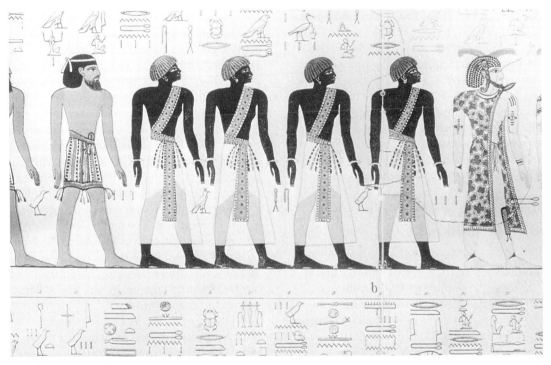

Egyptian tomb painting.

Because Judaism stressed God's special compact with the chosen Jewish people, there was no premium placed on converting non-Jews. This belief helps explain the durability of the Jewish faith itself; it also kept the Jewish people in a minority position in the Middle East as a whole. However, the elaboration of monotheism had a wide, if not immediate, significance. In Jewish hands, the concept of God became less human-like, more abstract. This represented a basic change in not only religion but also humankind's overall outlook. Jehovah had not only a power but also a rationality far different from what the traditional gods of the Middle East or Egypt possessed. These gods were whimsical and capricious; Jehovah was orderly and just, and individuals knew what to expect if they obeyed God's rules. God was also linked to ethical conduct, to proper moral behavior. Religion for the Jews was a way of life, not merely a set of rituals and ceremonies. The full impact of this religious transformation on Middle Eastern civilization was realized only later, when Jewish beliefs were embraced by other, proselytizing faiths. However, the basic concept of monotheistic religion was one of the legacies of the end of the first great civilization period to the new cultures that soon arose.

PATHS TO THE PRESENT

Some of the achievements of the early civilizations invoke a sense of awe that expresses our wonder at what people so long ago could achieve, but also our awareness of how separate they are from us today. We gape at pictures of the pyramids, and study how a society relying on human labor alone could build them; but we also know that the idea of building such monuments to individual leaders is a product of an earlier age.

Nonetheless, connections exist between the early civilizations and the present. Most obviously, early civilizations created a basic apparatus that has not required reinvention. Different writing systems emerged, but the idea of writing flows directly from these early systems. The same holds for basic concepts of government, including codes of law. Some parts of early law codes might strike us as pioneering even today—such as the idea of society compensating victims of crimes, which was part of the Hammurabic code. Money is another staple that has remained constant, albeit in shifting forms, throughout history. In these and other respects, the early civilizations created implements for human activity, in trade or government, that we take for granted.

There is debate about how many of the less tangible characteristics of human activity have survived from the early period. Does a Chinese interest in political order—strong still in China today—date back to the Shang dynasty, or was this a value that was instilled at a later time? The many rival groups and traditions in the Middle East today are not what they were 4000 years ago, but some of the components of these conflicts date back to the mixture of peoples and invasions operating at that point. Certainly, there is a straight line between the Jewish identity and religion forged late in the early civilization period and the Jewish people today. Historians debate how much legacy Egypt or Mesopotamia created for later history, much less for today, because of the impact of later cultures and institutions on these regions. But there are at least some connections, for example, in architectural styles and scientific ideas, beyond the apparatus of civilization itself.

SUGGESTED WEB SITES

To visit the Oriental Institute Museum, go to http://oi.uchicago.edu/OI/MUS/GALLERY/ EAST/New_East_Gallery.html; to explore ancient world cultures, see http://eawc.evansville.edu/; to learn more on the mysteries of Çatal Hüyük, go to www.smm.org/catal/top.php; visit the Weaving Art Museum and Research Institute at www.weavingartmuseum.org/.

SUGGESTED READINGS

Robert Chadwick, *First Civilizations: Ancient Mesopotamia and Ancient Egypt* (2005); Robert G. Morkot, *The Egyptians: An Introduction* (2005); Ian Shaw, *Exploring Ancient Egypt* (2003); Francis Joannès, *The Age of Empires: Mesopotamia in the First Millennium B.C.* (2004); Mu-chou Poo, *Enemies of Civilization: Attitudes Toward Foreigners in Ancient Mesopotamia, Egypt, and China* (2005); Kwang-chih Chang, *The Formation of Chinese Civilization: An Archaeological Perspective* (2005); "Formation of Chinese Civilization," found at www.china.org.cn/e-gudai/; Li Liu, *The Chinese Neolithic: Trajectories to Early States* (Cambridge, 2004); David N. Keightley, *The Ancestral Landscape: Time, Space, and Community in Late Shang China*, ca. 1200–1045 B.C. (Berkeley, 2000); Donald B. Redford, *From Slave to Pharaoh: The Black Experience of Ancient Egypt* (Baltimore, 2004).

On the environment, see I. G. Simmons, *Environmental History* (1993). On patterns of contact, see Philip D. Curtin, *Cross-Cultural Trade in World History* (1984); Xinru Liu, *Ancient India and Ancient China: Trade and Religious Exchanges* (1988); and Shereen Ratnagar, *Encounter: The Westerly Trade of the Harappan Civilization* (1981). The science and technology of the ancient world are discussed in Richard Bulliet, *The Camel and the Wheel* (1975); George Ifrah, *From One to Zero: A Universal History of Numbers* (1985); and Edgardo Marcorini, ed., *The History of Science and Technology: A Narrative Chronology* (1988). The nature and influence of early science, particularly from Egypt, is also covered in Dick Teresi's *Lost Discoveries: The Ancient Roots of Modern Science* (2002). See also M. E. Auber, *The Phoenicians and the West* (1996); Donald Redford, *Egypt, Canaan and Israel in Ancient Times* (1995); Gay Robbins, *Women in Ancient Egypt* (1993); and J. Curtis, *Ancient Persia* (1989).

3 Nomadic Societies

Not everyone nor every area was folded into the embrace of agricultural civilizations. World historians are paying increasing attention to nomadic herding peoples, whose economy and society contrasted with the more standard pattern. These smaller groups of people were capable of great impact because, of necessity, they moved around considerably. They were in a position to contact and influence civilizations, and to link civilizations through trade.

Nomadic populations, were smaller than those of the civilization; their economy offered limited support. This was one reason that nomads recurrently pressed into other areas, to relieve population pressure. Indeed, nomadic peoples show up in world history particularly when they migrated into more settled areas, or when they invaded. But they also, more systematically, provided trading contacts, through which ideas and techniques could spread. And they introduced some important techniques of their own.

▌ **KEY QUESTIONS** *How did nomadic societies differ from civilizations? Why might a herding economy be preferred over agriculture? What kinds of contacts did nomadic peoples have with civilizations?*

EARLY NOMADIC SOCIETIES

We do not know when nomadic societies developed, for they have left few written records and no real architectural monuments. They may have begun before the first civilizations emerged. Nomadic societies ultimately developed particularly in the huge grassy plains area of central Asia, on the fringes of the Sahara desert in Africa, and also in southern Arabia. Smaller nomadic societies

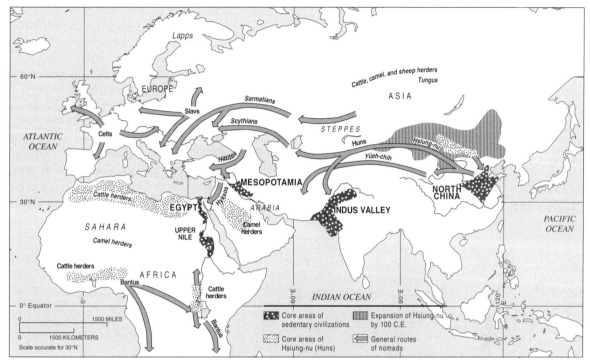

Earliest Civilizations and Migrations of Nomads

also developed in the Americas, in the Andes Mountains, the only place where there were relevant domesticated animals. Nomadic regions generally are characterized by sufficient rainfalls for developing grasslands but where rainfall is inadequate for settled agriculture.

The first groups of nomads to break into the historical record were the Indo-Europeans, who periodically intervened in the civilizations of the Middle East and India for a thousand years, beginning about 1500 B.C.E. Some Indo-European groups invaded civilized areas and established their own empires—such as the Hittites, who fit into the series of empire-invaders in Mesopotamia. Others, such as the Greeks, migrated into new territory and settled down, ultimately trying to fight off later groups of Indo-European invaders with whom they finally intermingled. Indo-European incursions into India increasingly threatened the later phases of Harappan civilization. Early Indo-Europeans used war chariots drawn by horses, but gradually they developed the equipment needed to ride horses directly.

Another early nomadic group that played an important role in larger world history, also from central Asia, was the Hsiung-nu, known in Europe as the Huns. The Hun invasions in China caused great devastation from the 4th century B.C.E. on. Like the Indo-Europeans before them, Hun movements were probably initially caused by droughts and internal warfare in central Asia, but then, achieving success, they took on a life of their own.

Other early nomadic groups included reindeer herders in northern Europe (the Lapps). More important were the camel herders in Arabia and north central Africa. The camel was domesticated by 1700 B.C.E. as a pack animal. Its capacity for traveling with huge loads, for more than 20 days without new water, was ideal for nomadic life in the deserts. Cattle-raising nomads also played a role in parts of Africa.

NOMADIC SOCIETY AND CULTURE

Seasonal travel was fundamental to the nomadic way of life. Harsh weather forced movement in search of adequate food, and too much time in one place exhausted the available vegetation. Most nomadic groups usually traveled the same routes, year after year. But droughts or other hardships could promote change. While nomadic groups usually respected each other's routes, problems could cause conflicts as one group tried to muscle into the territory of another.

Animals formed the core of the cultural interests of nomadic societies, with religion usually emphasizing animal sacrifices. Size of herd was the measure of wealth in nomadic societies. Animals were also the core of the nomadic economy. Nomads traded in leather, wool, milk products, and bone sculptures.

Desert nomads.

UNDERSTANDING CULTURES

NOMADIC ART

Nomadic economies developed in harsh environments. Elaborate resources for art were not available, and much art was strictly utilitarian. Sculptures and woven rugs, for example, often had animal themes, reflecting the immediate environment and also providing a sense of respect and control for these vital components of the nomadic economy. Many nomads claimed a particular animal as the originator of the kinship group and venerated it accordingly. In art, animals were frequently shown fighting or fleeing from danger. Art also had to be transportable, on rugs used in wagons or tents or as jewelry or belt buckles.

In fashion, nomads' great contribution to world history was the invention of trousers, introduced by the horse nomads in central Asia to facilitate riding.

Shading off from art to explicit technology was the nomads' invention of saddles, stirrups, and mouth bits, which were picked up by riders in civilizations once they learned how useful they were.

Nomads were also great storytellers, and their stories often explored the nature of different gods and goddesses. Stories in the Indo-European religion spread with nomadic migrations to Scandinavia, to Greece and Rome, and to India.

The harshness of the nomadic environment, plus periodic warfare, introduced a common note of violence into nomadic life. Nomadic societies emphasized the importance of honor, or what anthropologists call courage culture. Strong, warlike men dominated, and their leadership was dependent on a willingness to meet physical challenge. Nomadic cultures valued courage and heroic action above all other achievements. In addition to recognizing brave leaders, nomadic organization depended on kinship relations in small bands, usually of 30 to 150 people. These bands could, however, assemble into much larger groups in response to crisis.

Hospitality was another keynote of nomadic culture. Honor required that travelers be aided, a recognition of the harshness of the nomadic life. Acts of great generosity contributed to the reputation of leaders.

Nomads were outstanding fighters. Because their economic activity required much less time than that of agricultural peoples, there was more opportunity to train for battle. Easy familiarity with horses (or other animals) made for excellent military skills as well. Nomads' ability to ride for long distances often allowed them to draw the armies of civilizations out, where, exhausted, they could later be picked off. This technique was used successfully against Persian armies in the 6th century B.C.E., in western Asia, and against the British in 19th-century Africa.

Because of their fighting skills, nomads had a reputation for cruelty. This was sometimes exaggerated, but not always. Hun invaders in China had drinking cups made from the skulls of defeated rivals. Some nomadic groups routinely killed the wives and children of leaders they defeated.

Nomadic societies were male-dominated, with care of animals and skill in their use reserved for men. Marriages were arranged to promote the interests of kinship groups,

Mongol hunter in pursuit of game.

though nomads liked to tell stories about great romance and love of beautiful women. Polygamy was common for wealthier men. Women's tasks, besides childrearing, involved making and breaking camp, cooking, and sewing. In some nomadic societies, however, women held positions of greater prestige, occasionally even participating in wars and holding leadership positions.

NOMADS AND CIVILIZATIONS

Nomads are particularly famous in history when they invade. Civilized peoples, from the Chinese to the Romans, feared and condemned nomads as offspring of evil spirits, the ultimate barbarians. Without question, nomadic invasions were important, particularly when they were part of

Persian miniature depiction of a camp.

larger migrations that could change the population structure as well as political leadership. The role of the Indo-Europeans in shaking up civilizations in the Middle East and India is obvious, and this basic pattern repeated in the classical and postclassical periods.

But nomads often had a peaceful, mutually beneficial relationship with agricultural societies, and this pattern had its own historical significance. Nomads often traded with farmers for useful goods, including vegetables, silks, and iron tools and weapons. In turn, the meat and milk products provided by the nomads could supple-ment meager diets for frontier farming communities. Nomads also provided war-horses for civilizations in China, India, the Middle East, and sub-Saharan Africa.

Nomads often received tribute payments from agricultural societies, to keep them at bay. And they were often hired as mercenary soldiers by government leaders. At the end of the Roman Empire, nomads were hired to protect frontiers—Germans in Europe, Arabs in the Middle East. The Zhou, in China, began their careers as border guards for the Shang dynasty. Obviously, this practice could backfire when the

THE CONTRIBUTIONS OF NOMADS

Violence and war grab the history headlines where nomads are concerned, but they may not be the main point. Nomads pioneered all the great overland trade routes that joined civilized areas in Asia, Europe, and Africa, from the river valley period through the postclassical centuries. They showed the way across the Sahara desert, though other merchants and missionaries might follow. They cut through central Asia, along the fringe of the Himalayan Mountains.

To be sure, nomads often threatened the trade routes, and Roman or Chinese emperors might send troops against these land-based pirates. But they also served as facilitators along the routes, offering protection for merchant groups, providing animals and hospitable way-stations. Sometimes they traded directly; more often, they cooperated with merchant groups. At key points in world history, before the definitive rise of ocean-based transport and then the railroad, nomadic-shaped trade routes were the lifeline of connections among the major civilizations. Religions such as Buddhism and Islam spread peacefully along these routes, while artistic styles from centers such as Greece fanned out along the routes as well. The mobility of nomads was long fundamental to world trade.

Sometimes, when nomads picked up some additional pointers from civilizations with which they were in contact, contributions were more direct. Warfare against Chinese forces in western China in the 8th century, by nomadic armies that had converted to Islam, brought the capture of several Chinese craftsmen who knew how to make paper. This, in turn, resulted in the rapid spread of papermaking in the Middle East and north Africa, and then more widely.

Nomads also contributed to the spread of knowledge of new crops, even when they did not cultivate them directly. Sometimes they carried new diseases as well, the downside of contact. More obviously still, they recurrently added to the technology of war, with their equipment for horses and skill in hit-and-run attacks copied by the armies of civilizations.

How do the nomads compare to other intermediaries among early civilizations? What's the most accurate verdict on nomads' role in world history? What agents now serve the roles that nomads once did?

guards gained additional organizational skills and turned against the host society. Not surprisingly, many civilizations spent a great deal of money trying to keep nomads out—as with the Great Wall in China, or the frontier garrisons of the Roman Empire.

Nomadic invaders, including former border guards, often incorporated the institutions and values of a civilization when they were able to take over, changing more than the societies around them. It was often hard to maintain a nomadic identity. Many nomads feared the lures of civilization, worrying that they would become soft, and often pulled back lest they be corrupted. An Arab nomad put it this way: "A tent flapping in the desert air is dearer than [a] towering house, Wind rustling over the sandy waste has a sweeter sound than all the king's trumpets."

NOMADS AND GLOBAL PATTERNS

Nomadic peoples were sparse, compared to those of civilizations. But their skills and values gave them a world history role greater than numbers suggest. At the same time, their conditions of life made it impossible to develop durable civilizations of their own, or even to dominate farming societies for very long. Successful rule always depended on picking up the techniques, and much of the personnel, of established civilizations.

So the nomadic intrusions into world history tended to be dramatic but brief. Often, they caused more change by what they prompted agricultural societies to do in defense, in organizing government resources to guard against attack, than by what they did themselves. Most of human history has been made by agricultural peoples, not nomads, but the nomadic role has been crucial nevertheless.

PATHS TO THE PRESENT

In today's world, nomads are at most a curiosity, living on the fringes of settled societies, because agricultural civilizations gobbled up most of the nomadic lands 500 years ago or more, particularly in central Asia. Bedouin groups, for example, continue to roam the Middle East, but they are small and do not have much impact on the cultures around them. Despite nomads' modern invisibility, nomadic early contributions to world history were concrete. Nomadic societies challenged civilizations at various points through invasions and migrations, facilitating trade, and bringing new techniques and ideas.

Some societies retain a historical memory of a nomadic past. The nation of Mongolia understandably celebrates the achievements of nomadic Mongols, even though those achievements occurred 700 years ago. Other societies arguably retain particular traditions from earlier, nomadic ways. Arab hospitality, for example, is justly famous and possibly a nomadic legacy, even though most Arabs abandoned nomadism many centuries ago.

Contemporary world history has revived attention to one of the classic nomadic regions, central Asia. The collapse of the Soviet Union, and the crucial location of central Asia near Russia, the Middle East, India, and China, make the new nations of central Asia intriguing players in international relations. But the region gains attention now not because of nomadic economies, which have largely ended, but because of its rich resources, including oil, and its strategic position. Descendants of the nomads have new assets to affect the lives of the larger populations that surround them.

SUGGESTED WEB SITES

On the Silk Road Foundation, see http://www.silkroadfoundation.org/toc/index.html; to learn more about early nomads, go to http://www.hermitagemuseum.org/html_En/03/hm3_2_7.html; on nomadic challenges and civilized responses, see http://history-world.org/nomads.htm.

SUGGESTED READINGS

An excellent general work is A. M. Khazanov's *Nomads and the Outside World* (1984). Though not the explicit subject, the role of nomads in contacts is treated in Jerry Bentley, *Old World Encounters* (1993). See also Rene Grousset, *Empire of the Steppes: A History of Central Asia* (1970), and Richard Bulliet, *The Camel and the Wheel* (1975);

recent works include Ben Fitzhugh, ed., *Beyond Foraging and Collecting: Evolutionary Change in Hunger-Gatherer Settlement Systems* (2002); G. E. R. Lloyd, *Ancient Worlds, Modern Reflections: Philosophical Perspectives on Greek and Chinese Science and Culture* (2004); Steven Mithen, *After the Ice: A Global Human History, 20,000–5000 BC* (2004); Morris Berman, *Wandering God: A Study of Nomadic Spirituality* (2000); A. M. Khazanov, *Nomads in the Sedentary World* (2001); Peter S. Ungar, *Human Diet: Its Origins and Evolution* (2002); Steven A. LeBlanc, *Constant Battles: The Myth of the Noble Savage* (2003); and Richard Lee, *The Cambridge Encyclopedia of Hunters and Gatherers* (1999).

The Rise of Agriculture and Agricultural Civilizations

CONTACTS AND IDENTITIES

The most important global contacts during the early periods of human history involved the spread of techniques and foods, gradually, usually through ways we know little about. The diffusion of agriculture and iron use, from centers of initial invention, is the most important example. But foods also spread. For example, African farmers by 1000 B.C.E. were growing foods that originated in southeast Asia, which greatly enriched the variety available to them. This suggests some trade through the Indian Ocean, through which seeds or tubers were transported, but we don't know the mechanisms. Direct contacts among the river valley centers were less important, though trade and some warfare periodically brought Egypt and the Middle East into contact, and Harappan civilization traded widely. What resulted, beyond exchange of goods, is unclear. We have seen that Harappans ignored examples of technology available to them from societies with which they traded.

Because contacts were limited, it is also unclear how conscious people were of their identities. Egyptians surely had some sense of their culture and institutions when they encountered Kushites or peoples in the eastern Mediterranean; they often tried to impose some of their standards. The Middle East, so often invaded, must have seen efforts to retain identity. The Jewish people, certainly, worked hard to maintain their religion and language even when invaded by Assyrians and others; identity proved crucial in Jewish history from this point on. Many agricultural peoples were aware of different identities from the hunting or nomadic groups around them, and vice versa. We have seen that nomads, even when attracted by the more abundant wealth of civilizations, often insisted on the importance of maintaining their own values and greater simplicity. But surviving records make many identity issues a matter of speculation; here the Jewish experience, with its explicit chronicles, is atypical.

TENSIONS

The problem: Many aspects of the world today can be described in terms of the tensions between international exchanges and outside influences, on the one hand, and the clear human need to maintain identities, on the other. These tensions affect whole societies, which are called upon to decide how much identity to sacrifice in favor of possible benefits from wider interactions; groups; and individuals.

Americans sometimes (rarely) wonder whether they should give up their traditional measuring system and convert to metrics—the measurements used almost everywhere else in the world. Conversion cost some money in the short run, but probably saved money in the long run, so it seems a simple decision. But issues of identity also factor in: We are accustomed to our inches, miles, and quarts, and it might seem as though we were losing parts of our national self to give them up in favor of uniform global standards.

Several years ago, a French farmer won international attention and wide praise for driving his tractor into a local McDonald's to protest globalization of fast food. He struck a blow for traditional French identity and its connotation of creating fine cuisine. Yet, almost a third of French restaurant meals are taken in fast-food operations, either foreign or imitative-domestic—another case of an unresolved tension between global links and local identities.

The argument: Tensions between local practices and loyalties and the lure or inevitability of wider contacts are endemic to world history. The balance has gradually shifted toward the global, over the local—one sign is the disappearance, mainly in the past two centuries, of several thousand languages. But the tension remains. World history helps us understand how it evolved and helps explain why some societies and groups, even today, react to the tension in terms of identity protection while others are more open to the larger world.

The early history: The most striking point about the early human experience involves the wide dispersion of people, which explains how strong local identities emerged in the first place. Additionally, differences in economic systems, between agriculturalists and nomads for instance, provided bases for separate identities. Most polytheistic religions, to take one illustration, were highly regional in specific beliefs and practices, even if they shared wider elements because of the human need to explain the forces of nature or the inevitability of death. In contrast, the forces that pushed for wider contacts were usually more sporadic and diffuse.

Admittedly, we do not know as much about the nature and passion of early identities as we would like. Egyptians surely had some sense of their culture and institutions when they encountered Kushites or peoples in the eastern Mediterranean. They could and did identify non-Egyptians as "others" or outsiders. But we do not know details about the Egyptians' response to these outsiders. Phoenicians, to take another case, clearly had distinctive practices, which they exported to settlements in North Africa and southern Europe, providing a

Phoenician identity that supported wider trading ventures. Theirs was a case of a people who managed to further wider economic contacts but maintain a set of values and institutions separate from the groups they dealt with.

The most durable identity launched in this period was that of the Jewish people. Possessing a distinctive religion, and despite the lack of a durable Jewish state, Jewish people began quite early to maintain their sense of identity, even when overrun by conquerors such as the Assyrians. Maintenance of this identity, even amid wide geographic dispersion, was and is a fundamental feature not only of Jewish history, but of the role of Jews in the wider world.

Other identities took shape as well. Many Chinese scholars later claimed that some of their political and cultural features emerged with the Shang dynasty or even before, but it is hard to sort myth from reality. It is clear that a Chinese identity emerged and claimed deep historical roots, but it is not easy to sort out when this happened in fact. Another example of cultural identity is that of the Harappan people, who maintained an awareness of their values and achievements, even as their cities declined and Indo-European migrants overran their settlements. But this identity did not survive wider contacts. Similarly, Sumerians and other Mesopotamian groups, beset by invasions, left a legacy, in the form of surviving institutions and values, but not a durable identity.

Early human history illustrates and explains the process of identity formation in the various regions of the world. Migrations and diffusions challenged identities, but these larger connecting forces did not yet predominate. The tensions that resulted were sporadic, in contrast to the regular interactions with—and tensions that result from—global influences that form the framework of life today.

PART II

The Classical Period, 1000 B.C.E.– 500 C.E.

INTRODUCTION: NEW ISSUES FOR EXPANDING SOCIETIES

The classical period in world history began between 1000 and 800 B.C.E. and ended with the fall of great empires between the 2nd and 6th centuries C.E. So, it lasted about 1500 years, from roughly 1000 B.C.E. to roughly 500 C.E.

Slightly before 1000 B.C.E., the Zhou dynasty took shape in China. The Zhou began expanding Chinese territory; it was under them that characteristic Chinese cultural systems, such as Confucianism, emerged. In the Middle East, the Persian empire developed in the 6th century. A bit before this, Greek city-states emerged and began to spread settlements to other parts of the eastern Mediterranean. Classical Indian culture gained greater coherence between 1000 and 600 B.C.E. as key religious epics were written down, though the first Indian empires emerged only in the 4th century B.C.E. So, although starting points varied, the notion of a distinctive classical past gained traction in many parts of Asia, southern Europe, and north Africa from 1000 B.C.E. on.

At the other end, the classical period did not close tidily, at a single date; but it did close noisily. Majestic empires in China, the Mediterranean, and India all collapsed by or before 600 C.E. Clearly, an important human experience had ended, at least in part.

TIMELINE Classical Civilizations

China	India	Mediterranean (Greece and Rome)
		1700 B.C.E. Indo-European invasions.
	1500–1000 B.C.E. Recovery from Aryan invasions, Vedic Age, formative period.	**1400 B.C.E.** Kingdom of Mycenae.
1029–258 B.C.E. Zhou dynasty.	**1000–600 B.C.E.** Epic Age, beginnings of early Hinduism, *Upanishads*.	**800 B.C.E.** Rise of Greek city-states and economy; Homeric epics, *Iliad* and *Odyssey;* beginnings of Rome.
700 B.C.E. Zhou decline.	**c. 563–483 B.C.E.** Gautama Buddha.	**509–450 B.C.E.** Beginnings of Roman republic; Twelve Tables of Law.
551–478 B.C.E. Confucius.		**500–449 B.C.E.** Greek defeat of Persia; spread of Athenian Empire.
c. 500 B.C.E. Laozi and Daoism.		**470–430 B.C.E.** Athens at height; Pericles, Phidias, Sophocles, Socrates, etc.
c. 500 B.C.E. Editing of the Five Classics.		**431–404 B.C.E.** Peloponnesian Wars.
		330 B.C.E. ff. Macedonian Empire, Alexander the Great.
		330–100 B.C.E. Hellenistic period.
221–202 B.C.E. Qin dynasty, Great Wall.	**322–184 B.C.E.** Maurya dynasty.	**264–146 B.C.E.** Rome's Punic Wars.
202 B.C.E.–220 C.E. Han dynasty.		**133 B.C.E.** Decline of Roman republic.
140–87 B.C.E. Rule of Wudi; increased bureaucracy, examinations, spread of Confucianism.	**30 B.C.E.–220 C.E.** Kushan rule, Hindu beliefs develop.	**27 B.C.E.** Augustus Caesar, rise of Roman Empire.
c. 100 B.C.E. Invention of paper.		**180 C.E.** Death of Marcus Aurelius, beginning of empire's decline.
220–589 C.E. Nomadic invasions, disorder, considerable spread of Buddhism.	**320–535 C.E.** Gupta dynasty.	**313 C.E.** Constantine adopts Christianity.
		476 C.E. Fall of Rome.

THEMES

If the classical period has reasonably clear boundaries—a start and a finish—what did it contain? Amid a host of specific developments, two major themes emerge:

First, several societies gained the capacity to expand territorially, much more widely than the river valley civilizations had done. Indeed, all the classical civilizations covered the river valley territories but then went much farther. Territorial expansion was possible because of the experience gained from the earlier societies but also because of the use of iron tools and weapons, which were much more effective than bronze weapons had been.

Second, the leading classical societies worked hard to create values and institutions that would help internally tie these expanded territories together. They promoted internal trade, so different regions within the civilization could specialize effectively. Wheat-growing north China thus interacted with rice-growing south China. The societies promoted ideas and artistic styles that provided people across the civilization with common beliefs and expressions. Rome built its temples and coliseums from Iraq to Britain. Chinese leaders pressed elites in all regions to practice Confucian values. Finally, all the classical civilizations worked, at least periodically, toward political integration, seeking to meld the disparate expanded territories into a single political unit.

In the process of integration, all the classical societies created certain beliefs and institutions that had great survival power. Indian religions, Greek science, Chinese bureaucracy—these were achievements that continued to influence the regions in question long after the classical period was over. Some later influenced other regions. The classical period was thus a formative one, generating many practices that affected the experience of millions of people over many centuries.

Given classical societies' achievements and the durability, it is small wonder that many people look on them with awe and reverence. Our awe stems from wondering how people in early cultures could attain such greatness. Our reverence comes from wondering, if they did so much, can we also be inspired to great things?

In 2005, the nation of Iran was seeking, against considerable world resistance, to develop a nuclear power program, and possibly nuclear weaponry. Some young Iranians were interviewed amid the great temple ruins of Persepolis, the capital of the Persian Empire. They argued that if their classical ancestors built monuments that were the envy of the world, surely contemporary Iranians can claim their place in the international sun. This is a sentiment that many people experience—though without the nuclear twist—as they contemplate the classical pasts of their own societies, from Spain to China's Pacific coast.

Many people and regions continued apart from the major classical civilizations. Classical populations were unusually large: China's tripled to about 60 million; Rome at its height held sway over 54 million souls; and India contained about 50 million people. But during this period people lived elsewhere, in other parts of Africa, in northern Europe, in Japan, and, of course, in the Americas, who were not yet strongly influenced by the classical achievements, and whose histories were quite different. Even many of these regions, however, were later influenced by some of the ideas and institutions one or more of the classical civilizations had generated.

GLOBAL CONNECTIONS

Four major centers of classical civilization emerged: China, India, Persia, and the Mediterranean. Persia interacted with the Mediterranean and at one point was conquered by Greek armies, but on the whole it established and maintained a separate tradition.

Each of the classical civilizations influenced adjacent regions. Chinese power and example affected Korea. Mediterranean societies traded actively with Ethiopia, a pattern that explains why Ethiopia became predominantly Christian (though with a Jewish minority). Indian merchants influenced southeast Asia.

Aside from this regional outreach, the achievements of the classical civilizations rested on separate developments. This was the period in which durable but distinctive features in India, or in China, were created, though they may have utilized some earlier, river valley precedents. Of course the civilizations showed common tendencies: they all expanded, they all worked at integration, and they all relied heavily on social and gender inequality. But they implemented these common themes in different ways. This means, in turn, that a key feature of the classical period was internal development.

Yet contacts with other cultures were also important, even if they had limited impact in shaping specific institutions or cultures within each civilization. The contacts were significant enough at the time to inspire many, and later to ensure the maintenance of connective channels.

Trade opportunities increased as a result of these contacts between societies. During the classical period a series of overland routes developed from western China, through central Asia, into India and the Middle East (and thence to the Mediterranean). These routes are called the Silk Road, for merchants used them to carry Chinese silk westward, and to return with gold, exotic animals, and other products. Trade along the Silk Road was regional: one group of merchants carried goods through their region—nomads were sometimes involved—then another group took the goods to the next stage. Persian institutions such as a good road system and inns for travelers helped Asian goods reach the rest of the Middle East and Mediterranean.

Interregional trade also emerged in the Indian Ocean. Indian merchants actively traded with southeast Asia, including present-day Indonesia. Various Middle Eastern merchants developed commercial ties with India. So did the Romans, when they reached the eastern Mediterranean. Regular convoys were sent from the Red Sea, into the Indian Ocean, and on to India, seeking pepper and other spices; some Roman merchants resided in India to drum up trade. China also traded with India by sea. One emperor sent a special mission to India to buy a rhinoceros for his zoo.

Classical civilizations occasionally encountered each other more directly than via trade. Alexander the Great's conquests, in the 4th century B.C.E., brought Greeks not only to Persia but also to northwestern India (present-day Pakistan), where they set up the kingdom of Bactria. For two centuries Indians and Greeks interacted here, pooling mathematical knowledge, among other things. For a time, as a result, Indian artists in the region portrayed Buddha with Greek hairstyles and costumes.

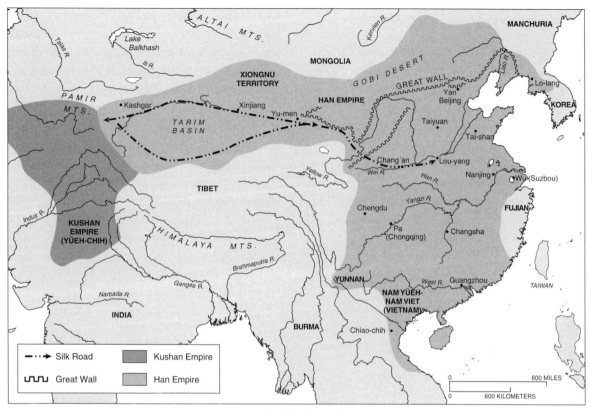

The Silk Roads

Late in the classical period, Chinese overland trade with India reached such a high level that Chinese merchants gained unusually active knowledge of Indian culture. Some began to convert to Buddhism, leading to other Chinese delegations being sent to India to learn more about this religion. Chinese importation of Buddhism was one of the great interregional cultural events in Chinese history.

Exchanges of products and ideas thus form an active part of the classical period, even amid the separate self-definitions of the key civilizations. There were limits to the exchanges, however. Greeks learned from Indian mathematicians,

and vice versa, but the Greeks did not import the efficient Indian numbering system—an odd omission, at least by our standards today. Also, while Roman elites valued silks from China, they had virtually no knowledge of China itself, and there is no definite evidence that anyone went from China to Rome or vice versa. Travelers did not venture too far outside their own region; the intensity of trade was rarely sufficient to inspire other kinds of exchange. Even the Greek-Indian interaction, in Bactria, led to few permanent achievements—for instance, the fad of dressing Buddhas in Greek attire lasted for only a century or so, then disappeared without much trace.

SUGGESTED READINGS

There are several useful treatments of cross-cultural themes and topics in antiquity. See, for example, Richard A. Gabriel, *War in the Ancient World* (1992); Milo Kearney, *The Indian Ocean in World History* (2004); W. H. McNeill, *Plagues and People* (1977); Irving Rouse, *Migrations in Prehistory* (1986); and Chester G. Starr, *The Influence of Sea-power on Ancient History* (1989). The role of women in the ancient world is the subject of A. Sharma, ed., *Women in World Religions* (1987); Bonnie S. Anderson and Judith P. Zinsser, *A History of Their Own: Women in Europe from Prehistory to the Present* (1988); and Bella Vivante, ed., *Women's Roles in Ancient Civilizations: A Reference Guide* (1999). The nature and impact of some of the most influential individuals of the classical world are the focus of S. N. Eisenstadt, ed., *The Origins and Diversity of the Axial Age* (1986). More recent works include Johann P. Arnason, *Axial Civilizations and World History* (Boston, 2005); Ralph W. Mathisen, *People, Personal Expression, and Social Relations in Late Antiquity, with Translated Texts from Gaul and Western Europe* (Ann Arbor, 2003); Barbara Sher Tinsley, *Reconstructing Western Civilization: Irreverent Essays on Antiquity* (Selinsgrove, 2006); and J. W. Roberts, *The Oxford Dictionary of the Classical World* (Oxford, 2005).

4 Classical Civilization: China

China generated the first of the great classical societies. The region remained somewhat isolated, despite its participation in Silk Road trade. This spared it frequent invasion and encouraged an intense, and distinctive, Chinese identity. The decline of the Shang dynasty did not result in as much internal chaos as did invasions of parts of the Middle East and particularly India. Hence, the Chinese could build more strongly on Huanghe precedents. Particularly important was a general, if somewhat vague, worldview developed by Huanghe thinkers and accepted as a standard approach in later Chinese thinking. This intellectual heritage stressed the basic harmony of nature: every feature is balanced by an opposite, every *yin* by a *yang*. Thus for hot there is cold, for male, female. According to this philosophy, an individual should seek a way, called *Dao,* to relate to this harmony, avoiding excess and appreciating the balance of opposites. Individuals and human institutions existed within this world of balanced nature, not, as in later Mediterranean philosophy, on the outside. Chinese traditions about balance, Dao, and yin/yang were intrinsic to diverse philosophies and religions established in the classical period, and they provided some unity among various schools of thought in China.

Despite important cultural continuity, classical China did not simply maintain earlier traditions. The formative centuries of classical Chinese history were witness to a great many changes. The religious and particularly the political habits of the Shang kingdom were substantially modified as part of building the world's largest classical empire. As a result of these new centuries of development, resulting in much diversity but often painful conflict, the Chinese emerged with an unusually well-integrated system in which government, philosophy, economic incentives, the family, and the individual were intended to blend into a harmonious whole.

■ **KEY QUESTIONS** *How did classical China fit the general definition of a classical civilization? Are there ways it did not fit? What were the main changes during the classical period: how was China different by 200 C.E. from what it had been 1200 years earlier; but, also, what had survived through the period as a whole?*

PATTERNS IN CLASSICAL CHINA

Of all the societies in the world today, it is China that has maintained the clearest links to its classical past—a past that has been a source of pride but also the cause of some problems of adaptation. Already in the period of classical Chinese history, a pattern was set in motion that lasted until the early part of the 20th century. A family of kings, called a "dynasty," began its rule of China with great vigor, developing strong political institutions and encouraging an active economy. Subsequently, the dynasty grew weaker and tax revenues declined, while social divisions increased in the larger society. Internal rebellions and sometimes invasions from the outside hastened the dynasty's decline. As the ruling dynasty declined, another dynasty emerged, usually from the family of a successful general, invader, or peasant rebel, and the pattern started anew. Small wonder that many Chinese conceive of history in terms of cycles, in contrast to the Western tendency to think of steady progress from past to present.

Three dynastic cycles cover the many centuries of classical China: the Zhou, the Qin, and the Han. The Zhou dynasty lasted from 1029 to 258 B.C.E. Although lengthy, this dynasty flourished only until about 700 B.C.E.; it was then beset by a decline in the political infrastructure and frequent invasions by nomadic peoples from border regions. Even during its strong centuries, the Zhou did not establish a powerful government, ruling instead through alliances with regional princes and noble families. The early Zhou and the introduction of a feudal system were discussed in Chapter 2. The dynasty initially came into China from the north, displacing its predecessor, the Shang rulers. The alliance systems the Zhou used as the basis for their rule were standard in agricultural kingdoms. (We will see similar forms later emerge in Japan, India, Europe, and Africa.) Rulers lacked the means to control their territories directly and so gave large regional estates to members of their families and other supporters, hoping that their loyalties would remain intact. The supporters, in exchange for land, were supposed to provide the central government with troops and tax revenues. This was China's feudal period, with rulers depending on a network of loyalties and obligations to and from their landlord-vassals. Such a system was, of course, vulnerable to regional disloyalties, and the ultimate decline of the Zhou dynasty occurred when regional landowning aristocrats solidified their own power base and disregarded the central government.

The Zhou did, however, contribute in several ways to the development of Chinese politics and culture in their active early centuries. First, they extended the territory of China by taking over the Yangzi River valley. This stretch of territory, from the Huanghe to the Yangzi, became China's core—often called the "Middle Kingdom." It provided rich agricultural lands plus the benefits of two different agricultures—wheat-growing in the north, rice-growing in the south—a diversity that encouraged population growth. The territorial expansion obviously complicated the problems of central rule, for communication and transport from the capital to the outlying regions were difficult. This is why the Zhou relied so heavily on the loyalty of regional supporters.

Despite these circumstances, the Zhou did actually heighten the focus on the central government itself. Zhou rulers claimed direct links to the Shang rulers. They also asserted that heaven had transferred its mandate to rule China to the Zhou emperors. This political concept of a mandate from heaven remained a key justification for Chinese imperial rule from the Zhou on. Known as Sons of Heaven, the emperors lived in a world of awe-inspiring pomp and ceremony.

The Zhou worked to provide greater cultural unity in their empire. They discouraged some of the primitive religious practices of the Huanghe civilization, banning human sacrifice and urging more restrained ceremonies to worship the gods. They also promoted linguistic unity, beginning the process by which a standard spoken language, ultimately called Mandarin Chinese, prevailed over the entire Middle Kingdom. This resulted in the largest single group of people speaking the same language in the world at this time. Regional dialects and languages remained, but educated officials began to rely on the single Mandarin form. Oral epics and stories in Chinese, many gradually recorded in written form, aided in the development of a common cultural currency.

Increasing cultural unity helps explain why, when the Zhou Empire began to fail, scholars were able to use philosophical ideas to lessen the impact of growing political confusion. Indeed, the political crisis spurred efforts to define and articulate Chinese culture. During the late 6th and early 5th centuries B.C.E., the philosopher known in the West as Confucius (see p. 62) wrote an elaborate statement on political ethics, providing the core of China's distinctive philosophical heritage. Other writers and religious leaders participated in this great period of cultural creativity, which later reemerged as a set of central beliefs throughout the Middle Kingdom.

Cultural innovation did not, however, reverse the prolonged and painful Zhou downfall. Regional rulers formed independent armies, ultimately reducing the emperors to little more than figureheads. Between 402 and 201 B.C.E., a period known aptly enough as the Era of the Warring States, the Zhou system disintegrated.

At this point, China might have gone the way of civilizations such as India, where centralized government was more the exception than the rule. But a new dynasty arose to reverse the process of political decay. One regional ruler deposed the last Zhou emperor and within 35 years made himself sole ruler of China. He took the title Qin Shihuangdi, or First Emperor. The dynastic name, Qin, conferred on the whole country its name of China. Qin Shihuangdi was a brutal ruler, but effective given the circumstances of internal disorder. He understood that China's problem lay in the regional power of the aristocrats, and like many later centralizers in world history, he worked vigorously to undo this force. He ordered nobles to leave their regions and appear at his court, assuming control of their feudal estates. China was organized into large provinces ruled by bureaucrats appointed by the emperor; and Qin Shihuangdi was careful to select his officials from nonaristocratic groups, so that they would owe their power to him and not dare to develop their own independent bases. Under Qin Shihuangdi's rule, powerful armies crushed regional resistance.

The First Emperor followed up on centralization by extending Chinese territory to the south, reaching present-day Hong Kong on the South China Sea and even influencing northern Vietnam. In the north, to guard against barbarian invasions, Qin Shihuangdi built a Great Wall, extending more than 3000 miles, wide enough for chariots to move along its crest. This massive mud wall, probably the largest construction project in human history up to that point, was built by forced labor, conscripted by the central bureaucracy from among the peasantry.

The Qin dynasty was responsible for a number of innovations in Chinese politics and culture. To determine the empire's resources, Qin Shihuangdi ordered a national census, which provided data for the calculation of tax revenues and labor service. The government standardized coinage, weights, and measures through the entire realm. Even the length of axles on carts was regulated to promote coherent road planning. The government also made Chinese written script uniform, completing the process of creating a single basic language in which all educated Chinese

China's Great Wall at Nanken. More than 6000 kilometers long, the Great Wall of China was built during the Qin dynasty. It used some smaller walls that regional rulers had constructed to try to keep out nomadic invaders. The Qin wall was made of mud; the wall shown here was built after 1450 C.E., though for the same basic purpose.

could communicate. The government furthered agriculture, sponsoring new irrigation projects, and promoted manufacturing, particularly for silk cloth. The activist government also attacked formal culture, burning many books. Thinking, according to Qin Shihuangdi, was likely to be subversive to his autocratic rule.

Although it created many durable features of Chinese government, the Qin dynasty was short-lived. Qin Shihuangdi's attacks on intellectuals, and particularly the high taxes needed to support military expansion and the construction of the Great Wall, made him fiercely unpopular. One opponent described the First Emperor as a monster who "had the heart of a tiger and a wolf. He killed men as though he thought he could never

finish, he punished men as though he were afraid he would never get around to them all." On the emperor's death, in 210 B.C.E., massive revolts organized by aggrieved peasants broke out. One peasant leader defeated other opponents and in 202 B.C.E. established the third dynasty of classical China, the Han.

It was the Han dynasty, which lasted more than 400 years, to 220 C.E., that rounded out China's basic political and intellectual structure. Han rulers retained the centralized administration of the Qin but sought to reduce the brutal repression of that period. Like many dynasties during the first flush of power, early Han rulers expanded Chinese territory, pushing into Korea, Indochina, and central Asia. This expansion gave rise to direct contact with India and also allowed the Chinese to develop contact with the Parthian empire in the Middle East, through which trade with the Roman Empire around the Mediterranean was conducted. The most famous Han ruler, Wudi (140-87 B.C.E.), enforced peace throughout much of the continent of Asia, rather like the peace the Roman Empire would bring to the Mediterranean region a hundred years later, but embracing even more territory and a larger population. Peace brought great prosperity to China itself. A Han historian conveys the self-satisfied, confident tone of the dynasty:

> The nation had met with no major disturbances so that, except in times of flood or drought, every person was well supplied and every family had enough to get along on. The granaries in the cities and the countryside were full and the government treasures

were running over with wealth. In the capital the strings of cash had stacked up by the hundreds of millions until . . . they could no longer be counted. In the central granary of the government, new grain was heaped on top of the old until the building was full and the grain overflowed and piled up outside, where it spoiled and became unfit to eat. . . . Even the keepers of the community gates ate fine grain and meat.

Under the Han dynasty, the workings of the state bureaucracy also improved and the government was linked to formal training that emphasized the values of Confucian philosophy. Reversing the Qin dynasty's policies, Wudi urged support for Confucianism, seeing it as a vital supplement to formal measures on the government's part; shrines were established to promote the worship of the ancient philosopher as a god.

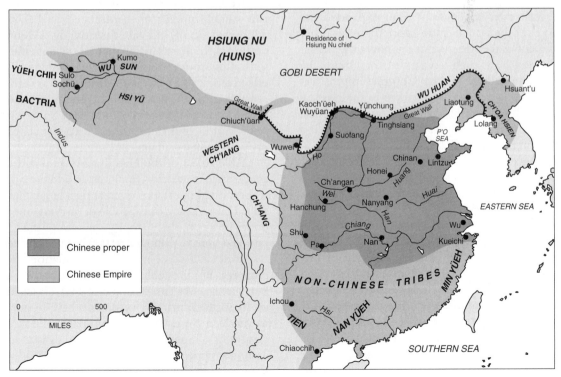

China Under Emperor Wudi, About 100 B.C.E.

The quality of Han rule declined after about two centuries. Central control weakened, and invasions from central Asia, spearheaded by a nomadic people called the Xiongnu, who had long threatened China's northern borders, overturned the dynasty entirely. Between 220 and 589 C.E., China was in a state of chaos. Order and stability were finally restored, but by then the classical or formative period of Chinese civilization had ended. Well before the Han collapse, however, China had established distinctive political structures and cultural values of unusual clarity, capable, as it turned out, of surviving even three centuries of renewed confusion.

POLITICAL INSTITUTIONS

The Qin and Han dynasties of classical China established a distinctive, and remarkably successful, kind of government. The Qin stressed central authority, whereas the Han expanded the powers of the bureaucracy. More than any other factor, it was the structure of this government that explained how such a vast territory could be effectively ruled—for the Chinese empire was indeed the largest political system in the classical world. This structure changed after the classical period, particularly in terms of streamlining and expanding bureaucratic systems and procedures, but it never required fundamental overhaul.

The political framework that emerged as a result of the long centuries of China's classical period had several key elements. Strong local units never disappeared. Like most successful agricultural societies, China relied heavily on tightly knit patriarchal families. Individual families were linked to other relatives in extended family networks that included brothers, uncles, and any living grandparents. Among the wealthy landowning groups, family authority was enhanced by the practice of ancestor worship, which joined family members through rituals devoted to important forebears who had passed into the spirit world. For ordinary people, among

whom ancestor worship was less common, village authority surmounted family rule. Village leaders helped farming families regulate property and coordinate planting and harvest work. During the Zhou dynasty, and also in later periods when dynasties weakened, the regional power of great landlords also played an important role at the village level. Landed nobles provided courts of justice and organized military troops.

Strong local rule was not the most significant or distinctive feature of Chinese government under the Qin and Han dynasties, however. Qin Shihuangdi not only attacked local rulers; he also provided a single law code for the whole empire and established a uniform tax system. He appointed governors to each district of his domain, who exercised military and legal powers in the name of the emperor. They, in turn, named officials responsible for smaller regions. Here indeed was a classic model of centralized government that other societies later replicated: the establishment of centralized codes and appointment of officials directly by a central authority, rather than reliance on arrangements with numerous existing local governments. The effectiveness of a central government was further enhanced by the delegation of special areas and decisions to the emperor's ministers. Some dealt with matters of finance, others with justice, others with military affairs, and so on.

Able rulers of the Han dynasty resumed the attack on local warrior-landlords. In addition, they realized the importance of creating a large, highly skilled bureaucracy, one capable of carrying out the duties of a complex state. By the end of the Han period, China had about 130,000 bureaucrats, representing 0.2 percent of the population. The emperor Wudi established examinations for his bureaucrats—the first example of civil service tests of the sort that many governments have instituted in modern times. These examinations covered classics of Chinese literature as well as law, suggesting a model of the scholar-bureaucrat that later became an important element of China's political tradition. Wudi also established a school to train men of exceptional talent and ability for the national examinations. Although most bureaucrats were drawn from the landed upper classes, who alone had the time to learn the complex system of Chinese characters, individuals from lower ranks of society were occasionally recruited under this system. China's bureaucracy thus provided a slight check on complete upper-class rule. It also tended to limit the exercise of arbitrary power by the emperor himself. Trained and experienced bureaucrats, confident in their own traditions, could often control the whims of a single ruler, even one who, in the Chinese tradition, regarded himself as divinely appointed—the "Son of Heaven." It was no accident then that the Chinese bureaucracy lasted from the Han period until the 20th century, outliving the empire itself.

Small wonder that from the classical period at least until modern times, and possibly still today, the Chinese were the most tightly governed people in any large society in the world. When it worked well—and it is important to recall that the system periodically broke down—Chinese politics represented a remarkable integration of all levels of authority. The edicts of an all-powerful emperor were administered by trained scholar-bureaucrats, widely respected for their learning and, often, their noble birth. Individual families also emphasized this strong principle of authority, with the father in charge, presumably carrying on the wishes of a long line of ancestors to which the family paid reverence. The Chinese were capable of periodic rebellions, and gangs of criminals more regularly came to disrupt the social scene—indeed, frequently harsh punishments reflected the need of the government to eradicate such deviant forces. Nevertheless, whether within the family or the central state, most Chinese in ordinary times believed in the importance of respect for those in power.

Government traditions established during the classical period included an impressive list of state functions. Like all organized states, the Chinese government operated military and judicial systems. Military activity fluctuated, as China did

not depend on steady expansion. Although classical China produced some enduring examples of the art of war, the state was not highly militaristic by the Han period. Judicial matters—crime and legal disputes—commanded more attention by local government authorities.

The government also sponsored much intellectual life, organizing research in astronomy and the maintenance of historical records. Under the Han rulers, the government played a major role in promoting Confucian philosophy as an official statement of Chinese values and in encouraging the worship of Confucius himself. The government developed a durable sense of mission as the primary keeper of Chinese beliefs.

The imperial government was also active in the economy. It directly organized the production of iron and salt. Its standardization of currency, weights, and measures facilitated trade throughout the vast empire. The government additionally sponsored public works, including complex irrigation and canal systems. Han rulers even tried to regulate agricultural supplies by storing grain and rice in good times to control price increases—and potential popular unrest—when harvests were bad.

China's ambitious rulers in no sense directed the daily lives of their subjects; the technology of an agricultural society did not permit this. Even under the Han, it took more than a month for a directive from the capital city to reach the outlying districts of the empire—an obvious limit on imperial authority. A revealing Chinese proverb held that "heaven is high, and the emperor is far away." However, the power of the Chinese state did extend considerably. Its system of courts was backed by a strict code of law; torture and execution were widely employed to supplement the preaching of obedience and civic virtue. The central government taxed its subjects and also required some annual labor on the part of every male peasant—this was the source of the incredible physical work involved in building canals, roads, and palaces. No other government had the organization and staff to reach ordinary people so directly until virtually

HISTORY DEBATE

WAR

Historians debate how to fit war and military developments into general patterns, beyond noting major wars as significant events. Military history is something of a specialty, and some historians stay away from it. Ironically, military history is the most popular kind of history with the general American public, as indicated by the History Channel and the purchases of books directed at a wide audience (but this is particularly true among males; females like this aspect of history less).

The classical period—classical China in particular—offers ways to relate military history to wider developments, while recognizing its importance and interest. Classical civilizations, with expanding territory and tax revenues, inevitably changed the ways wars were handled. Wider use of iron weaponry, a key underpinning for the classical period, had the same effect. Wars began to involve more soldiers, more casualties, and longer spans of time.

In most early civilizations, war had involved a good bit of ritual, along with contests among individual fighters. Leaders avoided war during harvest season or winter, they announced intentions of attack in advance, and they used priests to consult signs in order to determine when to strike. Battles involved contests among well-armed and trained elite warriors, along with a confused mass of ordinary foot soldiers who were peasants or slaves. Codes of honor dominated; it was not proper, for example, to strike from behind. There was great emphasis on heroic deeds, and early literature in India and the Mediterranean continued to highlight competition among individual heroes.

In the Shang and early Zhou dynasties, Chinese wars showed this common pattern. But Chinese leaders, with their concern for order, began to worry about the waste this system involved. In the 4th century B.C.E., one official, Sunzi, responded with a careful treatise, *The Art of War,* probably the most important book ever written in the military field. Sunzi urged that wars be carefully organized and moved away from macho contests among heroes. Armies should strike quickly, seeking to end wars rapidly. He recommended special schools to train military leaders. Chinese governments began to set these up. Under Sunzi's influence, a wider array of strategies were used in war, with the goals of winning and winning quickly. These strategies included bluffing, spying, sneak attacks, and committing sabotage. Psychological attacks to demoralize the enemy were also emphasized. At the same time, Chinese governments paid more attention to organizing large armies, including maintaining supply lines.

Sunzi's influence showed in the military success of the Qin dynasty. Quite independently, Greek armies began introducing similar kinds of careful organization and discipline, which underpinned their conquests and those of Alexander the Great. War as a contest among champions did not end—it showed up later in Europe and Japan—but the trend was clear, as war became part of the growing organization of government.

modern times, except in much smaller political units such as city-states. The power of the government and the authority it commanded in the eyes of most ordinary Chinese people help explain why its structure survived decline, invasion, and even rebellion for so many centuries. Invaders such as the Xiongnu might topple a dynasty, but they could not devise a better system to run the country, and so the system and its bureaucratic administrators normally endured.

RELIGION AND CULTURE

The Chinese way of viewing the world, as this belief system developed during the classical period, was closely linked to a distinct political structure. Upper-class cultural values emphasized a good life on earth and the virtues of obedience to the state, more than speculations about God and the mysteries of heaven. At the same time, the Chinese tolerated and often combined various specific beliefs, so long as they did not contradict basic political loyalties.

Rulers in the Zhou dynasty maintained belief in a god or gods, but little attention was given to the nature of a deity. Rather, Chinese leaders stressed the importance of a harmonious earthly life that maintained proper balance between earth and heaven. Harmony included carefully constructed rituals to unify society and prevent individual excess. Among the upper classes, people were trained in elaborate exercises and military skills such as archery. Commonly, ceremonies venerating ancestors and even marking special meals were conducted. The use of chopsticks began at the end of the Zhou dynasty; it encouraged a code of politeness at meals. Soon after this, tea was introduced, although the most elaborate tea-drinking rituals developed later on, in Japan more than China.

Even before these specific ceremonies arose, however, the basic definition of a carefully ordered existence was given more formal philosophical backing. Amid the long collapse of the Zhou dynasty, many thinkers and religious prophets began to challenge Chinese traditions. From this ferment came a restatement of the traditions that ultimately reduced intellectual conflict and established a long-lasting tone for Chinese cultural and social life.

Confucius, or Kong Fuzi (which means Master Kong), lived from roughly 551 to 478 B.C.E. His life was devoted to teaching, and he traveled through many parts of China preaching his ideas of political virtue and good government. Confu-

cius was not a religious leader; he believed in a divine order but refused to speculate about it. Chinese civilization was unusual, in the classical period and well beyond, in that its dominant values were secular rather than religious.

Confucius saw himself as a spokesman for Chinese tradition and for what he believed were the great days of the Chinese state before the Zhou declined. He maintained that if people could be taught to emphasize personal virtue, which included a reverence for tradition, a solid political life would naturally result. The Confucian list of virtues stressed respect for one's social superiors—including fathers and husbands as leaders of the family. However, this emphasis on a proper hierarchy was balanced by an insistence that society's leaders behave modestly and without excess, shunning abusive power and treating courteously those people who were in their charge. According to Confucius, moderation in behavior, veneration of custom and ritual, and a love of wisdom should characterize the leaders of society at all levels. And with virtuous leaders, a sound political life would inevitably follow: "In an age of good government, men in high stations give preference to men of ability and give opportunity to those who are below them, and lesser people labor vigorously at their husbandry to serve their superiors."

Confucianism was primarily a system of ethics—do unto others as your status and theirs dictate—and a plea for loyalty to the community. It confirmed the distaste that many educated Chinese had developed for religious mysteries, as well as their delight in learning and good manners. Confucian doctrine, carefully recorded in a book called the *Analects,* was revived under the Han emperors, who saw the usefulness of Confucian emphasis on political virtue and social order. Confucian learning was also incorporated, along with traditional literary works, into the training of aspiring bureaucrats.

The problems Confucius set out to rectify, notably political disorder, were approached through an emphasis on individual virtuous

WORLD PROFILES

CONFUCIUS, OR KONG FUZI
(c. 551–479 B.C.E.)

Confucius was the single most important thinker in Chinese history. He was responsible for developing an orderly political and social philosophy as the Zhou dynasty became more unstable. He believed that an emphasis on personal virtue would preserve Chinese tradition and restore what he regarded as the great days of the Chinese state. He spent much of his life traveling to many parts of China, preaching his ideas of personal virtue, which included respect for one's social superiors and a reverence for tradition. Tempering this emphasis on hierarchy, Confucius maintained that society's leaders must also exhibit personal virtue through moderation in behavior, veneration of custom and ritual, and a love of wisdom. The 18th-century Chinese nobleman who painted the image shown here depicts the philosopher with the costume and headdress of his own scholar-gentry class. What does the portrait suggest about the characteristics later generations attributed to Confucius?

Stone rubbing taken from an 18th-century Chinese painting of Confucius.

behavior, both by the ruler and the ruled. "When the ruler does right, all men will imitate his self-control. What the ruler does, the people will follow." According to Confucius, only a man who demonstrated proper family virtues, including respect for parents and compassion for children and other inferiors, should be considered for political service. "When the ruler excels as a father, a son, and a brother, then the people imitate him." Confucius thus built into his own system the links among many levels of authority that came to characterize larger Chinese politics at

their best. His system also emphasized personal restraint and the careful socialization of children.

Confucianism emphasized the importance of the gentleman, a member of what came to be known as the *shi* class. A superior man controlled his emotions, observed all the proper manners and rituals. He was a generalist, not a specialist, capable of serving in all sorts of government positions, capable of contributing also to art and poetry. His authority rested on his morality, not his expertise. Confucius believed that if such men ruled China, harmony would prevail forever.

For subordinates, Confucius largely recommended obedience and respect; people should know their place, even under bad rulers. However, he urged a political system that would not base rank simply on birth but would make education accessible to all talented and intelligent members of society. The primary emphasis still rested nonetheless on the obligations and desirable characteristics of the ruling class. According to Confucius, force alone cannot permanently conquer unrest, but kindness toward the people and protection of their vital interests will. Rulers should also be humble and sincere, for people will grow rebellious under hypocrisy or arrogance. Nor should rulers be greedy; Confucius warned against a profit motive in leadership, stressing that true happiness rested in doing good for all, not individual gain. Confucius projected the ideal of a gentleman, best described by his benevolence and self-control, a man always courteous and eager for service and anxious to learn.

Confucianism was accepted and amplified by many disciples. Mencius (Meng Ko) was an important figure who emphasized the goodness of human nature. People should be ruled in ways that brought out their goodness. Mencius' ideas, less hierarchical than pure Confucianism, set the basis for the belief that it was legitimate for peasants to rebel against oppressive rulers.

During the Qin and early Han periods, an alternate system of political thought, called "Legalism," sprang up in China. Legalist writers prided themselves on their pragmatism. They disdained Confucian virtues in favor of an authoritarian state that ruled by force. Human nature for the Legalists was evil and required restraint and discipline. In a proper state, the army would control and the people would labor; the idea of pleasures in educated discourse or courtesy was dismissed as frivolity. Although Legalism never captured the widespread approval that Confucianism did, it too entered the political traditions of China, where a Confucian veneer was often combined with strong-arm tactics.

Confucianists did not explicitly seek popular loyalty. Like many early civilizations, China did not produce a single system of beliefs, as different groups embraced different values, with the same individual even turning to contrasting systems depending on his or her mood. Confucianism had some obvious limits in its appeal to the masses and, indeed, to many educated Chinese. Its reluctance to explore the mysteries of life or nature deprived it of a spiritual side. The creed was most easily accepted by the upper classes, which had the time and resources to pursue an education and participate in ceremony. However, elements of Confucianism, including a taste for ritual, self-control, and polite manners, did spread beyond the upper classes. But most peasants needed more than civic virtue to understand and survive their harsh life, where in constant toil they eked out only a precarious and meager existence. During most of the classical period, polytheistic beliefs, focusing on the spirits of nature, persisted among much of the peasant class. Many peasants strove to attract the blessing of conciliatory spirits by creating statues and emblems, and household decorations honoring the spirits, by holding parades and family ceremonies for the same purpose. A belief in the symbolic power of dragons stemmed from one such popular religion, which combined fear of these creatures with a more playful sense of their activities in its courtship of the divine forces of nature. Gradually, ongoing rites among the ordinary masses integrated the Confucian values urged by the upper classes.

Classical China also produced a more religious philosophy—Daoism—which arose at roughly the same time as Confucianism, during the waning centuries of the Zhou dynasty. Daoism first appealed to many in the upper classes, who had an interest in a more elaborate spirituality. Daoism embraced traditional Chinese beliefs in nature's harmony and added a sense of nature's mystery. As a spiritual alternative to Confucianism, Daoism produced a durable division in China's religious and philosophical culture. This new religion, vital for Chinese civilization although never widely exported, was furthered by Laozi, who probably lived during the 5th century B.C.E. Laozi stressed that nature contains a divine impulse which directs all life. True human understanding comes in withdrawing from the world and contemplating this life force. Dao, which means "the way of nature," refers to this same basic, indescribable force:

> There is a thing confusedly formed,
> Born before heaven and earth.
> Silent and void
> It stands alone and does not change,
> Goes round and does not weary.
> It is capable of being the mother of the
>   world.
> I know not its name,
> So I style it "the way."

Along with secret rituals, Daoism promoted its own set of ethics. Daoist harmony with nature best resulted through humility and frugal living. According to this movement, political activity and learning were irrelevant to a good life, and general conditions in the world were of little importance.

Daoism, which combined with a strong Buddhist influence from India during the chaos that followed the collapse of the Han dynasty, guaranteed that China's people were not united by a single religious or philosophical system. Individuals did come to embrace some elements from both Daoism and Confucianism, and indeed many emperors favored Daoism. They accepted its spread with little anxiety, partly because some of them found solace in Daoist belief but also because the religion, with its otherworldly emphasis, posed no real political threat. Confucian scholars disagreed vigorously with Daoist thinking, particularly its emphasis on mysteries and magic, but they saw little reason to challenge its influence. As Daoism became an increasingly formal religion, from the later Han dynasty on, it provided many Chinese with a host of ceremonies designed to promote harmony with the mysterious life force. Finally, the Chinese government from the Han dynasty on was able to persuade Daoist priests to include expressions of loyalty to the emperor in their temple services. This heightened Daoism's political compatibility with Confucianism.

Confucianism and Daoism were not the only intellectual products of China's classical period, but they were the most important. Confucianism blended easily with the high value of literature and art among the upper classes. In literature, a set of Five Classics, written during the early part of the Zhou dynasty and then edited during the time of Confucius, provided an important tradition. They were used, among other things, as a basis for civil service examinations. The works provided in the Five Classics included some historical treatises, speeches, and other political materials, and a discussion of etiquette and ceremonies; in the *Classic of Songs,* more than 300 poems dealing with love, joy, politics, and family life appeared. The Chinese literary tradition developed on the basis of mastering these early works, plus Confucian writing; each generation of writers found new meanings in the classical literature, which allowed them to express new ideas within a familiar framework. Several thinkers during the Han dynasty elaborated Confucian philosophy. In literature, poetry commanded particular attention because the Chinese language featured melodic speech and variant pronunciations of the same basic sound, a characteristic that promoted an outpouring of poetry. From the classical period on, the ability to learn and recite poetry became the mark of an educated Chinese. Finally, the literary tradition established in classical China reinforced the Confucian emphasis on human life, although the subjects included romance and sorrow as well as political values.

Chinese art during the classical period was largely decorative, stressing careful detail and craftsmanship. Artistic styles often reflected the precision and geometric qualities of the many symbols of Chinese writing. Calligraphy became an important art form. In addition, Chinese artists painted, worked in bronze and pottery,

This elaborate bronze vase dates from the late Zhou dynasty (c. 300 B.C.E.). It might be compared with the simpler, more primitive Chinese designs depicted earlier from the Shang dynasty.

carved jade and ivory, and wove silk screens. Classical China did not produce monumental buildings, aside from the Great Wall and some imperial palaces and tombs, in part because of the absence of a single religion; indeed, the entire tone of upper-class Confucianism was such that it discouraged the notion of temples soaring to the heavens.

In science, important practical work was encouraged, rather than imaginative theorizing. Chinese astronomers had developed an accurate calendar by 444 B.C.E., based on a year of 365.5 days. Later astronomers calculated the movement of the planets Saturn and Jupiter and observed sunspots—more than 1500 years before comparable knowledge developed in Europe. The purpose of Chinese astronomy was to make celestial phenomena predictable, as part of the wider interest in ensuring harmony between heaven and earth. Chinese scientists steadily improved their instrumentation, inventing a kind of seismograph to register earthquakes during the Han dynasty. The Chinese were also active in medical research, developing precise anatomical knowledge and studying principles of hygiene that could promote longer life.

Horse figure from Han dynasty, 2nd century C.E. The Chinese imported new horse breeds as they expanded into central Asia. This statue celebrates the improvement over the early, short-legged horses that were known to the Chinese.

Chinese mathematics also stressed the practical. Daoism encouraged some exploration of the orderly processes of nature, but far more research focused on how things actually worked. For example, Chinese scholars studied the mathematics of music in ways that led to advances in acoustics. This focus for science and mathematics contrasted notably with the more abstract definition of science developed in classical Greece.

ECONOMY AND SOCIETY

Although the most distinctive features of classical China centered on politics and culture, developments in the economy, social structure, and family life also shaped Chinese civilization and

continued to have impact on the empire's history for a significant period of time.

As in many agricultural societies, considerable gaps developed between China's upper class, which controlled large landed estates, and the masses, farmer-peasants who produced little more than what was needed for their own subsistence. The difficulty of becoming literate symbolized these gaps, for landlords enjoyed not only wealth but also a culture denied to most common people. Prior to the Zhou dynasty, slaveholding may have been common in China, but by the time of the Zhou, the main social division existed between the landowning gentry—about 2 percent of the total population—and peasants, who provided dues and service to these lords while also controlling some of their own land.

The Chinese peasantry depended on intensive cooperation, particularly in the southern rice region; in this group, property was characteristically owned and regulated by the village or the extended family, rather than by individuals. Beneath the peasantry, Chinese social structure included a group of "mean" people who performed rough transport and other unskilled jobs and suffered from the lowest possible status. In general, social status was passed from one generation to the next through inheritance, although unusually talented individuals from a peasant background might be given access to an education and rise within the bureaucracy.

Officially then and to a large extent in fact, classical China consisted of three main social groups. The landowning aristocracy plus the educated bureaucrats formed the top group. This top group, first known as the shi, then the scholar-gentry, under the Han combined education and bureaucratic service, with landowning. Scholar-gentry families cooperated to run the estates and also provide bureaucrats. They were marked by special dress, including silks, which commoners were not supposed to wear. Most gentry families employed some toughs to help protect them and to make sure commoners stayed in their place, but they also received great deference from most ordinary people. Under the gentry next came the laboring masses, peasants and also urban artisans who manufactured goods. These people, far poorer than the top group and also condemned to a life of hard manual labor, sometimes worked directly on large estates but in other cases had some economic independence. Finally, were the mean people, the general category we have identified as applying to those without meaningful skills. Interestingly, performing artists were ranked in this group, despite the fact that the upper classes enjoyed plays and other entertainments provided by actors. Mean people were punished for crime more harshly than other groups and were required to wear identifying green scarves. Household slaves also existed within this class structure, but their number was relatively few and China did not depend on slaves for actual production.

Trade became increasingly important during the Zhou and particularly the Han dynasties. Much trade focused on luxury items for the upper class, produced by skilled artisans in the cities—silks, jewelry, leather goods, and furniture. There was also food exchange between the wheat- and rice-growing regions. Copper coins began to circulate, which facilitated trade, with merchants even sponsoring commercial visits to India. Although significant, trade and its attendant merchant class did not become the focal points of Chinese society, and the Confucian emphasis on learning and political service led to considerable scorn for lives devoted to money-making. The gap between the real importance and wealth of merchants and their officially low prestige was an enduring legacy in Confucian China.

If trade fit somewhat uncomfortably into the dominant view of society, there was no question about the importance of technological advance. Here, the Chinese excelled. Agricultural implements improved steadily. Ox-drawn plows were introduced around 300 B.C.E., which greatly increased productivity. Under the Han, a new collar was invented for draft animals, allowing them to pull plows or wagons without choking—this was a major improvement that became available to other parts of the world only many centuries later. Chinese iron mining was also well advanced, as pulleys and winding gear were devised to bring material to the surface. Iron tools and other implements such as lamps were widely used. Production methods in textiles and pottery were also highly developed by world standards. Under the Han, the first water-powered mills were introduced, allowing further gains in manufacturing. Finally, during the Han, paper was invented, which was a major boon to a system of government that emphasized the bureaucracy. In sum, classical China reached far higher levels of technical expertise than Europe or western Asia in the same period, a lead that it long maintained.

Peasants transplanting rice seedlings in south China.

Technological advances, emphasis on manufacturing, and the particular mastery of silk production also positioned China strongly in the world trade of the period. The quality of Chinese goods helped sustain the network of the Silk Roads.

The relatively advanced technology of classical China did not, however, steer Chinese society away from its primary reliance on agriculture. Farming technology helped increase the size of the population in the countryside; with better tools and seeds, smaller amounts of land could support more families. But China's solid agricultural base, backed by some trade in foodstuffs among key regions, did permit the expansion of cities and of manufacturing. There were many towns with more than 10,000 people; China was probably the most urbanized of the classical civilizations. Nonagricultural goods were mainly produced by artisans, working in small shops or

WORLD PROFILES

BAN ZHAO
(c. 48–117 C.E.)

Ban Zhao, now known as China's most famous woman scholar, was long esteemed as an advisor on female humility and an example of chaste widowhood. Her life and ideas illustrate the complexities of a patriarchal society in action, and also the several sides of Confucianism.

Ban Zhao was the daughter of a leading scholar, with two able brothers, one a historian, the other a general. She received a good education. Ban Zhao married and had a son but was widowed at an early age. Living with her historian-brother, she collaborated with him on a history of the Han dynasty. When her brother died, the emperor insisted she complete the history, and she seems to have been responsible for some of its most original sections. She also tutored women at the imperial court, in literature, history, mathematics, and astronomy, and exerted considerable influence when one of her students became empress, serving as regent for a time. Ban Zhao wrote widely, although most of her works have been lost over the centuries. Her most famous effort was *Lessons for Women*, reprinted and actively circulated in China through the 19th century. In this work, Ban Zhao urged humility and domestic skills, a point of view that seemed at odds with, although not in complete contrast to, her own life. Young girls, for example, were urged to sleep at the foot of a brother's bed, so they would begin to learn their proper station. Accepting a Confucian family hierarchy, Ban Zhao also insisted that men had specific obligations to women, particularly to provide an appropriate education—and she emphasized that this aspect of their reciprocal relationship was not being met. Still, the dominant tone of *Lessons for Women* was subservient. Her work raises obvious questions. Why would an educated, self-sufficient woman condone the notion of women's inferiority to men? How can the contradiction between Ban Zhao's life and her public views be explained?

This woodcut of Ban Zhao appeared in 1690, obviously long after her death. The drawing is a sign of her ongoing importance as an advisor on gender. Because it reflects no knowledge of what the famous author actually looked like, the drawing should be interpreted in terms of what symbolic qualities artists had decided to emphasize.

in their homes. Even though only a minority of the workforce was involved in such tasks that used manual methods for the most part, the output of tools, porcelain, and textiles increased considerably, aided in this case as well by the interest in improving techniques.

In all major social groups, tight family organization helped solidify economic and social views as well as political life. The structure of the Chinese family resembled that of families in other agricultural civilizations in emphasizing the importance of unity and the power of husbands and fathers. Within this context, however, the Chinese stressed authority to unusual extremes. Confucius said, "There are no wrongdoing parents"—and in practice, parents could punish disobedient children freely. Law courts did not prosecute parents who injured or even killed a disobedient son, but they severely punished a child who scolded or attacked a parent. In most families, the emphasis on obedience to parents, and a corresponding emphasis on wives' obedience to husbands, did not produce great friction. Chinese popular culture stressed strict control of one's emotions, and the family was seen as the center of such an orderly, serene hierarchy. Indeed, the family served as a great training ground for the principles of authority and restraint that applied to the larger social and political world. Women, although subordinate, had their own clearly defined roles and could sometimes gain power through their sons and as mothers-in-law of younger women brought into the household. The mother of a famous Confucian philosopher, Mencius, continually claimed how humble she was, but during the course of his life she managed to exert considerable influence over him. But the basic subordination was clear. A Confucian poet stated, "A woman with a long tongue is a stepping stone to disorder. Disorder does not come down from Heaven—It is produced by women." There was even a clear hierarchical order for children, with boys superior to girls and the oldest son having the most

enviable position of all. Chinese rules of inheritance, from the humblest peasant to the emperor himself, followed strict primogeniture, which meant that the oldest male child inherited property and position alike.

HOW CHINESE CIVILIZATION FIT TOGETHER

Classical Chinese technology, religion, philosophy, and political structure evolved with very little outside contact. Although important trade routes did lead to India and the Middle East, most Chinese saw the world in terms of a large island of civilization surrounded by barbarian peoples with nothing to offer save the periodic threat of invasion. Proud of their culture and of its durability, the Chinese had neither the need nor the desire to learn from other societies. Nor, except to protect their central territory by exercising some control over the mountainous or desert regions that surrounded the Middle Kingdom, did Chinese leaders have any particular desire to teach the rest of the world. A missionary spirit was foreign to Chinese culture and politics. Of course, China displayed key patterns that were similar to those of the other agricultural civilizations. Further, the spread of Buddhism from India, during and after the Han decline, was a notable instance of a cultural diffusion that altered China's religious map and also its artistic styles. Nevertheless, the theme of separators and superiority, developed during the formative period of Chinese civilization, was to prove persistent in later world history—in fact, it has not entirely disappeared to this day.

Chinese civilization was also noteworthy for the relative harmony among its various major features. We have, in this chapter, examined the pattern of leading historical events in classical China and then the systems of government, belief, economy, and social structure. All these facets were closely meshed. Although the centralized government, with its elaborate functions and far-reaching bureaucracy, gave the clearest unity and focus to Chinese society, it did not do so alone. Confucianism provided a vital supplement, making the bureaucracy more than a collection of people with similar political objectives, but rather a trained corps with some common ideals. In appreciation of distinctive artistic styles, poetry and the literary tradition added to this common culture. Cohesive government and related beliefs about human ideals and aesthetics were linked, in turn, to the economy. Political stability over a large and fertile land aided economic growth, and the government took a direct role in encouraging both agriculture and industry. A strong economy, in turn, provided the government with vital tax revenues. Economic interests were also related to the pragmatic Chinese view of science, whose aim was to determine how nature worked. Finally, social relationships reinforced all these systems. The vision of a stable hierarchy and tight family structures meshed with the strong impulse toward orderly politics and helped instill the virtues of obedience and respect that were important to the larger political system.

Not surprisingly, given the close links among the various facets of their civilization, the Chinese tended to think of their society as a whole. They did not distinguish clearly between private and public sectors of activity. They did not see government and society as two separate entities. In other words, these Western concepts that we have used to define classical China and to facilitate comparisons with other societies do not really fit the Chinese view of their own world. Confucius himself, in seeing government as basically a vast extension of family relationships, similarly suggested that the pieces of the Chinese puzzle were intimately joined.

A grasp of Chinese civilization as a whole, however, should not distract us from recognizing some endemic tensions and disparities. The division in belief systems, between Confucianism and Daoism, modifies the perception of an ultimately

tidy classical China. Confucianists and Daoists tolerated each other. Sometimes their beliefs coincided, so that an individual who behaved politically as a Confucianist might explore deeper mysteries through Daoist rituals. However, between both groups there was considerable hostility and mutual disdain, as many Confucianists found Daoists superstitious and over-excited. Daoism did not inherently disrupt the political unity of Chinese culture, but at times the religion did inspire attacks on established politics in the name of a mysterious divine will.

Tension in Chinese society showed in the way Confucian beliefs were combined with strict policing. Chinese officials believed in fundamental human goodness and the importance of ceremony and mutual respect. However, they also believed in the force of stern punishment, not only against criminals but also as warnings to the larger, potentially restless population. People arrested were presumed guilty and often subjected to torture before trial. The Chinese, in fact, early discovered the usefulness of alternating torture with benevolence, to make accused individuals confess. In the late Han period, a thief who refused to confess even under severe torture was then freed from chains, bathed, and fed, "so as to bring him in a happy mood"—whereupon he usually confessed and named his whole gang. In sum, both Confucianism and the Chinese penal system supported tight control, and the combination of the two was typically effective; however, they involved quite different approaches and quite different moral assumptions.

All of this suggests that classical China, like any vigorous, successful society, embraced a diversity of features that could not be fully united by any single formula. Elites and masses were divided by both economic interests and culture. Some shared the same values, particularly as Confucianism spread, and upper-class concern for careful etiquette and the general welfare of the population mitigated the tension. But such calm was a precarious balance, and when overpopulation or some other factor tipped the scale, recurrent and often violent protest could be the result.

Despite any divisions, the symbiosis among the various institutions and activities of many people in classical China deserves strong emphasis. It helps account for the durability of Chinese values. Even in times of political turmoil, families transferred beliefs and political ideals by the ways in which they instructed their children. The overall wholeness of Chinese society also helps account for its relative immunity to outside influence and for its creativity despite considerable isolation.

Chinese wholeness, finally, provides an interesting contrast to the other great Asian civilization that developed in the classical period. India, as fully dynamic as China in many ways, produced different emphases, but also a more disparate society in which links among politics and beliefs and economic life were less well defined. Many argue that this contrast between the two Asian giants persists to our own time.

PATHS TO THE PRESENT

The astonishing durability of the classical civilizations' features—a durability that extends to the present—is a key reason to study their formation and characteristics. Nowhere is this more the case than in China.

Huge changes have occurred, of course, between the fall of the Han dynasty and modern China, and it is important to examine later world history, to avoid stereotyping Chinese culture and people.

But the basic list of early China's enduring accomplishments is intriguing. China was once a center of world manufacturing, as evidenced by its centrality in Silk Roads trade, and modern China is reemerging into that role. Modern China, though no longer Confucian, continues

to emphasize the importance of political order and a strong state. Strong family structures, including in the countryside a preference for boys over girls, suggest additional links to the past; this has led in recent decades to a striking gender imbalance in contemporary Chinese society, which is a potentially serious problem. Even the current widespread enthusiasm for higher education—though in modern subjects, not traditional ones—likely builds on values created during the Han dynasty.

China's classical experience, in other words, forms part of the framework that has created China as it exists today. This raises vital questions about the reasons so many traditional elements survived so well—questions that can be answered by looking at the nation's experience in later world history periods.

SUGGESTED WEB SITES

For a view of the formation of Chinese civilization, see http://www.china.org.cn/e-gudai/; on Confucius, see http://plato.stanford.edu/entries/confucius/; for more information on the Great Bronze Age of China, see http://www.humanities-interactive.org/ancient/bronze/brochure_bronze_age.htm.

SUGGESTED READINGS

For recent scholarship, see Nicola DiCosmo, *Ancient China and Its Enemies: The Rise of Nomadic Power in East Asian History* (2002); Michael Loewe, ed., *The Cambridge History of Ancient China* (1999); Grant Hardy, *Worlds of Bronze and Bamboo: Sima Qian's Conquest of History* (1999); and Michael Neiberg, *Warfare in World History* (2001).

Several sources offer original materials on classical Chinese thought and politics: John Fairbank, ed., *Chinese Thought and Institutions* (1973); Wing-stit Chan, *A Source Book in Chinese Philosophy* (1963); and P. Ebrey, *Chinese Civilization and Society: A Sourcebook* (1981). Two excellent general surveys for this period and later ones are John Fairbank and Albert Craig, *East*

Asia: Tradition and Transformation (1993), and E. O. Reischauer and John Fairbank, *A History of East Asian Civilization*, Vol. 1: *East Asia, The Great Tradition* (1961); see also Arthur Cotterell, *The First Emperor of China* (1981). On more specialized topics, see E. Balazs, *Chinese Civilization and Bureaucracy* (1964); J. Needham, *Science and Civilization in China*, 4 vols. (1970); Richard J. Smith, *Traditional Chinese Culture: An Interpretive Introduction* (1978); Benjamin Schwartz, *The World of Thought in Ancient China* (1983); Michael Loewe, *Everyday Life in Early Imperial China* (1968); and Bella Vivante, ed., *Women's Roles in Ancient Civilizations: A Reference Guide* (1999); Steven Shankman, *Early China/Ancient Greece: Thinking Through Comparisons* (2002); Constance A. Cook, *Defining China: Image and Reality in Ancient China* (2004); Kwang-chih Chang and Sarah Allan, *The Formation of Chinese Civilization: An Archaeological Perspective* (2005); Steven Shankman and Stephen Durrant, *The Siren and the Sage: Knowledge and Wisdom in Ancient Greece and China* (2000); Paul Rakita Goldin, *The Culture of Sex in Ancient China* (2002); and Mu-chou Poo, *Enemies of Civilization: Attitudes Toward Foreigners in Ancient Mesopotamia, Egypt, and China* (2005).

5

Classical Civilization: India

The classical period of Indian history includes a number of contrasts to that of China—and many of these contrasts have proved enduring. Whereas the focus in classical China was on politics and related philosophical values, the emphasis in classical India shifted to religion and social structure; a political culture existed, but it was less cohesive and central than its Chinese counterpart. Less familiar but scarcely less important were distinctions that arose in India's scientific tradition and the tenor of the economy and family life. Here, too, the classical period generated impulses that are still felt in India today—and that continue to distinguish India from other major civilizations in the world.

India's distinctiveness was considerable, but a comparison must not be one sided. India was an agricultural society, and this dictated many similarities with China. Most people were peasant farmers, with their major focus on food production for their own family's survival. The clustering of peasants in villages, to provide mutual aid and protection, gave a strong localist flavor to many aspects of life in China and India alike. In addition, agriculture influenced family life, with male ownership of property creating a strongly patriarchal flavor, and women held as inferiors and often treated as possessions. As agricultural civilizations, both China and India produced important cities and engendered significant trade, which added to social and economic complexity and also created the basis for most formal intellectual life, including schools and academies. Both societies, finally, generated ideas that helped explain and confirm social inequality—though the cultural systems were rather different.

▌ **KEY QUESTIONS** *What were the main changes in India from the early classical period until the Gupta dynasty at the end? How did Hinduism and Buddhism relate in Indian history in this period? How did extensive merchant activity coexist with India's strong religious emphasis?*

THE FRAMEWORK FOR INDIAN HISTORY: GEOGRAPHY AND A FORMATIVE PERIOD

Important reasons for India's distinctive paths lie in geography and early historical experience. India was much closer to the orbit of other civilizations than China. Trading contacts with China expanded late in the classical period. India was also frequently open to influences from the Middle East and even the Mediterranean world. Persian empires spilled over into India at several points, bringing new artistic styles and political concepts. Briefly, Alexander the Great invaded India, and while he did not establish a durable empire, he did allow important Indian contacts with Hellenistic culture. Periodic influences from the Middle East continued after the classical age, prompting India to react and adapt in ways that China, more isolated, largely avoided.

In addition to links with other cultures, India's topography shaped a number of vital features of its civilization. The vast Indian subcontinent is partially separated from the rest of Asia, and particularly from east Asia, by northern mountain ranges, notably the Himalayas. Important passes through the mountains, especially in the northwest, linked India to other civilizations in the Middle East; although it lacked the isolation of China's Middle Kingdom, the subcontinent was somewhat set apart within Asia. At the same time, divisions within the subcontinent made full political unity difficult: India was thus marked by greater diversity than China's Middle Kingdom. The most important agricultural regions are those along the two great rivers, the Indus and the Ganges. However, India also has mountainous northern regions, where a herding economy took root, and a southern coastal rim, separated by mountains and the Deccan plateau, where an active trading and seafaring economy arose. India's separate regions help explain not only economic diversity but also the racial and language differences that, from early times, have marked the subcontinent's populations.

Much of India is semitropical in climate. In the river valley plains, heat can rise to 120° F during the early summer. Summer also brings torrential monsoon rains, crucial for farming. But the monsoons vary from year to year, sometimes bringing too little rain or coming too late and causing famine-producing drought, or sometimes bringing catastrophic floods. Certain features of Indian civilization may have resulted from a need to come to terms with a climate that could produce abundance one year and grim starvation the next. In a year with favorable monsoons, Indian farmers were able to plant and harvest two crops and could thus support a sizable population.

Indian civilization was shaped not only by its physical environment but also by a formative period, lasting several centuries, between the destruction of the Indus River (Harappan) civilization and the revival of full civilization elsewhere on the subcontinent. During this formative period, called the Vedic and Epic ages, the Indo-European migrants—nomadic herding peoples originally from central Asia, and sometimes called Aryans—gradually came to terms with agriculture but had their own impact on the culture and social structure of their new home. Also during the Vedic Age, from about 1500 to 1000 B.C.E., Indian agriculture extended from the Indus River valley to the more fertile Ganges valley, as the Aryans used iron tools to clear away the dense vegetation.

Most of what we know about this preclassical period in Indian history comes from literary epics developed by the Aryans, initially passed on orally. They were later written down in Sanskrit, which became the first literary language of the new culture. The initial part of this formative period, the Vedic Age, takes its name from the Sanskrit word *Veda*, or "knowledge." The first epic, the *Rig-Veda*, consists of 1028 hymns dedicated to the Aryan gods and composed by various priests. New stories, developed during the Epic Age between 1000 and 600 B.C.E., include the *Mahabharata,* India's greatest epic poem, and the *Ramayana,* both of which deal with real and mythical battles; these epics reflect a more settled agricultural society and better-organized political units than the *Rig-Veda.* The Epic Age also saw the creation of the *Upanishads,* epic poems with a more mystical religious flavor.

Aryan ideas and social and family forms also became increasingly influential. As the Aryans settled down to agriculture, they encouraged tight levels of village organization that came to be characteristic of Indian society and politics. Village chiefs, initially drawn from the leadership of one of the Aryan tribes, helped organize village defenses and also to regulate property relationships among families. Family structure emphasized patriarchal controls, and extended family relationships among grandparents, parents, and children were close.

The characteristic Indian caste system also began to take shape during the Vedic and Epic ages, as a means of establishing relationships between the Aryan conquerors and the indigenous people, whom the Aryans regarded as inferior. Aryan social classifications partly enforced divisions familiar in agricultural societies. Thus, a warrior or governing class, the *kshatriyas,* and the priestly caste, or brahmins, stood at the top of the social pyramid, followed by *vaisyas,* the traders and farmers, and *sudras,* or common laborers. Many of the sudras worked on the estates of large landowners. A fifth group gradually evolved, the untouchables, who were confined to a few jobs, such as transporting the bodies of the dead or hauling refuse. Handling leather hides was also in this category, because of Indian valuation of animals and disdain for people involved with killing them. It was widely believed that touching these people defiled anyone from a superior caste. Initially, the warrior group ranked highest, but during the Epic Age the brahmins replaced them, signaling the importance of religious links in Indian life. Thus, a law book stated, "When a brahmin springs to light he is born above the world, the chief of all creatures, assigned to guard the treasury of duties, religious and civil." Grad-

ually, the five social groups became hereditary, with marriage between castes forbidden and punishable by death; the basic castes divided into smaller subgroups, called jati, each with distinctive occupations and each tied to its social station by birth. India's caste system hardened with time, so what had been rather loose arrangements of social inequalities became life-determining. Only the highest three castes were directly authorized to read sacred texts. One of the heroes of Indian epics, Rama, was celebrated for cutting off the head of a peasant who read the Vedas while hanging upside down from a tree.

The *Rig-Veda,* the first Aryan epic, attributed the rise of the caste system to the gods:

> When they divided the original Man
> into how many parts did they divide him?
> What was his mouth, what were his arms,
> what were his thighs and his feet called?
> The brahmin was his mouth, of his
> arms was made the warrior.
> His thighs became the vaisya, of
> his feet the sudra was born.

The Aryans brought to India a religion of many gods and goddesses, who regulated natural forces and possessed human qualities. Thus, Indra, the god of thunder, was also the god of strength. Gods presided over fire, the sun, death, and so on. This system bore some resemblances to the gods and goddesses of Greek myth or Scandinavian mythology, for the very good reason that they were derived from a common Indo-European oral heritage. However, India was to give this common tradition an important twist, ultimately constructing a vigorous, complex religion that, apart from the Indo-European polytheistic faiths, endures to this day. During the epic periods, the Aryans offered hymns and sacrifices to the gods. Certain animals were regarded as particularly sacred, embodying the divine spirit. Gradually, this religion became more elaborate. The epic poems reflect an idea of life after death and a religious approach to the world of nature. Nature was seen as informed not only by specific gods but also by a more basic divine force. These ideas, expressed in the mystical *Upanishads,* added greatly to the spiritual power of this early religion and served as the basis for later Hindu beliefs. By the end of the Epic Age, the dominant Indian belief system included a variety of convictions. Many people continued to emphasize rituals and sacrifices to the gods of nature; specific beliefs, as in the sacredness of monkeys and cattle, illustrated this ritualistic approach. The brahmin priestly caste specified and enforced prayers, ceremonies, and rituals. However, the religion also produced a more mystical strand through its belief in a unifying divine force and the desirability of seeking union with this force. Toward the end of the Epic period one religious leader, Gautama Buddha, built on this mysticism to create what became Buddhism, another major world religion.

PATTERNS IN CLASSICAL INDIA

By 600 B.C.E., India had passed through its formative phase. Regional political units grew in size, cities and trade expanded, and the development of the Sanskrit language, although dominated by the priestly brahmin caste, furthered an elaborate literary culture. A full, classical civilization could now build on the social and cultural themes first launched during the Vedic and Epic ages.

Indian development during the classical era and beyond did not take on the convenient structure of rising and falling dynasties characteristic of Chinese history. Political eras were even less clear than in classical Greece. The rhythm of Indian history was irregular and often consisted of landmark invasions that poured in through the mountain passes of the subcontinent's northwestern border.

Toward the end of the Epic Age and until the 4th century B.C.E., the Indian plains were divided among powerful regional states. Sixteen major states existed by 600 B.C.E. in the plains of northern India, some of them monarchies, others republics dominated by assemblies of priests and warriors. Warfare was not uncommon. One regional state, Magadha, established dominance over a considerable empire. In 327 B.C.E., Alexander the Great, having conquered Greece and much of the Middle East, pushed into northwestern India, establishing the small border state called Bactria.

Political reactions to this incursion produced the next major step in Indian political history, in 322 B.C.E., when a young soldier named Chandragupta seized power along the Ganges River. He became the first of the Maurya dynasty of Indian rulers, who in turn were the first rulers to unify much of the entire subcontinent. Borrowing from Persian political models and the example of Alexander the Great, Chandragupta and his successors maintained large armies, with thousands of chariots and elephant-borne troops. The Mauryan rulers also developed a substantial bureaucracy, even sponsoring a postal service.

Chandragupta's style of government was highly autocratic, relying on the ruler's personal and military power. This style surfaced periodically in Indian history, just as it did in the Middle East, a region with which India had important contacts. A Greek ambassador from one of the Hellenistic kingdoms described Chandragupta's life:

> Attendance on the king's person is the duty of women, who indeed are bought from their fathers. Outside the gates [of the palace] stand the bodyguards and the rest of the soldiers. . . . Nor does the king sleep during the day, and at night he is forced at various hours to change his bed because of those plotting against him. Of his nonmilitary departures [from the palace] one is to the courts, in which he passed the day hearing cases to the end. . . . [When he leaves to hunt,] he is thickly surrounded by a circle of women, and on the outside by spear-carrying bodyguards. The road is fenced off with ropes, and to anyone who passes within the ropes as far as the women, death is the penalty.

Such drastic precautions paid off. Chandragupta finally designated his rule to a son and became a religious ascetic, dying peacefully at an advanced age.

Chandragupta's grandson, Ashoka (269-232 B.C.E.), was an even greater figure in India's history. First serving as a governor of two provinces, Ashoka enjoyed a lavish lifestyle, with frequent horseback riding and feasting. However, he also engaged in a study of nature and was strongly influenced by the intense spiritualism not only of the brahmin religion but also of Buddhism. Ashoka extended Mauryan conquests, gaining control of all but the southern tip of India through fierce fighting. His methods were bloodthirsty; in taking over one coastal area, Ashoka himself admitted that "one hundred and fifty thousand were killed (or maimed) and many times that number later died." But Ashoka could also be compassionate. He ultimately converted to Buddhism, seeing in the belief in *dharma,* or the law of moral consequences, a kind of ethical guide that might unite and discipline the diverse people under his rule. Ashoka vigorously propagated Buddhism throughout India, while also honoring Hinduism, sponsoring shrines for its worshippers. Ashoka even sent Buddhist missionaries to the Hellenistic kingdoms in the Middle East, and also to Sri Lanka to the south. The "new" Ashoka urged humane behavior on the part of his officials and insisted that they oversee the moral welfare of his empire. Like Chandragupta, Ashoka also worked to improve trade and communication, sponsoring an extensive road network dotted with wells and rest stops for travelers. Stability and the sheer expansion of the empire's territory encouraged growing commerce.

The Mauryan dynasty did not, however, succeed in establishing durable roots, and Ashoka's particular style of government did not have much later impact, although a strong Buddhist current persisted in India for some time. After Ashoka, the empire began to fall apart, and regional kingdoms surfaced once again. New invaders, the Kushans, pushed into central India from the

Column to Ashoka, 3rd century B.C.E.

northwest. The greatest Kushan king, Kanishka, converted to Buddhism but actually hurt this religion's popularity in India by associating it with foreign rule.

The collapse of the Kushan state, by 220 C.E., ushered in another hundred years of political instability. Then a new line of kings, the Guptas, established a large empire, beginning in 320 C.E. The Guptas produced no individual rulers as influential as the two great Mauryan rulers, but they may have had greater impact. One Gupta

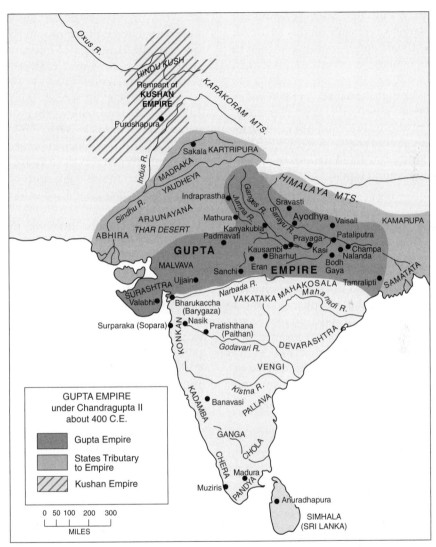

India, 400 C.E.

emperor proclaimed his virtues in an inscription on a ceremonial stone pillar:

> His far-reaching fame, deep-rooted in peace, emanated from the restoration of the sovereignty of many fallen royal families. . . . He, who had no equal in power in the world, eclipsed the fame of the other kings by the radiance of his versatile virtues, adorned by innumerable good actions.

Bombast aside, Gupta rulers often preferred to negotiate with local princes and intermarry with their families, which expanded influence without constant fighting. Two centuries of Gupta rule gave classical India its greatest period of political stability, although the Guptas did not administer as large a territory as the Mauryan kings had. The Gupta empire was overturned in 535 C.E. by a new invasion of nomadic warriors, the Huns.

Classical India thus alternated between widespread empires and a network of smaller kingdoms. Periods of regional rule did not necessarily suggest great instability, and both economic and cultural life advanced in these periods as well as under the Mauryas and Guptas.

POLITICAL INSTITUTIONS

Classical India did not develop the solid political traditions and institutions of Chinese civilization, or the high level of political interest that characterized classical Greece and Rome. The most persistent political features of India, in the classical period and beyond, involved regionalism, plus considerable diversity in political forms. Autocratic kings and emperors dotted the history of classical India, but there were also aristocratic assemblies in some regional states with the power to consult and decide on major issues.

As a result of India's diversity and regionalism, even some of the great empires had a rather shaky base. Early Mauryan rulers depended heavily on the power of their large armies, and they often feared betrayal and attack. Early rulers in the Gupta dynasty used various devices to consolidate support. They claimed that they had been appointed by the gods to rule, and they favored the Hindu religion over Buddhism because the Hindus believed in such gods. The Guptas managed to create a demanding taxation system, seeking up to a sixth of all agricultural produce. However, they did not create an extensive bureaucracy, rather allowing local rulers whom they had defeated to maintain regional control so long as they deferred to Gupta dominance. The Guptas stationed a personal representative at each ruler's court to ensure loyalty. A final sign of the great empire's loose structure was the fact that no single language was imposed. The Guptas promoted Sanskrit, which became the language of educated people, but this made no dent in the diversity of popular, regional languages.

The Guptas did spread uniform law codes. Like the Mauryan rulers, they sponsored some general services, such as road building. They also served as patrons of much cultural activity, including university life as well as art and literature. These achievements were more than enough to qualify the Gupta period as a golden age in Indian history.

The fact remains, however, that the political culture of India was not very elaborate. There was little formal political theory and few institutions or values other than regionalism that carried through from one period to the next. Chandragupta's chief minister, Kautilya, wrote an important treatise on politics, but it was devoted to telling rulers what methods worked to maintain power—somewhat like the Legalists in China. Thinking of this sort encouraged efficient authority, but it did not very widely spread political values or a sense of the importance of political service, in contrast to Confucianism in China and also to the intense interest in political ethics in Greece and Rome. Ashoka saw in Buddhism a kind of ethic for good behavior as well as a spiritual beacon, but Buddhist leaders in the long run were not greatly interested in affairs of state. Indeed, Indian religion generally did not stress the importance of politics, even for religious purposes, but rather the preeminence of holy men and priests as sources of authority. It was true, however, that some members of the brahmin caste served as advisors at royal courts and as administrators, though most brahmins served as priests to wealthy families or to peasant villages.

The limitations on the political traditions developed during this period of Indian history can be explained partly by the importance of local units of government—the tightly organized villages—and particularly by the essentially political qualities of social relationships under the caste system. Caste rules, interpreted by priests, regulated many social relationships and work roles. To a great extent, the caste system and religious encouragement in the faithful performance of caste duties did for Indian life what more conventional government structures did in many other cultures, in promoting public order.

India's caste system became steadily more complex after the Epic Age, as the five initial castes subdivided until ultimately almost 300 castes or jati subcastes were defined. Hereditary principles grew ever stronger, so that it became virtually impossible to rise above the caste in which a person was born or to marry someone from a higher caste. It was possible to fall to a lower caste by marrying outside one's caste or by taking on work deemed inappropriate for one's caste. Upward mobility could occur within castes, as individuals might gain greater wealth through success in the economic activities appropriate to the caste. The fact that brahmins replaced warriors as the top caste also indicates some flexibility. And rulers, like the Mauryans, might spring from the merchant caste, although most princes were warrior born. It is important not to characterize the caste system in an oversimplified way, for it did provide some flexibility. Nevertheless, the system gave India the most rigid overall framework for a social structure of any of the classical civilizations.

In its origins, the caste system provided a way for India's various races, the conquerors and the conquered, to live together without perpetual conflict and without full integration of cultures and values. Quite different kinds of people could live side by side in village or city, separated by caste. In an odd way, castes promoted tolerance, and this was useful, given India's varied peoples and beliefs. The caste system also meant that extensive outright slavery was avoided. The lowest, untouchable caste was scorned, confined to poverty and degrading work, but its members were not directly owned by others. The system also did not prevent mobility within castes, for example by earning more money.

The political consequences of the caste system derived from the detailed rules for each caste. These rules governed marriages and permissible jobs, but also social habits such as eating and drinking. For example, a person from one caste could not eat or drink with someone from a lower caste or perform any service for that person. This kind of regulation of behavior made detailed political administration less necessary. Indeed, no state could command full loyalty from subjects, for their first loyalty was to caste. By the end of the classical period, a person's life was tightly defined by caste position. People who refused to perform the duties of their caste could face beatings by the community, or even ostracism. If thrown out of the community, most people died, because no one, even a family member, was allowed to offer support to an "outcaste." Religious and political leaders enforced the system as a primary duty, believing that it was supernaturally ordained.

More of the qualities of Indian civilization rested on widely shared cultural values than was the case in China. Religion, and particularly the evolving Hindu religion as it gained ground on Buddhism under the Guptas, was the clearest cultural cement of this society, cutting across political and language barriers and across the castes. Hinduism embraced considerable variety; it gave rise to important religious dissent, and it never displaced important minority religions and other intellectual and artistic interests. However, Hinduism has shown a remarkable capacity to survive and is the major system of belief in India even today. It also promotes other features in Indian culture. Thus, contemporary Indian children are encouraged to indulge their imaginations longer than Western children are, and they are confronted less sharply with outside reality. Some observers argue that even Indian adults, on average, are less interested in general, agreed upon truths than in individually satisfying versions. A mindset of this sort goes back to the religious patterns created more than 2000 years ago in classical India, where Hinduism encouraged imaginative links with a

HISTORY DEBATE

INTERPRETING CIVILIZATION, ROUND TWO

World historians have frequently debated the validity of the concept of civilization. We saw in Chapter 1 that civilizations differ from other societies but that the boundary lines are fuzzy, and also that societies that were not civilizations might be interesting and, in some cases, important historically. In dealing with the classical period, the initial definition of *civilization* is extended. The term still designates societies that have cities, organized governments, and usually writing. However, now it also designates some degree of coherence and distinctiveness within a given region—hence, Chinese civilization is different from Indian civilization.

Coherence, however, is not always easy to define. Except for Mesopotamia after Sumer, the river valley civilizations are not too problematic. Egypt, for example, usually had a single government and religion. By the classical centuries, however, civilizations covered large areas and embraced much diversity. South China differed from the north, even under the same government; there was much ethnic and linguistic tension. India, never entirely united by a single government (except briefly under foreign rule, well after the classical period) and with widely varied castes, is an even tougher case. Here, no single religion ever fully dominated, although Brahmianism and then Hinduism were the most characteristic. Even modern-day India does not control the whole subcontinent, in large part because of religious divisions. Here, the idea of a coherent, distinct civilization denotes predominant values (including the important overlap between Hinduism and Buddhism) and social structures, not full unity or identity.

Treating major civilizations as tendencies that include important internal divisions and tensions, as entities that must be defined rather than assumed, helps capture the reality of how people have acted and continue to act in world history. Examining a classical civilization such as India or China even helps frame the other major themes of world history, including the degree of openness to outside influences. Here too, however, some world historians differ, seeing common human impulses and global forces as the whole story, with civilizations merely an invention of scholars unable to shake off the arrogant claims of particular societies such as China or, more recently, western Europe. Here, it is important to establish one's own position as to how useful or misleading the concept of civilization is, while recognizing the main alternatives.

One other complication: the basic features of a given civilization do not stand still, nor do its boundaries. The transitions from river valley to classical civilizations illustrate this kind of passage. Each major period of world history requires a renewed definition, still with the basic goal of testing coherence and a certain degree of distinctiveness. India can still be labeled a civilization today. How do its characteristics and territory compare with those of its classical counterpart?

higher, divine reality. It is this kind of tradition that illustrates how classical India, although not the source of enduring political institutions beyond the local level, produced a continuous civilization that retained its cultural cohesiveness from this point on—even through centuries in which political control escaped Indian hands almost completely.

RELIGION AND CULTURE

Hinduism, the religion of India's majority, developed gradually over a period of many centuries. Its origins lie in the Vedic and Epic ages, as the Aryan religion gained greater sophistication, with concerns about an overarching divinity supple-

menting the rituals and polytheistic beliefs supervised by the brahmin caste of priests. The *Rig-
Veda* expressed the growing interest in a higher
divine principle in its Creation Hymn:

> Then even nothingness was not, nor exis-
> tence. There was no air then, nor the heav-
> ens beyond it. Who covered it? Where was
> it? In whose keeping . . . ? The gods them-
> selves are later than creation, so who knows
> truly whence it has arisen?

Unlike all the other world religions, Hinduism had no single founder, no central holy figure from whom the basic religious beliefs
stemmed. This fact helps explain why the religion
unfolded so gradually, sometimes in reaction to
competing religions such as Buddhism or Islam.
Moreover, Hinduism pursued a number of religious approaches, from the strictly ritualistic and
ceremonial approach many brahmins preferred,
to the high-soaring mysticism that sought to
unite individual humans with an all-embracing
divine principle. Unlike Western religions or
Daoism (which it resembled in part), Hinduism
could also encourage political and economic
goals (called *artha*) and worldly pleasures (called
karma)—and important textbooks of the time
spelled out these pursuits. Part of Hinduism's success, indeed, was the result of its fluidity, its ability to adapt to the different needs of various
groups and to change with circumstance. With a
belief that there are many suitable paths of worship, Hinduism was also characteristically tolerant, coexisting with several offshoot religions that
garnered minority acceptance in India.

Under brahmin leadership, Indian ideas
about the gods gradually became more elaborate
(initially, the religion was simply called Brahmin-
ism). Original gods of nature were altered to represent more abstract concepts. Thus, Varuna
changed from a god of the sky to the guardian of
ideas of right and wrong. The great poems of the
Epic Age increasingly emphasized the importance
of gentle and generous behavior and the validity
of a life devoted to concentration on the Supreme

Brahmin (early Hindu) painting from an epic story:
Krishna playing the flute under the sacred tree.

Spirit. The *Upanishads,* particularly, stressed the
shallowness of worldly concerns—riches and
even health were not the main point of human
existence—in favor of contemplation of the
divine spirit. It was in the *Upanishads* that the
Hindu idea of a divine force informing the whole
universe, of which each individual creature's soul
is thought to be part, first surfaced clearly, in pas-
sages such as the following:

> "Fetch me a fruit of the banyan tree."
>> "Here is one, sir."
> "Break it."
>> "I have broken it, sir."
> "What do you see?"
>> "Very tiny seeds, sir."
> "Break one."
>> "I have broken it, sir."
> "What do you see now?"
>> "Nothing, sir."

"My son,. . . what you do not perceive is the essence, and in that essence the mighty banyan tree exists. Believe me, my son, in that essence is the self of all that is. That is the True, that is the Self."

However, the *Upanishads* did more than advance the idea of a mystical contact with a divine essence. They also attacked the conventional brahmin view of what religion should be, a set of proper ceremonies that led to good things in this life or rewards after death. From the Epic Age on, Hinduism embraced this clear tension between a religion of rituals, with fixed ceremonies and rules of conduct, and the religion of mystical holy men, seeking communion with the divine soul.

The mystics, often called *gurus* as they gathered disciples around them, and the brahmin priests agreed on certain doctrines as Hinduism became an increasingly formal religion by the first centuries of the common era. The basic holy essence, called *Brahma,* formed part of everything in this world. Every living creature participates in this divine principle. The spirit of Brahma enters several gods or forms of gods, including Vishnu, the preserver, and Siva, the destroyer, who could be worshipped or placated as expressions of the holy essence. The world of our senses is far less important than the world of the divine soul, and a proper life is one devoted to seeking union with this soul. However, this quest may take many lifetimes. Hindus stressed the principle of reincarnation, in which souls do not die when bodies do but pass into other beings, either human or animal. Where the soul goes, whether it rises to a higher-caste person or falls perhaps to an animal, depends on how good a life the person has led. The good life, in turn, was defined primarily in terms of living up to the duties of one's caste. Ultimately, after many good lives, the soul reaches full union with the soul of Brahma, and worldly suffering ceases.

Hinduism provided several channels for the good life. For the holy men, there was the meditation and self-discipline of *yoga,* which means "union," allowing the mind to be freed to concentrate on the divine spirit. For others, there were the rituals and rules of the brahmins. These included proper ceremonies in the cremation of bodies at death, appropriate prayers, and obedience to injunctions such as treating cows as sacred animals and refraining from the consumption of beef. Many Hindus also continued the idea of lesser gods represented in the spirits of nature, or purely local divinities, which could be seen as expressions of Siva or Vishnu. Worship to these divinities could aid the process of reincarnation to a higher state. Thus, many ordinary Hindus placed a lot of importance on prayers, sacrifices, and gifts to the gods that would bring them through reincarnation into a higher caste.

Hinduism also provided a basic, if complex, ethic that helped supply some unity amid the various forms of worship. The epic poems, richly symbolic, formed the key texts. They illustrated a central emphasis on the moral law of *dharma* as a guide to living in this world and simultaneously pursuing higher, spiritual goals. The concept of dharma directed attention to the moral consequences of action and at the same time the need to act. Each person must meet the obligations of life, serving the family, producing a livelihood and even earning money, and serving in the army when the need arises. These actions cannot damage, certainly cannot destroy, the eternal divine essence that underlies all creation. In the *Bhagavad Gita,* a classic sacred hymn, a warrior is sent to do battle against his own relatives. Fearful of killing them, he is advised by a god that he must carry out his duties. He will not really be killing his victims because their divine spirit will live on. This ethic urged that honorable behavior, even pleasure seeking, is compatible with spirituality and can lead to a final release from the life cycle and to unity with the divine essence. The Hindu ethic explains how devout Hindus could also be aggressive merchants or eager warriors. In encouraging honorable action, it could legitimize government and the caste system as providing the frameworks in which the duties of the world might be carried out, without distracting from the ultimate spiritual goals common to all people.

The ethical concept of dharma was far less detailed and prescriptive than the ethical codes associated with most other world religions, including Christianity and Islam. Dharma stresses inner study and meditation, building from the divine essence within each creature, rather than adherence to a fixed set of moral rules. The key feature of dharma, however, was to live up to the duties and status attached to the caste in which one was born. Defying this dharma was one of the greatest sins, fulfilling it the key preparation for advancement through reincarnation.

The spread of Hinduism through India and, at least briefly, to some other parts of Asia had many sources. The religion accommodated extreme spirituality. It also provided satisfying rules of conduct for ordinary life, including rituals and a firm emphasis on the distinction between good and evil behavior. The religion allowed many people to retain older beliefs and ceremonies, derived from a more purely polytheistic religion. It reinforced the caste system, giving people in lower castes hope for a better time in lives to come and giving upper-caste people, including the brahmins, the satisfaction that if they behaved well, they might be rewarded by communion with the divine soul. Even though Hindu beliefs took shape only gradually and contained many ambiguities, the religion was sustained by a strong caste of priests and through the efforts of individual gurus and mystics.

At times, however, the tensions within Hinduism broke down for some individuals, producing rebellions against the dominant religion. One such rebellion, which occurred right after the Epic Age, led to a new religion closely related to Hinduism. This religion, Buddhism, provided one of classical India's greatest contributions to world history. Buddhism played an important role in classical India itself, sharing features with Hinduism but disagreeing on key points. In the longer run, as Hinduism ultimately triumphed, Buddhism's greatest impact was in other parts of Asia.

This beautifully detailed sandstone statue of the Buddha meditating in a standing position was carved in the 5th century C.E. Note the nimbus, or halo, which was common in later Buddhist iconography. The calm radiated by the Buddhist's facial expression suggests that he has already achieved enlightenment. As Buddhism spread throughout India and overseas, a wide variety of artistic styles developed to depict the Buddha and key incidents of his legendary life. The realism and stylized robes of the sculpture shown here indicate that it was carved by artists following the conventions of the Indo-Greek school of northwestern India.

Around 563 B.C.E., an Indian prince, Gautama, was born who came to question the fairness of earthly life in which so much poverty and misery abounded. Gautama, later called Buddha, or "the enlightened one," lived as a Hindu mystic, fasting and torturing his body. After six years, he felt that he had found truth, then spent his life traveling and gathering disciples to spread his ideas. Buddha accepted many Hindu beliefs, but he protested the brahmin emphasis on ceremonies. In a related sense, he downplayed the polytheistic element in Hinduism by focusing on the supreme divinity over separate, lesser gods. Buddha believed in deeply spiritual rewards, seeing the ultimate goal as destruction of the self and union with the divine essence, a state that he called *nirvana*. Individuals could regulate their lives and aspirations toward this goal, without elaborate ceremonies. Great stress was placed on self-control: "Let a man overcome anger by love, let him overcome evil by good, let him overcome the greedy by liberality, the liar by the truth." A holy life could be achieved through individual effort from any level of society. Here, Buddhism attacked not only the priests but also the caste system; this was another sign of the complexity of Indian social life in practice. Consistently, Buddha and Buddhism focused on the problem of suffering, which was inevitably attached to things of this world, even those, indeed particularly those, that might seem pleasant. Escape from suffering could come only from ceasing to desire worldly goals. Enlightenment alone released one from suffering.

Buddhism spread and retained coherence through the example and teachings of groups of holy men, organized in monasteries but preaching throughout the world. Buddhism attracted many followers in India, and its growth was greatly spurred by the conversion of the Mauryan emperor Ashoka. Increasingly, Buddha was seen as divine. Prayer and contemplation at Buddhist holy places and works of charity and piety gave substance to the idea of a holy life on earth. Ironically, however, Buddhism did not witness a permanent following in India. Brahmin opposition was strong, and it was ultimately aided by the influence of the Gupta emperors. Furthermore, Hinduism showed its adaptability by emphasizing its mystical side, thus retaining the loyalties of many Indians. Buddhism's greatest successes, aided by the missionary encouragement of Ashoka and later the Kushan emperors, came in other parts of southeast Asia, including the island of Sri Lanka, off the south coast of India, and in China, Korea, and Japan. Still, pockets of Buddhists remained in India, particularly in the northeast. They were joined by other dissident groups who rejected aspects of Hinduism. Thus, Hinduism, although dominant, had to come to terms with the existence of other religions early on.

If Hinduism, along with the caste system, formed the most distinctive and durable products of the classical period of Indian history, they were certainly not the only ones. Even aside from dissident religions, Indian culture during this period was vibrant and diverse, and religion encompassed only part of its interests. Hinduism itself encouraged many wider pursuits.

Indian thinkers wrote actively about various aspects of human life. Although political theory was sparse, a great deal of legal writing occurred. The theme of love was important also. A manual of the "laws of love," the *Kama-sutra,* written in the 4th century C.E., is an unusually elaborate and expressive discussion of the sexual experience.

Indian literature, taking many themes from the great epic poems and their tales of military adventure, stressed lively story lines. The epics were recorded in final written form during the Gupta period, and other story collections, such as the *Panchatantra,* which includes Sinbad the Sailor, Jack the Giant Killer, and the Seven League Boots, produced adventurous yarns now known all over the world. Classical stories were often secular, but they sometimes included the gods and also shared with Hinduism an emphasis on imagination and excitement. Indian drama flourished also, again particularly under the Guptas, and stressed themes of romantic adventure in which lovers separated and then reunited after many perils. This literary tradition created a cultural framework that still survives in India. Even contemporary Indian movies reflect the tradition of swashbuckling romance and heroic action.

Classical India also produced important work in science and mathematics. The Guptas supported a vast university center—one of the world's first—in the town of Nalanda that attracted students from other parts of Asia as well as Indian brahmins. Nalanda had more than 100 lecture halls, three large libraries, an astronomical observatory, and a model dairy. Its curriculum included religion, philosophy, medicine, architecture, and agriculture.

At the research level, Indian scientists, borrowing a bit from Greek learning after the conquests of Alexander the Great, made important strides in astronomy and medicine. The great astronomer Aryabhatta calculated the length of the solar year and improved mathematical measurements. Indian astronomers understood and calculated the daily rotation of the earth on its axis, predicted and explained eclipses, and developed a theory of gravity, and through telescopic observation they identified seven planets. Medical research was hampered by religious prohibitions on dissection, but Indian surgeons nevertheless made advances in bone setting and plastic surgery. Inoculation against smallpox was introduced, using cowpox serum. Indian hospitals stressed cleanliness, including sterilization of wounds, while leading doctors promoted high ethical standards. As was the case with Indian discoveries in astronomy, many medical findings reached the Western world only in modern times.

Indian mathematicians produced still more important discoveries. The Indian numbering system is the one we use today, although we call it Arabic because Europeans imported it secondhand from the Arabs. Indians invented the concept of zero, and through it they were able to develop the decimal system. Indian advances in numbering rank with writing as key human inventions. Indian mathematicians also developed

the concept of negative numbers, calculated square roots and a table of sines, and computed the value of "pi" more accurately than the Greeks did.

Finally, classical India produced lively art, although much of it perished under later invasions. Ashoka sponsored many spherical shrines to Buddha, called *stupas*, and statues honoring Buddha were also common. Under the Guptas, sculpture and painting moved away from realistic portrayals of the human form toward more stylized representation. Indian painters, working on the walls of buildings and caves, filled their work with forms of people and animals, captured in lively color. Indian art showed a keen appreciation of nature, and some of it also suggested several of the erotic themes expressed in works such

Brahmin (early Hindu) sculpture: The god Siva Natarajah as the lord of dance.

UNDERSTANDING CULTURES

COMPARING SYSTEMS OF BELIEF

One of the key challenges in dealing with cultures in world history involves comparison. China and India during the classical period obviously developed very different cultural emphases. The contrast between Confucianism and Hinduism was sharp. Confucianists emphasized goals in this world and the primary quest for order; Hinduism focused on otherworldliness and encouraged spiritual intuition and imagination. Differences spilled into art, with India's sensuality and China's emphasis on more restrained, balanced portrayals of nature.

These differences, however, should not be exaggerated. Both civilizations produced diversity. Chinese Daoists used language similar to that of Hindus and Buddhists. Indian scientists, although more mathematically inclined than the Chinese, worked on some similar problems in astronomy and medicine.

Further, both civilizations used culture to help hold diverse populations together. Confucianism and Hinduism alike, although in very different ways, provided justifications for social inequality. According to Confucianism, inferiors should accept their lot, knowing that the upper classes will treat them responsibly and that orderliness is vital. According to Hinduism, inferiors should accept their lot, knowing that performing one's caste duty in this life will lead to spiritual advances in a subsequent existence. Contrast, in other words, must not monopolize a cultural comparison. Sometimes the functions of cultures are far more similar than their specific forms.

as the *Kama-sutra*. This was an art that could pay homage to religious values, particularly during the period in which Buddhism briefly spread, but could also celebrate the joys of life.

There was, clearly, no full unity to this cultural outpouring. Achievements in religion, legalism, abstract mathematics, and a sensual and adventurous art and literature coexisted. The result, however, was a somewhat distinctive overall tone, different from the more rational approaches of the West or the Chinese concentration on political ethics. In various cultural expressions, Indians developed an interest in spontaneity and imagination, whether in fleshly pleasures or a mystical union with the divine essence.

ECONOMY AND SOCIETY

The caste system described many key features of Indian social and economic life, as it assigned people to occupations and regulated marriages. Low-caste individuals had few legal rights, and servants were often abused by their masters, who were restrained only by the ethical promptings of religion toward kindly treatment. A brahmin who killed a servant for misbehavior faced a penalty no more severe than if he had killed an animal. This extreme level of abuse was uncommon, but the caste system did unquestionably make its mark on daily life as well as on the formal structure of society. The majority of Indians living in peasant villages had less frequent contact with people of higher social castes, and village leaders were charged with trying to protect peasants from too much interference by landlords and rulers. The peasantry grew steadily as the Indo-Europeans settled down, though large sections of classical India were still dominated by dense tropical rain forests. Peasant productivity increased with the use of new tools, and the class formed the majority of the total population.

Family life also emphasized the theme of hierarchy and tight organization, as it evolved from the Vedic and Epic ages. The dominance of husbands and fathers remained strong. One Indian code of law recommended that a wife worship her husband as a god. Indeed, the rights of women became increasingly limited as Indian civilization took clearer shape. Although the great epics stressed the control of husband and father, they also recognized women's independent contributions. As agriculture became better organized and improved technology reduced (without eliminating) women's economic contributions, the stress on male authority expanded. This is a common pattern in agricultural societies, as a sphere of action women enjoyed in hunting cultures was gradually circumscribed. Hindu thinkers debated whether a woman could advance spiritually without first being reincarnated as a man, and there was no consensus. The limits imposed on women were reflected in laws and literary references. A system of arranged marriage evolved in which parents contracted unions for children, particularly daughters, at quite early ages, to spouses they had never even met. The goal of these arrangements was to ensure solid economic links, with child brides contributing dowries of land or domestic animals to the ultimate family estates, but the result of such arrangements was that young people, especially girls, were drawn into a new family structure in which they had no voice.

Indian culture showed interesting ambiguities where women were concerned. On the one hand, they were often dismissed in the epics as weak and frivolous, often causing trouble. Good women were seen in terms of their service to fathers or husbands. But women were also described in the epics as strong willed and clever.

The rigidities of family life and male dominance over women were often greater in theory than they usually turned out to be in practice. The emphasis on loving relations and sexual pleasure in Indian culture modified family life, because husband and wife were supposed to pro-vide mutual emotional support as a marriage developed. The *Mahabharata* epic called a man's wife his truest friend: "Even a man in the grip of rage will not be harsh to a woman, remembering that on her depend the joys of love, happiness, and virtue." Small children were often pampered. "With their teeth half shown in causeless laughter, their efforts at talking so sweetly uncertain, when children ask to sit on his lap, a man is blessed." Families thus served an important and explicit emotional function as well as a role in supporting the structure of society and its institutions. They also, as in all agricultural societies, formed economic units. Children, after early years of indulgence, were expected to work hard. Adults were obligated to assist older relatives. The purpose of arranged marriages was to promote a family's economic well-being, and almost everyone lived in a family setting.

The Indian version of the patriarchal family was thus subtly different from that in China, although women were officially just as subordinate, and later trends—as in many patriarchal societies over time—brought new burdens. But Indian cultural allowance for resourceful women and goddesses contributed to women's status as wives and mothers. Stories also celebrated women's emotions and beauty. In the early part of the classical period, some women contributed directly to religious scholarship, though later they were banned from reading the sacred Vedic texts. Women also served as teachers, musicians, and artists, though the latter two activities were not highly esteemed. Generally, women had no respectable alternative to marriage, though groups of courtesans often surrounded the royal courts and, for Buddhists, monasteries provided opportunities for nuns. Women whose husbands died, particularly if they had not yet borne a son, were condemned to a difficult existence, often isolated in the compounds of the extended family.

The economy of India in the classical period became extremely vigorous, certainly rivaling China in technological sophistication and probably briefly surpassing China in the prosperity of its upper classes. In manufacturing, Indians invented new uses for chemistry, and their steel was the best in the world. Indian capacity in ironmaking outdistanced European levels until a few centuries ago. Indian techniques in textiles were also advanced, as the subcontinent became the first to manufacture cotton cloth, calico, and cashmere. Most manufacturing was done by artisans who formed guilds and sold their goods from shops.

Indian emphasis on trade and merchant activity was far greater than in China, and indeed greater than in the classical Mediterranean world. Indian merchants enjoyed relatively high caste status and the flexibility of the Hindu ethic. And, they traveled widely, not only over the subcontinent but, by sea, to the Middle East and east Asia. The seafaring peoples along the southern coast, usually outside the large empires of northern India, were particularly active. These southern Indians, the Tamils, traded cotton and silks, dyes, drugs, gold, and ivory, often earning great fortunes. From the Middle East and the Roman Empire, they brought back pottery, wine, metals, some slaves, and above all gold. Their trade with southeast Asia was even more active, as Indian merchants transported not only sophisticated manufactured goods but also the trappings of India's active culture to places such as Malaysia and the larger islands of Indonesia. In addition, caravan trade developed with China. India became something of a hub for the interregional trade of the period.

The Indian economy remained firmly agricultural at its base. The wealth of the upper classes and the splendor of cities such as Nalanda were confined to a small group, as most people lived near the margins of subsistence. But India was justly known by the time of the Guptas for its wealth as well as for its religion and intellectual life-always understanding that wealth was relative in the classical world and very unevenly divided. A Chinese Buddhist on a pilgrimage to India wrote:

The people are many and happy. They do not have to register their households with the police. There is no death penalty. Religious sects have houses of charity where rooms, couches, beds, food, and drink are supplied to travelers.

INDIAN INFLUENCE

Classical India, from the Mauryan period on, had a considerable influence on other parts of the world. In many ways, the Indian Ocean, dominated at this point by Indian merchants and missionaries, was the most active linkage point among cultures, although admittedly the Mediterranean, which channeled contact from the Middle East to north Africa and Europe, was a close second. Indian dominance of the waters of southern Asia, and the impressive creativity of Indian civilization itself, carried goods and influence well beyond the subcontinent's borders. No previous civilization had developed in southeast Asia to compete with Indian influence. And while India did not attempt political domination, dealing instead with the regional kingdoms of Burma, Thailand, parts of Indonesia, and Vietnam, Indian travelers or settlers brought to these locales a persuasive way of life. Many Indian merchants married into local royal families. Indian-style temples were constructed, and other forms of Indian art traveled widely. Buddhism spread from India to many parts of southeast Asia, and Hinduism converted many upper-class people, particularly in several of the Indonesian kingdoms. India thus serves as an early example of a major civilization expanding its influence well beyond its own regions.

Indian influence had affected China, through Buddhism and art, by the end of the classical period. Earlier, Buddhist emissaries to the Middle East stimulated new ethical thinking that informed Greek and Roman groups, such as the Stoics, and through them aspects of Christianity later on.

Within India itself, the classical period, starting a bit late after the Aryan invasions, lasted somewhat longer than that of China or Rome. Even when the period ended with the fall of the Guptas, an identifiable civilization remained in India, building on several key factors first established in the classical period: the religion, to be sure, but also the artistic and literary tradition and the complex social and family network. The ability of this civilization to survive, even under long periods of foreign domination, was testimony to the meaning and variety it offered to many Indians themselves.

CHINA AND INDIA

The thrusts of classical civilization in China and India reveal the diversity generated during the classical age. The restraint of Chinese art and poetry contrasted with the more dynamic, sensual styles of India. India ultimately settled on a primary religion, though with important minority expressions, that embodied diverse impulses within it. China opted for separate religious and philosophical systems that served different needs. China's political structures and values found little echo in India, whereas the Indian caste system involved a social rigidity considerably greater than that of China. India's cultural emphasis was, on balance, considerably more otherworldly than that of China, despite the impact of Daoism. Quite obviously, classical India and classical China created vastly different cultures. Even in science, where there was similar interest in pragmatic discoveries about how the world works, the Chinese placed greater stress on purely practical findings, whereas the Indians ventured further into the mathematical arena.

Beyond the realm of formal culture and the institutions of government, India and China may seem more similar. As agricultural societies, both civilizations relied on a large peasant class, organized in close-knit villages with much mutual cooperation. Cities and merchant activity, although vital, played a secondary role. Political power rested primarily with those who controlled the land, through ownership of large estates and the ability to tax the peasant class. On a more personal level, the power of husbands and fathers in the family—the basic fact of patriarchy—encompassed Indian and Chinese families alike.

However, Indian and Chinese societies differed in more than their religion, philosophy, art, and politics. Ordinary people had cultures along with elites. Hindu peasants saw their world differently from their Chinese counterparts. They placed less emphasis on personal emotional restraint and detailed etiquette; they expected different emotional interactions with family members. Indian peasants were less constrained than were the Chinese by recurrent efforts by large landlords to gain control of their land. Although there were wealthy landlords in India, the system of village control of most land was more firmly entrenched than in China. Indian merchants played a greater role than their Chinese counterparts. There was more sea trade, more commercial vitality. Revealingly, India's expanding cultural influence was due to merchant activity above all else, whereas Chinese expansion involved government initiatives in gaining new territory and sending proud emissaries to satellite states. These differences were less dramatic, certainly less easy to document, than those generated by elite thinkers and politicians, but they contributed to the shape of a civilization and to its particular vitality, its areas of stability and instability.

Because each classical civilization developed its own unique style, in social relationships as well as in formal politics and intellectual life, exchanges between two societies such as China and India involved specific borrowings, not wholesale imitation. India and China, the two giants of classical Asia, remain subjects of comparison to our own time, because they have continued to build distinctively on their particular traditions, established before 500 C.E. These characteristics, in turn, differed from those of yet another center of civilization, the societies that sprang up on the shores of the Mediterranean during this same classical age.

PATHS
TO THE PRESENT

Contemporary India, like contemporary China, shows many vestiges of its classical past. The Hindu religion, professed by the majority, forms an active link between present and past. The Indian state is modern and effective, but its federal system reflects the strong regionalism established many centuries ago—as does the absence of a single national language. Rural India links strongly to earlier social and cultural traditions.

India also grapples with its classical heritage in other respects. The caste system has been outlawed for more than half a century, but its traces persist. Efforts to promote people of lower-caste origins, for example, by providing special university scholarships, have been resisted by the former upper castes. And, women's inferiority is taken for granted still in many patriarchal families. As with racial issues in the United States and South Africa, it proves difficult to erase older, unequal social systems merely by implementing progressive laws.

Overall, the force of India's traditions, inherited in substantial part from the classical centuries, points in two directions. On the one hand, as a leading politician noted soon after India's independence, tradition forms a burden, limiting efforts at reform. On the other, tradition is a source of identity and pride, which many Indians successfully combine with fully contemporary activities in science and technology.

SUGGESTED WEB SITES

For more information on ancient India, see http://www.ancientindia.co.uk/, http://www.wsu.edu:8080/~dee/ANCINDIA/ANCINDIA.HTM, and http://www.mnsu.edu/emuseum/prehistory/india/; on the ancient Indus Valley, see www.harappa.com/.

SUGGESTED READINGS

There are fewer provocative surveys of Indian history than are available about China, but at least four competent efforts exist: P. Spear, *India* (1981); Stanley Wolpert, *A New History of India* (1994); Rhoads Murphey, *A History of Asia* (1992), and Jonardon Ganeri, *Philosophy in Classical India* (2001), an interesting recent study. See also Jennifer Howes, *The Courts of Pre-Colonial South India: Material Culture and Kingship* (2003); Suresh Ghosh, *The History of Education in Ancient India* (2001); and Romila Thapar, *History and Beyond* (2000). See also Thomas McEvilley, *The Shape of Ancient Thought: Comparative Studies of Greek and Indian Philosophies* (New York, 2002); Thomas R. Traultmann, *The Aryan Debate* (2005); Thomas William Rhys Davids, *Buddhist India* (1999); Jennifer Howes, *The Courts of Pre-Colonial South India: Material Culture and Kingship* (2003); Alfred S. Bradford, *With Arrow, Sword, and Spear: A History of Warfare in the Ancient World* (2001); and Daud Ali, *Courtly Culture and Political Life in Early Medieval India* (2001).

6 Classical Civilization in the Mediterranean and Middle East: Persia, Greece, and Rome

The classical civilizations that sprang up in Persia and on the shores of the Mediterranean Sea from about 800 B.C.E. until the fall of the Roman Empire in 476 C.E. rivaled their counterparts in India and China in richness and impact. Two major civilizations formed in the eastern Mediterranean and Middle East. A massive Persian empire developed, spurred initially by the kind of outside invasion that had earlier produced various Mesopotamian empires. But the Persian Empire grew far larger, illustrating the new capacities of the classical period. Durable political and cultural traditions were established that persisted in and around present-day Iran well beyond the classical period. Centered first in the peninsula of Greece, then in Rome's burgeoning provinces, the new Mediterranean culture did not embrace all of the civilized lands of the ancient Middle East. Greece rebuffed the advance of the mighty Persian Empire and established some colonies on the eastern shore of the Mediterranean, in what is now Turkey, but it only briefly conquered more than a fraction of the civilized Middle East. Rome came closer to conquering surrounding peoples, but even its empire had to contend with strong kingdoms to the east. Nevertheless, Greece and Rome do not merely constitute a westward push of civilization from its earlier bases in the Middle East and along the Nile—although this is a part of their story. They also represent the formation of new institutions and values that reverberated in the later history of the Middle East and Europe alike.

For most Americans, and not only those who are descendants of European immigrants, classical Mediterranean culture constitutes "our own" classical past, or at least a goodly part of it. The framers of the American Constitution were extremely conscious of Greek and Roman precedents. Designers of public buildings in the United States, from the early days of the American republic to the present, have dutifully copied Greek and Roman models, as in the Lincoln Memorial and most state capitols. Plato and Aristotle continue to be thought of as the founders of our philosophical tradition, and skillful teachers still rely on some imitation of the Socratic method. Our sense of debt to Greece and Rome may inspire us to find in their history special meaning or links to our own world; the Western educational experience has long included elaborate explorations of the Greco-Roman past as part of the standard academic education. But from the standpoint of world history, greater balance is obviously necessary. Greco-Roman history is one of the three major classical civilizations, more dynamic than its Chinese and Indian counterparts in some respects but noticeably less successful in others. The challenge is to discern the leading features of Greek and Roman civilization and to next compare them with those of their counterparts elsewhere. We can then clearly recognize the connections and our own debt without adhering to the notion that the Mediterranean world somehow dominated the classical period.

Classical Mediterranean civilization is complicated by the fact that it passed through two centers during its centuries of vigor, as Greek political institutions rose and then declined and the legions of Rome assumed leadership. Roman interests were not identical to those of Greece, although the Romans carefully preserved most Greek achievements. Rome mastered engineering; Greece specialized in scientific thought. Rome created a mighty empire, whereas the Greek city-states proved rather inept in forming an empire. It is possible, certainly, to see more than a change in emphases from Greece to Rome, and to talk about separate civilizations instead of a single basic pattern. And it is true that Greek influence was always stronger than Roman in the eastern Mediterranean, whereas western Europe encountered a fuller Greco-Roman mixture, with Roman influence predominating in language and law. However, Greek and Roman societies shared many political ideas; they had a common religion and artistic styles; they developed similar economic structures. Certainly, their classical heritage was used by successive civiliza-

tions without fine distinctions drawn between what was Greek and what was Roman.

■ KEY QUESTIONS *Three initial questions involve making sense out of variety. First, Persia established an important classical tradition; how can this also be seen in relationship to the Mediterranean? Second, on Mediterranean civilization itself: Greece and Rome tossed up a great mixture of political forms; what were the most important forms, and what was the political heritage of the classical Mediterranean for later societies? For the third question, keep in mind what Greece, Hellenistic society, and Rome had in common that defined classical Mediterranean civilization, while recognizing that important changes occurred from one period to another. What aspects of culture and social structure operated pretty consistently from Greece to Rome? Were the changes from Greece to Rome any greater than those from Zhou China to Han China, during the same classical period? A fourth, crucial comparative question involves the end of the classical period: Classical civilization in the Mediterranean did not survive as well as its counterparts in India and China—why?*

THE PERSIAN TRADITION

After the fall of the great Egyptian and Hittite empires in the Middle East by 1200 B.C.E., much smaller states predominated the area. Then new powers stepped in, first the Assyrians and then an influx of Iranians (Persians). A great conqueror emerged by 550 B.C.E. Cyrus the Great established a massive Persian Empire, which ran across the northern Middle East and into northwestern India. The new empire was the clearest successor to the great Mesopotamian states of the past, but it was far larger. The Iranians advanced iron technology in the Middle East.

Persian politics featured several characteristics, the first of which was tolerance. The Persian empire embraced a host of languages and cul-

Persian wall relief.

tures, and the early Persian rulers were careful to grant considerable latitude for this diversity. Second, however, was a strong authoritarian streak. Darius, successor to Cyrus, worked hard to centralize laws and tax collection. The idea of wide participation in politics was rejected. Third, and related to the centralization process, Persian rulers developed a vital infrastructure for the whole empire. A major system of roads reduced travel time, though it still took ninety days to go from one end of the empire to the other. An east-west highway, largely paved, facilitated commerce and troop movement from the Indian border to the Mediterranean, and another highway reached Egypt. The Persians established the first regular postal service, and they built a network of inns along their roads to accommodate travelers.

PATTERNS OF GREEK AND ROMAN HISTORY

Greece

Even as Persia developed, a new civilization took shape to the west, building on a number of earlier precedents. The river valley civilizations of the Middle East and Africa had spread to some of the islands near the Greek peninsula, although less to the peninsula itself. The island of Crete, in particular, showed the results of Egyptian influence by 2000 B.C.E., and from this the Greeks were later able to develop a taste for monumental architecture. The Greeks were an Indo-European people, such as the Aryan conquerors of India, who took over the peninsula by 1700 B.C.E. An early kingdom in southern Greece, strongly influenced by Crete, developed by 1400 B.C.E. around the city of Mycenae. This was the kingdom later memorialized in Homer's epics about the Trojan War. Mycenae was then toppled by a subsequent wave of Indo-European invaders, whose incursions destroyed civilization on the peninsula until about 800 B.C.E.

The rapid rise of civilization in Greece between 800 and 600 B.C.E. was based on the creation of strong city-states, rather than a single political unit. Each city-state had its own government, typically either a tyranny of one ruler or an aristocratic council. The city-state served Greece well, for the peninsula was so divided by mountains that a unified government would have been difficult to establish. Trade developed rapidly under city-state sponsorship, and common cultural forms, including a rich written language with letters derived from the Phoenician alphabet, spread throughout the peninsula. The Greek city-states also joined in regular celebrations such as the athletic competitions of the Olympic games. Sparta and Athens came to be the two leading city-states. The first represented a strong military aristocracy dominating a slave population; the other was a more diverse commercial state, also including the extensive use of slaves, justly proud of its artistic and intellectual leadership. Between 500 and 449 B.C.E., the two states cooperated, along with smaller states, to defeat a huge Persian invasion. It was during and immediately after this period that Greek and particularly Athenian culture reached its highest point. Also during this period, several city-states, and again particularly Athens, developed more colonies in the eastern Mediterranean and southern Italy, as Greek culture fanned out to create a larger zone of civilization.

It was during the 5th century B.C.E. that the most famous Greek political figure, Pericles, dominated Athenian politics. Pericles was an aristocrat, but he was part of a democratic political structure in which each citizen could participate in city-state assemblies to select officials and pass laws. Pericles ruled not through official position, but by wise influence and negotiation. He helped restrain some of the more aggressive views of the Athenian democrats, who urged even further expansion of the empire to garner more wealth and build the economy. Ultimately, however, Pericles' guidance could not prevent the tragic war between Athens and Sparta, which depleted both sides.

Political decline soon set in, as Athens and Sparta vied for control of Greece during the bitter Peloponnesian Wars (431–404 B.C.E.). Ambitious kings from Macedonia, in the northern part of the peninsula, soon conquered the cities. Philip of Macedonia won the crucial battle in 338 B.C.E., and then his son Alexander extended the Macedonian Empire through the Middle East, across Persia to the border of India, and southward through Egypt. Alexander the Great's empire was short-lived, for its creator died at the age of 33 after a mere 13 years of breathtaking conquests. However, successor regional kingdoms continued to rule much of the eastern Mediterranean for several centuries. Under their aegis, Greek art and culture merged with other Middle Eastern forms during a period called *Hellenistic,* the name derived because of the influence of the Hellenes, as the Greeks were known. Although there was little political activity under the autocratic Hellenistic kings, trade flourished and important scientific centers were established in such cities as Alexandria in Egypt. In sum, the Hellenistic period saw the consolidation of Greek civilization even after the political decline of the peninsula itself, as well as some important new cultural developments.

The Hellenistic period also provided an important opportunity for interregional contacts.

Greek-Indian interactions in the kingdom of Bactria were unusual for the time. More significant was the further exchange between Greek and Persian traditions, and between Greek and Egyptian as well. The advances in science and philosophy that resulted provided a shared intellectual legacy for the whole region, even after the Hellenistic political kingdoms collapsed.

Rome

The rise of Rome formed the final phase of classical Mediterranean civilization, for by the 1st century B.C.E. Rome had subjugated Greece and the Hellenistic kingdoms alike. The Roman state began humbly enough, as a local monarchy in central Italy around 800 B.C.E. Roman aristocrats succeeded in driving out the monarchy around 509 B.C.E. and established more elaborate political institutions for their city-state. The new Roman republic gradually extended its influence over the rest of the Italian peninsula, among other things conquering the Greek colonies in the south. Thus, the Romans early acquired a strong military orientation, although initially they may have been driven simply by a desire to protect their own territory from possible rivals. Roman conquest spread more widely during the three Punic Wars, from 264 to 146 B.C.E., during which Rome fought the armies of the Phoenician city of Carthage, situated on the northern coast of Africa. These wars included a bloody defeat of the invading forces of the brilliant Carthaginian general Hannibal, whose troops were accompanied by pack-laden elephants. The war was so bitter that the Romans in a final act of destruction spread salt around Carthage to prevent agriculture from surviving there. Following the final destruction of Carthage, the Romans proceeded to seize the entire western Mediterranean along with Greece and Egypt.

The politics of the Roman republic grew increasingly unstable, however, as victorious generals sought even greater power while the poor of the city rebelled. Civil wars between two generals led to a victory by Julius Caesar, in 45 B.C.E.,

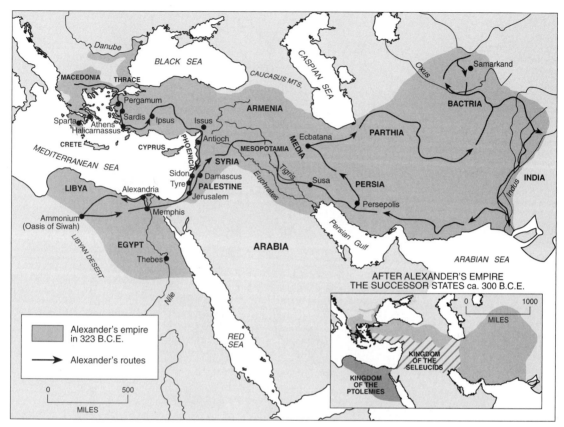

Alexander the Great and the Hellenistic World

and the effective end of the traditional institutions of the Roman state. Caesar's grandnephew, ultimately called Augustus Caesar, seized power in 27 B.C.E., following another period of rivalry after Julius Caesar's assassination, and established the basic structures of the Roman Empire. For 200 years, through the reign of the emperor Marcus Aurelius in 180 C.E., the empire maintained great vigor, bringing peace and prosperity to virtually the entire Mediterranean world, from Spain and north Africa in the west to the eastern shores of the great sea. The emperors also moved northward, conquering France and southern Britain and pushing into Germany. Here was a major, if somewhat tenuous, extension of the sway of Mediterranean civilization to western Europe.

Then the empire suffered a slow but decisive fall, which lasted more than 250 years, until invading peoples from the north finally overturned the government in Rome in 476 C.E. The decline manifested itself in terms of both economic deterioration and population loss: trade levels and the birth rate both fell. Government also became generally less effective, although some strong later emperors, particularly Diocletian and Constantine, attempted to reverse the tide. It was the emperor Constantine who, in 313, adopted the then somewhat obscure religion called Christianity in an attempt to unite the empire in new ways. However, particularly in the western half of the empire, most effective government became local, as the imperial administration could no longer

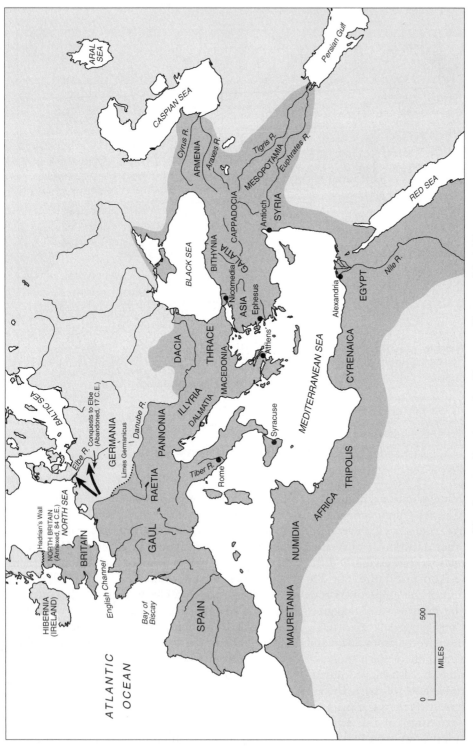

The Roman Empire at Its Greatest Extent, 98–117 C.E.

guarantee order or even provide a system of justice. The Roman armies depended increasingly on non-Roman recruits, whose loyalty was suspect. Then, in this deepening mire, the invasion of nomadic peoples from the north marked the end of the classical period of Mediterranean civilization—a civilization that, like its counterparts in Gupta India and Han China during the same approximate period, could no longer defend itself.

To conclude: the new Mediterranean civilization built on earlier cultures along the eastern Mediterranean and within the Greek islands, taking firm shape with the rise of the Greek city-states after 800 B.C.E. These states began as monarchies but then evolved into more complex and diverse political forms. They also developed a more varied commercial economy, moving away from a purely grain-growing agriculture; this spurred the formation of a number of colonial outposts around the eastern Mediterranean and in Italy. The decline of the city-states ushered in the Macedonian conquest and the formation of a wider Hellenistic culture that established deep roots in the Middle East and Egypt. Then Rome, initially a minor regional state distinguished by political virtue and stability, embarked on its great conquests, which earned it control of the Mediterranean, with important extensions into western and southeastern Europe plus the whole of north Africa. Rome's expansion ultimately overwhelmed its own republic, but the successor empire developed important political institutions of its own and resulted in two centuries of peace and glory.

GREEK AND ROMAN POLITICAL INSTITUTIONS

Politics were very important in classical Mediterranean civilization, from the Greek city-states through the early part of the Roman Empire. Indeed, our word *politics* comes from the Greek word for city-state, *polis,* which correctly suggests that intense political interests were part of life in a city-state in both Greece and Rome. The "good life" for an upper-class Athenian or Roman included active participation in politics and frequent discussions about the affairs of state. The local character of Mediterranean politics, whereby the typical city-state governed a surrounding territory of several hundred square miles, contributed to this intense preoccupation with politics. Citizens believed that the state was theirs, that they had certain rights and obligations without which their government could not survive. In the Greek city-states and also under the Roman republic, citizens actively participated in the military, which further contributed to this sense of political interest and responsibility. Under the Roman Empire, of course, political concerns were restricted by the sheer power of the emperor and his officers. Even then, however, local city-states retained considerable autonomy in Italy, Greece, and the eastern Mediterranean—the empire did not try to administer most local regions in great detail. The minority of people throughout the empire who were Roman citizens were intensely proud of this privilege.

Strong political ideals and interests created some similarities between Greco-Roman society and the Confucian values of classical China, although the concept of active citizenship was distinctive in the Mediterranean cultures. However, Greece and Rome did not develop a single or cohesive set of political institutions to rival China's divinely sanctioned emperor or its elaborate bureaucracy. So in addition to political intensity and localism as characteristics of Mediterranean civilization, we must note great diversity in political forms. Here the comparison extends to India, where various political forms—including participation in governing councils—ran strong. Later societies, in reflecting on classical Mediterranean civilization, did select from a number of political precedents. Monarchy was not a preferred form; the Roman republic and most Greek city-states had abolished early monarchies as part of their prehistory. Rule by individual strongmen was more common, and our word *tyranny* comes from this experience in classical Greece. Many tyrants were effective rulers, particularly in promoting public works and protecting the common people against the abuses of the aristocracy. Some of the Roman generals who seized power in the later days of the republic had similar characteristics, as did the Hellenistic kings who succeeded Alexander in ruling regions of his empire.

Greece

Democracy (the word is derived from the Greek *demos,* "the people") was another important political alternative in classical Mediterranean society. The Athenian city-state traveled furthest in this direction, before and during the Peloponnesian Wars, after earlier experiences with aristocratic rule and with several tyrants. In 5th-century Athens, the major decisions of state were made by general assemblies in which all citizens could participate—although usually only a minority attended. This was direct democracy, not rule through elected representatives. The assembly met every 10 days. Executive officers, including judges, were chosen for brief terms to control their power, and they were subject to review by the assembly. Furthermore, they were chosen by lot, not elected—on the principle that any citizen could and should be able to serve. To be sure, only a minority of the Athenian population were active citizens: women had no rights of political participation, and half of all adult males were not citizens at all, being slaves or foreigners. This, then, was not exactly the kind of democracy we envision today. But it elicited widespread popular participation and devotion, and certainly embodied principles that we recognize as truly democratic. The Athenian leader Pericles, who led Athens during its decades of greatest glory between the final defeat of the Persians and the agony of war with Sparta, described the system this way:

> The administration is in the hands of the many and not of the few. But while the law

secures equal justice to all alike in their private disputes, the claim of excellence is also recognized; and when a citizen is in any way distinguished he is preferred to the public service, not as a matter of privilege but as the reward of merit. Neither is poverty a bar, but a man may benefit his country whatever be the obscurity of his condition.

During the Peloponnesian Wars, Athens even demonstrated some of the potential drawbacks of democracy. Lower-class citizens, eager for government jobs and the spoils of war, often encouraged reckless military actions that weakened the state in its central dispute with Sparta.

Neither tyranny nor democracy, however, was the most characteristic political form in the classical Mediterranean world. The most widely preferred political framework centered on the existence of aristocratic assemblies, whose deliberations established guidelines for state policy and served as a check on executive power. Thus, Sparta was governed by a singularly militaristic aristocracy, intent on retaining power over a large slave population. Other Greek city-states, although less bent on disciplining their elites for rigorous military service, also featured aristocratic assemblies. Even Athens during much of its democratic phase found leadership in many aristocrats, including Pericles. The word *aristocracy,* which comes from Greek terms meaning "rule of the best," suggests where many Greeks—particularly, of course, aristocrats—thought real political virtue lay.

Rome

The constitution of the Roman republic, until the final decades of dissension in the 1st century B.C.E., which led to the establishment of the empire, tried to reconcile the various elements suggested by the Greek political experience, with primary reliance on the principle of aristocracy. All Roman citizens in the republic could gather in periodic assemblies, the function of which was not to pass basic laws but rather to elect various magistrates, some of whom were specifically entrusted with the task of representing the interests of the common people. The most important legislative body was the Senate, composed mainly of aristocrats, whose members held virtually all executive offices in the Roman state. Two consuls shared primary executive power, but in times of crisis the Senate could choose a dictator to hold emergency authority until the crisis had passed. In the Roman Senate, as in the aristocratic assemblies of the Greek city-states, the ideal of public service, featuring eloquent public speaking and arguments that sought to identify the general good, came closest to realization.

The diversity of Greek and Roman political forms, as well as the importance ascribed to political participation, helped generate a significant body of political theory in classical Mediterranean civilization. True to the aristocratic tradition, much of this theory dealt with appropriate political ethics, the duties of citizens, the importance of incorruptible service, and key political skills such as oratory. Roman writers such as Cicero, an active senator, expounded eloquently on these subjects. Some of this political writing resembled Confucianism, although there was less emphasis on hierarchy and obedience or bureaucratic virtues, and more on participation in deliberative bodies that make laws and judge the actions of executive officers. Classical Mediterranean writers also paid great attention to the structure of the state itself, debating the virtues and vices of the various political forms. This kind of theory both expressed the political interests and diversity of the Mediterranean world and served as a key heritage to later societies.

The Roman Empire was a different sort of political system from the earlier city-states, although it preserved some older institutions, such as the Senate, which became a rather meaningless forum for debates. Of necessity, the empire developed organizational capacities on a far larger scale than the city-states; it is important to remember, however, that considerable local autonomy prevailed in many regions. Only in rare cases, such as the forced dissolution of the independent Jewish state in 63 C.E. after a major local rebellion, did the Romans take over distant areas completely. Careful organization was particularly evident in the vast hierarchy of the Roman army, whose officers wielded great political power even over the emperors.

In addition to considerable tolerance for local customs and religions, plus strong military organization, the Romans emphasized carefully crafted laws as the factor that would hold their vast territories together. Greek and Roman republican leaders had already developed an understanding of the importance of codified, equitable law. Aristocratic leaders in 8th-century Athens, for example, sponsored clear legal codes designed to balance the defense of private property with the protection of poor citizens, including access to courts of law administered by fellow citizens. The early Roman republic introduced its first code of law, the Twelve Tables, by 450 B.C.E. These early Roman laws were intended, among other things, to restrain the upper classes from arbitrary action and to subject them, as well as ordinary people, to some common legal principles. The Roman Empire carried these legal interests still further, in the belief that law should evolve to meet changing conditions without, however, fluctuating wildly. The idea of Roman law was that rules, objectively judged, rather than personal whim should govern social relationships; thus, the law steadily took over matters of judgment earlier reserved for fathers of families or for landlords. Roman law also promoted the importance of commonsense fairness. In one case cited in the law texts of the empire, a slave was being shaved by a barber in a public square; two men were playing ball nearby, and one accidentally hit the barber with the ball, causing him to cut the slave's throat. Who was responsible for the tragedy: the barber, catcher, or pitcher? According to Roman law, the slave—for anyone so foolish as to be shaved in a public place was asking for trouble and bore the responsibility himself.

WORLD PROFILES

JULIUS CAESAR
(100–44 B.C.E.)

Julius Caesar was, along with his grandnephew Augustus, the leading figure in transforming the Roman republic into an imperial form of government ruled by one dictator. Caesar had become a minor political official by the age of 40. Then, however, he began to attain greater power, serving as governor of southern Gaul and northern Italy, from where he went on to conquer most of the territory now covered by France, Belgium, part of the Netherlands, and part of Germany. Opening these territories to classical Mediterranean civilization was his greatest and most lasting achievement. But his personal goals turned to ruling Rome itself, where he defied republican tradition, becoming Rome's dictator. He was killed by conservative members of the Senate for his ambition. His death did not save the republic—the kind of government he planned, including wider citizenship for the empire, came about 14 years later. The statue pictured here conveys an image of Caesar that became popular long after his death: calm, soldierly, and statesmanlike. Why was Caesar so idealized, not only in Rome but also in later European history?

No representations of Julius Caesar survive from his lifetime. This statue was made 100 years after his death.

Roman law codes spread widely through the empire, and with them came the notion of law as the regulator of social life. Many non-Romans were given the right of citizenship—although most ordinary people outside Rome itself preferred to maintain their local allegiances. With citizenship, however, came full access to Rome-appointed judges and uniform laws. Imperial law codes also regulated property rights and commerce, thus creating some economic unity in the vast empire. The idea of fair and reasoned law, to which officers of the state should themselves be subject, was a key political achievement of the Roman Empire, comparable in importance, although quite different in nature, to the Chinese elaboration of a complex bureaucratic structure.

The Greeks and Romans were less innovative in the functions they ascribed to government than in the political forms and theories they developed. Most governments concentrated on maintaining systems of law courts and military forces. Athens and, more durably and successfully, Rome placed great premium on the importance of military conquest. Mediterranean governments regulated some branches of commerce, particularly in the interest of securing vital supplies of grain. Rome, indeed, undertook vast public works in the form of roads and harbors to facilitate military transport as well as commerce. And the Roman state, especially under the empire, built countless stadiums and public baths to entertain and distract its subjects. The city of Rome itself, which at its peak contained more than a million inhabitants, provided cheap food as well as gladiator contests and other entertainment for the masses—the famous "bread and circuses" that were designed to prevent popular disorder. Colonies of Romans elsewhere were also given theaters and stadiums. This provided solace in otherwise strange lands such as England or Palestine. Governments also supported an official religion, sponsoring public ceremonies to honor the gods and goddesses; civic religious festivals were important events that both expressed and encouraged widespread loyalty to the state. However, there was little attempt to impose this religion on everyone, and other religious practices were tolerated so long as they did not conflict with loyalty to the state. Even the later Roman emperors, who advanced the idea that the emperor was a god as a means of strengthening authority, were normally tolerant of other religions. They only attacked Christianity, and then irregularly, because of the Christians' refusal to place the state first in their devotion.

Localism and fervent political interests, including a sense of intense loyalty to the state; a diversity of political systems together with the preference for aristocratic rule; the importance of

law and the development of an unusually elaborate and uniform set of legal principles—these were the chief political legacies of the classical Mediterranean world. The sheer accomplishment of the Roman Empire itself, which united a region never before or since brought together, still stands as one of the great political monuments of world history. This was a distinctive political mix. Although there was attention to careful legal procedures, no clear definition of individuals' rights existed. Indeed, the emphasis on duties to the state could lead, as in Sparta, to an essentially totalitarian framework in which the state controlled even the raising of children. Nor, until the peaceful centuries of the early Roman Empire, was it an entirely successful political structure, as wars and instability were common. Nonetheless, there can be no question of the richness of this political culture or of its central importance to the Greeks and Romans themselves.

RELIGION AND CULTURE

The Greeks and Romans did not create a significant, world-class religion; in this, they differed from India and to some extent from China. Christianity, which was to become one of the major world religions, did of course arise during the Roman Empire. It owed some of its rapid geographical spread to the ease of movement within the huge Roman Empire. However, Christianity was not really a product of Greek or Roman culture, although it was ultimately influenced by this culture. It took on serious historical importance only as the Roman Empire began its decline. The characteristic Greco-Roman religion was a much more primitive affair, derived from a belief in the spirits of nature elevated into a complex set of gods and goddesses who were seen as regulating human life. Greeks and Romans had different names for their pantheon, but the objects of worship were essentially the same: a creator or father god, Zeus or Jupiter, presided over an unruly assemblage of gods and

Greek sculpture: the god Zeus. Compare this work to the more sensual Hindu religious art illustrated on page 87.

goddesses whose functions ranged from regulating the daily passage of the sun (Apollo) or the oceans (Neptune) to inspiring war (Mars) or human love and beauty (Venus). Specific gods were the patrons of other human activities such as metalworking, the hunt, even literature and history. Regular ceremonies to the gods had real political importance, and many individuals sought the gods' aid in foretelling the future or in ensuring a good harvest or good health.

In addition to its political functions, Greco-Roman religion had certain other features. It tended to be rather human, of this world in its approach. The doings of the gods made for good storytelling; they read like soap operas on a superhuman scale. Thus, the classical Mediterranean religion early engendered an important literary tradition, as was also the case in India. (Indeed, Greco-Roman and Indian religious lore reflected the common heritage of Indo-European invaders.)

The gods were often used to illustrate human passions and foibles, thus serving as symbols of a serious inquiry into human nature. Unlike the Indians, however, the Greeks and Romans became interested in their gods more in terms of what they could do for and reveal about humankind on this earth than the principles that could elevate people toward higher planes of spirituality.

This dominant religion also had a number of limitations. Its lack of spiritual passion failed to satisfy many ordinary workers and peasants, particularly in times of political chaos or economic distress. "Mystery" religions, often imported from the Middle East, periodically swept through Greece and Rome, providing secret rituals and fellowship and a greater sense of contact with unfathomable divine powers. Even more than in China, a considerable division arose between upper-class and popular belief.

The gods and goddesses of Greco-Roman religion left many upper-class people dissatisfied also. They provided stories about how the world came to be, but little basis for a systematic inquiry into nature or human society. And while the dominant religion promoted political loyalty, it did not provide a basis for ethical thought. Hence, many thinkers, both in Greece and Rome, sought a separate model for ethical behavior. Greek and Roman moral philosophy, as issued by philosophers such as Aristotle and Cicero, typically stressed the importance of moderation and balance in human behavior as opposed to the instability of much political life and the excesses of the gods. Other ethical systems were devised, particularly during the Hellenistic period. Stoics, for example, emphasized an inner moral independence, to be cultivated by strict discipline of the body and by personal bravery. These ethical systems, established largely apart from religious considerations, were major contributions in their own right; they also were blended with later religious thought, under Christianity.

The idea of a philosophy separate from the official religion, although not necessarily hostile to it, informed classical Mediterranean political theory, which made little reference to religious principles. It also considerably emphasized the powers of human thought. In Athens, Socrates (born in 469 B.C.E.) encouraged his pupils to question conventional wisdom, on the grounds that the chief human duty was "the improvement of the soul." Socrates ran afoul of the Athenian government, which thought that he was undermining political loyalty; given the choice of suicide or exile, Socrates chose the former. However, the Socratic principle of rational inquiry by means of skeptical questioning became a recurrent strand in classical Greek thinking and in its heritage to later societies. Socrates' great pupil Plato accentuated the positive somewhat more strongly by suggesting that human reason could approach an understanding of the three perfect forms—the absolutely True, Good, and Beautiful—which he believed characterized nature. Thus, a philosophical tradition arose in Greece, although in very diverse individual expressions, which tended to deemphasize the importance of human spirituality in favor of a celebration of the human ability to think. The result bore some similarities to Chinese Confucianism, although with greater emphasis on skeptical questioning and abstract speculations about the basic nature of humanity and the universe.

Greek interest in rationality carried over an inquiry into the underlying order of physical nature. The Greeks were not outstanding empirical scientists. Relatively few new scientific findings emanated from Athens, or later from Rome, although philosophers such as Aristotle did collect large amounts of biological data. The Greek interest lay in speculations about nature's order, and many non-Westerners believe that this tradition continues to inform what they see as an excessive Western passion for seeking basic rationality in the universe. In practice, the Greek concern translated into a host of theories, some of which were wrong, about the motions of the planets and the organization of the elemental principles of earth, fire, air, and water, and into a considerable interest in mathematics as a means

Greek pottery. Depicting Greek soldiers (hoplites) fighting amid their chariots, this piece dates from 6th-century Athens.

of rendering nature's patterns comprehensible. Greek and later Hellenistic work in geometry was particularly impressive, featuring among other achievements the basic theorems of Pythagoras. Scientists during the Hellenistic period made some important empirical contributions, especially in studies of anatomy; medical treatises by Galen were not improved on, in the Western world, for many centuries. The mathematician Euclid produced what was long the world's most widely used compendium of geometry. Less fortunately, the Hellenistic astronomer Ptolemy produced an elaborate theory of the sun's motion around a stationary earth. This new Hellenistic theory contradicted much earlier Middle Eastern astronomy, which had recognized the earth's rotation; nonetheless, it was Ptolemy's theory that was long taken as fixed wisdom in Western thought.

Roman intellectuals, actively examining ethical and political theory, had nothing to add to Greek and Hellenistic science. They did help to preserve this tradition in the form of textbooks that were administered to upper-class schoolchildren. The Roman genius was more practical than the Greek and included engineering achievements such as the great roads and aqueducts that carried water to cities large and small. Roman ability to construct elaborate arches so that buildings could carry great structural weight was unsurpassed anywhere in the world. These feats, too, left their mark, as Rome's huge edifices long served as a reminder of ancient glories. But ultimately, it was the Greek and Hellenistic impulse to extend human reason to nature's principles that resulted in the most impressive legacy.

In classical Mediterranean civilization, however, science and mathematics loomed far less large than art and literature in conveying key cultural values. The official religion inspired themes for artistic expression and the justification for temples, statues, and plays devoted to the glories of the gods. Nonetheless, the human-centered qualities of the Greeks and Romans also registered, as artists emphasized the beauty of realistic portrayals of the human form and poets and play-

A great temple to Theseus, the legendary founder of Athens. This temple is an example of Doric architecture, the earliest Greek column style, in Athens during the 5th century B.C.E.

wrights used the gods as foils for inquiries into the human condition.

All the arts received some attention in classical Mediterranean civilization. Performances of music and dance were vital parts of religious festivals, but their precise styles have unfortunately not been preserved. Far more durable was the Greek interest in drama, for plays, more than poetry, took a central role in this culture. Greek dramatists produced both comedy and tragedy, indeed making a formal division between the two approaches that is still part of the Western tradition, as in the labeling of current television shows as either form. On the whole, in contrast to Indian writers, the Greeks placed the greatest emphasis on tragedy. Their belief in human reason and balance also involved a sense that these virtues were precarious, so a person could easily become ensnared in situations of powerful emotion and uncontrollable consequences. The Athenian dramatist Sophocles, for example, so insightfully portrayed the psychological flaws of his hero Oedipus that modern psychology long used the term *Oedipus complex* to refer to a potentially unhealthy relationship between a man and his mother.

Greek literature contained a strong epic tradition as well, starting with the beautifully crafted tales of the *Iliad* and *Odyssey,* attributed to the poet Homer, who lived in the 8th century B.C.E. Roman authors, particularly the poet Vergil, also worked in the epic form, seeking to link Roman history and mythology with the Greek forerunner. Roman writers made significant contributions to poetry and to definitions of the poetic form that was long used in Western literature. The overall Roman literary contribution was less impressive than the Greek, but it was substantial enough both to provide important examples of how poetry should be written and to furnish abundant illustrations of the literary richness of the Latin language.

In the visual arts, the emphasis of classical Mediterranean civilization was sculpture and architecture. Greek artists also excelled in ceramic work, whereas Roman painters produced realistic (and sometimes pornographic) decorations for

The Forum in Rome. In the ancient imperial city of Rome, the Colosseum was a triumph of Roman monumental architecture and a center for sports and ceremonies.

the homes of the wealthy. In the brilliant age of Athens' 5th century—the age of Pericles, Socrates, Sophocles, and so many other intensely creative figures—sculptors such as Phidias developed unprecedented skill rendering simultaneously realistic yet beautiful images of the human form, from lovely goddesses to muscled warriors and athletes. Roman sculptors, less innovative, continued this heroic-realistic tradition. They molded scenes of Roman conquests on triumphal columns and captured the power but also the human qualities of Augustus Caesar and his successors on busts and full-figure statues alike.

Greek architecture, from the 8th century B.C.E. onward, emphasized monumental construction, square or rectangular in shape, with columned porticos. The Greeks devised three embellishments for the tops of columns supporting their massive buildings, each more ornate than the next: the Doric, the Ionic, and the Corinthian. The Greeks, in short, invented what Westerners and others in the world today still regard as "classical" architecture, although the Greeks themselves were influenced by Egyptian models in their preferences. Greece, and later Italy, provided abundant stone for ambitious temples, markets, and other public buildings. Many of these same structures were filled with products

of the sculptors' workshops. They were brightly painted, although over the centuries the paint faded, so that later imitators came to think of the classical style as involving unadorned (some might say drab) stone. Roman architects adopted the Greek themes quite readily. Their engineering skill allowed them to construct buildings of even greater size, as well as new forms such as the free-standing stadium. Under the empire, the Romans learned how to add domes to rectangular buildings, which resulted in some welcome architectural diversity. At the same time, the empire's taste for massive, heavily adorned monuments and public buildings, while a clear demonstration of Rome's sense of power and achievement, moved increasingly away from the simple lines of the early Greek temples.

Classical Mediterranean art and architecture were intimately linked with the society that produced them. There is a temptation, because of the formal role of classical styles in later societies, including our own, to attribute a stiffness to Greek and Roman art that was not present in the original. Greek and Roman structures were built to be used. Temples and marketplaces and the public baths that so delighted the Roman upper classes were part of daily urban life. Classical art was also flexible, according to need. Villas or small palaces—built for the Roman upper classes and typically constructed around an open courtyard—had a light, even simple quality rather different from that of temple architecture. Classical dramas were not merely examples of high art, performed for the cultural elite. Indeed, Athens lives in the memory of many humanists today as much because of the large audiences that trooped to performances of plays by authors such as Sophocles as for the creativity of the writers and philosophers themselves. Literally thousands of people gathered in the large hillside theaters of Athens and other cities for the performance of new plays and for associated music and poetry competitions. Popular taste in Rome, to be sure, seemed less elevated. Republican Rome was not an important cultural center, and many Roman

UNDERSTANDING CULTURES

WHEN TWO BELIEF SYSTEMS MEET

One of the most interesting developments in world history involves points at which two quite different cultures encounter each other. Contact may result from trade, missionary activity, migration, or conquest. Its ramifications can be just as varied. The two cultures may detest each other, or one might try (or be forced) to copy the other. However, the most common result, even when one culture is promoted by force, is a certain blending. This blending is called *syncretism*.

When Alexander's conquests established a Hellenistic state for many decades in northwestern India, cultural contact ran high. Indians learned some additional mathematics from Greeks in the royal bureaucracy. They also admired Greek artistic styles. For some time, Buddhas in statues and other art forms were shown wearing Mediterranean-type hairdos and togas. Despite such displays, the Indians involved were not Hellenized. They maintained their own religion, for example, and their belief that art should serve this religion. Here was an early case of syncretism.

The impact on the Mediterranean was less clear. Indians grew more aware of the Middle East and sent Buddhist missionaries to the region. No major conversions resulted, but Buddhist ethical ideas may have influenced some Greek ethical systems and, through them, Christianity—it is simply not possible to be sure. Some obvious Indian developments, such as their superior numbering system, were ignored. Cultural borrowing is, among other things, oddly unpredictable.

leaders indeed feared the more emotional qualities of Greek art. The Roman Empire is known more for monumental athletic performances—chariot races and gladiators—than for high-quality popular theater. However, the fact remains that, even in Rome, elements of classical art—the great monuments if nothing more—were part of daily urban life and the pursuit of pleasure.

ECONOMY AND SOCIETY IN THE MEDITERRANEAN

Politics and formal culture in Greece and Rome were mainly affairs of the cities—which means that they were of intense concern only to a minority of the population. Most Greeks and Romans were farmers, tied to the soil and often to local rituals and festivals that were rather different from urban forms. Many Greek farmers, for example, annually gathered for a spring passion play to celebrate the recovery of the goddess of fertility from the lower world, an event that was seen as a vital preparation for planting and that also suggested the possibility of an afterlife—a prospect important to many people who endured a life of hard labor and poverty. A substantial population of free farmers, who owned their own land, flourished in the early days of the Greek city-states and later around Rome. However, there was a constant tendency, most pronounced in Rome, for large landlords to squeeze these farmers, forcing them to become tenants or laborers or to join the swelling crowds of the urban lower class. Tensions between tyrants and aristocrats or democrats and aristocrats in Athens often revolved around free farmers' attempts to preserve their independence and shake off the heavy debts they had incurred. The Roman republic declined in part because too many farmers became dependent on the protection of large landlords, even when they did not work their estates outright, and so no longer could vote freely.

Farming in Greece and in much of Italy was complicated by the fact that soil conditions were not ideal for grain growing, and yet grain was the staple of life. First in Greece, then in central Italy, farmers were increasingly tempted to shift to the production of olives and grapes, which were used primarily for cooking and wine making. These products were well suited to the soil conditions, but they required an unusually extensive conversion of agriculture to a market basis. That is, farmers who produced grapes and olives had to buy some of the food they needed, and they had to sell most of their own product in order to do this. Furthermore, planting olive trees or grape vines required substantial capital, for they did not bear fruit for at least five years after planting. This was one reason so many farmers went into debt. It was also one of the reasons that large landlords gained increasing advantage over independent farmers, for they could enter into market production on a much larger scale if only because of their greater access to capital.

The rise of commercial agriculture in Greece and then around Rome was one of the prime forces leading to efforts to establish an empire. Greek city-states, with Athens usually in the lead, developed colonies in the Middle East and then in Sicily mainly to gain access to grain production; for this, they traded not only olive oil and wine but also manufactured products and silver. Rome pushed south, in part, to acquire the Sicilian grain fields and later used much of north Africa as its granary. Indeed, the Romans encouraged such heavy cultivation in north Africa that they promoted a soil depletion, which helps account for the region's reduced agricultural fertility in later centuries.

The importance of commercial farming obviously dictated extensive concern with trade. Private merchants operated most of the ships that carried agricultural products and other goods. Greek city-states and ultimately the Roman state supervised the grain trade, promoting public works and storage facilities and carefully regulating the vital supplies. Other kinds of trade were vital also. Luxury products from the shops of urban artists or craftspeople played a major role in the lifestyle of the upper classes. There was some trade also beyond the borders of Mediterranean civilization, for goods from India and China. In this trade, the Mediterranean peoples found themselves at some disadvantage, for their manufactured products were less sophisticated than those of eastern Asia; thus, they typically exported animal skins, precious metals, and even exotic African animals for Asian zoos in return for the spices and artistic products of the east.

For all the importance of trade, merchants enjoyed a somewhat ambiguous status in classical Mediterranean civilization. Leading Athenian merchants were usually foreigners, mostly from the trading peoples of the Middle East—the descendants of Lydians and Phoenicians. Merchants had a somewhat higher status in Rome, clearly forming the second most prestigious social class under the landed patricians, but here, too, the aristocracy frequently disputed the merchants' rights. Overall, merchants fared better in the Mediterranean than in China, in terms of official recognition, but worse than in India; classical Mediterranean society certainly did not set in motion a culture that distinctly valued capitalist money-making.

Slavery was another key ingredient of the classical economy. Philosophers such as Aristotle produced elaborate justifications for the necessity of slavery in a proper society. Athenians used slaves as household servants and also as workers in their vital silver mines, which provided the manpower for Athens' empire and commercial operations alike. Sparta used slaves extensively for agricultural work. Slavery spread steadily in Rome from the final centuries of the republic. Because most slaves came from conquered territories, the need for slaves was another key element in military expansion. Here was a theme visible in earlier civilizations in the eastern Mediterranean, and within later societies in this

HISTORY DEBATE

MEDITERRANEAN CIVILIZATION AND "WESTERN" CIVILIZATION

The impulse to regard Greece and Rome as the origins of what is now called Western civilization runs very deep. Rome's glory and the power of Greek culture obviously impressed thinkers and statesmen in western Europe, who looked back to these times for inspiration. This was a key theme in European history after the classical period. From western Europe, fascination with the classical Mediterranean world later spread to North America.

All the classical civilizations left strong imprints on later developments. At the same time, these imprints require careful assessment, because none of the civilizations remained static. The nature and impact of the legacy must be weighed against innovations. This general analytical requirement is doubly important when considering classical Mediterranean culture, for the simple reason that, after Rome, Mediterranean civilization split apart. Some common features remained, including cultural aspects such as a strong emphasis on the defense of personal honor plus social-economic institutions such as relatively large villages; however, no Mediterranean civilization continued to exist as a whole.

Some historians argue that regarding Greece and Rome as the origins of Western civilization is completely off the mark. Greece, particularly, was proud of its own uniqueness, and when it sought to expand, it looked to the lands of the Middle East, not the West; Rome also ended up placing special value on its eastern holdings. Not surprisingly, Greek-Roman heritage lived on more directly in southeastern Europe than in the West. Certainly, the West does not have sole claim to Mediterranean heritage.

Nonetheless, selective Greek-Roman values and institutions did affect western Europe, either immediately or in later revivals. So the debate continues about positioning the classical Mediterranean civilization in light of later developments.

The issue involves both the facts and judgment. What were the most important surviving characteristics of classical Mediterranean civilization? Were they taken out of context as they helped shape later civilizations? Take democracy, for example: to what extent did Mediterranean democracy "cause" later democracy in the West? (And, if it was responsible for causing this democracy, why did the process take so long?) Your evaluation may focus on cultural and political achievements, but it must also address the social and economic framework of this third major classical civilization.

region as well, which helps explain the greater importance of military forces and expansion in these areas than in India or China. Actual slave conditions varied greatly. Roman slaves performed household tasks—including the tutoring of upper-class children, for which cultured Greek slaves were highly valued. They also worked the mines, for precious metals and for iron; as in Greece, slave labor in the mines was particularly brutal, and few slaves survived more than a few years of such an existence. Roman estate owners used large numbers of slaves for agricultural work, along with paid laborers and tenant farmers. This practice was another source of the steady pressure placed upon free farmers who could not easily compete with unpaid forced labor.

Partly because of slavery, partly because of the overall orientation of upper-class culture, neither

Greece nor Rome was especially interested in technological innovations applicable to agriculture or manufacturing. The Greeks made important advances in shipbuilding and navigation, which were vital for their trading economy. Romans, less adept on the water, developed their skill in engineering to provide greater urban amenities and good roads for the swift and easy movement of troops. But a technology designed to improve the production of food or manufactured goods did not figure largely in this civilization, which mainly relied on the earlier achievements of previous Mediterranean societies. Abundant slave labor probably discouraged concern for more efficient production methods. So did a sense that the true goals of humankind were artistic and political. One Hellenistic scholar, for example, refused to write a handbook on engineering because "the work of an engineer and everything that ministers to the needs of life is ignoble and vulgar." As a consequence of this outlook, Mediterranean society lagged behind both India and China in production technology, which was one reason for its resulting unfavorable balance of trade with eastern Asia.

Both Greek and Roman society emphasized the importance of a tight family structure, with a husband and father firmly in control. Women had vital economic functions, particularly in farming and artisan families. In the upper classes, especially in Rome, women often commanded great influence and power within a household. But in law and culture, women were held inferior. Families burdened with too many children sometimes put female infants to death because of their low status and their potential drain on the family economy. Pericles stated common beliefs about women when he noted, "For a woman not to show more weakness than is natural to her sex is a great glory, and not to be talked about for good or for evil among men." Early Roman law stipulated, "The husband is the judge of his wife. If she commits a fault, he punishes her; if she has drunk wine, he condemns her; if she has been guilty of

adultery, he kills her." (Later, however, such customs were held in check by family courts composed of members of both families.) Here was a case where Roman legal ideas modified traditional family controls. If divorced because of adultery, a Roman woman lost a third of her property and had to wear a special garment that set her apart like a prostitute. On the other hand, the oppression of women was probably less severe in this civilization than in China. Many Greek and Roman women were active in business and controlled a portion, even if only the minority, of all urban property.

Because of the divisions within classical Mediterranean society, no easy generalizations about culture or achievement can be made. An 18th-century English historian called the high point of the Roman Empire, before 180 C.E., the period in human history "during which the condition of the human race was most happy or prosperous." This is doubtful, given the technological accomplishments of China and India. And certainly, many slaves, women, and ordinary farmers in the Mediterranean world might have disagreed with this viewpoint. Few farmers, for example, actively participated in the political structures or cultural opportunities that were the most obvious mark of this civilization. Many continued to work largely as their ancestors had done, with quite similar tools and in very similar poverty, untouched by the doings of the great or the bustle of the cities except when wars engulfed their lands.

We are tempted, of course, exclusively to remember the urban achievements, for they exerted the greatest influence on later ages that recalled the glories of Greece and Rome. The distinctive features of classical Mediterranean social and family structures had a less enduring impact, although ideas about slavery or women were revived in subsequent periods. However, the relatively unchanging face of ordinary life had an important influence as well, as many farmers and artisans long maintained the habits and outlook they developed during the great days of the

Greek and Roman empires, and because their separation from much of the official culture posed both a challenge and opportunity for new cultural movements such as Christianity.

TOWARD THE FALL OF ROME

Classical Mediterranean society had one final impact on world history through its rather fragmentary collapse. Unlike China, classical civilization in the Mediterranean region was not simply disrupted only to revive. Unlike India, there was no central religion, derived from the civilization itself, to serve as link between the classical period and what followed. Furthermore, the fall of Rome was not uniform; in essence, Rome fell more in some parts of the Mediterranean than it did in others. The result, among other things, was that no single civilization ultimately rose to claim the mantle of Greece and Rome. At the same time, there was no across-the-board maintenance of the classical Mediterranean institutions and values in any of the civilizations that later claimed a relationship to the Greek and Roman past. Greece and Rome lived on, in more than idle memory, but their heritage was unquestionably more complex and more selective than proved to be the case for India or China.

PATHS TO THE PRESENT

In contrast to India and China, no relatively straight line connects the classical period in Persia or the Mediterranean to the present day. A Persian tradition was established, in art, for example, but many aspects of Persian politics and culture, including the Zoroastrian religion, were disrupted or later replaced.

As for the Mediterranean, its unity as a civilization ended with the fall of Rome. Certain cultural features remain, however, in southern Europe, North Africa, and the Middle East. For instance, these societies emphasize the importance of honor and the defense of honor, and relatively large peasant villages still exist, with a corresponding emphasis on market agriculture. These characteristics, however, although passed down from the classical period, are overshadowed by the current divisions in politics and religion.

If the classical Mediterranean world did not create a full heritage for the present, it did generate many features that were revived by later societies. Thus, when American leaders considered the styles for public buildings in the late 18th century, they could imagine no better model than the temples and theaters of Greece and Rome. Greek and Hellenistic emphasis on scientific and logical thinking also was later retrieved, as were the various Greek political forms, including democracy and the idea of a senate. We need to know about the classical Mediterranean to grasp the present, but less for reasons of literal survival than for the immense usefulness of selective revival.

Another factor complicates this classical-present relationship. Classical Mediterranean forms were revived not only in western Europe, but also—earlier and often more elaborately—in eastern Europe, including Russia, and in the Middle East and North Africa. This underscores the importance of the classical Mediterranean heritage, but its contribution to several later civilizations also complicates our understanding of it.

SUGGESTED WEB SITES

On the Roman Empire, see http://www.thebritishmuseum.ac.uk/world/rome/empire.html; on women in the ancient world, http://www.womenintheancientworld.com/index.htm and http://www.stoa.org/diotima/; for more on the ancient Greek world, see http://www.museum.upenn.edu/greek_world/Index.html.

SUGGESTED READINGS

Recent works include Nancy Demand, *A History of Ancient Greece* (1996), with a good bibliography; N. G. L. Hammond, *The Genius of Alexander the Great* (1997); Roger Brock, ed., *Alternatives to Athens: Varieties of Political Organization and Community in Ancient Greece* (2000); M. I. Finley, *Ancient Slavery and Modern Ideology* (expanded ed., 1998). See also Thomas Benediktson, *Literature and the Visual Arts in Ancient Greece and Rome* (2001); George Cawkwell, *The Greek Wars: The Failure of Persia* (New York, 2005); Gary Forsythe, *A Critical History of Early Rome: From Prehistory to the First Punic War* (2005); Alain M. Gowing, *Empire and Memory: The Representation of the Roman Republic in Imperial Culture* (2005); Callie Williamson, *The Laws of the Roman People: Public Laws in the Expansion and Decline of the Roman Republic* (2005); Richard Holland, *Augustus: Godfather of Europe* (2004); Harriet I. Flower, *The Cambridge Companion to the Roman Republic* (2004); G. E. R. Lloyd, *Ancient Worlds, Modern Reflections: Philosophical Perspectives on Greek and Chinese Science and Culture* (2004); Marilynn B. Skinner, *Sexuality in Greek and Roman Culture* (2005); I. M. Plant, *Women Writers of Ancient Greece and Rome: An Anthology* (2004); Fiona McHardy and Eireann Marshall, eds., *Women's Influence on Classical Civilization* (2004); and James I. Porter, *Classical Pasts: The Classical Traditions of Greece and Rome* (2006).

There are a number of excellent sources on classical Greece and Rome, even aside from translations of the leading thinkers and writers. See M. Crawford, ed., *Sources for Ancient History* (1983); C. Fornara, *Translated Documents of Greece and Rome* (1977); N. Lewis, *Greek Historical Documents: The Fifth Century B.C.* (1971); M. Crawford, *The Roman Republic* (1982); P. Green, *Alexander to Actium: The Historical Evolution of the Hellenistic Ages* (1990); and M. M. Austin, *The Hellenistic World from Alexander to the Roman Conquest* (1981). Important specialized works include M. Crawford and D. Whitehead, *Archaic and Classical Greece* (1983); Cyril Robinson, *Everyday Life in Ancient Greece* (1987); W. Burkert, *Greek Religions* (1985); G. E. R. Lloyd, *The Revolutions of Wisdom: Studies in the Claims and Practices of Ancient Greek Science* (1987); Sarah Pomeroy, *Goddesses, Whores, Wives, and Slaves: Women in Classical Antiquity* (1975); Renate Bridenthal and others, eds., *Becoming Visible: Women in European History* (1998); and A. R. Burn, *Persia and the Greeks* (1962). A recent book by Donald Kagan, *The Peloponnesian War* (2003), captures Greece's crisis moment. On Rome, see K. Christ, *The Romans: An Introduction to Their History and Civilization* (1984), which is eminently readable and provocative; J. Boardman et al., *Oxford History of the Classical World* (1986); and R. Saller, *The Roman Empire* (1987).

See also H. H. Schulhard, *A History of the Roman World, 753–146 B.C.* (1961). For social aspects of Greco-Roman culture, good sources include R. MacMullen, *Roman Social Relations, 50 B.C.–A.D. 284* (1981); P. Garnsey and R. Saller, *The Roman Empire: Economy, Society and Culture* (1987); K. Hopkins, *Conquerors and Slaves, Slaves and Masters in the Roman Empire* (1987); and K. R. Bradley and W. Philips Jr., *Slavery from Roman Times to the Early Transatlantic Trade* (1985).

7

The Classical Period: Directions, Diversities, and Declines by 500 C.E.

The basic themes of the three great classical civilizations involved expansion and integration. From localized beginnings in northern China, the Ganges region, or the Aegean Sea, commercial, political, and cultural outreach pushed civilization through the Middle Kingdom and beyond, through the Indian subcontinent, and into the western Mediterranean. The growth set in motion deliberate but also implicit attempts to pull the new civilizations together in more than name. Correspondingly, the most telling comparisons among the three classical civilizations—identifying similarities as well as differences—involve this same process of integration and some of the problems it encountered.

Throughout the classical world, integration and expansion faltered between 200 and 500 C.E. Decline, even collapse, began to afflict civilization first in China, then in the Mediterranean, and finally in India. These developments signaled the end of the classical era and ushered in important new themes in world history that defined the next major period. The response of major religions to political decline formed a leading direction for world history to come.

Classical civilizations (including Persia) had never embraced the bulk of the territory around the globe, although they did include the majority of the world's population. Developments outside the classical orbit had rhythms of their own during the classical period, and they gained new prominence as the great civilizations faltered. This describes the third historical theme—along with basic comparisons and the process of decline and attendant religious responses—that must be addressed in moving from the classical period to world history's next phase.

■ **KEY QUESTIONS** *Were there general causes and patterns in the decline of the classical civilizations? What was the relationship of religion to the process of decline, as cause or as effect? Finally, what were the key differences in patterns and what explains these differences?*

BEYOND THE CLASSICAL CIVILIZATIONS

Although the development of the three great civilizations is the central thread in world history during the classical period, significant changes also occurred in other parts of the world. On the borders of the major civilizations, as in northeastern Africa, Japan, and northern Europe, these changes bore some relationship to the classical world, although they were partly autonomous. Elsewhere, most notably in the Americas, new cultures evolved in an entirely independent way. In all cases, changes during the classical period set the stage for more important links in world history later on. Southeast Asia gained access to civilization during the classical period mainly through its contacts with India. Regional kingdoms had already been established, and agricultural economies were familiar on the principal islands of Indonesia as well as on the mainland. Participation in wider trade patterns developed through the efforts of Indian merchants. Hindu and particularly Buddhist religion and art also spread from India. Here was a case of the outright expansion of civilization without the creation of a fully distinctive or unified culture.

A similar case of expansion from an established civilization affected parts of sub-Saharan Africa; we have seen (in Chapter 2) the spread of government and new cultural forms to northeastern Africa south of Egypt. This society continued to develop during the classical period, in Kush and other centers. Monarchs continued to feature elaborate ceremonies illustrating a belief that the king was divine. The kingdom of Kush was defeated by a rival kingdom called Axum by about 300 B.C.E.; Axum ultimately fell to another regional kingdom, Ethiopia. Axum and Ethiopia had active contacts with the eastern Mediterranean world until after the fall of Rome. They traded with this region for several centuries. Some Ethiopians converted to Judaism after interacting with Jewish merchants, and a small minority of Ethiopians remain Jewish today. Greek-speaking merchants also had considerable influence, and it was through them that Christianity was brought to Ethiopia by the 4th century C.E. The Ethiopian Christian church, however, was cut off from mainstream Christianity thereafter, flourishing in isolation to modern times. Until the late 20th century, Ethiopia could boast of having the oldest continuous monarchy anywhere in the world.

It is not clear how much influence, if any, the kingdoms of the upper Nile had on the later history of sub-Saharan Africa. Knowledge of ironworking certainly spread, facilitating the expansion of agriculture in other parts of the continent. Patterns of strong, ceremonial kingship—sometimes called divine kingship—surfaced in other parts of Africa later, but whether this occurred through some contact with the Kushite tradition or independently is not known. Knowledge of Kushite writing did not spread, which suggests that the impact of this first case of civilization below the Sahara was somewhat limited.

For most of Africa below the Sahara, but north of the great tropical jungles, the major development up to 500 C.E. was the further extension of agriculture. Well-organized villages arose, often very similar in form and structure to those that still exist. Farming took earliest root on the southern fringes of the Sahara, which was less arid than it is today. Toward the end of the classical era, important regional kingdoms were forming in western Africa, leading to the first great state in the region—Ghana. Because of the barriers of dense vegetation and the impact of African diseases on domesticated animals, agriculture spread only slowly southward. However, the creation of a strong agricultural economy prepared the way for the next, more long-lasting and

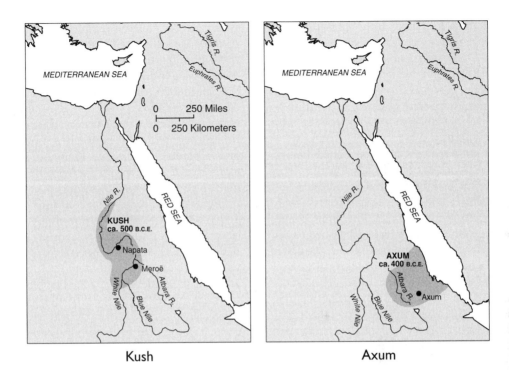

Kush   Axum

influential wave of African kingdoms, far to the west of the Nile. New crops, including root crops and plantains introduced through trade with southeast Asia about 100 C.E., helped African farmers push into new areas.

Advances in agriculture and manufacturing also occurred in other parts of the world besides sub-Saharan Africa. In northern Europe and Japan, there was no question, as yet, of elaborate contacts with the great civilizations, no counterpart to the influences that affected parts of southeast Asia and the upper Nile valley. Japan, by the year 200 C.E., had established extensive agriculture. The population of the islands had been formed mainly by migrations from the peninsula of Korea, over a 200,000-year span. These migrations had ceased by the year 200. In Japan, a regional political organization based on tribal chiefs evolved; each tribal group had its own god, thought of as an ancestor. A Chinese visitor in 297 described the Japanese as law-abiding, fond of drink, expert at agriculture and fishing; they observed strict social differences,

indicated by tattoos or other body markings. Japan had also developed considerable ironworking; the Japanese seem to have skipped the stage of using bronze and copper tools, moving directly from stone tools to iron. Finally, regional states in Japan became increasingly sophisticated, each controlling somewhat larger territories. In 400 C.E., one such state brought in scribes from Korea to keep records—this represented the introduction of writing in the islands.

Japan's religion, called *Shintoism,* provided for the worship of political rulers and the spirits of nature, including the all-important god of rice. Many local shrines and rituals revolved around Shinto beliefs, which became unified into a single national religion by 700 C.E. However, this was a simple religion, rather different in ritual and doctrine from the great world religions and philosophies developing in the classical civilizations. Something like national politics arose only around 400 C.E., when one regional ruler began to win the loyalty and trust of other local leaders;

this was the basis for Japan's imperial house, with the emperor worshipped as a religious figure. Such growing political sophistication and national cultural unity were just emerging by 600 C.E., however. It was at this point that Japan was ready for more elaborate contacts with China—a process that moved Japan squarely into the orbit of major civilizations.

Much of northern Europe lagged behind Japan's pace. Teutonic and Celtic peoples in what is today Germany, England, and Scandinavia, and Slavic peoples in much of eastern Europe, were loosely organized into regional kingdoms. Some, in Germany and England, had succumbed to the advances of the distant Roman Empire, but after Rome's decline the patterns of regional politics resumed. There was no written language, except in cases where Latin had been imported. Agriculture, often still combined with hunting, was rather primitive. Scandinavians were developing increasing skill as sailors, which led them into wider trade and pillage in the centuries after 600 C.E. Religious beliefs featured a host of gods and rituals designed to placate the forces of nature. This region changed, particularly through the spread of the religious and intellectual influences of Christianity. However, these shifts lay in the future, and even conversions to Christianity did not bring northern and eastern Europe into the orbit of a single civilization. Until about 1000 C.E., northern Europe remained one of the most backward areas in the world.

Yet another portion of the world was developing civilization by 600 C.E.—indeed, its progress was greater than that of much of Europe and Africa. In Central America, an Indian group called the Olmecs developed and spread an early form of civilization from about 800 until 400 B.C.E. The Olmecs seem to have lacked writing, but they produced massive, pyramid-shaped religious monuments.

The first American civilization was based on many centuries of advancing agriculture, expanding from the early cultivation of corn. Initially, in the wild state, corn ears were scarcely larger than strawberries, but patient breeding gradually con-

verted this grain into a staple food crop. In the Andes areas of South America, root crops were also grown, particularly the potato. The development of American agriculture was limited by the few domesticated animals available—turkeys, dogs, and guinea pigs in Central America. Nevertheless, Olmec culture displayed many impressive achievements. It explored artistic forms in precious stones such as jade. Religious statues and icons blended human images with those of animals. Scientific research produced accurate and impressive calendars. Olmec culture, in its religious and artistic emphases, powerfully influenced later American Indian civilizations in Central America. The Olmecs themselves disappeared without a clear trace around 400 B.C.E., but their successors soon developed a hieroglyphic alphabet and built the first great city—Teotihuacan—in the Americas, as a center for trade and worship. This culture, in turn, suffered setbacks from migrations and regional wars, but from its base developed a still fuller American civilization, starting with the Mayans, from about 400 C.E. on.

In essence, the Olmecs and their successors provided for the Central American region the equivalent of the river valley civilizations in Asia and the Middle East, although many centuries later. A similar early civilization arose in the Andes region in present-day Peru and Bolivia, where careful agriculture allowed the construction of elaborate cities and religious monuments. This culture led, later, to the civilization of the Incas. The two centers of early civilization in the Americas developed in total isolation from developments elsewhere in the world. As a result, they lacked certain advantages that come from the ability to copy and react to other societies, including such basic technologies as the wheel or the capacity to work iron. However, the early American Indian cultures were considerably ahead of most of those in Europe during the same period. And, they demonstrate the common, although not invariable, tendency of humans to move from the establishment of agriculture to the creation of the more elaborate trappings of a civilized society.

Another case of isolated development featured the migration of agricultural peoples to new island territories in the Pacific. Polynesian peoples had reached islands such as Fiji and Samoa by 1000 B.C.E. Further explorations in giant outrigger canoes led to the first settlement of island complexes such as Hawaii by 400 C.E., where the new settlers adapted local plants, brought in new animals (notably pigs), and imported a highly stratified caste system under powerful local kings.

Agriculture, in sum, expanded into new areas during the classical period. Early civilizations, or early civilizations contacts, were also forming. These developments were not central to world history during the classical period, but they folded into the larger human experience thereafter.

The herding peoples of central Asia also continued to contribute to world history, particularly toward the end of the classical period. Some nomadic groups gained new contacts with established civilizations, such as China, which brought changes in political organization as well as some new goals for conquest. Central Asian herders played a vital role in trade routes between east Asia and the Middle East, transporting goods such as silk across long distances. Other herding groups produced important technological innovations, such as the stirrup, which allowed mounted horsemen to aim weapons better. The herding groups thus enjoyed an important history of their own and also provided important contacts among the civilizations that they bordered. Finally, perhaps because of internal population pressure as well as new appetites and opportunities, nomadic groups invaded the major civilizations directly, helping to bring the classical period as a whole to an end.

DECLINE IN CHINA AND INDIA

Between 200 and 600 C.E., all three classical civilizations collapsed entirely or in part. During this four-century span, all suffered from outside invasions, the result of growing incursions by groups from central Asia. This renewed wave of nomadic expansion was not as sweeping as the earlier Indo-European growth, which had spread over India and much of the Mediterranean region many centuries before, but it severely tested the civilized regimes. Rome, of course, fell directly to Germanic invaders, who fought on partly because they were, in turn, harassed by the fierce Asiatic Huns. The Huns swept once across Italy, invading the city of Rome amid great destruction. It was another Hun group from central Asia who overthrew the Guptas in India, and similar nomadic tribes had earlier toppled the Chinese Han dynasty. The central Asian nomads were certainly encouraged by a growing realization of the weakness of the classical regimes, for Han China as well as the later Roman Empire suffered from serious internal problems long before the invaders dealt the final blows. And the Guptas in India had not permanently resolved that area's tendency to dissolve into political fragmentation.

By about 100 C.E., the Han dynasty in China began to enter a serious decline. Confucian intellectual activity gradually became less creative. Politically, the central government's control diminished, bureaucrats became more corrupt, and local landlords took up much of the slack, ruling their neighborhoods according to their own wishes. The free peasants, long heavily taxed, were burdened with new taxes and demands of service by these same landlords. Many lost their farms and became day laborers on the large estates. Some had to sell their children into service. Social unrest increased, producing a great revolutionary effort led by Daoists in 184 C.E. Daoism now gained new appeal, shifting toward a popular religion and adding healing practices and magic to earlier philosophical beliefs. The Daoist leaders, called the Yellow Turbans, promised a golden age that was to be brought about by divine magic. The Yellow Turbans attacked the weakness of the emperor but also the self-indulgence of the current bureaucracy. As many as 30,000 students

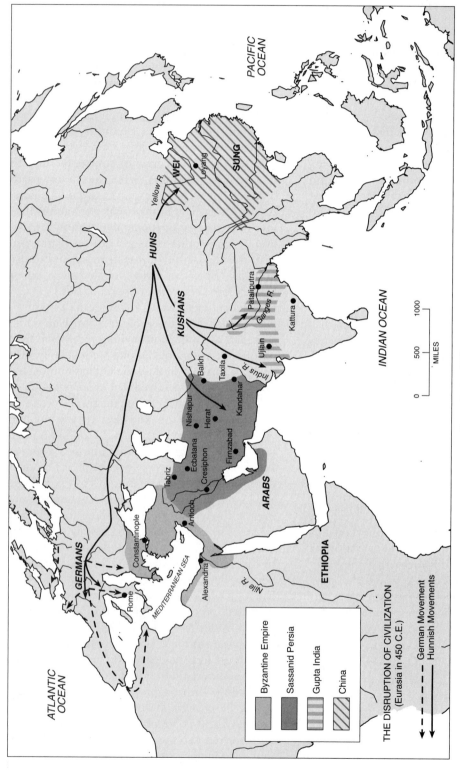

PACIFIC OCEAN

Yellow R.

WEI

Loyang

SUNG

HUNS

KUSHANS

Pataliputra

Ganges R.

Kattura

INDIAN OCEAN

Ujjain

Indus R.

Balkh

Taxila

Nishapur

Herat

Kandahar

Ecbatana

Cresiphon

Firuzabad

Tabriz

ARABS

Antioch

Constantinople

Alexandria

MEDITERRANEAN SEA

Nile R.

ETHIOPIA

Rome

GERMANS

ATLANTIC OCEAN

1000

500

MILES

0

THE DISRUPTION OF CIVILIZATION
(Eurasia in 450 C.E.)

Byzantine Empire

Sassanid Persia

Gupta India

China

German Movement

Hunnish Movements

Eurasia in 450 C.E.

demonstrated against the decline of government morality. However, their protests failed, and Chinese population growth and prosperity both spiraled further downward. The imperial court was mired in intrigue and civil war.

This dramatic decline paralleled the slightly later collapse of Rome, as we shall see. It obviously explained China's inability to push back invasions from borderland nomads, who finally overthrew the Han dynasty outright. As in Rome, growing political ineffectiveness formed part of the decline. Another important factor was the spread of devastating new epidemics, which may have killed up to half of the population. These combined blows not only toppled the Han but also led to almost three centuries of chaos—an unusually long span of unrest in Chinese history. Regional rulers and weak dynasties rose and fell during this period. Even China's cultural unity was threatened as the wave of Buddhism spread—one of the only cases in which China imported a major idea from outside its borders until the 20th century. Northern China, particularly, seemed near collapse.

Nonetheless, China did revive itself near the end of the 6th century. Strong native rulers in the north drove out the nomadic invaders. The Sui dynasty briefly ruled, and then in 618 C.E. it was followed by the Tang, who sponsored one of the most glorious periods in Chinese history. Confucianism and the bureaucratic system were revived, and indeed the bureaucratic tradition became more elaborate. The period of chaos left its mark somewhat in the continued presence of a Buddhist minority and new styles in art and literature. But, unlike the case of Rome, there was no permanent disruption.

The structures of classical China were simply too strong to be overturned. The bureaucracy declined in scope and quality, but it did not disappear during the troubled centuries. Confucian values and styles of life remained current among the upper class. Many of the nomadic invaders, seeing that they had nothing better to offer by way of government or culture, simply tried to assimilate the Chinese traditions. China thus had

to recover from a serious setback, but it did not have to reinvent its civilization.

The decline of classical civilization in India was less drastic than the collapse of Han China. The ability of the Gupta emperors to control local princes was declining by the 5th century. Invasions by nomadic peoples, probably Hun tribes similar to those who were pressing into Europe, affected some northern portions of India as early as 500 C.E. During the next century, the invaders penetrated much deeper, destroying the Gupta empire in central India. Many of the invaders were integrated into the warrior caste of India, forming a new ruling group of regional princes. For several centuries, no native ruler attempted to build a large Indian state. The regional princes, collectively called *Rajput,* controlled the small states and emphasized military prowess. Few political events of more than local significance occurred.

Within this framework, Indian culture continued to evolve. Buddhism declined further in India proper. Hindu beliefs gained ground, among other things converting the Hun princes, who had originally worshipped gods of battle and had no sympathy for the Buddhist principles of calm and contemplation. Within Hinduism, the worship of a mother goddess, Devi, spread widely, encouraging a new popular emotionalism in religious ritual. Indian economic prosperity also continued at high levels.

Although Indian civilization substantially maintained its position, another threat was to come, after 600 C.E., from the new Middle Eastern religion of Islam. Arab armies, fighting under the banners of their god Allah, reached India's porous northwestern frontier during the 7th century, and while there was initially little outright conquest on the subcontinent, Islam did win some converts in the northwest. Hindu leaders reacted to the arrival of this new faith by strengthening their emphasis on religious devotion, at the expense of some other intellectual interests. Hinduism also underwent further popularization; Hindu texts were written in vernacular languages such as Hindi, and use of the old classical language,

Sanskrit, declined. These reactions were largely successful in preventing more than a minority of Indians from abandoning Hinduism, but they distracted from further achievements in science and mathematics. Islam also hit hard at India's international economic position and affected its larger impact throughout Asia. Arab traders soon wrested control of the Indian Ocean from Tamil merchants, and India, though still prosperous and productive, saw its commercial dynamism reduced. In politics, regionalism continued to prevail. Clearly, the glory days of the Guptas were long past, although classical traditions survived particularly in Hinduism and the caste system.

DECLINE AND FALL IN ROME

The Roman Empire exhibited a great many symptoms of decay after about 180 C.E. There was statistical evidence in the declining population in addition to growing difficulties in recruiting effective armies. There were also political manifestations in the greater brutality and arbitrariness of many Roman emperors—victims, according to one commentator at the time, of "lustful and cruel habits." Tax collection became increasingly difficult, as residents of the empire fell on hard times. The governor of Egypt complained that "the once numerous inhabitants of the aforesaid villages have now been reduced to a few, because some have fled in poverty and others have died . . . and for this reason we are in danger owing to impoverishment of having to abandon the tax-collectorship."

Above all, there were human symptoms. Inscriptions on Roman tombstones increasingly ended with the slogan, "I was not, I was, I am not, I have no more desires," suggesting a pervasive despondency over the futility of this life and despair at the absence of an afterlife.

The decline of Rome was more disruptive than the collapse of the classical dynasties in Asia. For this reason, and because memories of the collapse of this great empire became part of the Western tradition, the process of deterioration deserves particular attention. Every so often, Americans or western Europeans concerned about changes in their own society wonder if there might be lessons in Rome's fall that apply to the uncertain future of Western civilization today.

We have seen that the quality of political and economic life in the Roman Empire began to shift after about 180 C.E. Political confusion produced a series of weak emperors and many disputes over succession to the throne. Intervention by the army in the selection of emperors complicated political life and contributed to the deterioration of rule from the top. More important in initiating the process of decline was a series of plagues that swept over the empire. As in China, the plagues' source was growing international trade, which brought diseases endemic in southern Asia to new areas such as the Mediterranean, where no resistance had been established even to contagions such as the measles. The resulting diseases decimated the population. The population of Rome decreased from a million people to 250,000. Economic life worsened in consequence. Recruitment of troops became more difficult, so the empire was increasingly reduced to hiring Germanic soldiers to guard its frontiers. The need to pay troops added to the demands on the state's budget, just as declining production cut into tax revenues.

Here, perhaps, is the key to the process of decline: a set of general problems, triggered by a cycle of plagues that could not be prevented, resulting in a rather mechanistic spiral that steadily worsened. However, there is another side to Rome's downfall, although whether it is a cause or result of the initial difficulties is hard to say. Rome's upper classes became steadily more pleasure-seeking, turning away from the political devotion and economic vigor that had characterized the republic and early empire. Cultural life decayed. Aside from some truly creative Christian writers—the fathers of Western theology—there was very little sparkle to the art or literature of the later empire. Many Roman scholars con-

This plaque portrays the Roman general Stilicho with his wife, Serena, and their son. Stilicho's energy and ability allowed him to become Master of Soldiers and Consul of Rome. But the facts that his father had been a Vandal and that he himself was not a Christian made him vulnerable to the rumors spread by his enemies, who said that he was intriguing against the interests of the Empire and intended to place his own son on the throne. In 408 he was imprisoned and his son, Eucherius, was murdered.

tented themselves with writing textbooks that rather mechanically summarized earlier achievements in science, mathematics, and literary style. Writing textbooks is not, of course, proof of absolute intellectual incompetence—at least, not in all cases—but the point was that new knowledge or artistic styles were not being generated, and even the levels of previous accomplishment began to slip. The later Romans wrote textbooks about rhetoric instead of displaying rhetorical talent in actual political life; they wrote simple compendiums, for example, about animals or

geometry, that barely captured the essentials of what earlier intellectuals had known, and they often added superstitious beliefs that previous generations would have scorned. This cultural decline, finally, was not clearly due to disease or economic collapse, for it began in some ways before these larger problems surfaced. Something was happening to the Roman elite, perhaps because of the deadening effect of authoritarian political rule, perhaps because of a new interest in luxuries and sensual indulgence. Revealingly, the upper classes no longer produced many offspring, for bearing and raising children seemed incompatible with a life of pleasure-seeking.

Rome's fall, in other words, can be blamed on large, impersonal forces that would have been hard for any society to control or a moral and political decay that reflected growing corruption among society's leaders. Probably elements of both were involved. Thus, the plagues would have weakened even a vigorous society, but they would not necessarily have produced an irreversible downward spiral had not the morale of the ruling classes already been sapped by an unproductive lifestyle and superficial values.

Regardless of precise causes, the course of Roman decay is quite clear. As the quality of imperial rule declined, as life became more dangerous and economic survival more precarious, many farmers clustered around the protection of large landlords, surrendering full control over their plots of land in the hope of military and judicial protection. The decentralization of political and economic authority, which was greatest in the western, or European, portions of the empire, foreshadowed the manorial system of Europe in the Middle Ages. The system of estates gave great political power to landlords and provided some local stability. But, in the long run, it weakened the power of the emperor and also tended to move the economy away from the elaborate and successful trade patterns of Mediterranean civilization in its heyday. Many estates tried to be self-sufficient. Trade and production declined further as a result, and cities shrank in size. The empire was locked in a vicious circle, in which responses to the initial deterioration merely lessened the chances of recovery.

Some later emperors tried vigorously to reverse the tide. Diocletian, who ruled from 284 to 305 C.E., tightened up the administration of the empire and tried to improve tax collection. Regulation of the dwindling economy increased. Diocletian also attempted to direct political loyalties to his own person, exerting pressure to worship the emperor as god. This was what prompted him to persecute Christians with particular viciousness, for they would not give Caesar preference over their God.

The emperor Constantine, who ruled from 312 to 337 C.E., experimented with other methods of control. He set up a second capital city, Constantinople, to regulate the eastern half of the empire more efficiently. He tried to use the religious force of Christianity to unify the empire spiritually, extending its toleration and adopting it as his own faith. These measures were not without result. The eastern empire, ruled from Constantinople (now the Turkish city of Istanbul), remained an effective political and economic unit. Christianity spread under his official sponsorship, although there were some new problems linked to its success.

None of these measures, however, revived the empire as a whole. Division merely made the weakness of the western half worse. Attempts to regulate the economy reduced economic initiative and lowered production; ultimately, tax revenues declined once again. The army deteriorated further. When the Germanic invasions began in earnest in the 400s, there was scant basis to resist. Many peasants, burdened by the social and economic pressures of the decaying empire, actually welcomed the barbarians. A priest noted that "in all districts taken over by the Germans, there is one desire among all the Romans, that they should never again find it necessary to pass under Roman jurisdiction." German kingdoms were established in many parts of the empire by 425 C.E., and the last Roman emperor in the west was displaced in 476 C.E. The Germanic invaders numbered at most 5 percent of the population of the empire, but so great was the earlier Roman decline that this small, poorly organized force was able to put an end to one of the world's great political structures.

The collapse of Rome echoed mightily through the later history of Europe and the Middle East. Rome's fall split the unity of the Mediterranean lands that had been so arduously won through Hellenistic culture and then by the Roman Empire itself. This was one sign that the end of the Roman Empire was a more serious affair than the displacement of the last classical dynasties in India and China, for Greece and

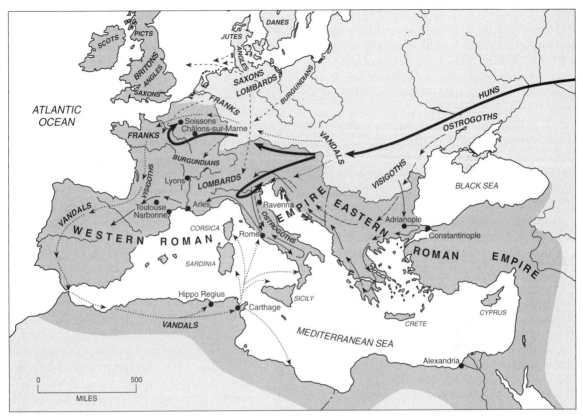

The Germanic Migrations, 4th to 6th Centuries

Rome had not produced the shared political culture and bureaucratic traditions of China that could allow revival after a period of chaos. Nor had Mediterranean civilization, for all its vitality, generated a common religion that appealed deeply enough, or satisfied enough needs, to maintain unity amid political fragmentation, as in India. Such religions reached the Mediterranean world as Rome fell, but they came too late to save the empire and produced a deep rift in this world—between Christian and Muslim—that has not been healed to this day.

However, Rome's collapse, although profound, was uneven. In effect, the fall of Rome divided the Mediterranean world into three zones, which formed the starting points of three distinct civilizations that developed in later centuries.

In the eastern part of the empire, centered now on Constantinople, the empire in a sense did not fall. Civilization was more deeply entrenched here than in some of the western European portions of the empire, and there were fewer pressures from invaders. Emperors continued to rule Greece and other parts of southeast Europe, plus the northern Middle East. This eastern empire—later to be known as the Byzantine Empire—was a product of late imperial Rome, rather than a balanced result of the entire span of classical Mediterranean civilization. Thus, although its language was Greek, it maintained the authoritarian tone of the late Roman rulers. But the empire itself was vibrant, artistically creative, and active in trade. Briefly, especially under the emperor Justinian (who ruled from 527 to 565 C.E.), the eastern emperors tried to recapture the whole heritage of Rome. However, Justinian was unable to maintain a hold in Italy and even lost the provinces of north Africa. He did issue one of the most famous compilations of Roman law, in the code that bore his name. But his was the last effort to restore Mediterranean unity.

The Byzantine Empire did not control the whole of the northern Middle East, even in its greatest days. During the late Hellenistic periods and into the early centuries of the Roman Empire, a Parthian empire had flourished, centered in the Tigris-Euphrates region but spreading into northwestern India and to the borders of Rome's holdings along the Mediterranean. Parthian conquerors had taken over this portion of Alexander the Great's empire. They produced little culture of their own, being content to rely on Persian styles, but they long maintained an effective military and bureaucratic apparatus. Then, around 227 C.E., a Persian rebellion displaced the Parthians and created a new Sassanid empire that more directly revived the glories of the earlier Persian empire. Persian religions, including Zoroastrianism, revived, although there was some conversion to Christianity. Persian styles in art and manufacturing experienced a brilliant resurgence. Both the Parthian and the Sassanid empires served as bridges between the Mediterranean and the East, transmitting goods and some artistic and literary styles between the Greek-speaking world and India and China. As the Roman Empire weakened, the Sassanids joined the attack, at times pushing into parts of southeastern Europe. Ultimately, however, the Byzantine Empire managed to create a stable frontier. The Sassanid empire preserved the important strain of Persian culture in the eastern part of the Middle East, and this continued to influence this region as well as India. The Sassanids, however, were finally overthrown by the surge of Arab conquest that followed the rise of Islam, in the 7th century C.E.

Rome's fall, then, did not disrupt the northern Middle East—the original cradle of civilization—

as much as might have been expected. Persian rule simply continued in one part of the region, until the Arab onslaught, which itself did not destroy Persian culture. Byzantium maintained many of the traditions of the later Roman Empire, plus Christianity, in the western part of the Middle East and in Greece and other parts of southeastern Europe.

The second zone that devolved from Rome's fall consisted of north Africa and the southeastern shores of the Mediterranean. Here, a number of regional kingdoms briefly succeeded the empire. While Christianity spread into the area—indeed, one of the greatest Christian theologians, Augustine, was a bishop in north Africa—its appearance was not so uniformly triumphant as in the Byzantine Empire or western Europe. Furthermore, separate beliefs and doctrines soon split north African Christianity from the larger branches, producing most notably the Coptic church in Egypt, which still survives as a Christian minority in that country. Soon this region was filled with the still newer doctrines of Islam and a new Arab empire.

Finally, there was the western part of the empire—Italy, Spain, and points north. Here is where Rome's fall not only shattered unities but also reduced the level of civilization itself. Crude, regional Germanic kingdoms developed in parts of Italy, France, and elsewhere. Cities shrank still further, and, especially outside Italy, trade almost disappeared. The only clearly vital forces in this region emanated not from Roman traditions but from the spread of Christianity. Even Christianity could not sustain a sophisticated culture of literature or art, however. In the mire of Rome's collapse, this part of the world forgot for several centuries what it had previously known.

In this western domain, what we call the fall of Rome was scarcely noted at the time, for decay had been progressing for so many decades that the failure to name a new emperor meant little. There was some comprehension of loss, some realization that the present could not rival the past. Thus, Christian scholars were soon apologizing for their inability to write well or to understand some of the doctrines of the earlier theologians such as Augustine. This sense of inferiority to classical achievements long marked the culture of this western zone, even as times improved.

THE NEW RELIGIOUS MAP

The end of the classical period is not simply the story of decay and collapse. This same period, from 200 to 600 C.E., saw the effective rise of many of the world's major religions. The devastating plagues caused new interest in belief systems that could provide solace amid rising death rates. From Spain to China, growing political instability clearly prompted many people to seek solace in joys of the spirit, and while the religious surge was not entirely new, the resulting changes in the religious map of Europe and Asia and the nature and intensity of religious interests were significant new forces. Christianity, born two centuries before Rome's collapse began, became a widespread religion throughout the Mediterranean region as the empire's political strength weakened. Buddhism, although launched still earlier, saw its surge into eastern Asia furthered by the growing problems of classical China. Thus, two major faiths, different in many ways but similar in their emphasis on spiritual life and the importance of divine power, reshaped major portions of Europe and Asia precisely as the structures of the classical period declined or disappeared. Finally, shortly after 600 C.E., an entirely new religion, Islam, surfaced and became the most dynamic force in world history during the next several centuries. In sum, the religious map of the world, although by no means completed by 500 C.E., was beginning to take on dramatic new contours. This means that while civilization in many ways declined, it was also being altered, taking new directions as well as losing some older strengths. Never before had single religions spread so widely, crossing so many cultural and political boundaries.

The newly expanding religions shared some general features. Christianity, Buddhism, and Hinduism, as well as Islam later on, all emphasized intense devotion and piety, stressing the importance of spiritual concerns beyond the daily cares of earthly life. All three offered the hope of a better existence after this life had ended, and each one responded to new political instability and to the growing poverty of people in various parts of the civilized world.

The spread of the major religions meant that hundreds of thousands of people, in Asia, Europe, and Africa, underwent a conversion process as the classical period drew to a close. Radically changing beliefs is an unusual human experience, symptomatic in this case of the new pressures on established political structures and on ordinary life. At the same time, many people blended new beliefs with the old, in a process called *syncretism*. This meant that the religions changed too, sometimes taking on the features of individual civilizations even while maintaining larger religious claims.

Despite these important common features, the major religions were very different. Hinduism, as we have seen, retained its belief in reincarnation and its combination of spiritual interest in union with the divine essence and extensive rituals and ceremonies. The religion experienced greater popular appeal after the fall of the Guptas, associated with the expanded use of popular languages and with the worship of the mother goddess Devi. Buddhism was altered more substantially as it traveled beyond India's borders, becoming only a small minority faith in India itself.

Buddhism

The chief agents of Buddhist expansion and leadership were monks, for Buddhism tended to divide the faithful among a minority who abandoned earthly life in favor of spiritual dedication and the larger number who continued to work in the world while doing the best they could to meet their spiritual obligations. Some centuries after Buddha's death, a doctrine of *bodhisattvas* developed, which held that some people could

HISTORY DEBATE

WHAT CAUSED DECLINE AND FALL?

Determining what causes major developments is never easy. Unlike laboratory science, repeated experiments, to narrow down the causes of a phenomenon, are not possible. It remains important to discuss causes as part of understanding what happened, and some plausible analysis is possible. However, debate is a vital part of the process.

In the case of the classical decline, particularly for Rome, debate has raged on and off for centuries. Even at the time, people wondered if perhaps the spread of Christianity was sapping Roman virtues and weakening the state (this is not a common explanation today). Other attempts to provide an appealing framework have included arguments that new patterns of sunspots reduced agricultural productivity (again, not widely believed now).

Current debates focus on inevitability and on external pressures versus internal decay. One of the great world historians of the 20th century, Arnold Toynbee, argued that civilizations inevitably undergo a life cycle in which prosperous middle age is followed by collapse. Loss of creativity, growing luxury, bureaucratic routine, and attacks from outside provide a law of history in which great empires finally shatter. Toynbee used Rome as one of his prime examples, and many historians concur with the approach. More recently, another well-known historian, David Kennedy, offered a slightly different interpretation: many societies, such as Rome's, overexpanded, and they ended up reducing their internal strength by trying to support impossibly wide frontiers.

On the other hand, some historians disagree with such sweeping explanations. The Roman Empire, after all, did not decline across the board—the eastern part survived quite well. It is important, in this counterargument, to look for more specific factors, on a case-by-case basis.

The internal-external quarrel runs like this: Many historians have long pointed to moral collapse as a key component of Rome's fall (and the argument can be applied to China and India too). Lower classes were sapped by bread and circuses, upper classes became greedy and pleasure-seeking, and the result was an inability to sustain vigorous institutions. There is evidence supporting this viewpoint, to be sure. But is the explanation necessary? The pressure of outside invasion plus the widespread impact of epidemic disease (particularly in Rome and China) may make the moral factors less salient. Some moral confusion may have resulted from growing death rates, rather than the other way around. The debate continues.

attain nirvana through their own meditation while choosing to remain in the world as saints and to aid others by prayer and example. Buddhism increasingly shifted from an original emphasis on ethics to become a more emotional cult stressing the possibility of popular salvation. The role of the bodhisattvas was crucial in this transformation, because it broadened the prospect of salvation for ordinary people by leading them in prayer and advising them on spiritual matters.

Buddhism evolved further as the religion spread seriously to China after the fall of the Han dynasty, when the idea of a celestial afterlife proved almost irresistible. Monasteries in India and the Himalaya Mountains continued to serve as spiritual centers for Chinese Buddhism, but the religion developed strong roots in east Asia directly, spreading through China and from there to Korea and Japan. The east Asian form of Buddhism, called *Mahayana,* or the Greater Vehicle, retained basic Buddhist beliefs. However, the emphasis on Buddha himself as god and savior increased in the Mahayana version. Statues devoted to Buddha as god countered the earlier Buddhist hostility to religious images. The religion improved its organization, with priests, tem-

Spread of Buddhism: A Buddhist grotto in China.

ples, creeds, and rituals. Buddhist holy men, or bodhisattvas, remained important. Their souls after death resided in a kind of super heaven, where they could receive prayers and aid people. Intense spirituality continued to inform Buddhist faith as well. But prayers and rituals could now help ordinary people to become holy. Buddha himself became a god to whom one could appeal for solace, "the great physician for a sick and impure world." East Asian Buddhism also spurred new artistic interests in China and, later, in Japan, including the pagoda style of temple design and the statues devoted to Buddha.

Buddhism had a fascinating impact on women in China, largely among families who converted. On the face of things, Buddhism should have disrupted China's firm belief in patriarchal power, because Buddhists believed that

women, like men, had souls. Indeed, some individual women in China captured great attention because of their spiritual accomplishments. But Chinese culture generated changes in Buddhism within the empire. Buddhist phrases such as "husband supports wife" were changed to "husband controls his wife," whereas "the wife comforts the husband"—another Buddhist phrase from India—became "the wife reveres her husband." Here was a vital case of cultural blending, or syncretism. Finally, many men valued pious Buddhist wives, because they might benefit the family's salvation and because Buddhist activity kept their wives busy, calm, and out of mischief. Buddhism was perhaps appealing to Chinese women because it led to a more meaningful life, but it did not really challenge patriarchy. A biography of one Buddhist wife put it this way: "At times of crisis she could be tranquil and satisfied with her fate, not letting outside things agitate her mind."

Buddhism was not popular with all Chinese. Confucian leaders, particularly, found in Buddhist beliefs in an afterlife a diversion from appropriate political interests. They disliked the notion of such intense spirituality and also found ideas of the holy life incompatible with proper family obligations. More important, Buddhism was seen as a threat that might distract ordinary people from loyalty to the emperor. When imperial dynasties revived in China, they showed some interest in Buddhist piety for a time, but ultimately they attacked the Buddhist faith, driving out many missionaries. Buddhism remained a minority current in China, and many villages worshipped in Buddhist shrines. Thus, China's religious composition became increasingly complex, but without overturning earlier cultural directions. Daoism reacted to Buddhism as well, by improving its organization and emphasizing practical benefits obtainable through magic. It was at this point that Daoism developed a clear hold on many peasants, incorporating many of their beliefs in the process. Buddhism had a greater lasting influence in the religious experience of other parts of east Asia, notably Japan, Korea, and Vietnam, than in China itself. And, of course, Buddhism had also spread to significant parts of southeast Asia, where it remained somewhat truer to earlier Buddhist concepts of individual meditation and ethics.

In the world today, some 255 million people count themselves as Buddhists. Most live in the areas of east and southeast Asia, where the religion had taken root by 500 C.E. Buddhism did not, by itself, dominate any whole civilization; rather, it lived alongside other faiths. However, it provided major additions to Asia's religious map and an important response to changing conditions in the troubled centuries after the classical period had ended.

Christianity

Christianity moved westward, from its original center in the Middle East, as Buddhism was spreading east from India. Although initially less significant than Buddhism in terms of the number of converts, Christianity ultimately proved to be one of the two largest faiths worldwide. And it played a direct role in the formation of two postclassical civilizations, those of eastern and western Europe. Despite important similarities to Buddhism in its emphasis on salvation and the guidance of saints, Christianity differed in crucial ways. It came to place more emphasis on church organization and structure, copying from the example of the Roman Empire. Even more than Buddhism, it placed a premium on missionary activity and widespread conversions. More, perhaps, than any other major religion, Christianity stressed the exclusive nature of its truth and was intolerant of competing beliefs. Such fierce confidence was not the least of the reasons for the new religion's success.

Christianity began in reaction to rigidities that had developed in the Jewish priesthood during the two centuries before the birth of Jesus Christ. A host of reform movements sprang up, some of them preaching the coming of a Messiah, or savior, who would bring about a Last Judgment on humankind. Many of these movements also stressed the possibility of life after death for the virtuous, which was a new element in Judaism. Jesus of Nazareth, believed by Christians to be the son of God sent to earth to redeem human sin, crystallized this radical reform movement. Combining extraordinary gentleness of spirit and great charisma, Jesus preached widely in Israel and gathered a group of loyal disciples around him. Initially, there seems to have been no intent on his or his followers' part to found a new religion. After Jesus' crucifixion, the disciples expected his imminent return and with it the end of the world. Only gradually, when the Second Coming did not transpire, did the disciples begin to fan out and, through their preaching, attract growing numbers of supporters in various parts of the Roman Empire.

The message of Jesus and his disciples seemed clear: there was a single God who loved humankind despite earthly sin. A virtuous life was one dedicated to the worship of God and fellowship among other believers; worldly concerns were secondary, and a life of poverty might be most conducive to holiness. God sent Jesus (called *Christ* from the Greek word *christos,* for "God's anointed") to preach his holy word and through his sacrifice to prepare his followers for the widespread possibility of an afterlife and heavenly communion with God. Belief, good works, and the discipline of fleshly concerns led to heaven; rituals, such as commemorating Christ's Last Supper with wine and bread, promoted the same goal.

Christianity's message spread at an opportune time. The official religion of the Greeks and Romans had long seemed rather sterile, particularly to many of the poor. The Christian emphasis on the beauty of a simple life and the spiritual equality of all people, plus the fervor of the early Christians and the satisfying rituals they created, captured growing attention. The great reach of the Roman Empire made it relatively easy for Christian missionaries to travel widely in Europe and the Middle East, to spread the new word, although as we have seen, they also reached beyond, to Persia, Axum, and Ethiopia. Then when conditions began to deteriorate in the empire, the solace this otherworldly religion provided resulted in its even wider appeal. Early Christian leaders made several important adjustments to maximize their conversions. Under the guidance of Paul, not one of the original disciples but an early convert, Christians began to see themselves as part of a new religion, rather than part of a Jewish reform movement, and they welcomed non-Jews. Paul also encouraged more formal organization within the new church, with local groups selecting elders to govern them; soon, a single leader, or bishop, was appointed for each city. This structure paralleled the provincial government of the empire. Finally, Christian doctrine became increasingly organized, as the writings of several disciples and others were collected into what became known as the New Testament of the Christian Bible.

During the first three centuries after Christ, the new religion competed among a number of eastern mystical religions. It also faced, as we have seen, periodic persecution from the normally tolerant imperial government. Even so, by the time Constantine converted to Christianity and accepted it as the one true legitimate faith, perhaps 10 percent of the empire's population had accepted the new religion. Constantine's conversion brought new troubles to Christianity, particularly some interference by the state in matters of doctrine. However, it became much easier to spread Christianity with official favor, and the continued deterioration of the empire added to the impetus to join this amazingly successful new church. In the eastern Mediterranean, where imperial rule remained strong from its center in Constantinople, state control of the church became a way of life. But in the West, where conditions were far more chaotic, bishops had a freer hand. A centralized church organization under the leadership of the bishop of Rome, called *Pope* from the word *papa,* or "father," gave the Western church unusual strength and independence.

By the time Rome collapsed, Christianity had thus demonstrated immense spiritual power and developed a solid organization, although one that differed from east to west. The new church faced a number of controversies over doctrine but managed to promote certain standard beliefs as against several heresies. A key tenet involved a complex doctrine of the Trinity, which held that the one God had three persons—the Father, the Son (Christ), and the Holy Ghost. Experience in fighting heresies promoted Christian interest in defending a single belief and strengthened its intolerance for any competing doctrine or faith. Early Christianity also produced an important formal theology, through formative writers such as Augustine. This theology incorporated many elements of classical philosophy with Christian belief and aided the church in its attempts to gain respectability among intellectuals. Theologians such as Augustine grappled with such problems as freedom of the will: if God is all-powerful, can mere human beings have free will? And if not, how can human beings be justly punished for

SAINT PAUL
(PAUL OF TARSUS)

Paul was a prominent Jewish official when early Christians were organizing their religion after the death of Christ. He was also a Roman citizen and proud of his connection to the empire. Paul was a member of a Jewish group called *Pharisees,* which organized around individual rabbis rather than the Jewish priesthood. Originally hostile to Christianity, he organized persecutions of Christians. But, presumably on the road to the city of Damascus, Paul had an intense conversion experience and began to assume a leadership role in this new religion. Against the opposition of some Christian leaders, Paul went on missions to convert non-Jews in what is now Greece and Turkey (between 48 and 55 C.E.), and Paul is credited with making the changes that began to move the religion from a Jewish reform movement to a world religion. He argued that non-Jews could be good Christians without conforming to Jewish law, and he emphasized baptism as the entry to religious faith. Paul also softened some of the radical stances of early Christians, for example placing more emphasis on the submission of women. And he worked on church organization, using Roman principles. He organized communities with overseers (bishops) and appointed ministers under them. Some of Paul's writings became part of the New Testament, as it was formulated, confirming his role in converting a passionate religious movement to an organized church.

Saint Paul (Paul of Tarsus).

sin? By working out these issues in elaborate doctrine, the early theologians, or church fathers, provided an important role for formal, rational thought in a religion that continued to emphasize the primary importance of faith. Finally, Christianity was willing to accommodate some earlier polytheistic traditions among the common people. The celebration of Christ's birth was thus moved to coincide with winter solstice, a classic example of syncretism, which allowed the new faith to benefit from the power of selective older rituals.

Like all successful religions, Christianity combined a number of appeals. It offered blind devotion to an all-powerful God. One church father, denying the validity of human thought, simply stated, "I believe because it is absurd." However, Christianity also developed its own complex intellectual system. Mystical holy men and women flourished under Christian banners, particularly in

Early Christian art: Figure of Christ on the door of a Roman church.

the Middle East. In the West, soon after the empire's collapse, this impulse was partially disciplined through the institution of monasticism, first developed in Italy under Benedict, who started a monastery among Italian peasants whom he lured away from the worship of the sun god Apollo. The Benedictine Rule, which soon spread to many other monasteries and convents, urged a disciplined life, with prayer and spiritual fulfillment alternating with hard work in agriculture and study. Thus, Christianity attempted to encourage but also to discipline intense piety, and to avoid a complete gulf between the lives of saintly men and women and the spiritual concerns of ordinary people. Christianity's success and organizational strength obviously appealed to political leaders. But the new religion never became the creature of the upper classes alone. Its

popular message of salvation and satisfying rituals continued to draw the poor, more than most of the great classical belief systems; in this regard, it was somewhat like Hinduism in India. Christianity also provided some religious unity among different social groups. It even held special appeal for women. Christianity did not create equality among men and women, but it did preach the equal importance of male and female souls. And it encouraged men and women to worship together, unlike many other faiths.

Christianity promoted a new culture among its followers. The rituals, the otherworldly emphasis, the interest in spiritual equality—these central themes were far different from those of classical Mediterranean civilizations. Christianity modified classical beliefs in the central importance of the state and of political loyalties.

Although Christians accepted the state, they did not put it first. Christianity also worked against other classical institutions, such as slavery, in the name of brotherhood (although later Christians accepted slavery in other contexts). Christianity may have fostered greater respectability for disciplined work than had been the case in the Mediterranean civilization, where an aristocratic ethic dominated. Western monasteries, for example, set forth rigid work routines for monks. Certainly, Christianity sought some changes in classical culture beyond its central religious message, including greater emphasis on sexual restraint. But Christianity preserved important classical values as well, in addition to an interest in solid organization and some of the themes of classical philosophy. Church buildings retained Roman architectural styles, although often with greater simplicity if only because of the poverty of the later empire and subsequent states. Latin remained the language of the church in the West, Greek the language of most Christians in the eastern Mediterranean. Through the patient librarianship of monks, monasticism played an immensely valuable role in preserving classical as well as Christian learning.

When the Roman Empire fell, Christian history was still in its infancy. The Western church soon spread its missionary zeal to northern Europe, and the Eastern church reached into the Slavic lands of the Balkans and Russia. By then, Christianity was already established as a significant world religion—one of the few ever generated. A world religion is defined as a faith of unusual durability and drawing power, one whose complexity wins the devotion of many different kinds of people. Major world religions, such as Christianity and Buddhism, are able to cut across different cultures, to win converts in a wide geographic area and amid considerable diversity.

Islam

Islam, launched in the 7th century, early in the postclassical period, initially surpassed Christianity as a world faith and has remained Christianity's most tenacious rival. With Islam, the roster of world religions was essentially completed. Changes followed, but no totally new religion of major significance arose—unless one counts some of the secular faiths, such as communism, that appeared in the last century. The centuries after Christianity's rise, the spread of Buddhism, and the inception of Islam saw the conversion of most of the civilized world to one or another of the great faiths, producing a religious map that, in Europe and Asia and even parts of Africa, did not alter greatly until our own time. Table 7.1 shows the distribution of major religions in the world today.

The spread of Hinduism in India, Buddhism in east and southeast Asia, a more popular Daoism in China, Christianity in Europe and parts of the Mediterranean world, and ultimately Islam was a vital result of the changes in classical civilizations brought on by attack and decay. Despite the important diversity among these great religions, which included fierce hatreds, particularly between Christian and Muslim, their overall development suggests the way important currents could run through the civilized world, crossing political and cultural borders—thanks in part to the integrations and contacts built by the classical civilizations. Common difficulties, including invading forces that

Table 7.1
MAJOR RELIGIONS AND THEIR DISTRIBUTION IN THE WORLD TODAY*

Religion	Distribution
Christianity	2 billion
Islam	1.3 billion
Hinduism	780 million
Buddhism	350 million
Shintoism	3 million
Daoism	31 million
Judaism	18 million

*Figures for several religions have been reduced, over the past 50 years, by the impact of communism in eastern Europe and parts of Asia.

journeyed from central Asia and contagious epidemics that knew no boundaries, help explain parallel changes in separate civilizations. Trade and travel also provided common bonds. Chinese travelers learned of Buddhism through trading expeditions to India, whereas Ethiopians learned about Christianity from Middle Eastern traders. The new religions spurred a greater interest in spiritual matters and resulted in a greater tendency to focus on a single basic divinity instead of a multitude of gods. Polytheistic beliefs and practices continued to flourish as part of popular Hinduism and popular Daoism, and they were not entirely displaced among ordinary people who converted to Christianity, Buddhism, or Islam. But the new religious surge reduced the hold of literal animism in much of Asia and Europe, and this too was an important development across boundaries.

THE WORLD AROUND 500 C.E.

Developments in many parts of the world by 500 C.E. produced three major themes for world history in subsequent centuries. First, and particularly in the centers of classical civilization, there was a response to the collapse of classical forms. Societies in China, India, and around the Mediterranean faced the task of reviving or reworking their key institutions and values after internal decline and external invasion. Second, in these areas but also in other parts of Africa, Europe, and Asia was the need to react to the new religious map that was taking shape, to integrate new religious institutions and values into established civilizations or, as in northern Europe, to use them as the basis for a civilization that had previously been lacking. Finally, increased skill in agriculture and the creation of early civilizations or new contacts—such as the Japanese import of writing—prepared parts of Europe, Africa, Asia, and the Americas for new developments in the centuries to come. The centers of classical civilization still held a dominant

position in world history after 500 C.E., but their monopoly was increasingly challenged by the spread of civilization to other areas.

PATHS TO THE PRESENT

The decline of the great empires signaled the end of an era, rather than the launching of new themes that might survive to the present. The legacies of China, India, Persia, and the Mediterranean, discussed in earlier sections, obviously had to survive the declines in order to participate in framing later world history.

The decline phenomenon itself connects to the present in three ways. First, alterations in the world's map, set in motion by the fall of the Roman Empire, proved durable. A few efforts to reconstitute a unified Mediterranean—by an eastern Roman emperor, and later, to an extent, by Arab leaders—failed. The Mediterranean world remains divided to this day.

Second, the promotion of greater religious interest and new conversions that resulted in part from the failure of earthly empires helped set a religious map for Asia, North Africa, and Europe that has lasted, with a few modifications, to the present day. This religious configuration had not been achieved by the end of the classical decline period, but the process of its formation was in motion.

Third, the fact of collapse—particularly for people aware of the Roman legacy—added to humans' recurrent anxieties. If such great achievements could fail, what were the prospects of more recent gains? People in various parts of Europe and the Mediterranean might wonder whether their societies would follow the path of Rome, seeing a period of success followed by disintegration and collapse. Some observers in Western Europe and the United States during the past century have noted the analogy between weaknesses in their societies, for example, the overextension of finances and natural resources, the moral decay, and Rome's—and wondered about the ultimate implications of that analogy. It is sometimes hard to avoid and shake off the thought—and this is a legacy of the collapse period in its own right.

SUGGESTED WEB SITES

On the invention of antiquity, see http:// www.brynmawr.edu/library/exhibits/antiquity/ index2.htm; on the decline of the Roman Empire, see http://www.roman-empire.net/decline/ decl-index.html; on the origins of Germany, see http://mars.wnec.edu/~grempel/courses/germany/ lectures/01origins.html; on the history of Christianity, see http://history-world.org/ world%20religions%20development_of.htm.

SUGGESTED READINGS

The fall of the Roman Empire has generated rich and interesting debate. For modern interpretations and discussion of earlier views, see A. H. M. Jones, *The Decline of the Ancient World* (1966); J. Vogt, *The Decline of Rome* (1965); and F. W. Walbank, *The Awful Revolution—The Decline of the Roman Empire in the West* (1960). On India and China in decline, worthwhile sources include R. Thaper, *History of India*, Vol. 1 (1966); R. C. Majumdar, ed., *The Classical Age* (1966); Raymond Dawson, *Imperial China* (1972); J. A. Harrison, *The Chinese Empire* (1972); and Twitchett and Fairbanks, eds., *The Cambridge History of China*, Vol. 3, Part 1 (1979). On Africa, see K. Shillington, *History of Africa* (1989); Graham Connal, *African Civilizations: Precolonial Cities and States in Tropical Africa, an Archeological Perspective* (1987). On the role of disease, W. McNeill, *Plagues and Peoples* (1977), is useful. For the rise or spread of new religions, consult Lewis M. Hopke, *Religions of the World*

(1983); N. C. Chandhuri, *Hinduism: A Religion to Live By* (1979); S. Renko, *Pagan Rome and the Early Christians* (1986); M. Hengel, *Acts and the History of Earliest Christianity* (1986); A. Sharma, ed., *Women in World Religions* (1987); D. Carmody, *Women and World Religions* (1985); G. Clark, *Women in Late Antiquity: Pagan and Christian* (1993); and B. Witherington, *Women in the Earliest Churches* (1988). Peter N. Stearns, *Gender in World History* (2001), deals with women and world religions. The recent new edition by Peter Brown, *The Rise of Western Christendom* (2003), is a vital contribution.

The causes of the rise and fall of civilizations are addressed in Jared Diamond, *Guns, Germs and Steel: The Fate of Human Societies* (1997); Christopher Chase-Dunn and Thomas D. Hall, *Rise and Demise: Comparing World-Systems* (1997); H. M. Jones, *The Decline of the Ancient World* (1966); Joseph A. Tainter, *The Collapse of Complex Societies* (1988); and Norman Yoffee and George L. Cowgill, *The Collapse of Ancient States and Civilizations* (1991). Other recent work includes J. H. W. G. Liebeschuetz, *Decline and Fall of the Roman City* (2001). For an overview of the development of Christianity and the spread of world religions: David Shotter, *The Fall of the Roman Empire* (2005); Noel Lenski, ed., *The Cambridge Companion to the Age of Constantine* (2006); Dale B. Martin and Patricia Cox Miller, *The Cultural Turn in Late Ancient Studies: Gender, Asceticism, and Historiography* (2005); Edward Gibbon, *The Christians and the Fall of Rome* (2005); P. J. Heather, *The Fall of the Roman Empire: A New History of Rome and the Barbarians* (2006); Bryan Ward-Perkins, *The Fall of Rome: And the End of Civilization* (2005); A. H. Merrils, *History and Geography in Late Antiquity* (2005); Charles Freeman, *The Closing of the Western Mind: The Rise of Faith and the Fall of Reason* (2002); and Andrew Bell-Fialkoff, *The Role of Migration in the History of the Eurasian Steppe: Sedentary Civilization vs. "Barbarian" and Nomad* (2000).

The Classical Period, 1000 B.C.E.–500 C.E.

CONTACTS AND IDENTITIES

The most obvious change in the tension between local identities and the advantages or inevitabilities of contact came with the formation of the classical civilizations themselves, because of the stress the integration efforts caused fro smaller cultural and institutional systems. As the Chinese included southern China, for example, leaders from the north put forth massive efforts to reduce the separateness of southern Chinese ethnic groups, including sending many settler groups from north China to reduce local attachments. The conquering leaders insisted on common education and that elites speak Mandarin. Finally, something of a larger Chinese identity was forged. This did not mean that all local identities were lost—southerners continued to speak a different form of Chinese, even when they learned Mandarin to use for certain purposes—but they were modified. Only on the frontiers, particularly in the west, did Chinese leaders face ongoing problems of locals vigorously retaining non-Chinese identities.

Similar tensions arose in the Mediterranean, though Greek and Roman leaders were somewhat more tolerant of local variations, including religious variations. Roman military settlers were posted to different parts of the empire, where they helped keep order; the lifestyles they established, including entertainments and the classic Roman public baths, attracted some locals, but there was usually no effort to break down local identities entirely. Romans themselves remained conscious of their own identity within the larger empire. They worried, for example, about corruption by Greek influences, because the Greeks were held to be softer and less manly and military, even as Greek artistic styles and intellectual practices spread. A few local identities were perceived as subversive because they loudly refused to place loyalty to the Roman state first: the Jews, particularly, were uprooted from Jerusalem and its surroundings because of this clash of identities.

Identity issues surfaced in India as Indian civilization spread to the whole subcontinent. They were modified, however, by great tolerance of local variants, including languages. Even the caste system protected separate identities within the discrete castes.

Still, the tension between previously established languages, beliefs, and customs, and the new power of integrating civilizations, was real. This meant a considerable extension of the tension itself throughout the world, compared to the previous period when smaller river valley societies had predominated.

A larger tension, however, than that of the friction between local identity and assimilation into a larger culture, existed in the classical period, although less clearly so. To some degree, particularly among elite social groups, the major civilizations themselves formed identities: Chinese had some sense of what was "Chinese," Greeks of what was "Greek." Leaders celebrated these identities by contending that people outside the civilizations were "barbarians"—a clear sense of difference from, and superiority to, the rest of the known world.

These new civilizational identities were not, however, severely tested by the contacts among civilizations. Silk Roads trade and commerce in the Indian Ocean continued to exchange goods, but not with the intensity that brought a wider sense of outside influence against which established identities had to be more sharply defined. Even when Greeks and Indians encountered each other, there is little record of the contact having generated identity issues. Indians briefly borrowed a few Greek styles, which modified their artistic identity for some decades, but there was little sense of a deep clash between the cultures.

Relationships between Greeks and Persians were another matter, something of an exception in the classical period. These two societies frequently interacted and fought. Greeks formed definite prejudices about the Persians. They tended to argue, particularly, that Persian government was more arbitrary, its rulers more unrestrained, than was true in Greece—and that the Persian system was decidedly inferior. Here was a rare case in which identity was sharpened by larger regional contacts. Alexander, of course, hoped to fuse Greeks, Persians, and other cultures in the larger Middle East, which was another response to the tension between identity and contact, but his effort fell short. Indeed, some Greek companions tried to insult Alexander by calling him a "Persian"—a clear sign that identities had not been significantly modified.

Identity was tested, again, at the end of the classical period when Buddhism moved into China. Here was a case, for several centuries, in which the attractions of an outside influence—a religion—outweighed Chinese insistence on preserving their own identity. Even here, however, as we have seen, the Chinese quickly modified Buddhism to make it more compatible with their view of what was proper. Only later, under a subsequent dynasty, did leadership largely turn against the religion on the grounds it was incompatible with Chinese values.

The classical period produced signs, in other words, that distinct civilizations were forging identities that might clash with other cultural identities as a result of contact. But, as we have seen, not all civilizations framed the tensions around identity in the same way: Chinese values insisted more fiercely on identity preservation than did the more tolerant Indian approach. For the most part, however, contacts among the civilizations were light enough that identity issues did not surface too harshly. Also, many merchants and consumers found the advantages of interregional trade, particularly along the Silk Roads, too great to sacrifice to relatively minor identity concerns. Starker tests of civilizational identities awaited the future.

PART III

The Postclassical Period, 500–1450 C.E.

INTRODUCTION: MARKING THE NEW ERA

The postclassical period of world history runs from roughly 500 C.E. to about 1450. Its beginning was marked by the final stages of decline of the classical empires and their aftermath. With this came the spread of world religions, the definition of a strong remnant of the Roman Empire in the east (the Byzantine Empire), and, soon, the rise of the Arabs.

The end of the period saw a decline of Arab political and commercial power, despite the continued importance of Arab peoples and culture; the end of the Byzantine Empire; and the end of a series of post-Arab frameworks for interregional trade. By 1450 western Europeans were well launched in a series of explorations and trading expeditions that propelled them into a new role in world history, while China had developed production capacities that long affected world trade.

THEMES: RELIGION AND LONG-DISTANCE TRADE

The postclassical period was defined, internally, by two major themes. First was the expansion of the world religions, and their impact on a variety of fields. Thanks to unprecedented missionary fervor from Buddhist, Christian, and Islamic leaders, hundreds of thousands of people changed their beliefs in fundamental ways. Polytheistic religions declined; the expanding monotheistic faiths showed the capacity to cut across religious and political boundaries. New religious emphasis tended to eclipse political interest; there were fewer bold political ventures, certainly fewer empires, in this period than in the preceding classical centuries, in part because more resources and talent went into religious than into political ideas and institutions. World religions also affected social structure, tempering continued inequality with new ideas about the religious value of poverty and the universality of souls.

The period's second main theme was the acceleration of interregional trade and the establishment of new, regular commercial routes. The key trade axis now ran east-west, from the Middle East through the Indian Ocean to southeast Asia and China. In addition, seaborne trade moved along Africa's eastern coast. Overland trade ran from north to south from northern Europe through western Russia, reaching the Middle East; and also from south to north in west Africa. Japan began trading regularly with Korea and China. A final regular route, established a bit later, brought western European merchants into the Mediterranean, again linking up with the Arab routes. Travel increased: By the 13th century venturesome individuals might go widely into Africa and Asia; the most tireless example, Ibn Battuta from north Africa, journeyed more than 86,000 miles. Accounts of distant places, along with better maps, both reflected and encouraged the new emphasis on long-distance commerce.

New technologies did not cause the expanding trade, but they did support it. Arabs improved ship design. The Chinese introduced the compass, which by the 13th century was being widely adopted in southeast Asia, the Middle East, and Europe. Trade also promoted the spread of other technologies and ideas. Arabs learned of papermaking from China, of a more efficient numbering system from India. Other groups, trading with the Arabs, later adopted these gains in turn.

The twin themes of the period, religion and trade, were an odd pairing in some ways. Religious leaders worried about too much devotion to commerce and money-making, and some merchants repented of their careers, turning to religion at the end of life. But the themes supported each other as well. The spread of major religions created larger cultural zones, while beliefs in a single divine framework or plan made long-distance trade seem less risky. Merchants often brought religion with them, as when Islam accompanied Arab commerce to the islands of present-day Indonesia or through the Sahara to west Africa. And commercial success helped persuade many people that religious change was worthwhile, linking conversion with worldly success as well as spiritual gain.

The two themes might also have had additional, diverse impacts. The three major world religions taught that women had souls, along with men. All provided new opportunities for religious expression, even some religious leadership, for women. But women's conditions also deteriorated in several places during the postclassical period. The practice of footbinding spread in China, and women in India and the Middle East became more secluded. Many societies used growing prosperity—the result of new trade-to place women in a more purely ornamental role, particularly women in the upper classes. The complexity of gender trends in several regions shows the unexpected impact of religion and commerce.

The world religions and trade both also supported the theme of growing contacts. The world religions all promoted wide interactions. Buddhist scholars traveled extensively in Asia, seeking enlightenment in different locations from India to Vietnam. Muhammad urged his followers to "seek knowledge, even unto China," and pilgrimages maintained wide connections through the expanding Islamic world. Christian pilgrims moved across borders within Europe, and some also sought to visit the Holy Land. The religions also, of course, set up new separations among religious zones—unlike trade, in this respect—but the spur to contact was substantial, as well.

A NEW GEOGRAPHY

The postclassical period was marked by another important theme: the number of civilizations, and the geographical areas they covered, both expanded. The four initial centers of civilization continued to exert impact: Mediterranean values and institutions showed up both in Byzantium and the Arab world, and the Indian and Chinese legacies also played a major role in these regions. Persian traditions persisted as well, though modified by Arab conquest and widespread conversion to Islam. But civilization, as a form of human organization, now spread to additional parts of Africa, to the eastern and western portions of northern Europe, to Japan, and to further sections of southeast Asia. Expansion occurred in the Americas as well, from centers in Central America and the Andes.

With these extensions, and the division of the Mediterranean world, the tally of civilizations changed as well, from the original four (east Asia, south Asia, the Middle East, and north Africa) to seven, with the addition of sub-Saharan Africa, eastern Europe, western Europe, and the Americas. Different definitions—for example, were Japan and China part of the same civilization?—could further expand the list.

Against this complexity, however, it is important to remember that most of these civilizations, whether old or new, were affected by the major themes of religious and commercial change. These themes linked the various cultures, even if each society reacted to the influences in different ways. Furthermore, as we will see, many new regions began actively to imitate some of the older civilizational centers. This final key process in the postclassical period provides a framework in which several otherwise disparate societies can be coherently analyzed and compared.

TIMELINE The Extension of Civilization, 500–1400 C.E.

The Middle East	India and Southeast Asia	Western Europe	The Americas
	200 ff. Spread of Indian influence in Southeast Asia.		
	500s Hun invasions; beginning of the Rajput (princedoms) period.	**500–800** "Dark Ages," missionary work in northern Europe.	
570–632 Muhammad and the foundation of Islam.			
632–634 Abu Bekr, first caliph.			
632–738 Islamic expansion beyond Arabia.			
661–750 Umayyad caliphate.	**700 ff.** Spread of Hinduism in southern India.		
750–1258 Abbasid caliphate.	**711** Arab raids begin.	**732** Franks defeat Muslims in France.	
906 ff. Decline of caliphate, growing Turkish influence.		**800–814** Charlemagne's empire.	**7th century** End of Olmec culture; rise of Mayans in Central America.
			900 Movement north by Mayans; intermingling with Toltecs.
1095 ff. Attacks by Western crusaders.			
	1192 ff. Muslim invasions, leading to Delhi sultanate.		
		1066 Norman conquest of England; strong feudal monarchy.	
		1073–1085 Reform papacy of Gregory VII.	**1100 ff.** Rise of Incas.
1200 ff. Rise of the Sufi movement.	**1253** Formation of Thai state (Siam).	**1096 ff.** Crusades.	**1200 ff.** Mayan decline.
1258 Mongol conquest of Baghdad, fall of Abbasid caliphate.			
		1200–1274 Thomas Aquinas and flowering of scholasticism.	
	1338 ff. Decline of Delhi sultanate.		**1350 ff.** Formation of Aztec empire.
		1265 English parliament.	**1400** Height of Incan empire.
		1338–1453 Hundred Years War.	**1493** Beginnings of Spanish government in the Americas (second voyage of Columbus).
		1479 Formation of single Spanish monarchy.	

Sub-Saharan Africa	East Asia	Byzantium and Eastern Europe
		527–569 Justinian emperor.
	589–618 Sui dynasty.	
	600 ff. Increasing Japanese contact with China. **618–907** Tang dynasty.	
		718 Defeat of Arab attack on Constantinople.
c. 800–1200 Empire of Ghana at its height. **800 ff.** Bantu migrations.		**855** According to legend, Rurik king of Kievan Russia.
	960–1279 Song dynasty.	**864** Beginning of missionary work of brothers Cyril and Methodius in Slavic lands. **980–1015** Conversion of Vladimir I of Russia to Christianity.
		1054 Schism between Eastern and Western Christianity. **1100 ff.** Byzantine decline; growing Turkish attack.
	1161 Use of explosives in war.	
1210–1400 Empire of Mali.	**1185–1333** Kamakura shogunate, Japan. **1206** Temujin named Chingghis Khan of Mongols; Mongol invasions of China. **1279** Toppling of Song dynasty by Kubilai Khan and Mongols.	**1203–1204** Capture of Constantinople by fourth crusade. **1236** Capture of Russia by Mongols (Tatars).
1300 Height of Zimbabwe. **1312–1337** King Mansa Musa.	**1281** Failure of second Mongol invasion of Japan; "divine wind" typhoon. **1368** Mongols driven from China by Ming dynasty. **1405–1433** Chinese expeditions.	**1453** Turkish capture of Constantinople; end of Byzantine Empire. **1480** Expulsion of Tatars from Russia.
1500–1591 Kingdom of Songhai.		

Chapters in this section deal first with the rise of Islam in the Middle East and north Africa, then with the two other societies most affected by Islam and by Muslim trade: south Asia and Africa. The two European regions, explored next, were less deeply touched by Islam, though trade links with Islamic cultures were vital. The latter chapters deal with another major, though more regional, set of interactions within the new world network, with the spread of east Asian culture, with the separate development of the Americas, and with the impact of the Mongol period in providing additional links between east Asia and other parts of Eurasia. The last chapter also examines developments around 1450, in transition from the postclassical period to the next era in world history.

The postclassical period was a busy one in world history. Key changes during this time, especially in commerce and culture—particularly the cultural impacts of the world religions—organized much of the experience of many societies.

GLOBAL CONNECTIONS

Both of the dominant themes of the postclassical period generated new connections among different regions. The world religions are so called precisely because they spread over geographic and cultural barriers. Missionaries fanned out from the Middle East to India and Africa, from Constantinople to east-central Europe and Russia. Ultimately, of course, the religions created barriers of their own. While Muslims and Christians often coexisted peace-fully, collaborating actively in places such as pre-conquest Spain, the two religions also experienced new hostilities. Buddhism was less confrontational, but it too created divisions with other belief systems.

Trade cut across boundaries even more thoroughly than the new religions did. Muslims, Buddhists, and Confucianists interacted via trade in China, southeast Asia, and the Middle East. Sometimes warily, Christians and Muslims traded as well.

Thanks to religion, but even more so to the new trade routes, it was during the postclassical period that the balance of world history shifted from separateness to convergence. Individual societies' local values and institutions still shaped many aspects of human experience, but increasingly, contacts among societies helped forge binding economic and cultural relationships.

Take, for example, the role of Islam. Islam and Arab politics and trade were the most dynamic set of forces during the early centuries of the postclassical period. Here was, in many ways, the first world power. The results touched literally every civilization in Africa, Europe, and Asia. Europe, including Russia, largely rejected Islam, but Europeans had to decide what to do about Islam's power and how to trade with Arab merchants despite rejecting the merchants' religion. Islamic invasions and commerce helped create a new and important Islamic minority in India. Conversions in Central Asia were even more widespread. Chinese and Islamic armies fought in western China, where another Islamic minority was planted, which created a complicating factor for China that still affects Chinese policies today. Islam became a predominant force in the Middle East/north Africa and in parts of southeast Asia; a significant force in several other societies; and a challenging force for contact more widely still. Islam's role as cultural connector is clear.

The new importance of contact showed also in the decision by leaders in many societies to imitate features of their neighbors' cultures. Many leaders sent delegations into neighboring provinces to further this process. Japan decided to copy China. Russia, slightly less formally, learned from the Byzantine Empire. Sub-Saharan Africa culled characteristics from Islam and the Arab world. Western Europe imported ideas and technologies from several sources, including Islam. And direct borrowing was practiced among the older civilization centers, as when Arabs adopted Chinese technology and Indian mathematics. Connections counted. What had been gradual and informal processes of cultural diffusion now shifted gears with this deliberate interaction, becoming relatively rapid.

By around 1000, a world network was being created that drew in societies from Africa to Russia, England to Japan. To be sure, the key interactions still occurred in stages. For instance, although England and Japan were involved in the network, neither had knowledge or or contact with the other. Trade between these societies occurred through intermediaries, particularly Arab and other merchants in the Indian Ocean, and the English and Japanese focused on relations with neighbors such as France and China, respectively, rather than on the larger exchange routes or each other.

It is revealing, however, that when one framework for interregional contact faltered, another sprang up in its stead. By the 13th century, Arab political power was declining, Arab merchants faced increasing challenges, and the organization of the east-west trade routes became less clear-cut. But it was also in the 13th century that the Mongol conquests in central Asia created an alternative network. Interlocking Mongol empires, or *khanates*, developed from China to east-central Europe, directly affecting trade in the Middle East, southeast Asia, Europe, and Japan. The organization of this huge territory, combined with the Mongol's tolerance of outsiders, allowed unprecedented travel and exchange among various parts of Asia and with Europe, using both overland and Indian Ocean routes.

When the Mongol structure began to collapse by the later 14th century, another alternative briefly surfaced to spearhead international trade: a new pattern of Chinese sea routes emerged during the first half of the 15th century. Clearly, by the latter part of the postclassical period, the advantages of wide trade and contact had become so obvious that the world network no longer depended on a single set of trade routes. When one pattern of routes faltered, another soon took its place—and this proved true again, after 1450, when Chinese policy changed in favor of more domestic focus.

The acceleration of contacts among disparate cultures was the most significant feature of the postclassical period, but despite this fact, the contact was not yet global. Several major societies operated in effective isolation outside the world network. The American civilizations, particularly, proved creative in generating complex economies and elaborate political structures; they had no need to participate in the network to achieve impressive results. But isolation inevitably creates vulnerability, and this too became visible soon after 1450—providing another illustration, though a negative one, of how important contacts had become to the rest of the world.

8

The Rise of Islam: Civilization in the Middle East

We begin with what became the center of the postclassical world: the Islamic Middle East and north Africa. Military conquests and a new empire, the caliphate, were one key ingredient. More important were an explosion of trade activity and the new religion of Islam. "There is no God but Allah, and Muhammad is his prophet." This prophet, an Arab born in the city of Mecca, intended to perfect a religion that focused on the power of a single god more clearly than any other religion—and by many measures he succeeded. The new faith of Islam sought to place its believers under the tutelage of an all-powerful divinity. Common Islamic names still reflect this orientation; many names include the Arabic word *Abd,* meaning "slave," to indicate subjugation to God. The religion's name, Islam, means "submission to the will of God." Islam quickly became the fastest-growing religion in the world, maintaining this pace throughout the postclassical period.

Islam was born among the Arab people and served to carry their influence over much of the Middle East. This Semitic people had long existed on the southern fringes of Middle Eastern civilization, from their center in and around the Arabian desert. They had considerable experience in trade because of their proximity to the main routes between the Mediterranean and the wealth of India. They had undertaken agriculture, although some (called *bedouins*) remained nomadic herders with a tribal organization under their warrior chiefs, or *shaykhs.* The Arabs had developed writing and a literature. They had also produced great works of art. Their religion was polytheistic, with priests organizing prayers and sacrifices to the various gods.

The rise of Islam and the Arabs supported major changes in Middle Eastern civilization from the 6th century on. A vital new religion spread over this region and beyond, although minorities of Christians and Jews remained. While Islam ultimately pushed beyond the Arabs, it initially served as a vehicle for Arab assertion against states such as Persia and Christian Byzantium that had long dominated the region. Arabs brought a new language as well, although again, pockets of other languages persisted. However, there was important continuity. Muhammad, Islam's founder, viewed himself as a prophet who spoke in God's voice. He deliberately built on other religions in the Middle East, notably Judaism and Christianity. Furthermore, older traditions survived in other respects. Middle Eastern culture, although altered by Islam, retained some of the traditions of Hellenistic philosophy and science. Arab merchants extended Middle Eastern commercial patterns, but they built on the trading practices that had already made the Middle East a vital commercial link between the Mediterranean and Asia. The Middle East, in sum, displayed new powers with the rise of Islam

and the Arabs, but it relied heavily on the earlier achievements of civilization in the region.

KEY QUESTIONS *Comparing Islam with the other world religions is a vital starting point: what was distinctive about Islam? Keeping religion in perspective is another challenge: What developments in Middle Eastern civilization during the postclassical period are not primarily explained by Islam? Finally, why did the vigor of Arab society begin to lag somewhat by the 13th century?*

THE ADVENT OF ISLAM

The Arabs' burst into larger Middle Eastern history started with the life of Muhammad, who

---

UNDERSTANDING CULTURES

THE IMPACT OF WORLD RELIGIONS

Because the postclassical period provides an unusual focus on international cultural change, several questions arise. Causation is one: why would cultures change in similar directions—toward one of the major religions—in otherwise very different regions? Missionary activity combined with political deterioration and the impact of disease probably supplies the basic answer, but the issue remains intriguing.

What about results? Change in religious affiliation, from one of the many versions of polytheism to Buddhism, Islam, or Christianity, involved more than a shift in ritual and belief, or even an increased focus on spiritual goals, although all this was important. There were also political implications. What happened to governments when many people came to believe that religion was more important than politics (and how would powerful state traditions, as in China, react in

turn)? Were there implications for trade? Religion might question the profit-seeking motives of merchants, but religion and trade also often spread in tandem, suggesting a more complex connection. The major religions all promoted spiritual equality for believers. They raised questions about previous social and gender divisions—but what were the concrete consequences, if any?

Finally, how did people individually manage cultural change? One key, common in periods of cultural transition, involved syncretism, the blending of old and new. Thus, China adapted Buddhism to fit its traditions, and many people retained their distinct identities while becoming Muslim or Christian. The magnitude of religious transformation in the postclassical period inevitably brought complexities in its wake.

around 570 C.E. was born of poor parents in Mecca, a trading city that already had some religious significance for the Arabs. First a camel driver, then a businessman happily married to a wealthy woman, Muhammad increasingly turned his thoughts to religious subjects. He experienced a conversion that brought him a sense of immediate understanding of Allah. He was fascinated by the Christian and Jewish faiths, both of which had many followers in Mecca, but he sought a purer statement of God's divinity—one uncluttered, for example, by complex doctrines such as the Christian Trinity—and a statement that was uniquely Arab. Writing what he believed were God's words, he argued that Allah, previously a rather vague Arab divinity, was the one true God and that Jewish and Christian leaders had merely been earlier prophets of Allah's truth. In Muhammad's view, the Jewish Old Testament and the work of Jesus, seen as a preacher but not as divine, provided a basis for the true religion. A series of ecstatic revelations convinced Muhammad that he had been called upon to organize this religion and to persuade others. He began attracting converts, whom he called *Muslims* ("surrendered to God").

Chased from Mecca by authorities who feared that he was organizing insurrection against them, Muhammad fled in 622 to Medina, whose citizens looked to him for religious and political leadership. His flight to Medina, called the *Hejira,* is regarded as the year 1 in the Islamic calendar. In Medina, Muhammad built a mosque for Muslim worship, while also attempting to join Muslims, Christians, and Jews in a single community. This early example of Muslim tolerance for peoples sharing religious traditions also brought frustrations at incomplete conversions to Islam. Muhammad also led Medina's government in a war with Mecca. Medina won, and many Arab tribesmen began to then negotiate peace with Muhammad. In one such negotiation, Mecca yielded to Islam but retained its status as the chief holy place. Muhammad, who had first ordered his followers to pray in the direction of Jerusalem, now told the supplicants to face toward Mecca. His decision was eased by the fact that most Jews, whom he had hoped to convert, rejected the new faith.

Muhammad died in 632. The revelations he received from Allah, via the intermediary of the archangel Gabriel, formed the Muslim holy book, called the *Qur'an* (or Koran). To loyal Muslims from this time on, the Qur'an has stood as the direct word of God, brooking no contradiction. It is God's "full and complete" statement of a perfect religion, including the "pillars of faith," or basic religious obligations. These provided further guidance for a proper life. After his death, Muhammad's disciples also began to assemble the Hadith, based on multiple recollections of the prophet's sayings and other rules and regulations for the Islamic community. These provided further guidance for an upright life.

Muhammad's death thus did not disrupt his religious message. As one of his disciples said, "Whoso worshippeth Muhammad, let him know that Muhammad is dead. But whoso worshippeth God, let him know that God liveth and dieth not." However, the new religion, and the political organization Muhammad had formed in Medina, needed new leadership. One of Muhammad's closest followers, Abu Bakr, was selected as *caliph,* or successor. Abu Bakr restructured his regional state and what was still a regional religion into a war machine, using small but brilliantly led armies to vanquish a series of rebellions against the rule of the Muslim states. The Arab people became firmly converted as a result. A rift developed, however, during the conversion process. A minority group, the Shiites, favored a direct descendant of Muhammad over Abu Bakr, whose followers formed the majority Sunni tradition. Shiite Muslims generally contended that they followed Muhammad's teachings more closely than their Sunni rivals.

Even with this important split, conversion seemed to galvanize the Arabs into several generations of conquest. Religion and a desire for material gain, through conquest, made for a powerful mixture. Muhammad had encouraged military

WORLD PROFILES

MUHAMMAD
(570–632 C.E.)

Muhammad is a fascinating historical figure. He was born into a poor family but later served as camel driver to a wealthy widow, whom he eventually married. No official portrait exists, but he was described as a handsome man with piercing black eyes and a full beard. Not an active businessman, Muhammad spent 15 years happily married and, in the eyes of local merchants, was regarded as somewhat indolent. Despite a lack of formal learning, he contemplated religious matters, experiencing a conversion that brought him an immediate understanding of Allah, a rather shadowy divinity in Arab tradition, as sole God. Future visions impelled Muhammad to convert others to his faith. These efforts culminated in the conversion of most of the Arabian peninsula by his death in 632. Muhammad and the Qur'an continued to be central reference points in Islam in life and law. Today, Muhammad is the most common male name in the world.

Islam's disapproval of representational art limited attempts to depict Muhammad even in an idealized fashion. But this miniature, in the Persian artistic tradition, shows the prophet building a mosque in Medina with his disciples.

effort in the name of Islam, claiming that anyone killed in a *jihad,* or holy war in defense of the faith, automatically attained an afterlife in heaven. Most historians believe that the economic desire of a poor people to gain access to the wealth of their neighbors provided a more important motive. Indeed, for most Muslims the concept of Jihad came to emphasize an internal struggle for religious purity. The Arab armies were not particularly large, nor did they benefit from advanced weaponry. They were ably led, however, by the generals who served under Abu Bakr and several subsequent caliphs. And they profited from the weakness of their neighbors, who had been ineffectually ruled from Constantinople since the fall of Rome. Egypt and north Africa lacked strong governments. To the north, the Byzantine Empire and the Persians had exhausted each other by repeated wars. As a result, there was territory ripe for the plucking.

PATTERNS OF ISLAMIC HISTORY

During the decades following Muhammad's death and the creation of a government by his successors, called the *caliphate,* swift expansion continued. The speed and extent of Arab victories rivaled the earlier sweep of Alexander the Great. Islamic forces first turned northward to the heart of the Middle East. In 635, they defeated a larger Byzantine army and conquered Syria and Palestine. The Muslims also defeated the Persians after a three-day battle during which Arab poets chanted war songs and pious Muslims recited the Qur'an. This victory pushed the borders of the Islamic caliphate north to the Caucasus mountains and east to the frontiers of India. The Arabs also turned west, attacking Egypt and establishing a new capital on the Nile. Then, later in the 7th century, the Arabs invaded the rest of north Africa, conquering or assimilating the native Berber peoples. Berber opposition, at first fierce, eased as the people converted to Islam and gradually accepted the Arab language. Finally, aided by Berber troops, the Muslims invaded Spain in 711, defeating a weak Germanic kingdom there.

Only beyond the Pyrenees were the Muslims stopped—Frankish leader Charles Martel defeated their forces in 732—although it was the strain on Muslim troops and supplies, not Frankish power, that turned the tide. Most of Europe thus remained outside the Islamic orbit, although Spain and parts of southern Italy were Muslim-ruled for several centuries. The Muslims also failed to conquer Byzantium and began to encounter new resistance in northwestern India. These various

setbacks ended the period of Arab conquest by the second quarter of the 8th century.

Nevertheless, even as it settled into a period of consolidation after the conquests, the Islamic caliphate ruled a larger territory and more people than the Romans had. The orders of the caliph were obeyed from Spain to the western borders of India and China. Organizing this huge area was no small matter. The second caliph, Umar, who spearheaded early Arab conquests, began the process of forming a larger government apparatus.

One source of control was the leadership of the Arab military. As leaders fanned out in conquest, they acquired considerable wealth and became something of a local ruling class. Islamic belief, holding that all land belonged to Allah, justified their seizure of property, but in fact most Arabs were content to leave the land in the hands of the original owners, collecting a tax instead. This tax became the main financial support for not only the new Arab ruling class, but also the government of the caliphate.

The Islamic conquerors were also tolerant of other religions. They believed that Judaism and Christianity were kindred faiths, just not aware or accepting of the complete truth. This policy of tolerance facilitated Islamic rule, resembling earlier Roman policies. However, Islam did win many new converts because of the purity of its doctrine and admiration for Arab success in conquest. Most converts, such as the north African Berbers, learned Arabic, for Islamic leaders were reluctant to see the Qur'an translated into other languages. Thus, not only a process of conversion to Islam, but also the development of a larger common culture began throughout much of the Middle East and north Africa. This, too, consolidated Arab rule.

The actual government of the caliphate was not strikingly original. Under Umar, the caliph claimed great authority, down to the amount of pension each soldier was to receive. However, the assertions of authority were not backed up with

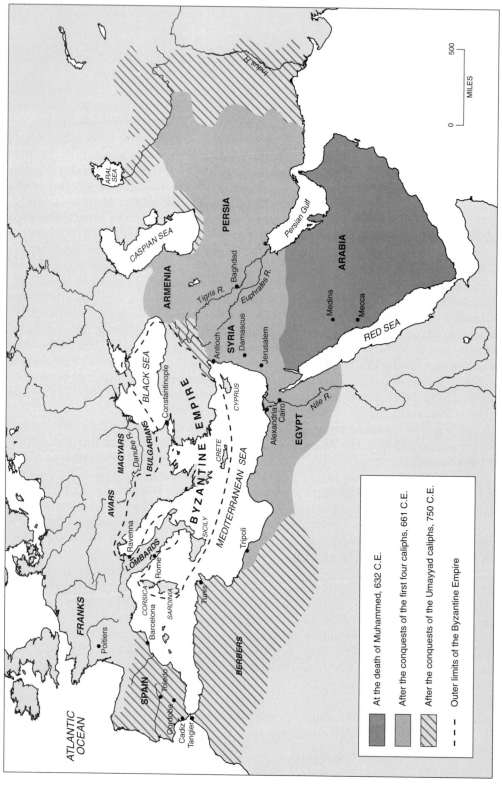

The Expansion of Islam

Legend:
- At the death of Muhammed, 632 C.E.
- After the conquests of the first four caliphs, 661 C.E.
- After the conquests of the Umayyad caliphs, 750 C.E.
- Outer limits of the Byzantine Empire

Map labels:
ATLANTIC OCEAN · FRANKS · Poitiers · SPAIN · Toledo · Cordoba · Cadiz · Tangier · Barcelona · CORSICA · SARDINIA · LOMBARDS · Rome · Ravenna · AVARS · MAGYARS · Danube R. · BULGARIANS · BLACK SEA · Constantinople · BYZANTINE EMPIRE · SICILY · Tunis · BERBERS · MEDITERRANEAN SEA · Tripoli · CRETE · CYPRUS · EGYPT · Alexandria · Cairo · Nile R. · Jerusalem · Damascus · SYRIA · Antioch · RED SEA · Mecca · Medina · ARABIA · Persian Gulf · Euphrates R. · Tigris R. · Baghdad · ARMENIA · PERSIA · CASPIAN SEA · ARAL SEA · Indus R.

500 MILES · 0

solid power. Many caliphs were assassinated; others proved to lack political talents. A recurrent difficulty was the lack of agreement, in Arab custom, over procedures for succession to the throne after a ruler died. Umar established an election process, but it was soon ignored in favor of heredity. Throughout the history of Middle Eastern civilization in the postclassical period, assassinations and plots frequently disrupted political tranquility.

One dynasty did establish power over the caliphate for about a century (661-750). This dynasty, under the Umayyad family, transferred the caliph's government to Damascus, Syria, where greater prosperity allowed a more luxurious court. But another family, the Abbasids, seized power in 750, although a few regions including Spain remained in Umayyad hands. The Abbasid dynasty moved the capital still farther east, to Baghdad. It also began the use of professional soldiers and slaves for troops, a sign that the military zeal of the Arabs was beginning to falter. This policy, like that of Rome before it, was risky in the long run. The use of mercenary troops from a central Asian people called the Turks proved particularly questionable, as Turkish influence in the Middle East gradually began to increase.

But Abbasid power remained solid for several centuries, despite some important rebellions and even though the dynasty was often severely troubled by plots and counterplots. The Abbasids continued the process of broadening Islam's base in the Middle East beyond the Arab peoples alone. Abbasid rulers held that all Muslims, Arabs or not, were equal in the sight of God and roughly equal in law as well. Further, any Muslim who spoke Arabic was regarded as Arab—a move that solidified the hold of the Arab language over most of the Middle East and north Africa. Only in Persia did conversion to Islam not bring acceptance of Arabic; Persia, now Iran, remains one of the only non-Arab-speaking parts of the region even today.

The Abbasids not only extended Islam and the Arab language as unifying elements in their vast empire, but they also served as sponsors of art and literature. The greatest flowering of Islamic creativity took place under their auspices, with Baghdad as its center.

Politically, however, Abbasid rule began to decline before the year 1000, although the dynasty officially lasted until 1258. A number of internal revolts rocked the royal family. The hold of mercenary troops and Turkish advisors became increasingly important. As more non-Arab people converted to Islam, the special tax revenues levied on nonbelievers declined—an ironic effect of Muslim success. Several key provinces broke away, including Egypt and Spain. European troops reconquered southern Italy (in 1061) and began to push back the Muslim rulers of Spain. The weakness of the Abbasid government allowed Christian crusaders in the 11th and 12th centuries to conquer parts of the Holy Land, establishing the short-lived kingdom of Jerusalem. More ominous still, Turkish nomads, already converted to Islam, began to move in from central Asia, causing Abbasid power to erode further.

The long and painful decline of the Abbasids did not, initially, signal a decline in the larger Islamic-Arab culture. Creative works in art, literature, and theology survived into the 13th century. Gradually, however, political difficulties had a severe impact. Islam still reigned. Indeed, political chaos served to extend its hold on the common people, particularly those in the countryside, some of whom had been only superficially touched by the new religion previously. But religious devotion increasingly monopolized Arab culture, to the detriment of other outlets. After 1200, a new movement, Sufism, gained growing influence; it expanded Islam's spiritual power while narrowing other interests in the name of piety. The Sufi leaders were holy men who experienced mystical visions of God. They gathered followers and inspired them by their holiness, using highly emotional rituals, including elaborate dances. The spread of the Sufi movement signaled important changes in Middle Eastern civilization, especially in Arab culture, even as it deepened the hold of Islam in the countryside and inspired missionary movements in other parts of the world.

The decline of the Abbasids did not signify a permanent disruption of the Middle East. A few areas were lost. The last Muslims were driven from Spain in 1492, but Christianity had won back most of this country beforehand. The northwestern tip of North Africa, the kingdom of Morocco, although firmly Islamic, became independent. But the rise of Turkish military power soon brought new and in some ways more effective government to most of the Islamic Middle East. What the Abbasid decline did result in, however, was a prolonged political eclipse of the Arab world. The caliphate was toppled by a brutal invasion of Mongol troops in 1258. From that point until after World War II, most Arabs were governed by others. Initially, the rulers were Turks and Muslims, but even they looked down on their Arab subjects because of their political and military fall from power.

The story of Arab civilization is thus one of swift rise and extension and equally swift, though incomplete, decline. Despite these sudden changes, the civilization that was partially redefined by the Islamic religion and Arab leaders produced durable institutions and values in the Middle East. Other regions were affected as well. By 1300, Islam was spreading to parts of Africa south of the Sahara, to India, and to southeast Asia. Here, the agents of diffusion were not military conquerors, but traders who brought religion and a sophisticated lifestyle along with their wares and fervent missionaries, including those inspired by the new Sufi movement. Military conquest played little role in Islam's surge beyond the borders of the Middle East. But Islam's entry into other civilizations, while creating some similarities to Middle Eastern society, is, in part, a separate story to be taken up in later chapters. Before 1300, the greatest impact of Islam lay in reshaping Middle Eastern civilization itself.

ISLAMIC POLITICAL INSTITUTIONS

Muhammad and his immediate followers generated significant political ideals. In their view, shaped in part by Muhammad's own experience in running the city of Medina, a perfect state should be governed by a religious leader—there was no differentiation between secular aims and religious goals. The state and its leader should put the faith first and serve as agents of Allah.

Islam was born connected to the state, in contrast to Christianity, and the difference mattered. Political ideals were an important and durable vision in the new Middle Eastern civilization. Political movements even during the 20th century returned to the idea that state and religion are one. In practice, however, the ideal did not usually prove feasible. Umayyad and Abbasid rulers did not always keep the interest of the faith foremost, particularly as their taste for luxury and for cultural patronage increased. But Islam did not formulate clear principles to guide a state that fell short of the ideal. Should Muslims obey any government, regardless of quality? Muhammad had declared this for the sake of emphasizing attention to religion. Or should Muslims try to work toward a government more attuned to Islamic ideals? These are questions still debated in Islam.

Officially, of course, the caliphs continued a tradition of combining political rule with the enforcement of religious law. Many Abbasid caliphs were indeed personally pious, which aided their popularity. Cultural achievements occurred in a variety of fields, from art to leisure. However, Abbasid governments, in fact, depended heavily on the whims of an individual ruler. A number of caliphs were cruel and arbitrary, often ordering the execution of not only potential rivals for the throne but also chief ministers. A leading Abbasid caliph, the pious Harun al-Rashid, provided an important period of peace and stability for much of the Middle East, but a

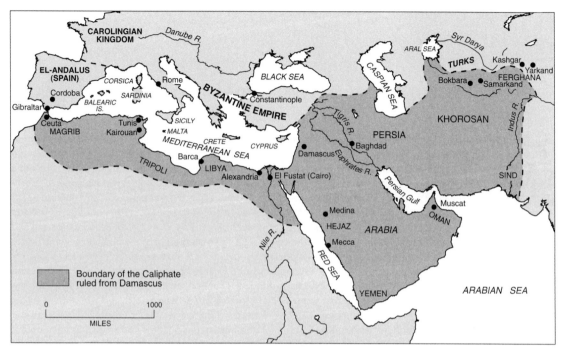

The Caliphate at Its Greatest Extent, About 750 C.E.

study of his regime also reveals the use of arbitrary power. He is reported to have ordered the execution of his favorite minister on sudden impulse. Then, overcome with remorse, he put the executioner to death because he could not bear to look on the man who had slain his favorite. Many caliphs impressed their subjects as much with their luxury—traveling in public surrounded by an escort of parasol carriers, flag bearers, and musicians—as by their religious fervor or political acumen. Harun al-Rashid won a great reputation by frequent acts of generosity, including his support to writers. An Arab admirer wrote: "No Caliph had been so profusely liberal to poets, lawyers, and divines, though as the years advanced he wept over his extravagance among his other sins."

The caliphate could provide effective rule. Harun was an able soldier, conquering rebellions and maintaining the upper hand in warfare with the Byzantine Empire. The absence of a strong titled aristocracy, with claims on political power, facilitated central administration. However, the Abbasid caliphs did suffer for their reliance on slaves and foreigners as chief bureaucrats. Many bureaucratic positions became virtually hereditary, unless their occupants were unseated by assassination. Thus, it was small wonder that the Abbasid dynasty lost effective control of its own government and that important new groups, particularly the Turks, established regional administrations of their own.

In fact, the caliphate, especially under the later Abbasids, became increasingly remote, not even very actively commanding its provincial bureaucracy. Local administrators, although appointed by the central court, had substantial autonomy, so long as they returned satisfactory tax revenues to the caliph in Baghdad. Reliance on mercenary troops and slave soldiers reduced

HISTORY DEBATE

POLITICAL IMPLICATIONS OF ISLAM

Historians find various messages in the political ideals and early experience of Islam. There is no question that the ideals differed from those in Christian western Europe, where a separate church institution reduced the theoretical importance of the state. In asking for a state that pursued religious goals first and foremost, Islam set a high standard. The real debate involves what Islam should encourage if the standard is not met. Muhammad specifically urged obedience to the state no matter what, for the goals of a religious person transcended political problems. Some historians have argued that this stance, plus the development of a separate system of religious law and increasing popular piety, produced a political passiveness among Muslims. This, it is argued, accounts for the frequent authoritarian governments in the Middle East, the common use of non-Muslims in the bureaucracy, and (some contend, by extension) the difficulties for modern democracy to take root. However, other leading historians try to show that Islam suggested two paths, not one. Passivity might be replaced by an eager desire to make the state better, to bring it closer to the religious ideal—and this, in a modern context, could even generate support for the goal of democratic political participation, so that the true Muslim voice can be heard.

Comparison with Christianity usefully supplements the debate, for despite their mutual hostility, Christianity and Islam shared a host of features. Christianity, like Islam, might be involved in political movements against a state regarded as evil. But Christianity also urged obedience, and the Catholic church established a model of authority, not participation. Zealous Christians could ignore political life. Thus, the complexity of Islam is not unique, and attempts to use the religion to explain current political practices may be risky or overly simplistic. All three world religions generated complex political impulses, and Islam needs to be assessed within this framework.

the need to recruit directly from the Arab population. The caliph's growing use of Turkish, Persian, and even Christian advisors, although designed to limit the power of upper-class Arabs, underscored the remoteness of the government from most people. To be sure, all governments in agricultural societies, even in China, were remote by modern standards: they had little contact with most peoples' day-to-day lives. But the caliphate, and the lack of political ideals in Islam that helped legitimize an "imperfect" or not simply religious state, intensified this remoteness. The combination hastened Abbasid decline after several centuries of splendor.

However, the limitations of the government established by the caliphate were not the whole story of Islamic politics. Islamic political ideals were far more closely realized in the religiously run legal system that spread throughout the Middle East. Islam did not establish an elaborate, centralized organization outside the state. But local religious leaders, schooled in Islamic law, did more than lead prayers. Building on the Qur'an and the Hadith, Islamic leaders gradually developed an elaborate body of law known as the *Sharia,* or "straight path." This law reflected a mixture of Qur'anic principles with interpretations offered in the Hadith. Sharia law regulated many aspects of social behavior, including family relations, economic contacts, and outright crimes. It was interpreted and extended by groups of Islamic scholars and religious leaders known as the *ulema.* The ulema, which initially arose spontaneously and was then encouraged by

This photograph shows pilgrims during the holy night of Ramadan at the Kabaa in Mecca in Saudi Arabia.

mind, body, and soul. In contrast, the Muslim hell was full of the darkest pain and torture, surpassing most Christians' visions of Satan's torments.

Islam was not a constant, although its basic principles persisted. As the Sufi movement gained ground, from 1200 on, mystical leaders, called dervishes, played a growing role in inspiring the faithful. Their activities bore some resemblance to those of monks in Christianity, but there was no general discipline of the Benedictine sort. Spiritual and emotional example gave new force to Islam. It also helped inspire missionary activity.

The religious fervor Islam could generate, plus the local quality of much of the religious organization, guaranteed religious division. The Sunni/Shiite split continues from the 7th century, with the Shiite Muslims revering the memory of Muhammad's son-in-law, Ali, and lamenting the martyrdom of his son Huseyn. They also believed that they were truer to Islamic law than the majority group, called the Sunni. Shiites continued to expect additional prophecies. And they formed a clearer religious structure than the majority group, identifying religious leaders, such as the ayatollahs in Persia, who could direct the faithful and select and instruct local religious officials. The Shiite minority gained particular strength in the north, in the present-day countries of Iran and Iraq, but elements of Shiite culture may be found in many parts of the region. Their special religious fervor remains an important factor in Middle Eastern life in the early 21st century. The Shiite-Sunni split frequently encouraged political disunity in the Middle East, including periodic assassinations and other acts of violence. This penchant, too, recurred in modern times, with each side viewing the other as heretical.

Islamic leaders often delighted in discussing the meaning of a virtuous life. Arab religious thinkers also detailed their ideas about heaven, coming up with a seven-stage scheme often represented in art. However, here were fewer discussions about the nature of God or problems of free will than in Christianity. Islamic theology was mainly confined to the search for truths in the Qur'an and to the study of the traditions of Muhammad and his early followers. Simply keeping track of the various traditions and laws of the Sharia was no easy task. By the time of the Abbasid dynasty, Muslim scholars found it necessary to collect the traditions that had developed. One scholar spent 16 years touring the Middle East, gathering 600,000 customs and beliefs, which he reduced to 7275 regarded as authentic religious truths. This code helped promote the Islamic emphasis on charity and the importance of God's rules for humankind, one of the important attractions of Islamic faith. But the task of interpreting the traditions of Islam remained a challenging assignment. Strict Muslims believed that no other intellectual enterprise was valid, for faith alone was all that Allah required.

Nevertheless, a wider philosophy persisted in Middle Eastern civilization, inspired in part by knowledge of older Greek and Persian learning still available in the region. By the 9th century, a host of scholars were busy translating Greek and Persian sources into Arabic. Huge libraries were erected in cities such as Baghdad. This bustling cultural life was aided by the introduction of paper from China, which made book production more extensive and cheaper.

Greek tradition, of course, contradicted the strictest Islamic belief system, for it held that people could understand a great deal through the use of reason. Arab philosophers grappled with this schism for several centuries, and many urged a rationalistic approach without breaking with Islam. A similar disparity arose later in the Christian West, in part because of the Arab precedent. By the 1100s, many Arab philosophers were trying to build a rationalistic framework for all knowledge, mixing religious truth, science, mathematics, and rational speculation. This work both preserved and extended the Hellenistic heritage.

As in philosophy, the fine arts were strongly influenced by Islamic rules—but not entirely constrained by them. Muhammad, eager to develop the purest possible focus on Allah, forbade idols, and later the ulema extended prohibitions against all representation of human or animal forms. The goal was to purge Muslims of any impulse to worship lesser images. As a result, most Islamic art centered on the nonrepresentational. Only a few artists, particularly those in Persia, continued to create sculpture or painting involving human or animal figures. Muslim artists instead placed distinctive geometric designs and the flowing patterns of Arab script on pottery, metalware, textiles, and leather and on buildings' tile and stucco. Mosques, which are the Muslim houses of prayer, and palaces were especially covered with glazed tile and stucco relief in intricate designs. This powerful artistic style spread beyond the Middle East to influence art in Spain and Portugal, even after the expulsion of the Muslims, and in India. In the Middle East itself, concern for rich decorative images on buildings and in the form of a host of artifacts remained central to the arts.

Middle Eastern architects learned much from the earlier classical styles of the Mediterranean. Palaces often reflected a Roman influence, with an open courtyard and fountain surrounded by separate rooms. For mosques, Muslim architects created a distinctive kind of tower, the minaret,

Arab calligraphy: A leaf from the Qur'an, dating from the 8th or 9th century, illustrates the Kufic form of Arabic calligraphy.

from which the faithful were called to prayer at the appointed hours. Most mosques were domed buildings, preceded by a hall of columns with distinctive, horseshoe-shaped arches. These innovations in arches and towers helped inspire the Gothic style that later emerged in western Europe. Both Muslims and Christians sought structures that directed the eye toward heaven.

Music also received considerable attention. Muhammad and his followers frowned on the frivolity of music, which was not part of Islamic prayer services. However, most people in the Middle East did not take this particular prohibition too seriously. As one writer put it, "Wine is as the body, music as the soul, and joy is their offspring." Musicians, and particularly singers, gained in respect. The singer Tways, who lived from 632 to 710, was the originator of the high-pitched, nasal singing style popular in the Arab world. He introduced new rhythms and was the first to sing with accompaniment—a tambourine. Other

instruments commonly used were the lute and guitar. Arab rhythm and instrumentation influenced Spanish musical styles, which in turn influenced the styles later developed in Latin America.

Middle Eastern literature emphasized poetry above all. Most cultivated Arabs and Persians have rated poetry as the highest achievement of their civilization after Islam itself. Arab poetry predated Muhammad. But, as the Arabs came into contact with other peoples in the Middle East, their literary efforts became more polished. Abbasid caliphs patronized scores of poets, and the knowledge of poetry and ability to express oneself in verse became the mark of a cultivated person—as in Confucian China.

Poets wrote on many themes, most of them nonreligious, as in Omar Khayyam's *Rubaiyat*. A black ex-slave in Baghdad gained great popularity with poems that poked fun at the traditional Arab emphasis on heroism. Many Persian poets, writing in Arabic, used sensual themes, praising

WORLD PROFILES

OMAR KHAYYAM
(c. 11TH–12TH CENTURIES)

The vitality of Islamic intellectual life shows in the career of the Persian Omar Khayyam, the type of person who in Western culture might be known as a "Renaissance man." Omar's early life is obscure; his last name means "tentmaker," which may suggest his father's occupation. He obtained an extensive education and came to the attention of the Turkish sultan then ruling the region (despite the continuance of the Abbasid caliphate). The sultan sponsored his scientific work. Omar became a royal astronomer and helped reform the Islamic calendar. His books on algebra were particularly notable, as he classified equations of the first degree. He is best known in the world at large for his poems, which were collected in *The Rubaiyat* and translated into English during the 19th century. These quatrains feature complex, multiple rhymes in the first, second, and fourth lines. Their subject matter emphasized the pleasures of this life. Omar was at times humble toward Allah, at other times defiant; he was also very critical of Islamic extremists, such as the Sufis, who nonetheless adapted his work. The main theme of *The Rubaiyat* was the beauty of earthly existence; God created humans as he is, so he will not punish; a person should enjoy the only life we can be sure of. How does Omar Khayyam fit the main themes of Middle Eastern culture during the postclassical period?

This representation of Omar Khayyam is based on an English painting by H. M. Burton. It reflects a later Western interpretation of the great poet and scientist and his setting. Omar Khayyam is shown working out a calendar, surrounded by samples of his philosophic aphorisms and astronomical work.

the joys of hunting and drinking, but also expressing some religious sentiments.

Overall, Arabic poetry showed a growing concern for polished manners and a life of refinement, characteristic of an aristocracy that was becoming more devoted to culture and the good life than to military prowess. The poetry also revealed an unusual interest in pure style, as poets strove for perfection in each individual line and, by Western literary standards, seemed more preoccupied with their stylistic devices than content. Frequent changes of subject, word associations, and images were the hallmarks of this poetry, which focused on both nature and human experience. Thus, one poet praised the lion-mouthed fountain at an Arab palace in Grenada, Spain (a palace that still exists). His description served as a trigger for all sorts of word associations:

And lions people this official wood
encompass the pools with thunder
and profuse over aureate-banded
bodies their skulls gush glass. . . .
Sun is tinder to the stirred
colors, is light to long tongues,
is a hand to unsheathe the lunging
blades that shiver out in a splash.

However, Arab poetry could also be terse and humorous, as in this verse, "The Radish":

The radish is a good
And doubtless wholesome food,
But proves, to vex the eater,
A powerful repeater.
This only fault I find:
What should be left behind
Comes issuing instead
Right from the eater's head.

Science, including history and geography, provided the final outlet for the high culture of the Middle East. A scientific interest followed, of course, from the rationalistic concerns of the leading philosophers and from the Hellenistic heritage. Arabs found a practical application for it in the study of medicine, astronomy, and geography. Medicine could cure. Knowledge of the stars, it was believed, might help predict the future—hence, interest in astrology ran high. And geography served the direct needs of Arab trade. Abbasid caliphs supported considerable scientific study in all these areas, in addition to the translation of earlier Greek and Persian scholarship.

Arab astronomers made no major advances, in part because they relied heavily on the theories of the Hellenistic astronomer Ptolemy and his claim that the earth was the center of the universe. However, observatories checked the accuracy of various Greek measurements, and scientists acquired more precise knowledge of eclipses and the length of the solar year. Arab scientists, aware that the earth was a sphere, also calculated the planet's circumference. In medicine, a host of empirical observations were recorded. Doctors in Baghdad chose the location for the central hospital by carefully studying environmental conditions. Although in medical science, too, there were no new general theories, the idea of contagion was strongly suggested as a practical finding. As one doctor wrote: "The result of my long experience is that if a person comes into contact with a patient, he is immediately attacked by the disease with the same symptoms." In a similar pragmatic spirit, doctors described the symptoms of a variety of common diseases and the properties of hundreds of therapeutic drugs. Finally, some advances were made in the study of chemical elements, and Greek and Indian discoveries in chemistry and physics were assimilated within this body of knowledge. Without question, Arab science predominated in the world by 1200, with only Chinese scholarship a near rival.

Arab scholars also showed some interest in mathematics, taking over the Indian numbering system. Particular advances were made in algebra, which is an Arab-derived word. The text written by the greatest Arab mathematician, al-Khwarismi, was translated and used in European universities until the 16th century. It established new territory in algebraic multiplication and division and in equations of the second degree.

Because of their extensive travels, Arab merchants and missionaries produced more abundant geographical knowledge than the world had ever known—or was to know again until the age of European exploration began in the 15th century. In history, the north African Ibn Khaldun, writing in the 14th century and building on a long tradition of narrative accounts of the past, achieved an understanding of the dynamics of social behavior that has had few rivals before or since.

Overall, Arab scientists were not as adept at formulating general theories as they were at recording careful observation and preserving the learning of their own scholars and scholars of the past. Nonetheless, they contributed to a flourishing intellectual life, in which not only scholars but also aristocrats and other wealthy urbanites gained an extensive education that combined the Muslim faith with a healthy enjoyment of secular culture. In this spirit, an unusually large elite became literate and a series of major universities were founded, as in Egypt in the 10th century and in Baghdad in 1065. Schools and universities taught religion, poetry, philosophy, the sciences, and history—a fair sampling of the cultural knowledge Middle Eastern civilization had created.

ECONOMY AND SOCIETY IN THE MIDDLE EAST

A lively economy was a vital part of the new Middle Eastern civilization, and it built on earlier traditions of agriculture and trade. Economic activity served as a key element in the spread of Islam to Africa and southeast Asia. It also set the stage for the bustling cities, the educated elite, and the luxurious court life of the caliphate.

Agriculture, long established in this area, remained highly productive. The Abbasid caliphate drained swamps, extended systems of irrigation, and otherwise supported agricultural development. Wheat, barley, and rice were the main crops, whereas dates and olives constituted important secondary goods. A free peasant class did most of the farming, and under the early Abbasids the conditions of the peasants improved somewhat. Most peasants remained poor, however, and they owed heavy taxes to the state and local landlords. The Abbasid caliphate provided more equitable treatment by assessing a percentage of the crops produced, rather than a fixed fee, as taxes, so that peasants would not suffer unduly when harvests were bad.

The Islamic empire had substantial mineral holdings, including iron and precious metals.

Some large private mining operations arose; one, in the 10th century, employed 10,000 miners.

Manufacturing was extensive and, like agriculture, won encouragement from the state. Textile production, including carpets and other luxury items, gained ground steadily. Persian rugs became particularly famous. City centers were crowded with artisans who manufactured in and sold from their own homes. The bustle of a Middle Eastern marketplace, or bazaar, reflected the abundant production of craft goods and vigorous trade.

There were, however, few significant technological improvements in Middle Eastern agriculture or manufacturing. The Arabs did import papermaking from China. The manufacture of fine iron products, particularly of swords, made Damascus famous. But careful organization and vigorous activity, not innovation in techniques, served as the hallmarks for this economy.

Commerce, nevertheless, flourished, and a strong merchant spirit was a central feature of this renewed civilization. To be sure, governments often seemed to consider merchants mainly as subjects for taxation and did little to encourage transportation or trade. However, a large merchant class evolved, both for the local trade at bazaars and for international operations. Most overseas trade centered on luxury products, but some basic goods, such as timber from India and slaves from Africa and Europe, were also involved. Merchants brought silks, spices, and tin from India, China, and southeast Asia, for use at home and for sale to Europe and Africa. One source lists the goods brought from China: perfumes, silks, crockery, paper, ink, peacocks, swift horses, saddles, felt, cinnamon, and rhubarb; from the Byzantine Empire: gold and silver, drugs, slave girls, engineers, marble workers, locks, and trinkets; and from India: tigers, panthers, elephants, skins, rubies, sandalwood, ebony, and coconuts.

Islamic sailors were quite at home in all the Asian waters from the 8th century on, aided by good mapmaking. Improved sailing ships facilitated commerce also, particularly in the Indian

Ocean; Arab dhows had both speed and considerable capacity. By sailing into the Black and Caspian seas, Muslims traded with Russians and Scandinavians. Thousands of Muslim coins have been found in Sweden, brought back from this trade; indeed, the first Swedish coins copied Muslim models. Active trade developed with Africa. Overland expeditions imported gold, salt, and slaves. Slave marches were brutal affairs, with many thousands perishing. Islamic ships also traded with ports farther down the east African coast. Trade with western Europe was less active, because the Europeans had few goods of interest to the more sophisticated Middle East. However, there was some exchange, often undertaken by Jewish entrepreneurs, through which the Middle East obtained cloth, furs, and slaves. Here, technology did play a role. Mapmaking and navigational instruments changed as well.

Far-flung trade led to improvements in banking. Some Baghdad banks had branch offices in other cities. It was thus possible, for example, to draw a check in Baghdad and cash it in Morocco.

Islamic culture gave merchants considerable esteem—more than in any other civilization at that time. The Islamic religion did not see profitmaking as a contradiction of spirituality or honor, so long as active charity ensued. Muhammad, with merchant experience of his own, proclaimed merchants to be models of a virtuous life: "On the day of judgment, the honest, truthful Islamic merchant will take rank with the martyrs of the faith," and "Merchants are the couriers of the world and the trusted servants of God upon earth." One caliph supposedly said: "There is no place where I would be more gladly overtaken by death than in the marketplace, buying and selling for my family." Manuals were written to encourage good commercial and investment practices.

The commercial zeal of Islam, along with the religion itself, made the new Middle Eastern civilization the most significant force in the world for many centuries. Although India, southeast Asia, and east Africa were most closely affected,

more remote parts of Europe and Africa also experienced the impact of this unusual dynamism. Economic life solidified important values in the Middle East and brought luxury and wealth to the upper classes. The attractiveness of the urban marketplaces, as evidenced in the vital role that trade came to play in city life, survives to the present day. Even more than artistic achievement, trade expressed a central quality of the Middle East.

Socially, Middle Eastern civilization displayed many of the features expected in a prosperous agricultural region. A landlord class flourished, as had long been the case in the Mediterranean world. Arab conquerors, some of them former merchants, assumed the landlord role in many areas. Urban artisans, as well as the merchants, were numerous and well organized. Although some peasants worked entirely for landlords, we have seen that, in the most prosperous centuries before the Abbasid decline, a significant free peasant class existed.

The social order was complicated by three factors. First, the mixture of racial groups and minority religions added to the region's diversity. Even among Muslims, tensions often surfaced between Arabs and non-Arabs. Second, Islam maintained a strong egalitarian theme. Muslims believed that all people were basically equal under God. Such a doctrine made some adherents uncomfortable with existing social inequality, and it spurred some lower-class elements to revolt in the name of religion itself. But Muhammad had not intended to preach social equality. His insistence on the importance of charity acknowledged, in fact, that there would always be the rich and the poor in this life. However, the spiritual equality that Muhammad avowed sometimes added bitterness and confusion to the society shaped by Islam.

The third complicating factor in the civilization of the Middle East was the substantial presence of slavery. Islamic civilization during this period depended more heavily on slave labor than did any of the other major civilizations except Central America. In India, slavery had been largely displaced by the caste system, whereas in east Asia and Europe slavery, although it did exist, was confined primarily to occasional household service. The existence of slavery was, to be sure, less important in the Islamic Middle East than it had been under the Roman Empire. Agriculture, for example, did not rely on slave labor. But slaves provided domestic service, manual labor for many of the mines and sailing vessels, and above all, troops for military operations. As we have seen, the Abbasids also used elite slaves as soldiers and bureaucrats. Furthermore, Islam developed an extensive slave trade. Initially, most slaves in the Middle East had been taken in conquest, as had been the case in most other slaveholding societies. However, the need for slaves did not cease when Arab conquests stopped, and the active trading impulse of the Arabs provided a clear alternative. Slaves formed the most sought-after goods in sub-Saharan Africa and parts of Europe. Their use, particularly in the armies of the caliphate, made them virtually indispensable. Some slaveholding survived in the Middle East until quite recent times.

In principle, slaves could not be Muslim; their being so contradicted the spiritual equality of all believers. But slaves who converted to Islam were not promised their liberty—although the freeing of slaves was considered a pious act that could win rewards in heaven.

Slave uprisings were rare, but they did occur. Black slaves revolted between 869 and 889. Inspired by a leader aware of Islamic values, the slaves claimed that "God would save them" and "make them masters of slaves and wealth and dwellings." Their leader was executed, his head brought to Baghdad on a pole as a warning against similar uprisings. This was, to be sure, an unusual rising. Slaves used for other functions, including palace service and the army, were better positioned to exert pressure. Periodic revolts involved military troops who were legally slaves.

Peasant revolts also occurred in the name of greater equality. Some of these had racial over-tones, with non-Arab Muslims protesting Arab control. One of the goals of the rebellions was the sharing of property; the peasants argued that social equality should match religious equality. A poet thus captured the spirit of peasant rebellions in the 10th century:

> By God, I shall not pray to God while I am
> bankrupt . . .
> Why should I pray—where are my wealth,
> my mansion
> And where are my horses, trappings, golden
> belts?
> Were I to pray, when I do not own
> An inch of earth, then I would be a
> hypocrite.

Peasant uprisings were always vanquished, but they cropped up recurrently.

Families served as a basic institution for the upper class, merchants, and peasants alike. Family discipline was tight, although often tempered by affection. One caliph described how he wanted a tutor to treat his son:

> Be not strict to the point of stiffening his faculties nor lenient to the point of making him enjoy idleness. Treat him as much as thou canst through kindness and gentleness. Fail not to resort to force and severity should he not respond.

The position of women was particularly noteworthy in the Muslim family. Muhammad carefully stated the spiritual importance of women, noting that they had souls just the same as men. And he introduced some rules designed to protect women. For example, he granted women the right to divorce men and not simply the reverse. He tried to prevent the killing of female babies, a common practice in many agricultural societies where women were regarded as less useful than men and female infanticide was a means of population control. Women could also own property, and their property rights within marriage were carefully defined. Despite Muhammad's attention to certain conditions of women, Islam helped maintain the pronounced inferiority of females within the Islamic family. Women worshipped separately, and the Hadith characterized them as particularly likely to become sinners. As in Christianity, spiritual equality warred with disdain in its views of women.

One sign of the subjugation of women was polygamy. A woman could take but one spouse, whereas a man could have up to four wives. In fact, only the very wealthy could contemplate more than one wife, because Islamic law insisted that a man support his children, so polygamy was never widely practiced. Other rules were more important. A man could divorce his wife far more easily than the other way around. A woman typically married early, at the age of 13 or 14, according to an arrangement made by her father. Once she was married, the duty of a wife was "the service of the husband, care of the children, and the management of the household." In public life, the segregation of the sexes increased steadily, for as in many advanced agricultural societies, inequalities increased over time. By the 10th century, urban women rarely left their household compound. In the 11th century, a caliph decreed that women had to wear a veil when mixing with men and in all public places, extending the pre-Muslim Arab and Middle Eastern custom. Many people came to believe that veiling was part of Islam.

In this segregated situation, Muslim women established intricate social contacts with each other, particularly among other women in the same extended household. Furthermore, the severest limitations on women were not always strictly imposed. Especially in peasant households, where women's work was vital, the total seclusion and veiling of women were often ignored. Nevertheless, a strict differentiation between men and women, in the family and beyond, developed during this formative period and persisted as a basic feature of Middle Eastern civilization.

Even as women's public position deteriorated, however, complexity remained. Many individual women were highly educated. With their property rights, they often ran businesses, though hampered by constraints on their appearing in public. Political roles were limited. A young wife of Muhammad, Aisha, had led armies in battle, but she ultimately failed and her example was widely questioned.

THE DECLINE OF MIDDLE EASTERN CIVILIZATION

After about the year 1200, Middle Eastern civilization began to display a number of symptoms of decline. We have seen that, at the top, the Abbasid caliphate was already in a compromised position, losing control over its provinces and about to collapse completely. However, disintegration ran even deeper than this. At the same time, the decline of Arab civilization was never complete—not like the fall of Rome. What was occurring involved a loss of vitality and diversity, and political problems were only one symptom.

By 1300, a shift in intellectual life was noteworthy. Increasingly, religious leaders gained the upper hand over poets, philosophers, and scientists. The earlier tension among diverse cultural elements yielded to the predominance of the faith. The new piety associated with the rising Sufi movement was both the cause and result of this development. In literature, an emphasis on secular themes, such as the joys of feasting and hunting, gave way to more strictly religious ideas. Persian poets, writing now in their own language instead of Arabic, led the way. Religious poetry, and not poetry in general, became part of the education of upper-class children. In philosophy, the rationalistic current encountered new attack. In Islamic Spain, the philosopher Ibn Rushd (known as Averroës in Europe) espoused Greek rationalism, but his efforts were largely ignored in the Middle East. European scholars were, in fact, more heavily influenced by his teachings. In the Middle East proper, a more typical philosopher now claimed to use Aristotle's logic to show that it was impossible to discover religious truth by human reason—in a book revealingly, if not subtly, titled *The Destruction of Philosophy*.

The Sufi movement was a reaction to both the secularism and corruption of the declining caliphate and the formalism of Islam. The movement emphasized individual contact with God, and at first it surfaced in purely personal formulations. Sufi groups began to form in the 12th and 13th centuries, often among outlying peoples such as the Turks. They reflected an interesting cultural syncretism, borrowing several features from the Christian monastic movement and others from Buddhism. Some Sufi groups stressed works of charity, but others practiced auto-hypnotism that could allow people to swallow burning embers or pass knives through their bodies; these groups also featured impassioned dances. Sufism contradicted traditional Islam in emphasizing saints or holy men, but in so doing, it provided an outlet for a vital religious impulse. It not only furthered the Islamic missionary effort but also increased the piety of ordinary people.

Increasingly, then, Middle Eastern scholarship focused on religion and the Islamic legal tradition. Some interest in science remained, although it too began to fade. In its place, many Sufi scholars wrote excitingly of their mystical contacts with God and the stages of their religious transformation. This narrowing of Middle Eastern cultural life had less impact on the arts. Artisans' production continued to flourish in many centers, maintaining the Middle East's distinctive commitment to richly decorated rugs, leather goods, and other wares.

Changes in society and the economy were still more subtle, but in many ways at least as ominous as the shifts in politics and intellectual life. As the authority of the caliphate declined, landlords seized greater power over the peasantry. From about 1100 on, peasants increasingly lost their freedom, becoming serfs on large estates. This loss was not the peasants' alone, for agricultural productivity suffered as a result. Landlords turned to draining whatever profit they could from their estates, rather than trying to develop a more vital agriculture; peasants had little incentive and no means to do better, as they were tied to the land and obligatory labor and production output for the landlords. With this gradual social deterioration came fewer tax revenues for the state and less of a basis for flourishing trade. Indeed, Arab traders began to lose ground. Few Arab coins have been found in Europe dating from later than 1100; European merchants were beginning to control their own turf and soon began to challenge the Arabs in other parts of the Mediterranean. Arab commerce remained active in the Indian Ocean, but the time fast approached when it faced new competition there as well, from Chinese and southeast Asian merchants, many of whom had converted to Islam.

The main point is clear, however. Between 600 and 1400, a significant new culture arose in the Middle East. It was unquestionably the most dynamic in the world during most of the period. Important ingredients of this culture remained dominant in the region even after 1400, for this was a durable new society. Even after 1400, the region's role in a complex set of international relationships continued, for Middle Eastern society galvanized a new set of contacts that ran from China in the east to Spain in the west.

PATHS TO THE PRESENT

Many aspects of present-day Middle-Eastern and north African culture trace back to developments in the postclassical period—including the fact that most people in the region, for all their diversity, regard themselves as Arabs and Muslims. Traditionalists in the region maintain styles of dress developed or revived in this period, including veiling for women. Lively commercial traditions, including bustling markets and price bargaining, persist as well. Islamic law remains a vital factor in business relations and family conduct. The Sunni-Shiite split remains vivid, deeply affecting current political prospects in places in Iraq.

The vigor of the Islamic heritage is undeniable, but it is also complex. Islam—as do other religions—contains profound self-contradictions. The Qur'an emphasizes peace and the humane treatment of others. Yet the concept of jihad justifies militancy in the name of Allah, in the postclassical centuries and today. Under Islam, women gained important protections—to such a degree that some contemporary Muslim feminists argue that true Islam provides an appropriate basis for gender equity. But other traditions from the postclassical period seem to enforce the inferiority of women. It is also vital to remember that Islam is not the only legacy from this period of the region's history. Vigorous commerce and sophisticated urban life also link present to past in many parts of Middle-Eastern/north African civilization.

SUGGESTED WEB SITES

For more on medieval Islamic cultures, see http://www.sfusd.k12.ca.us/schwww/sch618/ Islam_New_Main.html, http://www.fordham.edu/ halsall/sbook1d.html, and http://www.wsu.edu:8080/ ~dee/ISLAM/MED.HTM.

SUGGESTED READINGS

An important recent work is Mahmoud Ayoub's *Islam: Faith and History* (2004) on issues in the early history of Islam and its outreach. General texts include Francis Robinson, ed., *The Cambridge Illustrated History of the Islamic World* (1998); Sheldon Watts, *Disease and Medicine in World History* (2003); and Leila Ahmed, *Women and Gender in Islam* (1992). B. Lewis, *The Arabs in History* (1966), offers a brief and provocative survey. A splendid interpretation is M. Hodgson, *The Venture of Islam* (1975). On the development of Islam, see T. Andrae, *Mohammed: The Man and His Faith* (1970), and W. M. Watt, *What Is Islam?* (1968). Good sources for other topics include G. E. Von Grunebaum, *Medieval Islam* (1961); Roman Ghirshman, *Iran from the Earliest Times to the Islamic Conquest* (1961); and Seyyed H. Nasr, *Science and Civilization in Islam* (1968). Ira M. Lapidus, *A History of Islamic Societies* (2002), is a masterful survey. See also M. M. Ahsan, *Social Life Under the Abbasids* (1979); Bernard Lewis, *Race and Slavery in the Middle East* (1990); Lois Beck and Nikki Keddi, eds., *Women in the Muslim World* (1978); and F. Mermiss, *The Veil and the Male Elite: A Feminist Interpretation of Women's Rights in Islam* (1992). Two useful source collections are Eric Schroeder, *Muhammad's People* (1955), with Arabic poetry, and W. M. Watt, trans., *The Faith and Practice of Al-Ghazali* (1953). The Qur'an has also been widely translated. See also, Jonathan P. Berkey, *The Formation of Islam: Religion and Society in the Near East* (2003); Donna Lee Bowen, ed., *Everyday Life in the Muslim Middle East* (2002); and Charles Lindholm, *The Islamic Middle East* (2002).

9

India and Southeast Asia Under the Impact of Islam

The impact of Islam extended to many areas besides the Middle East and north Africa. Some military activity, plus trade and missionary outreach, installed Islam in central Asia, as far as western China. Sub-Saharan Africa was another important case, where trade and missionary endeavor were largely responsible for Islamic success; we turn to the African experience in the next chapter. This chapter deals with two other areas of Islamic impact: India and southeast Asia. Islam provided a key new ingredient in these regions, along with growing levels of world trade. The results persist to the present day.

The force of Islam and growing involvement in the world network did not result in the exact replication of Middle Eastern patterns in these other locations. Africa and southeast Asia, for instance, retained distinctive characteristics. The real challenge is for us to understand how change combined with the patterns of still-separate civilizations during the postclassical period.

Such a combination is even more central to the experience of postclassical India, where Islam provided a new political force and a new religious minority, but in a civilization already well established. Key features of classical India, including the Hinduism of the majority, the caste system, high levels of trade, and regional politics, all continued. Hinduism adjusted somewhat, in order to remain a vital force in the face of Islamic competition. Indian traders also adapted to the growing dominance of Arab commerce in the Indian Ocean. Significant trade and manufacturing survived, and India was a key participant in the world network as the Indian Ocean became the most important center for world commerce.

Developments in southeast Asia partially paralleled those on the Indian subcontinent. This was no accident, for Indian trade and culture left a strong mark on several parts of this extensive region as Indian influence radiated before the arrival of Islam. Hinduism receded in Indonesia, but the Buddhist influence that had spread out from India established deep roots in Burma (present–day Myanmar) and Thailand and on the island of Sri Lanka. Like India, southeast Asia operated under decentralized or regional governments—there was no great empire. Like India, southeast Asia participated actively in Indian Ocean trade, producing spices and other goods for a wide market.

The dynamic impact of Islam began to be felt from the 7th century on. Neither India nor southeast Asia completely fell under Islam's sway, although a minority of Indians converted and several areas in southeast Asia became fervently Muslim—indeed, the largest single Islamic nation in the world today, Indonesia, began its conversion process during this period. The elaboration of a new and rather complex religious map in India and southeast Asia was a major development in the centuries between 600 and 1400. Through Islamic contacts and growing trade links, parts of southeast Asia were drawn more fully into the mainstream of world history than ever before, another specific illustration of civilization's general spread during the centuries after the classical age. Thus, this period holds a significant place in southern Asian history.

■ **KEY QUESTIONS** *There are two main challenges. Why is it obvious that India remained a separate civilization despite growing Muslim impact? How can the vast region of southeast Asia, never unified in a single political or religious unit, best be defined in world history?*

THE DEVELOPMENT OF INDIAN CULTURE

Even during the classical age, India had never functioned as a single political unit. Unity came closest during the Maurya dynasty, but even then it was incomplete. After the Hun invasions, regional political units characteristically prevailed for many centuries. In northern India, a few vigorous states

were formed. One military leader in the north, Harsha, conquered a number of territories early in the 7th century. A Buddhist, Harsha through his conquests helped extend this religion to Tibet. However, although Harsha was an able administrator, he was unable to extend his bureaucracy throughout the empire, and after his death regional units resurfaced. In general, northern India was dotted with small states ruled from capital cities by princes, called *Rajput* when they came from the dominant military caste. The princes maintained few paid officials, rewarding their administrators with land grants instead. This system produced limited governments with few functions. Frequent wars pitted these feeble states against each other, for in conquest the princes sought new lands with which to reward new followers.

The political situation in southern India was somewhat different. This area had not been a center of Indian culture previously. During the classical age, most attention, and the most vigorous political forms, focused on the great river valleys of the north. After about 600 C.E., however, stronger kingdoms arose in southern India, particularly among Tamil-speaking peoples. Less subject to invasion than northern India, this region also maintained more active trading contracts with other societies, especially parts of southeast Asia. Trade, and the merchant wealth it produced, provided the financial basis for the new southern kingdoms. Here, too, regional units prevailed; there was no single southern Indian state. Few of the governments developed tightly centralized systems even within their own boundaries, and local autonomy for landlords and peasant villages remained considerable. A few kingdoms had regional assemblies of landlords, merchants, and even artisans to provide advice; assemblies took place also at the village level. Taxes, which in theory ranged from one-tenth to one-sixth of all agricultural produce, in fact provided only a limited income. Hence, southern kingdoms were also likely to engage in warfare to secure the means to support their armies and administrators. Some of the southern states also maintained navies and occasionally fought with states of southeast Asia, including one empire that developed on several islands in present-day Indonesia.

Ironically, during the very period when regional politics predominated, greater cultural unity emerged than ever before. As in the West, cultural unity, based on religion, spread even amid divided, sometimes chaotic, politics. Buddhism, already a fading religion in India, was virtually eliminated after the 7th century. In the north, Hun invaders disliked the contemplative emphasis of Buddhism, preferring the more varied approach provided by Hinduism. Hinduism also spread to the south with increasing force, after some earlier interest in Buddhism within this region. Hindu temples spread, often administering landed estates and frequently backed by local political leaders. In addition, the caste system gained acceptance in the south; many of the new regional kings saw it as a good means of organizing society and providing greater stability. With the caste system came greater influence from the brahmin or priestly caste, which further encouraged Hinduism. Hindu leaders controlled a flourishing educational system. Schools and colleges were attached to the Hindu temples. Some minority religions, including Buddhism, still survived in India, but before the Muslim challenge the influence of Hinduism became increasingly pervasive.

Hinduism also tended to reach out, more clearly than before, to the ordinary Indian. Although Sanskrit remained the literary language of the brahmins, a substantial literature—not all of it religious—also arose in more popular languages such as Hindi and Tamil. This ensured that India was not unified linguistically, but it increased the service of Hinduism as a cultural bond across linguistic and political boundaries. Various Hindu thinkers worked within the basic tradition of the Vedas. The philosopher Shankara argued that the world is an illusion, or *maya,* which obstructs pure perception. He established a number of centers to promote his teachings. Another philosopher, Ramanuja, emphasized devotion rather than pure intellect as the path to

God. Writing in the 11th century, he inspired devotional groups all over the subcontinent.

Religion guided important artistic activity. A number of temples were constructed, with painted walls depicting religious stories and legends. Around the temples clustered not only schools but also centers for dance and music, and a host of stores and banks. Ornate designs and statues adorned many temple complexes.

Along with the religion-centered culture, characteristic economic and social forms predominated throughout the subcontinent, supported of course by the pervasive caste system. Urban society, although open only to a minority of the whole population, continued to flourish during this period of Indian history. Many merchants worried about their religious lives, often contributing to temples to help cleanse themselves, but their status were higher in India than in early Christian Europe. Indian merchants exchanged goods with southeast Asia and participated in caravan trade with China and the Middle East. Indian cities harbored artisans and small shopkeepers. Some artisans were of a low caste. Leatherworkers, for example, because they handled the skins of dead animals, were members of the untouchable caste, even though their products were essential. Artisans such as carpenters and brick makers enjoyed higher status.

Throughout most of India, the caste system solidified into the form that was to persist into our own century. The four major groups, brahmins, warriors, peasants, and untouchables, had subdivided, in part according to precise occupation, so that more than 3000 castes and jati subcastes had come into existence. Each caste had a governing body to enforce caste rules and make sure no caste member was "polluted" by inappropriate contact with other caste members. Caste organization also provided some mutual assistance to its members. Even more than before, this system in many ways replaced government in regulating relations among Indians.

For those at the bottom of the caste system—the untouchables—life in some ways differed little

This 8th-century temple pavilion at Ellora, dedicated to Siva, was constructed from living rock.

from that of menial slaves or serfs in other societies. For them, there was perhaps a more varied routine and a greater sense of belonging to a partly separate society, but a similar vulnerability to great poverty and harsh treatment by superiors existed. Overall, however, the caste system produced a distinctive society, by differentiating social rules and contacts for all groups and so providing a clear identity at all social levels. Even aside from the sheer number of castes, the system was complex. A class system coexisted within castes, so that in some cases people who were brahmins could be found not serving as priests but as peasants tilling the soil. Inherited status protected their caste membership but did not prevent confusing occupational differentiation and

mobility within a caste. Wealth could vary greatly for families within a single caste.

Family ties continued to serve as a focal point for Indians of all castes. Considerable loving attention was lavished on children, particularly boys. Literacy was fairly widespread in wealthier groups, so that even the children of prosperous farming families could often read and write. Increasingly, Indian parents arranged marriages for their children at an early age, in part to ensure that girls were virgins on their wedding night. Thus, most girls were legally married before they reached puberty, often to men they had never seen. The actual wedding, however, was delayed until after puberty, when the wife could start a family of her own. Despite the arranged marriage

HISTORY DEBATE

THE CASE SYSTEM

Two features of India's caste system, spreading and solidifying during the postclassical period, continue to draw debate. Both reflect the extent to which the system seems strange in modern eyes. First, historians argue over the system's precise definition. Many now argue that the basic castes were not as important, in actually regulating relations among peoples, as the subcastes or *jati*. These units, it is argued, played a greater role in defining who could eat or socialize with whom, and how tasks were divided. Even the untouchables were divided, with sweepers looking down on manure handlers, who in turn despised leatherworkers.

The second debate involves the "livability" of a system that differs from the way most modern people, officially at least, think society should be organized. Some Indian historians, while not defending the system, urge that it allowed different groups some autonomy and cultural identity, through separate caste structure and rituals. This limited outright prejudice, they suggest, or the direct imposition of one group's authority over others that slavery, for example, entailed. Castes are now illegal in India, but caste background still counts, to the advantage of some groups or the disadvantage of others. Figuring out and evaluating the system's past is not just a historical exercise. How do the caste system and slavery compare?

practice, it was assumed that husbands and wives could learn to love each other. Hindu law recommended that couples forgo sex for the first three nights of their marriage so they could get to know each other and form an emotional bond before a physical union was attempted. As wives, women were expected to obey their husbands and were usually confined to household activities. Within the warrior caste, a practice called *sati* developed in these centuries, whereby wives were expected to throw themselves on the funeral pyre of their husbands, confirming in death that the two could have no life apart. This practice was never widespread, and some argue that it developed to protect widows against rape or imprisonment by invaders. It nevertheless indicates some intensification of India's particular version of a patriarchal system.

In practice, however, many Indian women developed a strong role in the family based on their household authority. One Indian poem showed the power of a vigorous wife:

But when she has him [her husband] in her clutches, it's all housework and errands. Fetch a knife to cut this gourd. Get me some fresh fruit. We want wood to boil the greens, and for a fire in the evening. Now paint my feet. Come and massage my back.

THE MUSLIM CHALLENGE IN INDIA

The weakness of Indian political structures after the Hun invasions left the subcontinent a tempting target for subsequent attack. Arab forces approached northwestern India during their great military campaigns following Muhammad's death. Arab and Turkish armies pushed into the Indus valley. The purpose combined religious zeal, as against Hindus regarded as idolaters, and desire for plunder. There was no durable conquest at this point. However, conversions to Islam took place in the northwestern region, which, because of its proximity to the Islamic Middle East, was to be the center of Islam in India proper. This first threat helped convince Hindu leaders that they needed to develop clearer popular ties in their own religion, thus encouraging some of the cultural changes that affected India more generally.

A second wave of Islamic invasion occurred toward the end of the 10th century. Again, the path lay through the valleys of northwestern India. But the Muslim armies this time were composed of Turks, not Arabs. While some Turks had been moving from their original home in central Asia into the Middle East, influencing the caliphate and, as we will see, also attacking the Byzantine Empire, others remained in the East, although they too had converted to Islam from their earlier animist beliefs. A Turkish kingdom in present-day Afghanistan provided the starting point for the invasions into India. A Turkish chieftain named Sabuktigin, a devout Muslim, raided as far as the Ganges valley, attacking many Hindu shrines and statues because they represented false gods.

Once again, invasion did not lead to conquest. But then, in 1192, a new line of Turkish kings in Afghanistan mounted an attack, this time with plans to annex the conquered territory rather than simply raiding it. Turkish forces seized the city of Delhi, in the Ganges valley, and extended their control throughout most of northern India. Again, Hindu shrines and statues were destroyed, and Buddhist centers were also demolished. Tens of thousands of monks were killed at the Buddhist university center in Nalanda, effectively ending Buddhism in India, while Hindu centers were also attacked. A Turkish general established a new regional kingdom, called the Delhi sultanate, that produced additional territory in central and southern India. This Islamic kingdom represented a deliberate imposition of minority rule over the Hindu majority. Most administrators were brought in from the Middle East. Mosques were constructed in many places, changing the face of Indian architecture.

A temple sculpture dating from the 11th century in central India. The sensual aspect of Indian art is evident here.

Under the encouragement of the Delhi sultanate, Islam gained a solid hold on northwestern India—what is now Pakistan. Here, Islam had the appeal of a conquering force. It also won Indian converts from the lower castes, for Islamic belief had no place for the caste system. Elsewhere in India, though, Hinduism largely prevailed, even though divided political units could muster no unity against Islamic armies. Most Indians viewed the Delhi sultans as merely another outside force that could be largely endured. Governed by the regulations of the separate castes, Indians could ignore foreign rule more readily than other people. Later Delhi sultans also were more tolerant. Furthermore, Hinduism had deep roots that were not easily shaken.

Hindus objected to Islam on many grounds. Its rituals conflicted with Hindu practice. Muslims shunned pork, which Hindus often enjoyed, whereas Muslims saw no reason to avoid beef.

UNDERSTANDING CULTURES

COMPARISON AND CONTACT

The results of encounters between different cultures constitute one of the leading topics in world history, and the issues apply to all time periods, not just the modern centuries. Differences between Middle Eastern and Indian traditions can be seen in the treatment of women. Veiling of women in the Middle East contrasted with customs of greater public freedom and a greater emphasis on female sensuality in India. Muslims often commented on these aspects of India, even after the postclassical period. One Arab observer in 1595 noted that Indian women often dealt with political officials, and "chief public transactions fall to the lot of women." Islam did not, in other words, immediately transform gender relations in India. Even women who converted to Islam did not adopt all the gender habits characteristic of the Middle East, and of course the majority of Indians, male and female, remained Hindu. Strong contact between cultures does not necessarily produce blending.

Over time, however, Islamic example had more effects in India, even on many Hindus. Islam was a conquering force in many parts of India, and this might have influenced even Hindus to believe that some aspects of this culture should be copied. Furthermore, both Hinduism and Islam were strongly patriarchal, although in different specific ways. It was not surprising, then, that many Indians, despite their rejection of Islam, welcomed its support of an officially patriarchal system.

Thus, by the late postclassical period and beyond, contact had more effects. Indian Muslim women began to adopt the veil, and gradually their patterns of working alongside men in agricultural tasks were also limited. But Indian women, including Muslims, persisted in wearing colorful dress, in contrast to the dark tones of women's clothing in the Middle East. Even among Hindus, at least in the upper castes, customs of greater isolation gained ground. In the system called *purdah*, women were not permitted to leave their own sections of the home except under careful male supervision. Purdah persisted into the 20th century, when it was attacked by Indian nationalists eager for women's support. The challenge here is obvious: to realize that over time, initial differences can be eroded by the example of another culture. The results often have a profound impact on even very personal aspects of life.

Hindus also saw no virtue in abstaining from alcohol or avoiding religious music or statues created to honor the gods. Turkish attacks on Hindu religious centers obviously added to the clash between the two religions. Finally, Hindus disagreed with the Muslim practice of veiling and secluding women.

The Delhi sultanate did not consistently attack the Hindu faith, although the destruction of leading Hindu shrines during their invasions could not be reversed. (One result was that present-day India has few remaining examples of earlier Hindu monumental architecture.) Islamic rulers, while not viewing Hinduism as embodying as much of the true faith as Christianity or Judaism, did see some religious validity in Hindu spirituality. Hence, the Muslim impulse of religious tolerance was given some sway. Increasing Hindu emphasis on popular devotion to key Hindu gods encouraged intense religious piety among the masses of Hindu faithful, which helped solidify the religion among about 70 percent of the subcontinent's population.

The Delhi sultanate encountered the characteristic problems of any regime seeking control over India, for smaller political units soon reemerged. Southern kingdoms arose by the 1330s, confining the sultanate once more to the north. A new Turkish raid in 1398 weakened the sultanate in the north, and by 1400 India was again politically divided, with the Delhi sultanate merely a regional kingdom.

The first waves of Islamic invasions thus brought no permanent political change to India. Moreover, although they created a new religious minority, of great importance to India's future, they encouraged the hold of Hinduism on the majority and actually stimulated a growing piety among the general population.

SOUTHEAST ASIA

Even before the end of India's classical age, civilization in southeast Asia had developed under considerable stimulus from the subcontinent. Hindu traders brought Indian artistic as well as religious forms to several centers in the islands of Indonesia. Buddhism had already begun to spread overland, to other parts of southeast Asia. Furthermore, the southeast Asian form of Buddhism, with its emphasis on personal devotion and meditation, remained truer to the Buddhist ideal than the Buddhist variants adopted in China and Japan. However, southeast Asia was not purely and simply an extension of Indian culture. Hinduism did not gain a durable hold in the region. Nor did the caste system develop, because among other factors, Buddhists were always hostile to this brahmin-devised structure.

Indian influences did penetrate more widely in southeast Asia between about 650 and 1250, nonetheless. Buddhist missionaries and Indian (particularly Tamil) merchants played a leading role in this movement. Indian emissaries in many places encountered new peoples moving into the region from the north. Their relations with most of these peoples were peaceful, but there were some important wars between southern Indian kingdoms and local states on the Malay Peninsula and the islands of the Indian Ocean.

In one part of the region, tribes of Thai people pushed southward in the 8th century, estab-lishing the Buddhist kingdom of Thailand. Their language was related to Chinese, but they adopted an Indian derived writing system. Another people, the Burmese, set up a kingdom in the 9th century. Yet another people, the Khmers, established a Cambodian empire in 782, which long served as the largest political unit on the southeast Asian mainland. This empire, again largely Buddhist and heavily influenced by India, began to decline around 1200. Buddhist leaders did sponsor the massive temple complex of Angkor Wat in this country. Cambodian kings adapted Hindu ideas about divine sources for political power, using the temple building to consolidate their authority. In the process, religious leadership passed from priests to Buddhist monks.

On the main Indonesian islands of Borneo, Sumatra, and Java, another empire took shape, the Srivijaya. At its height, this empire also controlled the southern part of the Malay Peninsula. The empire was weakened in the 11th century by attacks from a leading kingdom in southern India. During the 13th century, traders from China began to exert influence in the region as well, crippling the power of the local merchant group. By the 14th century, local kingdoms governed most parts of Indonesia.

Thus, diverse and largely regional kingdoms became characteristic of southeast Asia during the centuries of civilization's expansion. In contrast to India, there was never even a brief tradition of political unity. Cultural unity was somewhat greater, although it was affected by competing influences from India and China. Indian artistic forms helped inspire a number of great temples, particularly in Cambodia and Indonesia. Indian literature and legends spread widely. Southeast Asian monarchs, greatly attracted to Indian culture, passed it along to their subjects.

Buddhism was the clearest winner in this process of cultural diffusion. Buddhist emphasis on direct contact with ordinary people, its strong missionary impulse, and its intense focus on religious devotion and ethical behavior gave it a clear edge over Hinduism in southeast Asia. Many

The great temple at Angkor Wat, in Cambodia.

southeast Asians made pilgrimages to Buddhist centers in India and on the island of Sri Lanka, which further confirmed the religion's influence. Many rulers, inspired by Buddhist promptings toward an ethical life as preparation for nirvana, offered humane government to their subjects.

Indian influence also surfaced in the area of economics. Indian merchants, many of them Muslims, encouraged the considerable production of spices and other goods for a wider market, which brought southeast Asia firmly into contact with the central routes of world trade. From this point on, southeast Asian goods played a vital role in world trade. Merchants from the region became increasingly active in east-west trade in the Indian Ocean, quickly adapting advances such as the canpos. The region also sponsored considerable piracy against Chinese, Arab, and even Japanese shippers.

Then, by about 1300, a third influence added new complexity to the southeast Asian mix. By this point, Arab traders had gained increasing significance in southeast Asian trade, displacing many Indian merchants. Southeast Asian spices and teas were brought to the Middle East and even Europe in Arab vessels or through Arab intermediaries. This merchant influence was particularly strong in the Indonesian islands, as well as in the southern part of the Philippine islands and on the Malay Peninsula. The reduction of Indian independence, during the Delhi sultanate, added to the possibility of growing Islamic activity in this region. Then the new missionary spirit that arose in the Middle East with the Sufi movement sent another vigorous signal to southeast Asia. Increasing numbers of Malays, Indonesians, and Filipinos converted to Islam. By 1400, Buddhism had been almost entirely eliminated in these places, while Hinduism was displaced except on a few islands, such as Bali, where it continues to be practiced.

By this point, the diverse religious map of southeast Asia had become established fact. Hinduism was a minor strand, but Buddhism held great importance in most of the regional kingdoms of the mainland. On the islands, however, as on the Malay Peninsula, Islam was becoming dominant. Written forms were similarly diverse. Writing for many of the southeast Asian languages derived from scripts used in India, including Sanskrit. However, Malay writing developed under Arabic influence, whereas in Vietnam writing derived from Chinese ideographs. In essence, many features of southeast Asian culture were derivative, but they came from no one center, despite the special importance of Indian influences. At the same time the area played a vital role in the world network. Its goods were highly valued and its merchants provided increasing competition for the Arabs in the Indian Ocean.

PATHS TO THE PRESENT

As with other parts of Afro-Eurasia, south and southeast Asia experienced enduring religious changes during this period. Buddhism and Islam predominated in different parts of southeast Asia, blending with diverse local cultures. Indonesian Muslims, for example, did not adopt Middle Eastern styles of women's dress as they converted to Islam, reserving the wearing of a veil for strictly religious occasions. Regional identities formed during this period, in places such as Thailand and many parts of Indonesia, have persisted to the present.

The creation of a Muslim minority in India, and the alternation of tolerance and tension in its relationship with the Hindu majority, set an important framework for the future. Political divisions on the subcontinent today, particularly between India and Pakistan, form the latest product of several centuries of jockeying. A great deal of India's artistic heritage, which is today regarded as traditional, stems from this period and its blending of Hindu, Islamic, and Persian styles.

SUGGESTED WEB SITES

On Muslim mysticism in India (the poet Kabir), see http://goto.bilkent.edu.tr/gunes/KabirPoems.htm. On the spread of Islam in south and southeast Asia, see http://users.erols.com/zenithco/indiamus.htm. On Sufism, see http://www.geocities.com/Athens/5738/intro.htm.

SUGGESTED READINGS

For Indian history in this period, see Romila Thapar, *A History of India* (1966), and the relevant chapters of Rhoads Murphy's *History of Asia* (4th ed., 2002). India's wider influence is examined in H. B. Q. Wales, *The Indianization of China and Southeast Asia* (1967). An excellent summary on southeast Asia is D. G. E. Hall, *A History of Southeast Asia* (1981). On Indian Ocean trade patterns, see J. L. Abu-Lughod, *Before European Hegemony: The World System A.D. 1250–1350* (1988). For a good recent work, see Richard M. Eaton, *India's Islamic Traditions* (2003). See also Richard C. Martin, *Approaches to Islam in Religious Studies* (2001); and Bruce B. Lawrence, ed., *Beyond Turk and Hindu: Rethinking Religious Identities in Islamic South Asia* (2000). See also Jackson, *The Delhi Sultanate* (Cambridge, 1999); Osborne, *Southeast Asia: An Illustrated Introductory History* (London, 1997); and Sar Desai, *Southeast Asia Past and Present* (Boulder, 1997).

10 Africa and Islam

During the postclassical period, Africa participated actively in the expansion of civilization and in new contacts with the developing world network. Islam's sweep across north Africa effectively joined this region to the Middle East in a single, if sometimes politically fragmented, civilization. Below the Sahara desert, Islam also gained important influence although, as in southern Asia, it competed with other beliefs. Sub-Saharan Africa remained an area of independent civilization, even as it participated in the radiation of religion, commerce, and politics from Islam. A distinct set of African identities persisted. At the same time, portions of sub-Saharan Africa borrowed more than from Islam than India did, importing not only religion but also Arabic writing. Africa in this sense imitated the more established centers of civilization, as did Russia, Japan, and western Europe during this same postclassical period. Parts of the African economy were more closely tied to the Arab world than was true in India, as Africans sent gold, raw materials, and slaves in return for horses and some luxury craft items.

█ **KEY QUESTIONS** *There are three main challenges in approaching this vital period in African history. The first involves any lingering stereotypes that Africa was uncivilized or that no developments of significance occurred before European penetration. In contrast, African developments rivaled or surpassed those in western Europe at this point. The second challenge involves the need to combine an appreciation of great diversity with some shared features in African civilization. What did (many) Africans have in common, and where do generalizations break down in the face of distinctive local societies? Finally, how does this case of Islamic influence compare with those in India and southeast Asia, and in the Middle East itself? How can the African place in the Islamic world best be defined?*

SUB-SAHARAN AFRICA AND THE WORLD NETWORK

Because of its diverse sources and the vast territory involved, sub-Saharan African history, before the modern centuries, is not easy to grasp. Because most African societies did not develop writing, the formal historical record is sparse, gleaned from accounts of non-African travelers (notably the Muslims), archeological remains, and the detailed stories and family histories that many African peoples transmitted by word of mouth. Technology, although benefiting from the extensive use of iron—introduced below the Sahara by 1000 B.C.E.—lagged behind Asian standards. Animal diseases, including that spread by the dreaded tsetse fly, limited livestock and animal transportation. Although political organization featured monarchies in many parts of Africa—emerging at about the same time and in some of the same ways that monarchies arose in western Europe—there were more African societies without formal politics beyond villages and tribes than was the case in Asia and Europe.

Furthermore, African societies were diverse. The continent, even below the Sahara, is vast. It includes huge deserts such as the southern Sahara and, in the south, the Kalahari; extensive mountains in the east; grasslands below the Sahara and again in the south; and the dense tropical jungle in the center. Large African empires developed, but none ever embraced more than a fraction of the sub-Saharan region. Fragmentation produced considerable diversity. No religion has ever swept over the whole of sub-Saharan Africa, nor has any language provided unified communication.

However, diversity was not absolute. Although there are more than 1000 languages in use in sub-Saharan Africa, they derive from no more than four or five basic tongues, which means that many of the languages are closely related to one another. While political unity was never achieved, there were some recurring polit-

ical trends in many parts of the continent. Although a single religion never flourished, a strong polytheistic leaning resulted in some basic common ground where the African religious experience was concerned. Similarities of this sort, while they cannot be pressed too far, highlight certain tendencies in African civilization— tendencies that reached fuller expression when civilization itself began to spread widely, although not universally, from about the year 600 C.E.

The impetus for this spreading civilization was twofold, involving prior achievements and new connections. As with other early civilizations, several African societies built on foundations already established. Civilization had flourished in the northeast for more than a millennium. Agriculture had been well entrenched in the northern and western regions of sub-Saharan Africa even longer. It had not, by 500 C.E., reached into or through the equatorial jungles, where small hunting-and-gathering groups persisted. Thus, the southern part of the continent, ultimately a fertile agricultural region, remained untouched. But in the north and west, long centuries of agriculture had provided a solid economic base. Ironworking was also well established. Village organization was tightly knit, and the local communities, along with firm ties among kinship or extended family groups, provided a durable political base for further cultural achievements. In some African societies, the stable local units and tight links among family members sufficed to ensure order. Family or lineage bonds were a distinctive feature, and Africans devoted great attention to memorizing elaborate family trees so that relatives could be identified even in fairly distant regions. In many kinship groups, or clans, certain vocations were inherited, such as the work of traders, peasants, political officials, and even slaves. The importance of clans explains the often unstructured quality of African government.

Finally, religion, although varying widely in specific local forms, gave Africans an explanation of the workings of nature, including rites and beliefs to deal with illness and natural disasters, and also a firm sense of their own identity. Each clan had its own sacred animal that expressed a divine spirit and could not be killed by clan members. Because most African religions included both the worship of spirits in nature and a veneration of ancestors, they served a social as well as mystical function.

In sum, the first context for expanding civilization in Africa was the solid foundation formed by an agricultural economy many centuries old and a supportive religious and political culture. Stronger kingdoms, such as Ghana in west Africa, began to emerge as early as 300 C.E. on these bases. The expansion of civilization in Africa started even before the postclassical period.

A crucial development, beginning before the postclassical period but continuing through it, involved the great Bantu migration. Bantu peoples, from west-central Africa, gradually moved south and southeast, spreading agriculture through these parts of the continent. They also brought the use of iron. Most African languages are Bantu in origin, reflecting this huge movement. The word *Bantu* means "many peoples." Civilization areas that emerged in the south in this period, notably Zimbabwe, reflected the Bantu impact, as did later societies.

The second stimulus for the spread of civilization resulted from trading contacts that developed between the 7th and the 10th centuries. New levels of interregional exchange established two principal channels. On Africa's east coast, Islamic sailors from southern Arabia set up urban centers. Trade to and from these centers, across the Indian Ocean, became extensive. Ivory and gold, plus some slaves, were exported to the Middle East, India, and even China, in return for manufactured products including Chinese porcelain. Although this commerce remained largely in non-African hands, the Arab traders settled in the east African cities, intermarried extensively, and provided the foundation for a number of city-states and local kingdoms. They even devel-

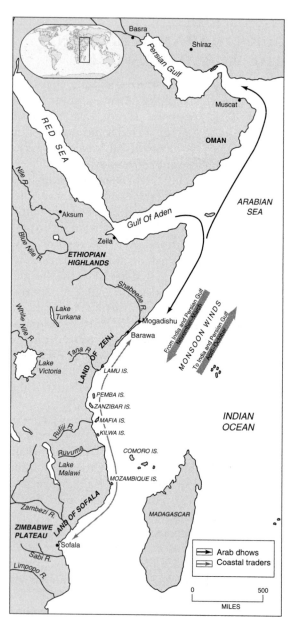

East African Trade Routes

oped a language, Swahili, that combined Arab and African features to promote wider communication. East African cities did not have extensive contacts with the interior, which limited

WORLD PROFILES

SUNDIATA

One of the greatest postclassical kingdoms in west Africa, Mali, was formed when the Malinke people broke away from the state of Ghana in the 13th century. Its leader was Sundiata, a brilliant warrior and statesman. His exploits launched a great oral tradition. The griots, professional oral historians who advised kings and kept their traditions, began their histories of Mali with this "Lion Prince."

> Listen then sons of Mali, children of the black people, listen to my word, for I am going to tell you of Sundiata, the father of the Bright Country, of the savanna land, the ancestor of those who draw the bow, the master of a hundred vanquished kings. . . . He was great among kings, he was perfect among men; he was beloved of God because he was the last of the great conquerors.

Sundiata had a difficult childhood, amid great family feuds. He created a unified state, setting basic rules for Malinke society and outlining the government of Mali. He established groups of freemen who could bear arms, another group of priests, and several classes of artisans, including the historian griots. These divisions were not new, but Sundiata won credit for them. He allowed for regional and ethnic differences but also set up garrisons to keep order in his large kingdom. He worked to protect travelers and punish crime—both important in a society

Mansa Musa.

that depended on secure trade. Sundiata died about 1260, but his successors carried his achievements still further.

their impact in Africa, but they were also a noteworthy development.

More significant was the second trade channel, across the Sahara from Muslim north Africa. Here, caravans traveled, by camel and by foot, on arduous journeys. Although the domestication of camels occurred earlier, widespread African use of camels began about 200 C.E. and revolutionized trading opportunities. By 700, Muslim traders were seeking gold, ivory, salt, and some

slaves from sub-Saharan Africa. They also traded for the cola nut, a stimulant not mentioned in the Qur'an and therefore permitted to the faithful. The wealth that resulted permitted the development of thriving African cities. Timbuktu, in the southern Sahara, was the greatest center, boasting a large military force, a huge treasury, and—in the words of an early European visitor—"many magistrates, learned doctors, and men of religion." The city became an integral part of the Islamic intellectual world. More broadly, west African-Arab interaction stimulated growing trade, the manufacture of cloth and precious metals, and new social and political patterns in a wide stretch of Africa below the Sahara. African merchants expanded their operations through many parts of West Africa. Social divisions began to form, between rich and poor, between soldiers, artisans, and farmers, some of which cut across traditional kinship lines.

Africa was thus part of the Islamic orbit and a growing participant in international trade. It was also one of the first societies to imitate other civilizations, using its trade contacts and selective borrowings from Islam to accelerate aspects of its historical development. The postclassical period saw distinctive characteristics persist in Africa, but also the increasing influence of larger world trends.

THE GREAT KINGDOMS

Not surprisingly, the first great African kingdoms—not counting the states in the upper Nile—arose in the region of the southern Sahara and the grasslands below. This area is called the Sudan (from the Arab word for "black"); in these centuries, however, it stretched all along the southern Sahara rather than the upper Nile area that is now the nation of Sudan. The Sudanese kingdoms exacted some tribute from merchants, which provided considerable wealth without an extensive taxation of the peasant class.

Ghana was the earliest of a series of Sudanic kingdoms. Its origins extended to the classical period, but its clearer development from about 800 related to the growth of cross-Saharan trade and the expansion of salt and gold mining in the region. The kingdom, built around several cities that have since vanished, served as a crossroads between north Africa and the gold and ivory producers of the grassland and forest areas to the south. Kings of Ghana imposed taxes on the trade that crossed their region. According to one Arab

writer, "All pieces of gold that are found in this empire belong to the king." This monopoly carefully protected against the unauthorized production of gold that might flood the market and supplemented the direct tax (also to be paid in gold) levied on every donkey or camel bearing salt. With these resources, the Ghanese king sustained a lavish court, offering banquets to thousands of guests and surrounding himself with luxurious trappings. Ceremony and ritual helped the king express his power; so did the related belief that the king was in some sense divine, descended from and protected by the gods. The features of divine kingship, as it has been called, became common in African political organization during this period and beyond.

Ghana developed a complex relationship with the Islamic world. Its kings hired Arabs to keep records, which helped them develop the bureaucracy necessary for the expansion of the state. Trade with Islamic north Africa was needed not only for tax revenues but also as a source for horses, on which military activities, notably the cavalry, depended (local horse breeding was limited by the presence of the tsetse fly). The cavalry allowed the state to expand into the plains of the Sudan, to exact tribute and acquire slaves. However, these contacts with Islam and a growing dependence on trade also made Ghana vulnerable to nomadic raiders and invasions from states to the north. The kingdom's wealth inevitably drew attention from north Africa, while local Islamic residents may have invited the presence of fellow Muslims. The kingdom of Ghana, always loosely organized through alliances between king and local leaders, lacked the ability to survive this situation. Although its wealth was great, Ghana's defense depended on arrangements with local military groups, rather than professional soldiers. And the kingdom maintained only a rudimentary bureaucracy, understandably focused on tax collection. Weakened by military raids from outside its borders, the kingdom collapsed around 1200.

A number of other kingdoms had already formed in the Sudan region, some of them organized with councils as well as kings. Copper production and textiles flourished in several of these kingdoms, a few of which endured into the 19th century. A number of African trading companies developed, sometimes organized along hereditary lines so that their administration remained within the same extended family across generations. Some of these companies, too, survived into present times. Thriving market centers assumed a major place in the life of west Africa, in portions of contemporary nations such as Nigeria.

The clearest successor state to Ghana, however, emerged during the 13th century. Its regional basis was slightly different from that of Ghana, and its political organization was better developed. It too, however, relied on cavalry, trade, and contact with Islam. The kingdom of Mali was established under the leadership of an able general named Sundiata, who defeated a number of smaller states and ruled for about a quarter century until his death in 1260. Sundiata's state rested on the wealth derived from trade with north Africa, and also on the unusual fertility of the Gambia River valley, where rice and several other crops thrived. Sundiata and his successors were regarded as divine monarchs, similar to the pattern in Ghana, where a ruler's religious authority and magical power were emphasized. They also formed alliances with a variety of local leaders. But Sundiata converted to Islam, partly as a gesture of goodwill toward his north African trading partners. Although he did not force Islam on his subjects, he and his successors employed Islamic bureaucrats and popularized the use of Arabic script. As a religion of the elite, Islam provided a sense of coherence and also skills in law and writing that allowed the development of a more extensive bureaucracy and legal system than had prevailed in Ghana.

The rulers of Mali also accrued great wealth. One successor to Sundiata, Mansa Musa, making a pilgrimage to Mecca in 1334–35, dazzled Egyptians and other Arabs with the gold and ornaments of his entourage. His staff loaded 90 camels with gold dust, each load weighing 300 pounds, to provide spending money for the trip. Several thousand subjects accompanied Mansa Musa on the pilgrimage. He offered substantial gifts to people he met along the way and to the holy cities of Mecca and Medina. Not surprisingly, his reputation spread widely. (Also not surprisingly, he ran out of gold and had to borrow in Egypt; the size of the loan, quickly repaid, threw Egyptian banks into some confusion.) A French map, some decades later, recalled Mansa Musa's name, adding provocatively that "so abundant is the gold that is found in his land that he is the richest and most noble king of all the area." But Mansa Musa was more than a big-spending pilgrim. He organized a pool of many Muslim scholars, from as far away as Egypt, in his capital city; his government engaged in diplomacy, including the exchange of ambassadors, with other north African countries and possibly other even more distant nations.

Mali became one of the great nations of the Islamic world, extending from the Atlantic deep into the interior of the Sudan. Mali emperors promoted active trade and also patronized Islamic learning; Timbuktu served as a major center of Islamic scholarship, where books, it was said, were valued above gold. Regular scholarly exchange connected Timbuktu with centers in Morocco and Egypt, linking West Africa more firmly with the Mediterranean and Islamic world. Laws were strictly enforced, and the Mali empire enjoyed a long period of peace and prosperity. The great trading families extended their commercial skills. An Arab visitor noted, "Neither the man who travels nor he who stays at home has anything to fear from robbers or men of violence."

Mali began to decline, however, by about 1400. Its place was taken by a third great Sudanese kingdom, Songhai, which flourished from the late 15th century to 1591. Songhai, although somewhat smaller than Mali, continued the development of a civil service to supplement the personal authority of the king. This state, too, was Islamic, though again, most of the inhabitants remained true to their polytheistic traditions, and in the freedom granted women, especially in

The spread of Islam in Africa is represented by the great mosque at Jenne on the Niger River in what is now the Republic of Mali. Jenne was a major center of ironworking and trade. Along with Timbuktu, 200 miles to the north, it was also a center of Islamic learning and scholarship.

public, and in other respects, it greatly offended Islamic purists. Rather than depending on alliances with local lords, the kings of Songhai built armies that owed loyalty only to them; some of their soldiers were slaves, the personal possessions of the monarchy. Many new territories were gained by conquest. The kingdom of Songhai collapsed only as a result of new attacks from north Africa, notably from the kingdom of Morocco, and internal rebellion. With its downfall, the great period of the Sudanic kingdoms came to an end, although in fact a variety of new kingdoms formed in subsequent centuries. Basic west African political patterns proved quite durable.

Partly through the example of the Sudanic kingdoms, by the 14th century a number of other states formed in northern and western sub-Saharan Africa. Most were monarchies, with kings claiming the authority and trappings of divine right. Characteristically, such divine claims were balanced by rather weak control over most subjects and by councils of local leaders and townspeople that provided, although informally, something of the same pattern of government existing in the early parliamentary institutions of Europe during the same period. The kingdoms that spread into the forested areas of west Africa, in parts of present-day Nigeria and other states, also benefited from the trading and craft skills of the Sudanic peoples. Particularly in the loosely organized kingdom of Benin, an important artistic tradition developed in woodcarving and metal sculpture,

Bust of a king from Benin, west Africa, center of some of the most imaginative African art. Gold-braided hair and necklace show the man's royal status.

featuring powerful portrayals of divine spirits and human forms alike.

By about 1400, then, much of northern and central Africa south of the Sahara was organized into regional kingdoms, with an especially potent imperial tradition in the Sudan. Most states were not tightly organized. Some were Muslim in leadership, others strictly polytheistic. Boundaries among states were not firmly set, in part because bureaucracies were too small to enforce them, in part because political rule still depended heavily on personal loyalties and alliances. And there were areas, including many active trading centers and artistic cultures, organized on a purely local basis in addition to the city-states of east Africa. The forested regions of west Africa contrasted with the large states of the Sudan, in part because

their geography prevented the travel and operation of any cavalry. These were stateless societies in terms of structures beyond village and family levels. Clearly, however, agriculture and advances in crafts, manufacturing, and trade were spreading ever more widely into the tropical forests, and with this came a tendency toward more formal and effective political administration.

Even more widely, the Bantu migrations continued. As early as 860 C.E., some Bantu farmers had reached territory in what is now the nation of South Africa. Bantus also spread into the rich agricultural plateaus of eastern Africa, in present-day Kenya and Uganda. This was a gradual migration, spurred by recurring land shortages. Until 1500, many of the Bantu settlements were short-lived, as farming problems or conflicts

---

HANDLES FOR AFRICAN HISTORY

Until fairly recently, most Westerners viewed Africa as a land of considerable mystery and backwardness, the "dark continent," and assumed that most of it had little history until the arrival of Europeans. Important research and scholarly work on African history has proved this imperialistic attitude wrong. More recently, some scholars have blasted what they see as consistent efforts to belittle the African past, arguing that the continent's great achievements, beginning with ancient Egypt, need far more emphasis and that Western criteria for measuring a society's success are distorted and narrow.

In between some of these debates, a number of historians seek explanations for some general features of African civilization in the postclassical period and beyond. Comparison can help. One scholar has noted how similar African and western European societies were around 1200. Both imitated more advanced centers in the Mediterranean. Both had fairly loose political organizations, although African kingdoms were larger than their European counterparts; tribal loyalties were important in both regions. Both saw the rapid advance of trade and merchants. Of course, differences exist, particularly in the degree of impact world religions have had and in the extent of writing, but the similarities are revealing. Two hundred years later, the comparison changes shape: Europe was beginning to explore more widely, whereas Africa maintained established patterns to a greater extent. Africa had never emphasized ocean-going activity, in part because (particularly on the Atlantic coast) it did not have a rich network of navigable rivers. Its relations with Islam were smooth, in contrast to Christian Europe, where a dependence on Islam for trade was viewed negatively. Unlike Europe, Africa gained little from new knowledge of Asian technologies. This represents a complex mix of factors, reflecting some African limitations by European standards, but also an absence of some of the problems that beset postclassical Europe. Does a society largely content with its substantial achievements—as African leaders were by 1400—require special explanation?

---

with local hunting groups forced periodic movement. As a result, not many large political units developed until a later point. A few kingdoms arose, often with Bantu overlords ruling a subject local people; two such kingdoms, Rwanda and Burundi, have survived into the 21st century.

One great empire flourished for a time in Zimbabwe. This was a gold-producing region, with links to the trading cities of east Africa. Powerful kings built a huge stone-walled city, the ruins of which fascinated archeologists in later ages. The sheer size of the stone monuments of Zimbabwe rivals the buildings of ancient Egypt and the Mayans. Concepts of divine kingship prevailed in this great state, which at its height around 1300 ruled a vast territory in southeast-

ern Africa. Zimbabwe declined, as mysteriously as it rose, after about 1400. Although unique in its monument-building capacity, it serves as additional evidence of the spread, however uneven, of new political organization across much of Africa.

FEATURES OF AFRICAN CIVILIZATION

African civilization, as it had developed by the 15th century, was characterized by obvious diversity and disunity on the one hand, and common general themes on the other. In politics, the tendency to embrace a divine monarch, but to temper this form of government with some kind of advisory councils, set a clear—although again far from uniform—political pattern. Africans in many regions were acquiring skills in the art of state-building. In the Sudanic kingdoms, increasingly sophisticated forms of organization were devised, and, on the whole, African political development shows a progression much like that of western Europe during the Middle Ages.

Africans were also creating a significant commercial tradition, particularly, of course, on the east coast and in the Sudan. There were no institutional innovations, such as banking networks, but the family-based trading companies had genuine cohesion. Landowning lords emerged in many parts of Africa, and in some cases one tribal group was controlled by an upper class from another tribe; this was true in some areas settled by the Bantu. In general, however, African farmers were freer than their counterparts in western Europe during most of the Middle Ages; there was no manorial system to dispute peasants' control of property. At the same time, slavery was practiced in a number of areas. Many slaves were taken in the frequent wars that occurred during early African history. Some families, however, were enslaved on a hereditary basis. Slaves were used for a variety of tasks, ranging from personal service to mining and soldiering.

The African economy was bounded by limitations on technology. Despite the displays of great wealth in some states, there was less wealth overall than in the civilizations of Asia, and populations were smaller as a result. African farmers established irrigation systems and developed considerable knowledge of a variety of crops. Mining techniques improved steadily, as Africans discovered ways to sink deeper shafts and refine gold more efficiently. By the 15th century, west African miners had produced a total of perhaps 5500 tons of gold, and they produced as much again during the next four centuries. Copper and ironworking also had developed extensively, although overall, by 1400, manufacturing technology (as opposed to artistic creativity) was lagging behind Eurasian

standards, in part because Africans imported fewer technologies from Asia.

African society characteristically featured tight family structures. The links among extended kin, even in different villages, formed one of the key bonds of African society even when political structures, in a more formal sense, were weak. African families, moreover, devoted considerable time to children. Mothers typically carried infants while at work, in contrast to the Western tendency to separate mother and child as early as possible. Women were officially inferior in the African family, and some African groups controlled women's behavior rigorously. In general, however, women had considerable status in not only the family but also public functions such as operating shops in the open market. Their diverse roles in agriculture and commerce stood in contrast to their place in most Asian societies.

Women's public freedom and colorful dress, as we have seen, differed from the Islamic traditions of north Africa and the Middle East. The famous 14th-century Arab traveler, Ibn Battuta, an admirer of African wealth, political power, and piety, was nonetheless shocked by what he saw among women. "With regard to their women, they are not modest in the presence of men, they do not veil themselves in spite of their perseverance in the prayers. . . . The women there have friends and companions among men." Here was another case where contact and even imitation did not erase regional traditions. Although Africans participated in the spread of Islam, and such involvements resulted in real change, they did so in their own way.

By 1400, religious divisions were important in sub-Saharan Africa. Ethiopia maintained its Christianity. Islam had spread to various parts of the Sudan and to the port cities on the Indian Ocean. Islam was not yet a mass religion in Africa, but its hold over a substantial portion of the north and west was already established.

Africans converted to Islam for several reasons, including personal piety and engagement with Islamic intellectual life. Some leaders saw political benefits in Islam, using Muslims for their skills in writing and in bureaucracy. Some leaders, however pious, also maintained older commitments to "divine kingship" to supplement Islamic political principles. Many Africans were attracted to Islam through its role in trade. Some men found benefits in Islam's espousal of polygamy. Some African women valued the protection of property rights in the dowry that was established in Islamic law.

Most Africans, even in the sub-Saharan Islamic states, remained polytheists. As in many other agricultural societies, Africans relied heavily on magical explanations of natural occurrences that they could not otherwise explain. African polytheism was elaborate and comprehensive in its scope, which helps account for its durability even when competing against monotheistic religions such as Islam. It involved belief in a supreme being, who was responsible for creating the universe and a corresponding set of beliefs, and subsidiary gods and spirits, good and evil, who actually managed daily affairs such as crops and wars. These lesser gods, who had the greatest influence on people's lives, received the most attention. Religious rituals, organized by medicine men, played an important role in treating illness. At the same time, Africans had a certain sense of skepticism; too much religious fervor was regarded with suspicion. A Nigerian proverb held that when a person displayed excessive religious belief, "people can tell him the wood he is made of"—that is, they can remind him that he is only mortal.

Religion played a significant role in directing African artistic achievements. Work in wood, ivory, and terra-cotta had advanced steadily by 1400, particularly in west Africa. Many masks and statues had religious significance and were used in dances of worship and other ceremonies. African art emphasized strong, stark portrayals, without intricate detail. Artists had an important place in urban society, along with most other artisans. In certain areas, such as the Bantu regions, African art displayed a particular interest in the circle, rather than in other shapes, as the basic geometric unit for art and architecture. Many homes and great temples—in Zimbabwe, for instance—were built in a circular form. Even today, many African children readily draw perfect circles, in contrast to the great reliance on squares and angles characteristic of European and Asian education.

African development was proceeding actively by 1400. New kingdoms endured for many centuries, as did artistic, religious, and family traditions. European contacts altered the face of some regions in Africa increasingly after about 1500, but without the overwhelming disruption of an entire society that occurred in the Americas. Among other things, Africans had maintained sufficient ties with other cultures to develop adequate immunity to some of the great diseases of Europe and Asia; hence, the population was not decimated through plagues, as happened among the native peoples of the Americas. The arrival of Europeans by the late 15th century thus represents a partial break in African history. However, European explorers and settlers interacted with a highly developed African society, and for many centuries basic trends established during the formative period of civilization south of the Sahara continued.

PATHS TO THE PRESENT

Sub-Saharan Africa did not establish a single "great tradition," in contrast to key civilizations in Asia and Europe. Most notably, it adapted world religions from other regions, rather than establishing its own. This complicates African legacies as they affect the contemporary world. Furthermore, European imperialism in modern Africa overran many African institutions, including political boundaries, disrupting Africans' connection with their past.

Still, African developments during the post-classical period have continuing impact. They provided monuments with which contemporary Africans can identify—hence the use of older names such as *Ghana* and *Mali* for modern nations. They provided enduring political themes. Many observers note an ongoing African penchant for the leadership of "big men" in government and believe it may link to older ideas and symbols associated with divine kingship. The creative art forms pioneered in west Africa survive in African art today and have influenced artistic styles in other places as well, including Europe and North America. Patriarchal ideas about gender persist, though their complexity resists facile description. Some African feminists praise the strong role some women have achieved in traditional Africa, while also believing in validity of the protections provided by solid community life and family ties. Some male-dominated African courts, in places such as Zimbabwe, have recently evoked African traditions which gave men the ownership of all family property—which includes women and children. Finally, Islam continues to play a vigorous role in sub-Saharan African culture, building from the basis established in the postclassical centuries.

SUGGESTED WEB SITES

On medieval African kingdoms, see http://score.rims.k12.ca.us/score_lessons/ medieval_african_kingdoms/; on Africa during the Middle Ages, see http://www.medieval-life.net/ africa.htm; on African heritage, see http:// whc.unesco.org/exhibits/afr_rev/toc.htm.

SUGGESTED READINGS

On sub-Saharan Africa, several source collections are interesting reading: G. S. P. Freeman-Greenville, *The East African Coast: Select Documents from the First to the Earlier Nineteenth Century* (1962); D. T. Niane, *Sundiata: An Epic of Old Mali* (1986); and Ross Dunn, *Adventures of Ibn Battuta, A Muslim Traveler of the Fourteenth Century* (1986). Recent works include Graham Connah, *African Civilizations: An Archaeological Perspective* (2001); Philip Curtin et al., *African History from Earliest Times to Independence* (1995). See also B. Davidson, *Africa in History* (1974); J. D. Fage, *Africa Discovers Her Past* (1970); Richard Olaniyan, *African History and Culture* (1982); R. S. Smith, *Warfare and Diplomacy in Pre-Colonial West Africa* (1969); J. D. Fage, *A History of West Africa* (1969); N. Leutzion and Hopkins, eds., *Ancient Ghana* (1981); Anne Hilton, *The Kingdom of the Kongo* (1985); David Birmingham and Phyllis Martin, *History of Central Africa*, 2 vols. (1983); Derek Nurse and Thomas Spear, *The Swahili: Reconstructing the History and Language of an African Society* (1985); and J. Middleton, *The World of the Swahili and African Mercantile Civilization* (1992). On women, refer to N. Hafkin and E. Bay, *Women in Africa* (1976), and H. Loth, *Women in Ancient Africa* (1992). See also A. H. M. Jones and Elizabeth Monroe, *A History of Ethiopia* (1955), and two studies by one of the pioneers in using new sources to reexamine early African history, J. Vansina, *The Children of Woot: A History of the Kuba People* (1978), and *Art History in Africa* (1984). On trade patterns, see Richard W. Bulliet, *The Camel and the Wheel* (1975). An interesting recent work is *The Civilizations of Africa: A History to 1800* (2002). See also Eva Evers Rosander, ed., *African Islam and Islam in Africa* (1997); Timothy Insoll, *The Archeology of Islam in sub-Saharan Africa* (2002); and Ahmend S. Bangura, *Islam and the West African Novel* (2000).

11

East European Civilization: Byzantium and Russia

Important civilizations expanded in Europe during the postclassical period. They linked actively with the world trade network, while interacting with Islam even as they developed different world religions. Eastern Europe initially led the way. The existence, in Byzantium, of a successor empire to Rome, in the northeastern Mediterranean, served as a beacon to emerging kingdoms in eastern Europe, particularly among many Slavic groups.

Two major Christian zones arose in Europe during the postclassical centuries. Each represented a distinctive version of that faith, symbolized by the formal split between the Eastern Orthodox and Western Catholic churches in the 11th century. Similar beliefs, some shared memories of classical Greece and Rome, and their geographical position as neighbors produced some common features in east and west European civilizations. On the whole, however, the two societies took different forms, and the centuries after 500 saw these differences develop and then solidify.

Indeed, Byzantium had much the same kind of outreach that India and China demonstrated during the postclassical period, as it helped shape other parts of eastern Europe in establishing basic cultural and political patterns. Byzantium, at its height, approximated the economic and political sophistication of the Asian civilizations, as evidenced by its great capital city, Constantinople. Like its purely Asian counterparts, Byzantium built on classical foundations while responding to new religious fervor. East European civilization, initially centered in the Byzantine Empire, had the closest contacts with the traditions of the classical Mediterranean world. As a result, for many centuries this east European civilization greatly surpassed the West in political sophistication, culture, and economic vitality. Like its neighbor to the west, however, it had one important feature: a strong desire to expand, particularly through the Christian religion. Blocked from expansion to the east and south by the rise of the Islamic caliphate, the

Byzantine emperors and church patriarchs turned their eyes to the northern peoples. The spread of Orthodox Christianity in eastern Europe rivaled that of Roman Catholicism in the West, with key contacts running south to north in each case.

■ **KEY QUESTIONS** *This chapter presents east European society as a different civilization from that of western Europe, despite the spread of Christianity in both regions. Is this framework more accurate than dealing with a single Christian Europe? What were the main differences between east and west? (Answering this question involves this chapter and the next.) How did each society use its Greco-Roman heritage? Another comparison is useful: how did imitation in eastern Europe stack up against African imitation of the Middle East (or Japanese use of Chinese models)? What was copied, and what was not? Finally, what were the causes and results of east European decline toward the end of the postclassical period?*

THE BYZANTINE PHASE

The development of the Byzantine Empire effectively began in the 4th century C.E. It was at this point that the Roman Empire established its eastern capital in Constantinople, which quickly became the most vigorous center of the otherwise fading empire. The emperor Constantine ordered the construction of many elegant buildings, including Christian churches, in his new city, which was built on the foundations of a previously modest town called Byzantium. Soon, separate eastern emperors ruled from this city, even before the western portion of the empire fell to Germanic invaders. Constantinople was responsible for the Balkan Peninsula, the northern Middle East, the Mediterranean coast, and north Africa. Although for several centuries Latin served as the court language of the Eastern empire, Greek was the common tongue and, after the emperor Justinian, it became the official lan-

guage as well. Indeed, in the eyes of Easterners, Latin became an inferior, barbaric means of communication. Knowledge of Greek enabled educated people in the Eastern empire to read the philosophical and literary classics of ancient Athens and the Hellenistic culture.

As the Eastern empire took shape, Christianity also began its split between East and West. In the West, the Roman pope controlled basic church organization. But there was no comparable leader in the Eastern church. The patriarch, or bishop, of Constantinople held top prestige, but there were three other patriarchs in the East, none of whom had political control over the church. For several centuries, the Eastern church in principle acknowledged the authority of the pope, but in practice papal directives had no hold over the Byzantine church. Rather, the Eastern emperors regulated church organization, creating a pattern of state control over church structure quite different from the tradition that developed in the West, where the church insisted, although not always successfully, on its independence. Disputes over doctrine, including such issues as the recipe used to make bread for the *eucharist,* the sacramental celebration of Christ's sacrifice in the mass, further divided the two churches. Even the two churches' monastic movements differed, following separate rules.

The early history of the Eastern empire, which came to be known as *Byzantine* after the capital city's name, was marked by the constant threat of invasion. The Eastern emperors vanquished Sassanid Persian and Germanic attacks. Early emperors developed a solid military base, recruiting local soldiers in addition to hiring some mercenaries. Upper-class Greeks, recapturing their lapsed military tradition, provided a series of able generals. The Emperor Justinian tried, of course, to regain Roman territories in western Europe and north Africa, but despite brief successes, his effort left the Eastern empire exhausted and financially drained. The empire was successful, however, in expanding a bit to the north. A major fort in the Crimea, for example,

WORLD PROFILES

THE EMPEROR JUSTINIAN
(527–565 C.E.)

The Emperor Justinian attempted to revive the Roman Empire; he achieved considerable although short-term success. He also served, somewhat unintentionally, as a founding figure in the Byzantine Empire that long survived. Justinian and his generals briefly succeeded in regaining Roman territories in western Europe and north Africa. The law code compiled during his reign assembled and reconciled the laws and legal precedents of the later Roman Empire, thus preserving and clarifying Roman law for all of Europe. Justinian also oversaw the construction of Saint Sophia, the great church of Constantinople that influenced Byzantine and Islamic architecture for centuries. Despite his desire to restore Roman culture, it is interesting to note the revealing differences between his image in art and the more traditional portrayal of the Roman Caesars (see Chapter 6). In the mosaic shown here, Justinian's costume, and the surrounding group of church and court officials, indicated the unity of the Byzantine state and the Orthodox church, as the emperor is portrayed as both king and priest. How does this depiction compare with the Roman political tradition?

This mosaic of Justinian is from San Vitale in Ravenna, Italy. Ravenna was one of the many cities Justinian recaptured in western Europe, a city that also served at times as the capital of the Western empire.

north of the Black Sea, helped prevent Germanic invasions. Justinian's monumental law code, assembling and reconciling the law and legal precedents of the later Roman Empire, was of vital service in preserving and clarifying Roman law for both eastern and western Europe. However, Justinian's ideas on territorial expansion were less fortunate. He was a somber personality, autocratic by nature, and prone to grandiose conceptions. A contemporary historian named Procopius, no friend of the emperor, described him as "at once villainous and amenable; as people say colloquially, a moron. He was never truthful with anyone, but always guileful in what he said and did, yet easily hoodwinked by any who wanted to deceive him." The emperor was also heavily influenced by his wife, Theodora, of humble origin but willful and eager for power. Justinian, urged on by Theodora, contended successfully with massive popular unrest at one point by putting 30,000 rebels to death.

Later emperors were eager to consolidate the Eastern territories alone, recognizing that grander visions were unrealistic. The Persians were defeated early in the 7th century, and the newer threat, from the Arabs, was also averted, although not without the loss of most of the Mediterranean portions of the empire south of Constantinople. Arab armies besieged the capital city, but they were repelled in part through the use of a flammable weapon called "Greek fire," a mixture of petroleum, quicklime, and sulfur. Greek fire was shot through long copper tubes and could, among other things, burn enemy ships. The result of these battles was an empire about half the size of the previous eastern half of the Roman Empire, united around its Greek and Balkan populations. Once more, carefully organized military recruitment served the embattled empire well, because strong army officers were often able to control weak emperors. After a final invasion attempt, in 718 C.E., the Arabs never seriously threatened Constantinople again.

Soon after this, the Byzantine Empire began to seek new territories and cultural allies in the vast stretches of eastern Europe. The attractions of Hellenistic culture remained strong. Many regional rulers in southeastern Europe, such as the kings of Bulgaria, admired its accomplishments and often were educated at Constantinople. They were not easy neighbors, however, sometimes seeking territory at the empire's expense and, during the many disputes over legitimate ascendancy to the Byzantine throne, occasionally claiming imperial rule directly. A Bulgarian king in the 10th century took the title of *tsar*, a Slavic version of "caesar." However, diplomacy, intermarriage, and, above all, war eroded regional kingdoms such as Bulgaria. In the 11th century, the Byzantine emperor Basil II, known appropriately enough as Bulgaroktonos, or slayer of the Bulgarians, used the empire's wealth to bribe many Bulgarian nobles and generals. He defeated the Bulgarian army in 1014 and blinded as many as 15,000 captive soldiers—the sight of whom later brought on the Bulgarian king's death. Thus, Bulgaria became part of the empire, its aristocracy settling in Constantinople and merging with the leading Greek families.

Even more important than Byzantine expansion into the Balkans—an area stretching between the present-day nations of Slovenia in the west and Bulgaria and Romania in the east—was the extension of Eastern, or Orthodox, Christianity to these regions and beyond. A major missionary effort was mounted to convert the Slavic and other peoples in the Balkans and points north to Eastern, or Orthodox, Christianity. In 864, the government sent the missionaries Cyril and Methodius to the territory that is now the Czech Republic and Slovakia. The conversion attempt failed in this region, where Roman Catholic missionaries were more successful. But the Byzantine missionaries did pull back into the Balkans and southern Russia, where their ability to speak the Slavic language greatly aided their efforts. They devised a written script for this language, derived from Greek letters; to this day, the Slavic alphabet is known as *Cyrillic*.

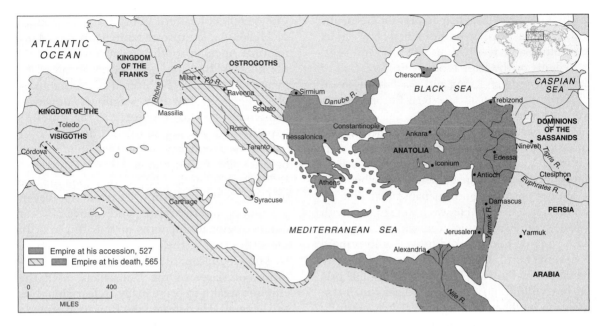

Empire at his accession, 527
Empire at his death, 565

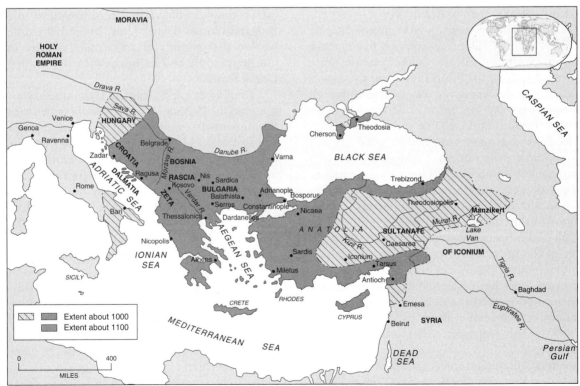

Extent about 1000
Extent about 1100

The Byzantine Empire and Its Decline

Use of "Greek fire" by a 9th-century Byzantine fleet against an invader.

The Byzantine Empire entered a particularly stable period during the 9th and 10th centuries under a family dynasty from Macedonia. This dynasty managed to avoid the quarrels over succession that had beset earlier ruling families. The result was growing prosperity as well as solid political rule. The luxury of the court and its buildings steadily increased. Elaborate ceremonies and rich imperial processions created a magnificence designed to dazzle the empire's subjects. The Macedonian dynasty also extended the empire's territories in central Asia and the Balkans. Substantial trade with Asia developed, along with a thriving production of silk. Constantinople, in the northeastern corner of the Mediterranean and at the entrance to the Black Sea, was an ideal location for trade, both east to west and south to north. The empire became the hub of a new trade northward, through Russia to Scandinavia. Not only silks but also other luxury products such as gold and jewelry gave the empire a favorable trading position with less sophisticated lands. Briefly, at the end of the 10th century, the Byzantine emperor may have been the most powerful single monarch on earth, with a capital city whose rich buildings and abundant popular entertainments awed visitors from western Europe.

It was at the end of this vigorous period that Byzantium broke fully with Western Catholicism.

There had been no serious contact between the two branches of Christianity for several centuries, but neither side had cared to make a definitive statement on this fact. In 1054, however, an ambitious patriarch in Constantinople raised a host of old disputes, including the quarrel over what kind of bread to use for mass. He also attacked the Roman Catholic practice of insisting on celibacy for its priests; Eastern Orthodox priests could marry. Delegations of the two churches discussed the disputes, but this led only to renewed bitterness. The Roman pope finally excommunicated the patriarch and his followers; the patriarch, in turn, excommunicated all Roman Catholics. Thus, the split between the Roman Catholic Church and Eastern Orthodoxy, which came to include several Orthodox churches—the Greek, the Russian, and the Serbian, among others—became formal; it has endured to this day. The schism was not, despite the drama, a sudden or total break. But there was growing estrangement between the two branches of Christianity.

Shortly thereafter, the Byzantine Empire entered a long period of decline. Turkish invaders began to attack the eastern borders, having already gained increasing influence in the Islamic caliphate. In the later 11th century, Turkish troops seized almost all the Asiatic provinces of

Saint Sophia, the great church in Constantinople built under Justinian. It was converted to a mosque by the Turks after their successful conquest. At that point, the minarets were added.

the empire, thus cutting off the most prosperous sources of tax revenue as well as the territories that had supplied most of the empire's food. The empire eked by for another four centuries, but its doom was virtually sealed. At one point, a force of crusaders from Italy and other west European territories even captured Constantinople, on the pretext that they were seeking reconquest of the Holy Land. This fourth crusade, in 1204, destroyed three-quarters of the city and also furthered a process by which Western, particularly Italian, merchants came to dominate trade with the Middle East, reinforcing the economic decline of Byzantium. Then a new group of Turks, the Ottomans, invaded, closing in on Constantinople by the early 15th century. The

Turks finally laid siege to the city in 1453, using the largest cannon ever constructed up until that point. Byzantine efforts to obtain help from western Europe failed, because the Western and Eastern churches could not agree on religious terms. The city fell, becoming the capital of a new Ottoman Empire. The great cathedral built by Justinian, St. Sophia, was converted to a magnificent Islamic mosque. As the Turks took control of the final remnants of the empire in the Balkans, in the eight years after 1453, the long history of Byzantium finally closed.

Elements of its heritage, however, lived on. If Byzantium achieved nothing else, its contribution to forming a new civilization among many of the Slavic peoples of eastern Europe alone justifies its place in history. With the decline and fall of the Byzantine Empire, the focus of east European civilization passed northward, particularly to Russia.

THE EARLY RUSSIAN PHASE: KIEVAN RUS'

Slavic peoples had moved into the sweeping plains of Russia and eastern Europe during the time of the Roman Empire. They were already familiar with the use of iron, and they extended agriculture in the rich soils of what is now western Russia. Their political organization long rested in family tribes and villages; they maintained a polytheistic religion with gods for the sun, thunder, wind, and fire. Gradually, some loose regional kingdoms formed among the Slavs.

During the 6th and 7th centuries, traders from Scandinavia began to journey to the Slavic lands, moving along the great rivers of western Russia, particularly the Dnieper. Through this route they were able to reach the Byzantine Empire, and a flourishing trade developed between Scandinavia and Constantinople. The Scandinavian traders, who were militarily superior to the Slavs, gradually established some governments along their trade route. A monarchy emerged, and according to legend, Rurik, a native of Denmark, became the first king of Russia, ascending to the throne around 855. This kingdom soon established its center in the city of Kiev, which remained the capital of Russia until the 12th century. Kievan Rus' centered in what is now the Ukraine, but its contacts affected Russia proper as well. It was the Scandinavian traders, indeed, who coined the term *Russia*—possibly from a Greek word for "red," referring to the hair color of many of the northern people. The Scandinavians gradually mingled with the larger Slavic population.

Contacts between Kievan Russia and Byzantium extended steadily. Russia became one of the several societies during the period that freely imitated Byzantine civilization. Kiev, because of its central location, became a prosperous trading cen-

ter, channeling goods, from the Muslim lands as well as from Byzantium, that had first passed through Constantinople. Many Russians visited Constantinople. These exchanges led to a growing knowledge of Christianity. King Vladimir I (980–1015) finally took the step of converting to Christianity, not only in his own name but in that of all his people. Vladimir was eager to avoid the influence of Roman Catholicism, because he feared papal control as being competitive with his own power; he was also influenced by rivalries with his neighbor, the king of Poland, who had recently converted to Catholicism. In addition, Russian awe at the splendor of religious services in

The Cathedral of St. Dmitry was built from 1194–1197, during the reign of Prince Vsevolod III. Its famous white stone carvings celebrate the myths and heroes of many cultures as well as the beauty of the biblical God's creation through the portrayal of numerous plants and animals.

Constantinople may have played a role. Vladimir certainly wanted the link to the Byzantine Empire. Rebuffed when he asked to marry the emperor's daughter, he conquered Byzantine territory in the Crimea, promising to give it back if he could marry the princess. And the court obliged. Once converted to Christianity, Vladimir proceeded to organize mass baptisms for his subjects, forcing conversions by military pressure when necessary. Remnants of the old religion were incorporated into Russian Orthodoxy, as when gods of nature were made into Christian saints.

An early Russian chronicle described the conversion of Vladimir and his subjects to Christianity as follows:

> For at this time the Russes were ignorant pagans. The devil rejoiced thereat, for he did not know that his ruin was approaching. He was so eager to destroy the Christian people, yet he was expelled by the true cross even from these very lands. . . . Vladimir was visited by Bulgars of the Mohammedan faith. . . . [He] listened to them for he was fond of women and indulgence, regarding which he heard with pleasure. But . . . abstinence from pork and wine were disagreeable to him. "Drinking," said he, "is the joy of the Russes. We cannot exist without that pleasure." [Russian envoys sent to Constantinople] were astonished [by the beauty of the churches and the chanting], and in their wonder praised the Greek ceremonial. . . .
>
> [Later, Vladimir was suffering from blindness; a Byzantine bishop baptized him] and as the bishop laid his hand upon him, he straightway recovered his sight. Upon experiencing this miraculous cure, Vladimir glorified God, saying, "I have now perceived the one true God." When his followers beheld this miracle, many of them were also baptized. Thereafter Vladimir sent heralds throughout the whole city to proclaim that if any inhabitant, rich or poor, did not betake himself to the river [for mass baptism]

> he would risk the Prince's displeasure. When the people heard these words, they wept for joy and exclaimed in their enthusiasm, "If this were not good, the Prince and his nobles would not have accepted it." . . . There was joy in heaven and upon earth to behold so many souls saved. But the devil groaned, lamenting, "Woe is me. How am I driven out hence . . . my reign in these regions is at an end."

By this point, Kievan Russia was the largest state in Europe, although it remained loosely organized. Rurik's descendants tried to avoid damaging fights over succession to the throne. The Russian kings were able to issue a formal law code, borrowed in part from Byzantium; this code among other things reduced the severity of traditional punishments in Russia and replaced personal vendettas with state-run courts.

The Kievan kingdom began to decline from about 1100 on. Rival princes established their own regional governments. Invaders from Asia whittled away at Russian territory. The eclipse of Byzantium reduced Russia's wealth, for the kingdom had always depended heavily on the greater prosperity and sophisticated manufacturing of its southern neighbor. A new kingdom was briefly established around a city near present-day Moscow, but by 1200, Russia was weak and disunited. The final blow, in this stage of Russian history, came in 1236, when a large force of Mongols from central Asia moved through Russia, hoping to add not only this country but also the whole of Europe to their growing empire. The Mongols, or *Tatars* as they are called in Russian history, easily captured the major Russian cities and moved into other parts of eastern Europe, including Poland, ending their invasions only because of political difficulties in their own homeland. For more than two centuries, Russia remained under Tatar control, although regional differences increased as both the Baltic peoples and Ukrainians began to emancipate themselves from Mongol-dominated Russia proper.

HISTORY DEBATE

A RUSSIAN CIVILIZATION?

Russia in the postclassical period was just beginning to shape an identity. It was not, by itself, a major player in world history. Many historians treat Russia as a part—often, a minor part—of Europe as a whole. Certainly Russia's distinctive features, compared to other parts of Europe, have changed over time. In the postclassical period, differences in religious and political styles, and trade routes, predominated. East European art, though similar in Christian subject matter, was also different. Later, social differences in distinguishing Europe east and west loomed larger, along with politics. Today, just to add a final complication, many Russians (though not all) hope to become more Western, and earlier distinctions may fade. Decisions about characterizing Russia have never been easy. This is not a self-evident case of civilization coherence, unlike that represented by China.

Discussions about Russia, finally, spill over to neighboring parts of east central Europe, where patterns have sometimes resembled those in Russia, sometimes more those of the West. Without much doubt, the boundary between eastern and western Europe has changed with time—the past 15 years included.

EAST EUROPEAN POLITICAL INSTITUTIONS

The postclassical period was a formative one for what proved to be a durable east European civilization, particularly in Russia. Even the era of Mongol rule did not displace basic characteristics established in Russia in part through Byzantine influence, including, of course, Orthodox Christianity. Obviously, much was yet to happen in the development of east European civilization, as Russia came into its own again in the late 1400s. Furthermore, as in other cases of cultural diffusion during the postclassical period, the great influence Byzantium exerted on Russia did not result in complete assimilation. Nevertheless, especially in politics and culture, some customs and traditions dating from Byzantine and early Russian history still echo in east European civilization to the present day.

The Byzantine and early Russian political system emphasized authoritarian rule under an emperor or king. A key ingredient of this author-itarianism involved the state's control over the Orthodox churches. Unlike the West, where the church remained partly separate from the state, and unlike the Muslim lands, where the ulema maintained separate religious institutions, east European rulers expected to be able to regulate church organization and even intervene in doctrinal disputes. This did not lessen the intense piety of Orthodox Christianity, but it unquestionably enhanced the power of the state.

In Byzantium, that power was also exemplified by the elaborate ceremonies and luxury of the imperial court. The functions of government were also extensive. As a state almost constantly at war, the Byzantine Empire naturally stressed strong military organization and recruitment. It also attended to economic affairs. The state directly operated an immense silk factory and was active in regulating trade. An elaborate bureaucracy supported the various state functions. Its efficiency was sometimes questionable, as complex deals had to be struck to conduct new policies or even to make simple arrangements. In the

English language, the term *byzantine* came to suggest a pattern of bargaining and bribing rather than straightforward procedures.

The early Russian monarchy, ruling over a less prosperous area, could not rival Byzantine splendor or the functions that the imperial government maintained. Yet Russian rulers, too, were attracted to luxurious ceremonies and to the idea, if not yet the reality, that the state should have widespread duties and a sweeping range of activity. The Russian bureaucracy remained small, as regional rulers owing allegiance to the king performed most administrative duties, but some features of Byzantine bureaucratic procedures later surfaced in Russia.

Russian authoritarianism was more directly enhanced by the Byzantine example through a sense of special mission. Byzantine rulers understandably claimed their imperial mantle as the heritage of the great Roman Empire. Early Russian kings acknowledged this, calling the Byzantine ruler tsar, or caesar. But when Byzantium fell, and when the Russian monarchy extricated itself from Tatar rule after 1450, Russian rulers took on the title tsar for themselves and claimed a new sense of imperial mission.

EAST EUROPEAN RELIGION AND CULTURE

The dominant feature of east European culture, in this early period, was of course Orthodox Christianity—the Greek Orthodox church established under the patriarch of Constantinople and the Russian and other Slavic Orthodox churches formed as a result of missionary efforts and state-led conversions.

Organizationally, the Orthodox churches, under some direction by the state, established bishoprics, and they assigned priests to conduct worship and maintain the faith. Many early Russian bishops were appointed by the patriarch in Constantinople, but the Russian church acquired increasing independence. Leading bishops were

characteristically appointed by the king or a regional prince; this was a chief mechanism of state control even though the bishops then maintained considerable powers through appointments and the administration of church property and church law in their own right.

Orthodox Christianity conveyed a vivid sense of the power of God. A large number of saints, holy men and women whom the church recognized for their religious example, also commanded the attention of the faithful, becoming objects of prayer and veneration. Orthodox Christianity emphasized the importance of ritual. Churches were usually ornate, filled with the pungent smell of incense. Icons—pictures of religious figures, including the saints—helped direct religious devotion. Some Orthodox leaders attacked the use of icons, fearing that they would become religious objects in and of themselves, but their creation and use persisted.

In addition to ritual and the adoration of holy figures, Orthodox religion stressed Christian morality and charity toward the poor and unfortunate. Rulers as well as ordinary people were encouraged to behave ethically. Traditional practices, such as polygamy among the early Russians, gradually yielded to the Christian family ethic, which held that a man should take only one wife. Almsgiving to the poor and aid to institutions that comforted the sick received great emphasis, in Kiev as well as in Constantinople. Good works of this sort were seen as a vital component of faith and worship. The strong tradition of personal almsgiving as a means of gaining God's grace actually delayed the development of more formal charitable and welfare organizations in imperial Russia.

Orthodox Christianity did not encourage an elaborate theology—that is, an intricate examination of the nature of God and the universe. Even in Byzantium, despite the accessibility of Greek philosophical texts, no extensive tradition of rational speculation or scientific inquiry developed. The importance of faith and good works seemed to preclude this kind of activity. Certainly

Interior of Saint Sophia, in the domed style characteristic of Eastern Orthodox churches and cathedrals. Calligraphy and other details show the church's conversion to a mosque.

in Russia, which remained intellectually more backward than its Byzantine exemplar, most religious writing continued to be strictly devotional, full of praises to the saints and invocations of the power of God. Disasters, according to Russian writers, came as just expressions of the wrath of God against the wickedness of humanity; success in war involved the aid of God and the saints, in the name jointly of Russia and the Orthodox faith. Beliefs of this sort were common in western Europe as well as in the east European zone, but the absence of other kinds of philosophical and scientific inquiry proved to be a distinctively Eastern trait.

The special cultural attributes of Eastern Orthodoxy showed clearly in the monastic move-ment, both in the Byzantine Empire and Kievan Russia. Monasteries received large grants of property from charitable donors. Some monks, to be sure, maintained an existence as hermits, an Eastern tradition of mortification of the flesh that was not so widely adopted in the West. But most monks lived in congregations, under rules established by St. Basil of Cappadocia in the 4th century. Orthodox monks lived their lives performing useful works, presiding over hospitals, orphanages, and homes for the aged, and administering extensive charity to the poor. Unlike Western monks, they did not devote much attention to intellectual activities, seeing a life of zealous faith and good works as sufficient service to God.

The spread of Christianity to Russia and the development of the Cyrillic alphabet facilitated the creation of Russian literature. A strong tradition of oral history existed already, although many sagas were not recorded until later. Early Russian literature consisted primarily of chronicles by members of the clergy, who sought to record the histories of their region and what they perceived as God's work in the world. The first of these narratives dates from the 12th century. Some secular poetry also described wars and the activities of the princes.

Byzantine art and architecture, brought to Russia along with Christianity, established a rich decorative tradition. Orthodox churches were typically built in the form of a cross, surmounted by a dome. Many early Russian churches were wooden and have not survived, but some stone buildings were also constructed. For decoration, the Byzantines and early Russians used elaborate mosaics, depicting religious figures and scenes from the lives of the saints. Some paintings were created, particularly in the form of frescoes (wall paintings), and there were abundant icons, usually picturing the heads of saints. Following the Byzantine example, a Russian tradition of icon painting arose in Kiev, along with some fine work in illuminated manuscripts; this technique featured attention to detail and miniature figures.

Music also played a vital role in Russian culture, and Russian kings and princes maintained court musicians. In Orthodox religious services, chants helped move the spirits of the faithful.

Along with the religiously oriented art and literature, a vigorous popular oral tradition continued, combining music, street entertainments, and some theater. The Russian church constantly tried to suppress these forms, because they contained pre-Christian elements, but it was not entirely successful in this regard.

Overall, this formative period in east European civilization saw the development of a powerful religious sentiment. Religion and art alike developed quite separately from the forms of west European culture during the same time period. Cultural distance long supplemented geographical distance in keeping east European religious and intellectual life on its own wavelength. During much of the period from 500 to 1400, the fact that Byzantium so clearly outshone the West in art and some branches of literature only enhanced east European indifference to available Western models. Then, the long period of Tatar rule, while it did great harm to levels of cultural life in Russia, added to the differentiation of East and West in Europe, for the West was spared this kind of invasion and control.

EAST EUROPEAN ECONOMY AND SOCIETY

During most of the postclassical centuries, eastern Europe was well ahead of the West in technology and commerce; even Russia and the Balkans dominated iron manufacturing and other key processes. However, from about the 12th century on, the balance began to shift—as western European dominance over Constantinople in the Mediterranean amply signified. After centuries of Mongol rule, Russia emerged as distinctly inferior to the West in terms of levels of manufacturing and commercial skills. Thus, the leading economic achievements of this period did not create a significant legacy for east European society later on.

There were, however, some features worthy of note in the economy and social patterns of eastern Europe at this point. In both the Byzantine Empire and Russia, a large free peasantry was the dominant social class. This contrasted with the serfdom of many west European peasants and contributed to the productive agriculture of eastern Europe. Both Byzantium and Russia tolerated some slavery, a practice that was rarer in the West at this time. Widespread slavery persisted in Russia through the 17th century, although the Orthodox church tried to curtail it.

An important aristocracy developed in eastern Europe as well. Aristocrats in Russia, called *boyars*, had less political power than their counterparts in western Europe, except when kings were weak. Nevertheless, the nobility exerted some authority. Along with the church, aristocrats controlled considerable land, and their hold over the land only increased in later centuries, thus reducing the holdings of the free peasantry. Unlike the feudal pattern of western Europe (or Japan), aristocrats did not join together in bonds of mutual loyalty.

Socially and economically, as in other ways, eastern Europe developed according to its own dynamic; it was not simply a distant echo of western European civilization. Even when east European social trends later shifted, this characteristic, on the whole, remained.

EAST EUROPEAN CIVILIZATION IN ECLIPSE

The period that had seen an early east European civilization raise and extend its borders ended with that same civilization in apparent disarray. The collapse of the Byzantine bastion and Tatar control of Russia might well have destroyed the civilization outright. It is certainly true that the active south-north trade that had linked the various centers of eastern Europe never reoccurred. Even within Russia, commerce fell off and the levels of manufacturing deteriorated.

Cultural activity withered as well. Some chronicles continued to be written, but literacy declined; many priests did not know how to read. In this respect as well as in economics, eastern Europe emerged after 1400 with a great deal of catching up to do.

Although Byzantine society was never restored, the decline of east European civilization overall proved only temporary. In Russia, key political traditions, major social groups including the boyar aristocracy, and religious and artistic traditions emerged virtually unscathed. In this sense, Tatar domination, although frightening to Russians, was fairly superficial in its effects. There were also some benefits, such as the introduction of a postal system and paper money. Russia also gained new trade contacts with Asia.

One final point requires clarification, as it relates to both the formative east European centuries and more recent developments. East European civilization initially developed within the context of large empires: first the Byzantine, then the Russian. However, the civilization, both before 1400 and since, also spilled over to other parts of eastern Europe that never formed durable empires. Orthodox Christianity and a Cyrillic rather than Latin alphabet thus spread to Bulgaria and Serbia as well as to Russia. Yet other east European territories, such as Poland and Bohemia (now the Czech Republic and Slovakia), had more contacts with the West than the East. Although Slavic, these countries used a Latin alphabet and largely adopted Roman Catholicism. Their regional kingdoms, at points quite extensive, long existed as a sometimes uncomfortable buffer between Russia and the monarchies of western Europe. In other words, the boundary between west and east European civilizations was somewhat fluid, and it has shifted at different points over the centuries. The existence of a "border region" between Russia and the West was itself an important product of the spread of civilization northward in Europe from distinct Eastern and Western bases during the postclassical period.

PATHS TO THE PRESENT

Even though the Byzantine Empire is a thing of the past, East European postclassical history leaves traces in today's world apart from the splendid existing examples of Byzantine art.

Postclassical Eastern Europe was defined in terms of Christianity, but the dominance of religion has faded in some parts of the region during the past century. Areas that were Orthodox Christian, such as Russia, developed a tight link between church and state that, many historians believe, has encouraged an authoritarian approach to government. Current differences between Russia and the West were hardly predetermined by the east-west European split in the postclassical period, but they are affected by it.

Russia was shaped by its contacts with Byzantium in other ways as well. Russian territorial expansion—which ultimately motivated the creation of one of the world's great landed empires—might have occurred without Byzantine example. But there is no doubt that Russian leaders were impressed with Byzantium's imperial claims and its legacy from the Roman Empire. The results of this are visible today in a country that stretches across 11 time zones.

The postclassical period also contributed to defining a fluid zone in east-central Europe, with potential ties both eastward and westward. The region was divided between Roman Catholicism and Orthodoxy, and between the Cyrillic and the Latin alphabets. This, along with the area's geographical position between Russia and western Europe, which has made it something of a borderland from the postclassical period on, helps explain the fluctuations in the region's orientation in recent decades. Currently, its alignments seem decidedly Western, with participation in the movements toward European unity; but the longstanding divisions have not been entirely mended, and questions of east-central Europe's orientation might reopen.

SUGGESTED WEB SITES

On Byzantine studies, see http://
www.fordham.edu/halsall/byzantium/,
http://www.doaks.org/Byzantine.html, and
http://www.byzantium1200.com/; on Kievan
Rus', see http://www.mnsu.edu/emuseum/
history/russia/kievanrus.html.

SUGGESTED READINGS

Recent work includes Michael Maas, *The Cambridge
Companion to the Age of Justinian* (2005); Timothy Gre-
gory, *A History of Byzantium* (2005); Helen C. Evans,
ed., *Byzantium: Faith and Power (1261–1557)* (2004);
Rowena Loverance, *Byzantium* (2004); Carolyn L.
Connor, *Women of Byzantium* (2004); Ioli Kalavrezou,
Byzantine Women and Their World (2003); Gilbert
Dagron, *Emperor and Priest: The Imperical Office in
Byzantium* (2003); Jonathan Harris, *Byzantium and the
Crusades* (2003); Lucy-Anne Hunt, *Byzantium, East-
ern Christendom and Islam: Art at the Crossroads of the
Medieval Mediterranean* (1998); Anthony Cutler,
Byzantium, Italy and the North (2000); and Robert

Geraci, *Of Religion and Empire: Missions, Conversions
and Tolerance in Tsarist Russia* (2001).

For studies on the Byzantine Empire, see J. Hussey,
The Byzantine World (1982); A. A. Vasiliev, *History of the
Byzantine Empire* (1968); S. Runciman, *Byzantine Civi-
lization* (1956); Norman Baynes and H. St. L. B. Moss,
eds., *Byzantium* (1961); G. Every, *The Byzantine Patriar-
chate, 451–1204* (1978); D. M. Nicol, *Church and Society
in the Last Centuries of Byzantium* (1979); E. Kitzinger,
Byzantine Art in the Making (1977); and H. J. Magoulia,
Byzantine Christianity: Emperor, Church and the West (1982).
An excellent analysis of Byzantine influence in Eastern
Europe is D. Obolensky's *The Byzantine Commonwealth:
Eastern Europe, 500–1453* (1971). See also S. Runciman,
A History of the First Bulgarian Empire (1930). On Russian
history, the best survey is Nicholas Riasanovsky and Mark
Steinberg, *A History of Russia*, 7th ed. (2005); it also
includes a good bibliography. See also J. H. Billington, *The
Icon and the Axe: An Interpretive History of Russian Culture*
(1966); Wladyslaw, *Viking Rus: Studies on the Presence of
Scandinavians in Eastern Europe* (2004); Valerie A. Kivelson
and Robert H. Greene, *Orthodox Russia: Belief and Practice under the Tsars* (2003); and Sergei M. Soloviev, ed.,
Russian Society: 1389–1425 (2001).

12 Western Civilization: The Middle Ages

In contrast to eastern Europe, conditions deteriorated markedly in western Europe after Rome's fall. The deterioration of political forms, trade, city life, and intellectual endeavor reduced the achievements of classical Mediterranean civilization to only a faint memory. Between 700 and 1400 C.E., however, western Europe revived, creating new institutions and styles to accompany the selective adoption of earlier Roman and Greek traditions. Active interchange both with Byzantium and with the Arab world was a crucial part of this process. During most of this period, the area remained backward by standards of the great civilizations of the world. But, with the advantage of hindsight, we see that Western civilization was not only taking shape but also beginning to develop growing dynamism, particularly from the 11th century on.

Like other societies on the borders of the former classical world—Japan, Russia, the Sudanic kingdoms, and southeast Asia—western Europe borrowed actively during the postclassical period, although in ways that preserved a distinctive identity. There was no single source for imitation in this case, however, as west Europeans looked to Islam and Byzantium as well as the earlier traditions of Greece and Rome for guidance. The availability of several models may have been an advantage. Certainly, it helped open west Europeans to the importance of maintaining international contacts, even as they experienced fierce rivalries with many neighboring civilizations. In certain respects, however, western Europe resembled other borrowing societies, not only in its eagerness to imitate but also in its relatively loose political framework and the limitations (compared to the most advanced centers) on urban and manufacturing forms.

The postclassical period in western Europe thus saw the establishment of a largely new civilization and its extension northward. During much of the time, the leading centers of activity were in France, the Low Countries, Germany, and England—areas at best peripheral to civilization in Roman days. Spain lay in Muslim hands; Italy, although the center of the Catholic church and usually active in trade, was somewhat outside the Western mainstream in other respects. The usual label for this era of Western history is *medieval,* or the *Middle Ages.* The term is, in some sense, misleading; it suggests a way station between classical times and the more modern versions of Western civilization that took shape only after 1300 or 1400. Rather than being "between" two grander eras, the Middle Ages, in fact, witnessed the development of a largely new civilization and its presence in parts of Europe that had previously been isolated. But it is true that some of the institutions and values developed in the Middle Ages were unique to the period. Thus, in viewing these centuries as formative for a new Western civilization, we must also distinguish between important but peculiar features of medieval life on the one hand and, on the other, significant customs and traditions created by medieval people that shaped Western society even in later periods of development.

■ **KEY QUESTIONS** *It is often hard to sort out a dominant theme from other important developments. Christian culture was western Europe's unifying feature as it emerged in this period as a civilization. Did it shape all the main features of society and politics? Change is another central point: how did this phase of European history differ from the Greco-Roman (classical) past? What were the most important changes within the period itself, including its last two centuries? Finally, what are the most revealing comparisons with other postclassical societies? How did western Europe resemble, and how did it differ from the other imitative societies of the period?*

EARLY PATTERNS IN WESTERN CIVILIZATION

From 500 to almost 1000, major events in western Europe were few and far between. Effective political organization was largely local, although Germanic kings ruled some territories, such as a portion of present-day France. Most people lived on self-sufficient agricultural estates called *manors.* They received some protection from their landlords, including the administration of justice, and in return they were obligated to turn over part of the goods they produced and to remain on the land. The manorial system had originated in the later Roman Empire; it was strengthened by the decline of trade and the lack of larger political structures.

Landlords themselves formed some alliances. Greater lords provided protection and aid to lesser lords, called *vassals,* who in turn owed their lords military service, some goods or payments, and advice. This system formed the beginnings of the European version of feudalism. However, early feudalism did not prevent a great deal of disorder. Many local wars occurred. In addition, western Europe was often raided by Viking pirates from Scandinavia and other groups. Because of the disarray, poverty, and general educational decline from the late Roman Empire on, few cultural developments of any note took place. The scattered intellectuals who existed, all members of the clergy, were busy trying to preserve and understand older Christian and classical learning.

During these centuries, the Catholic church provided the only extensive example of solid organization. Roman popes built a careful hierarchy through their control over local bishops. The popes did not always appoint the bishops, for monarchs and local lords often claimed this right, but they did nonetheless issue directives and receive important information. The popes also regulated doctrine, successfully undermining several heresies that threatened a unified Christian faith. Moreover, they sponsored extensive missionary activity. Papal missionaries converted the English and Irish to Christianity. They brought the religion to northern and eastern Germany, beyond the borders of the previous Roman Empire, and ultimately, by the 10th century, to Scandinavia. They were active, of course, in the border regions of eastern Europe, sometimes competing directly with Orthodox missionaries. The solid structure of the church, which gave it a vital organizational edge over what secular government there was in the West, and the spread of Christianity constituted significant developments in the history of the West. Christian values increasingly became the essential cement of the newly developed civilization that covered virtually the whole of western Europe.

One significant political development occurred during these difficult centuries, sometimes called the Dark Ages. The royal house of a Germanic people, the Franks, grew in strength during the 8th century. A new family, the Carolingians, assumed the monarchy of these people, which was based in northern France, Belgium, and western Germany. One founder of the Carolingian line—Charles Martel, or Charles the Hammer—was responsible for defeating the Muslims in the Battle of Tours in 732. This defeat helped confine the Muslims to Spain and, along with the Byzantine defeat of the Arabs during the same period, preserved Europe for Christianity.

A later ruler in this same royal line, Charles the Great, known as Charlemagne, established a substantial empire in France, the Low Countries, and Germany around the year 800. Briefly, it looked as if a new Roman Empire might revive in the West, and indeed the term *Holy Roman Empire* ("Holy" denoted that it was firmly Christian) was later used by Charlemagne's successors in Germany. Charlemagne helped to restore some church-based education in western Europe, and the level of intellectual activity began a slow recovery, in part due to these efforts. When Charlemagne died in 814, however, his empire did not survive him. Rather, it was split into three geographic sectors—the outlines of modern France, Germany, and a middle strip consisting of the Low Countries, Switzerland, and northern Italy. Several of Charlemagne's successors, with nicknames such as "the Bald" or "the Fat," were not models of political dynamism even in their regional kingdoms.

From this point on, the essential political history of western Europe consisted of the gradual emergence of national monarchies. This was to be a civilization with strong cultural unity, initially centered in Catholic Christianity, but with pronounced political division.

The royal houses of several lands gained new power soon after Charlemagne's empire split. At first, the emperors who reigned over Germany and northern Italy were in the strongest position. It was they who claimed the title Holy Roman Emperor, beginning around the 12th century. By this time, however, their rule had become increasingly shallow, precisely because they relied too much on their imperial claims and did not build a solid monarchy from regional foundations. The future lay elsewhere, with the rise of monarchies in individual states—states that ultimately became nations.

From the 900s on, the kings of France began to assume growing authority. They amassed territory around their base in Paris, directly under their control; they formed feudal alliances with great lords in other parts of France, creating what is called a feudal monarchy. Regional monarchies began to form in Spain as Christian lords were able to push back the Muslims, from 1018 on, but a national royal house was formed only in the 15th century with the marriage of Ferdinand and Isabella. In England, an invasion from the French province of Normandy occurred in 1066. The Duke of Normandy, who was of Viking descent, had already built a strong feudal domain in northwestern France, and he now extended this system to England. William the Conqueror and his successors thus tied the great lords of England to the royal court by bonds of feudal loyalty, giving them estates in return for their military service.

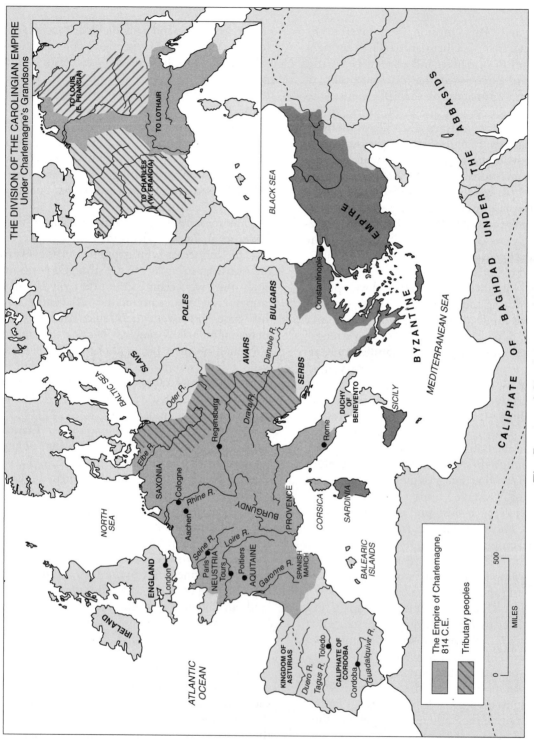

THE DIVISION OF THE CAROLINGIAN EMPIRE
Under Charlemagne's Grandsons

TO LOUIS
(E. FRANCIA)

TO LOTHAIR

TO CHARLES
(W. FRANCIA)

BLACK SEA

ABBASIDS

THE

UNDER

BAGHDAD

OF

CALIPHATE

BYZANTINE

EMPIRE

Constantinople

MEDITERRANEAN SEA

POLES

SLAVS

BALTIC SEA

Oder R.

Elbe R.

AVARS

Drava R.

Danube R. BULGARS

SERBS

Regensburg

DUCHY
OF
BENEVENTO

Rome

SICILY

SAXONIA

BURGUNDY

PROVENCE

CORSICA

SARDINIA

Cologne

Rhine R.

Aachen

Seine R.

Paris

NEUSTRIA

Tours

Loire R.

Poitiers

AQUITAINE

Garonne R.

SPANISH
MARCH

BALEARIC
ISLANDS

NORTH
SEA

ENGLAND

London

IRELAND

ATLANTIC
OCEAN

KINGDOM OF
ASTURIAS

Duero R.

Tagus R. Toledo

CALIPHATE OF
CORDOBA

Guadalquivir R.

Cordoba

The Empire of Charlemagne,
814 C.E.

Tributary peoples

0   500

MILES

The Empire of Charlemagne, 814 C.E.

The development of stronger feudal units and some powerful monarchies increased the orderliness of European life, starting in the 10th century. Invasions by the Vikings ceased; both trade and intellectual pursuits began to revive rapidly. The growth in the west European population reflected the new stability and encouraged improvements in agriculture and commerce. City life perked up gradually, as metropolitan areas became the centers for economic and cultural activity. Medieval Europe blossomed, and the centuries between 1000 and 1300 form the high point of this early version of Western civilization. It was during this period that the West began to show its muscle beyond its borders; a series of Crusades set out, from 1096 until the early 14th century, to reconquer and defend the Holy Land from the Muslims. The Crusades had only limited success in achieving their explicit goal, as a Kingdom of Jerusalem was established for about two centuries; even this success did not demonstrate real Western superiority against Muslim civilization, for the West remained backward. But as an expression of a combination of religious zeal—the Crusades were initiated by the pope—and growing commercial and military vigor on the part of the knights and merchants who organized the largest efforts, the Crusades unquestionably showed the distinctive spirit of the Western Middle Ages at their height. They also helped open the West to new cultural and economic influences from the Middle East, a major spur to further change.

As medieval society developed, the Catholic church went through several periods of decline and renewal. At times, church officials and the leading monastic groups became preoccupied with their holdings in land and their political interests. Reform-minded popes, such as Gregory VII (1073-1085), sought to purify the church more generally. They began to insist that all priests remain unmarried, to separate the priesthood from the ordinary world of the flesh. Gregory also endeavored to free the church from any vestige of state control. He quarreled vigorously with the Holy Roman Emperor, Henry IV, over the prac-

tice of state appointment, or investiture, of bishops in Germany. Ultimately, by excommunicating the emperor from the church, Gregory won his point. Gregory and several later popes made clear their beliefs that the church was to be not only free from state interference but also superior to the state in its function as the direct communicator of God's word. These claims were not entirely accurate, as governments influenced religious affairs still, but they were not altogether untrue. It was this sort of affirmation, indeed, that enabled the church to inspire kings and warriors to fight in the Crusades and also to war against several heresies that arose during the same centuries.

Monasteries and convents played a vital role in postclassical Europe. They served as centers of piety, and they provided men and women an alternative to ordinary life in the world. They also controlled much land and wealth. This sometimes led to corruption, which could in turn cause movements of reform and renewal, with the formation of new monastic orders. Some orders worked in the growing cities, or joined in attacks on heresy. Overall, monastic movements helped preserve and further learning and also provided examples of best available practices in agriculture. These functions might relate quite directly. As monks used parchment made from sheepskin, they had to raise or acquire as many as 500 sheep simply to produce a single copy of the Christian Bible.

Even in the centuries of its greatest strength, the church was by no means the only institution of importance during the High Middle Ages. As feudal monarchs extended their power, particularly in France and England, they became increasingly involved in the administration of justice and, through taxation, in the economic affairs of their subjects. Growing military strength made it possible for the royal families to assert their power against the claims of the church. Early in the 14th century, the French king actually imprisoned the pope in a dispute over taxation rights. Finally, the raising of armies by the national monarchs led to the beginning of a long series of wars in Europe. The chief rivals were the kings of France and

England. The English throne claimed large sections of French territory, from the days when they also had been dukes of Normandy; French kings steadily pressed against these territories. This rivalry evolved during the 14th and 15th centuries into a long, intermittent struggle called the Hundred Years War, in which France ultimately triumphed. From this point on, no century was to pass without major warfare among the leading nations of western Europe.

MEDIEVAL POLITICAL INSTITUTIONS

The characteristic political structure of the High Middle Ages, and the one of greatest importance for the later history of Western civilization, was the feudal monarchy. This was not, of course, the only political form in existence. Territories such as Germany and Italy remained more loosely organized, despite the grandiose claims of the Holy Roman Emperors. Feudal monarchy itself was a gradual development, not a carefully planned institution. It reflected a balance between the principles of feudalism pure and simple and the growing claims of the leading royal families. The result was an effective but distinctly limited government.

The monarchies of France, England, and ultimately Spain acquired several key functions during and after the 11th century, in addition to a general if vague recognition that kings and queens deserved some special loyalty. Medieval royal families, from the 10th and 11th centuries on, used the lands under their direct control to pay for armies and a small central bureaucracy. Often, they chose urban business or professional people to serve in this bureaucracy, partly because such people had expertise in financial matters and partly because, unlike the aristocracy, they owed allegiance to the crown alone. French and English monarchs began to introduce bureaucratic specialties, so that some of their ministers handled justice, others finance, still others military mat-

ters. They found ways to send centrally appointed emissaries to the provinces, to supervise tax collection and the administration of justice. In England, from the Norman Conquest on, kings appointed local sheriffs to oversee the administration of justice. None of these activities gave the monarchs extensive contacts with ordinary subjects; for most people, effective governments were still local. But once the principle of central control was established, a steady growth of state-sponsored rule followed. By the end of the Middle Ages, monarchs were gaining the right to tax their subjects directly. And they were beginning to recruit professional armies, instead of relying solely on an aristocratic cavalry, whose loyalties depended on feudal bonds or alliances. Several medieval kings also gained a solid reputation as lawgivers, which allowed the gradual centralization of legal codes and court systems. Rediscovery of Roman law, in countries such as France, encouraged this centralization effort.

However, feudal monarchy was a delicately balanced institution, of which the central government formed only one of the key ingredients. The power of the church served to check royal ambitions. As we have seen, the church could often win in a clash with the state by excommunicating rulers and thus threatening to turn the loyalties of the population against them. Although the church entered a period of decline at the end of the Middle Ages, the principle was rather clearly established, as part of feudal monarchy, that there were areas of belief and morality that were not open to manipulation by the state.

The second limitation on the royal families came from the traditions of feudalism and from the landed aristocracy as a powerful class. Aristocrats tended to resist too much monarchical control in the West. And they had the strength to make their objections heard, for these aristocrats, even when they were vassals of the king, had their own economic base and their own military force—sometimes, in the case of certain powerful nobles, an army greater than that of the king. The growth of the monarchy reduced aristocratic

HISTORY DEBATE

WESTERN CIVILIZATION

For some time, Americans have talked about "Western civilization." The concept of the West was actively used in the cold war with the Soviet Union, yet it is hard to define. We have seen that the classical Mediterranean did not directly identify a "Western" civilization, and this classical heritage was used most selectively by postclassical western Europe. Further, the consistent absence of political unity in western Europe complicates any definition of common structures.

West Europeans could not have identified Western civilization in the postclassical period, but they would have recognized the concept of Christendom, along with some difference between their version of this religion and that of eastern Europe. The first definition of this civilization was primarily religious, although artistic forms associated with religion also figured in this definition. Regional cultures varied, of course, and there was no linguistic unity, but cultural developments in one area—for example, the creation of universities, which started in Italy—surfaced elsewhere fairly quickly. Supplementing culture were some reasonably common social structures—such as manors and guilds—and trade patterns that increasingly joined northern and much of southern Europe. The resulting civilization was by no means as coherent as Chinese civilization; many of its members detested each other—for example, the English and French, who were often in conflict and sometimes engaged in name-calling (the English were "les goddams" because they swore so much, and the French were "frogs" because of what they ate).

Until very recently, Europeans thought in terms of distinctive national histories, not European ones. But it is possible to define some common features that differed from those of neighboring civilizations. Even as the civilization began to change, late in the postclassical period, it preserved some common directions. Debate continues about the balance between the Western and more purely national features. Debate also continues about how much the West borrowed from others, particularly the Arabs.

power, but this led to new limits on kings. In 1215, an unpopular English king, John, faced opposition to his taxation measures from an alliance of nobles, townspeople, and church officials. Defeated in battle, John was forced to sign the Great Charter, or Magna Carta, which confirmed basically feudal rights against monarchical claims. John promised to observe restraint in his dealings with the nobles and the church. The few references to the general rights of the English people against the state that were included in the Magna Carta largely served to show where the feudal concept of mutual limits and obligations between rulers and the ruled could later lead.

This same feudal balance led, late in the 13th century, to the creation of parliaments, as bodies representing not individual voters but privileged groups such as the nobles and the church. The first full English parliament convened in 1265, with the House of Lords representing the nobles and the church hierarchy and the Commons made up of elected representatives from wealthy citizens of the towns. The parliament institutionalized the feudal principle that monarchs should consult with their vassals. In particular, parliaments gained the right to rule on any proposed changes in taxation; through this power, they could also advise the crown on other policy issues. While the parliamentary tradition became strongest in England, similar institutions arose in France, Spain, and several of the regional governments in Germany. Other countries, as we have seen, used councils in government. However, it was Western feudalism alone that led to the more formal institutions of parliament.

Medieval government was not modern government. People had rights according to the estate into which they were born; there was no general concept of citizenship. Thus, parliaments represented only a minority, and even this minority only in terms of three or four estates (nobles, clergy, urban merchants, sometimes wealthy peasants), not some generalized group of voters. But by creating a concept of limited government and some hint of representative institutions, Western feudal monarchy produced the beginnings of a distinctive political tradition. This tradition differed from the political results of Japanese feudalism discussed in the next chapter, which emphasized group loyalty more than checks on a central power. Nonetheless, remnants of medieval traditions, embodied in institutions such as parliaments and ideas such as the separation between God's authority and state power, defined a basic thread in the Western political process even into the 21st century.

One other feature of medieval politics deserves note: its unusual focus on war. Although feudal monarchies created increasing internal order within individual countries, the idea of the state as an institution for warfare remained strong. Given the failure to develop any lasting political unity in Europe, this penchant ensured recurrent conflict within Western civilization. It is true that, during the Middle Ages, warfare continued to be a fairly limited activity. The basic military force was composed of the landed nobility, who alone could afford horses, weapons, and armor and the training needed for skill in battle. However, this interest in war sparked attention in improved weaponry. During the Hundred Years War, states learned to use archery and, particularly, the longbow, which opened the way to larger armies and began to limit the effectiveness of the aristocratic cavalry. At about the same time, the introduction of gunpowder stimulated still more portentous developments, as Europeans by

the 14th century improved cannons so they could project firepower over considerable distances. Now, not only cavalry but also the fortified castles of the aristocracy became increasingly vulnerable. Warfare thus stimulated technological advances in Western society, which ultimately enhanced the power of the state and increased the means available for destruction. The inclination to rely on the battlefield to settle disputes also proved a durable part of the Western political tradition. It contrasted particularly with the lower level of interest of civilizations such as China in matters of military goals and technologies.

MEDIEVAL RELIGION AND CULTURE

As in eastern Europe and Islam during these centuries, religion was the focal point of medieval cultural life. But Western Christianity spawned a number of cultural tensions and increasingly diverse intellectual and artistic movements, so that a substantial array of interests describes the philosophy and literature of the High Middle Ages.

During the centuries before about 1000, a small number of theologians continued the efforts of preserving and interpreting past wisdom, particularly the writings of church fathers such as Augustine, as well as some non-Christian Latin authors. During Charlemagne's time, a favorite practice was to gather quotations from ancient writers around key subjects. Efforts of this sort showed little creativity, but they gradually produced a fuller understanding of past thought and improvements in Latin writing style and in organizing philosophical materials. Interest in the classical principles of rhetoric and, particularly, logic reflected the concern for coherent organization; Aristotle, known to the Middle Ages as *the* Philosopher, was valued because of his clear exposition of rational thought.

From 1000 on, a series of outstanding clerics advanced the logical exposition of philosophy and theology to new levels. They stressed the importance of absolute faith in God's word, but they believed that human reason could move mankind toward an understanding of some aspects of religion and the natural order as well. Thus, according to several theologians, it was possible to prove the existence of God, to use logic to help explain the Trinity, and to develop certain moral principles. A concomitant interest in collecting Roman law and codifying church law (called *canon law*) also promoted the use of careful logical exposition. Fascination with logic led some intellectuals to a certain zeal in pointing out inconsistencies in past wisdom, even in the writings of church fathers. In the 12th century, Peter Abelard, in Paris, wrote a treatise called *Yes and No,* in which he highlighted a number of logical contradictions in established doctrine.

This logical-rationalist current in Western philosophy was hardly unopposed. Quite apart from the fact that most ordinary Christians knew nothing of these debates, seeing their religion as a matter of beliefs not to be questioned, appointed sacraments, and comforting rituals that removed sin and promoted salvation, many church leaders emphasized the role of faith alone. A powerful monk, St. Bernard of Clairvaux, challenged Abelard and had him condemned. Bernard was an intellectual of a different sort, who stressed the importance of a mystical union with God, which was attainable even on this earth in brief moments of blissful enlightenment, rather than rationalist endeavor.

However, the thirst to assimilate rational philosophy with Christian faith was a dominant medieval theme. By the 12th century, the zeal for knowledge produced several distinctive results. First, a number of universities were founded in Italy and France, then in England and Germany. Some specialized in law or medicine, but the most prestigious centers, such as those in Paris and Oxford, emphasized philosophy and theology. Degrees granted to aspiring scholars, ranging from the bachelor's to the doctorate, originated the system still in use today in Western universities. These schools were under

church control, but already they produced great intellectual diversity as well as a serious quest for knowledge. Another key development was the translation of newly discovered texts from Greek and Arabic philosophy and science. Translators in Spain and Constantinople could barely keep up with the growing Western demand to discover everything there was to know. It was in culture that western Europe ranked as one of the great imitative societies of the postclassical period.

With much fuller knowledge of Aristotelian and Hellenistic science, plus the work of Arab rationalists such as Ibn Rushd (Averroës), Western philosopher-theologians in the 13th century proceeded to the final great synthesis of medieval learning. The leading figure was Thomas Aquinas, an Italian-born monk who taught at the University of Paris. Aquinas maintained the basic belief that faith came first, but he greatly expanded the role of reason. Through reason alone, humans could know much of the natural order, moral law, and the nature of God. Thomas had complete confidence that all essential knowledge could be coherently organized, and he produced a number of treatises, called *Summas,* that disposed, through careful logic, of all possible objections to truth as revealed by reason and faith alike. Here was a masterful demonstration of medieval confidence in the fundamental orderliness of not only learning but also God's creation. Essentially, this work restated in Christian terms Greek efforts to seek a rationality in nature that corresponded to the rational capacities of the human mind.

Medieval philosophy did not encourage a great deal of new scientific work. The emphasis on mastering past learning and organizing it logically led to perhaps an overemphasis on previous discoveries, rather than much new empirical research. However, toward the end of the 13th century, a current of practical science developed. At Oxford, members of the clergy such as Roger Bacon performed experimental work with optics, pursuing research earlier done by Muslim scholars. An important by-product of this interest was

Adoration of the Magi: 12th-century French enamel.

the invention of eyeglasses, an indispensable aid to many Western (and other) scholars ever since. During the 14th and 15th centuries, experimentalists also advanced knowledge in chemistry and astronomy. This early work set the stage for the flourishing of Western science later on.

Like most philosophy, medieval art and architecture were intended to serve the glory of God. Western painters used religious subjects almost exclusively. Painting mainly on wooden panels, artists in most parts of western Europe depicted Christ's birth and suffering and the lives of the saints using stiff, stylized figures. By the 14th and 15th centuries, artists improved their ability to render natural scenes realistically and portrayed a host of images of medieval daily life as backdrops to their religious subjects. Designs and scenes in stained-glass windows for churches were another important form of artistic expression.

Medieval architecture initially followed Roman models, particularly in church building, by utilizing rectangular (Romanesque) style, sometimes surmounted by domes. During the 11th century, however, a new style termed *gothic* took hold, which was far more original (although it benefited from the knowledge of Muslim arches). Gothic architects, taking advantage of growing engineering expertise, built soaring church spires and massive, arched windows. Although their work focused on the creation of large churches and great cathedrals, some gothic architects created civic buildings and palaces, using the same design motifs. The gothic was one of the three main architectural styles ever developed in Western culture (the others being the earlier classical and the later modern). Music for church use also flourished during the Middle Ages.

Medieval literature reflected strong religious interests. Most Latin writing dealt with points of philosophy, law, or political theory. There was little concern with style for its own sake. But alongside writing in Latin came the development of a growing literature in the spoken languages, or vernaculars, of western Europe. A number of oral sagas were written down, dealing with the deeds of great knights and mythic figures from the past. From this tradition evolved the first known writing in early English, *Beowulf,* and in French, the *Song of Roland.* Late in the Middle Ages, a number of writers created adventure stories, comic tales, and poetry in the vernacular tongues, such as Chaucer's *Canterbury Tales.* Much of this work, and also a number of plays written for performance in the growing cities, reflected a tension between Christian values and a desire to portray the harshness of life on this earth. Chaucer's narrative, in its colorful language, thus shows a willingness to poke fun at the hypocrisy of many Christians as well as an ability to capture some of the tragedies of human existence. In France, a

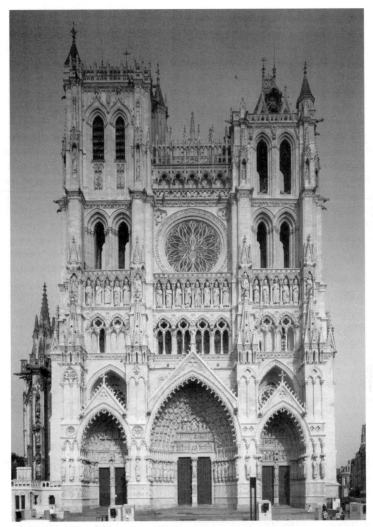

The cathedral of Notre-Dame (Our Lady) at Amiens, France, is a grand example of gothic architecture, which flourished during the later Middle Ages in western Europe. The cathedral, which dwarfs the surrounding buildings, was built between 1220 and 1402 and was the tallest building in Europe at the time of its completion.

long poem called the *Story of the Rose* wove together various kinds of sexual imagery, while the poet Villon wrote, in largely secular terms, of the terror and poignancy of death. Finally, again in vernacular language, a series of courtly poets (troubadours), based primarily in southern France, wrote hymns to the love that could flour-ish between men and women. Although such verses stressed platonic devotion rather than sexual love, and paid homage to courtly ceremonies and polite behavior, the troubadours' concern with love was the first sign of the new value this emotional experience had taken on in the Western tradition.

UNDERSTANDING CULTURES

CHRISTIANITY AND SYNCRETISM

It is accurate to see Christianity as the key ingredient in Western culture, indeed in the whole of Western society, in the postclassical period. Preserving Christian purity was a major focus. Various internal heresies were rooted out violently, in local crusades, because they contradicted the definitions of the church. Thus a lower-class purity movement against corruption among priests was put down by military expeditions in the second half of the 12th century, in what was called the Albigensian Crusade in southern France. Non-Christians, particularly Jews, were often mistreated as well.

Christianity was not, however, the only cultural component in western Europe at the time. The earthiness of some literature, delighting in bawdy humor and sexual references, was also a genuine part of Western culture in this period and beyond.

Christianity also combined with pre-Christian elements, in a process called *syncretism*. Syncretism is a common outcome when a new culture meets well-established popular beliefs. Most ordinary Christians thus still believed in magic and witches, even though the church officially frowned on these ideas. Witches were seen as beautiful women, in contrast with later Western imagery. And they were not always evil: White magic, to help cure disease or produce a good marriage, was the most common form of magic practiced by good witches. The newer Christian calendar often incorporated older beliefs about seasonal change and revelry to define its holidays. This was a key reason that Christmas was scheduled in later December, to overlap older celebrations of the winter solstice and, for instance, the Roman celebration of Saturnalia. The widespread revival of paganism during the 20th century indicates that, even after many centuries, official Christianity has not entirely won out. This adds to the challenge and interest of interpreting Western culture in this formative period.

Medieval intellectual and artistic life, in sum, created a host of important themes. Religion served as the centerpiece, but it did not curtail a growing range of interests from science to romantic poetry. Medieval culture was a rich intellectual achievement in its own right. It also set in motion a series of developments—in rationalist philosophy, science, artistic representations of nature, and vernacular literature—that served as building blocks for later Western thought and art.

ECONOMY AND SOCIETY

Medieval thinkers liked to picture their society in rather simple terms, not unlike the metaphors of classical India. Borrowing from classical Greek and Roman concepts, John of Salisbury, an English churchman, likened society to the human body. Peasants were the feet, without which society could not function. Knightly warriors were the hands, to defend. Priests provided heart and soul, the king the head. Each part was essential, but each fit into a clear hierarchy in which subordinates were properly ruled by their superiors.

In fact, medieval society was far more complicated, and it evolved toward ever-greater complexity. In the early Middle Ages, and to some extent throughout the period, the key social relationship, as far as most people were concerned, was that between landlord and serf. Just as feudal relationships described contacts among the landlords, so manorialism described contacts between those who ruled the landed estates and those who

Peasants and lords work near a fictional late-medieval castle in the Loire valley of France. (Illuminated manuscript from the *Très Riches Heures du duc de Berry*.)

performed the manual labor of farming. There were a few free farmers in the early Middle Ages, but most peasants were serfs, clustered in villages on the lords' estates. From the lords, the peasant-serfs received some military and judicial protection, and some aid, where possible, during periods of poor harvest. To the lords, they owed a portion of their harvests and considerable work service. Serfs were not free to leave their land, but they were not outright slaves, because in normal circumstances they could not be evicted from their land. Most land was, in this sense, jointly owned, with both the serf and lord having some control over it—although the lords and church owned some estates outright, which they worked mainly through the serfs' labor.

This agricultural society was quite primitive. Tools were simple. Peasants had to leave a third or more of their land fallow each year, to replenish the soil. Most estates produced mainly for their own subsistence, and there was little market activity.

By the 9th and 10th centuries, partly because of the restoration of order, the agricultural economy began to improve. New techniques developed through contacts with eastern Europe and Asia. A heavier plow was devised, the moldboard, which made it much easier to till the heavy soils of Europe. The horse collar, first invented in Asia but now finally introduced in the West, allowed for the use of horses as well as oxen to pull plows and carts. Advances of this sort increased agricultural productivity and promoted a steady growth of population, which lasted until the 14th century. This rising population, in turn, encouraged the settlement of new lands in various parts of Europe, as forests were cleared and swamps drained. To attract farmers to the new lands, the conditions of serfdom were relaxed. There was great variety in this process; in many parts of western Europe, a strict manorial system lasted well beyond the Middle Ages. However, by the 12th and 13th centuries, many peasants retained very few obligations to their lords, often little more than rent (which also reflected the fact that

many peasants were now able to directly sell part of their produce to the market). Some peasants owned their land outright and could sell it if they wished. Compared to east European and most Asian civilizations by 1400, the west European peasantry was unusually free, and although its agricultural techniques were not as advanced as those in some areas, such as east Asia, there had nonetheless been considerable improvement in this regard.

Shifts in agriculture promoted and reflected changes in commerce. With rising agricultural productivity, from about 1000 on, a minority of people were able to concentrate on other economic activities. In parts of Italy, the Low Countries, England, and northern Germany, about 20 percent of the population could now be supported away from the farms. This meant new possibilities for trade and for the expansion of cities. New commercial opportunities, in turn, inspired some peasants and landlords to turn more fully to the market, rather than concentrate on subsistence agriculture. The use of money spread steadily, to the dismay of many Christian moralists and many ordinary people who preferred the more direct, personal methods of traditional society.

Rising trade took a number of forms. Western Europe exchanged goods with other parts of the known world and became an active part of the world network, which allowed the cultural borrowings from Byzantium and Islam and stimulated commerce. Wealthy Europeans developed a taste for some of the spices and luxury goods of Asia; the Crusades played a role in bringing these products to wider attention. A Mediterranean trade redeveloped, mainly in the hands of Italian merchants dealing with Arab traders, in which European cloth and some other products were exchanged for the higher-quality goods of the East. Commerce within Europe involved exchanges of timber and grain from the north for cloth and metal products manufactured in Italy and the Low Countries. England, at first an exporter of raw wool, developed some manufactured goods for exchange by the later Middle Ages. Huge fairs in northern

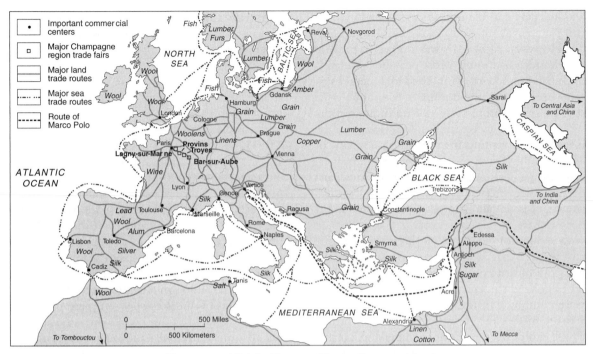

European–Middle Eastern Trade Connections

France and the Low Countries brought together merchants from various parts of Europe. Commercial alliances developed. Cities in northern Germany and southern Scandinavia united in the Hanseatic League to encourage trade. Banking facilities spread, particularly through the efforts of the Italians. It thus became possible to organize commercial transactions throughout much of western Europe. Bankers, including a number of Jewish businessmen, were valued for their service in lending money to monarchs and to the papacy. The growth of trade and banking in the Middle Ages served as the genesis of capitalism in Western civilization. The greater Italian and German bankers, the long-distance merchants of the Hanseatic cities, were clearly capitalistic in their willingness to invest considerable sums of money in trading ventures with the expectation of substantial profit.

This was not, by world standards, a totally unprecedented merchant spirit. European traders were still less venturesome and less wealthy than some of their Muslim counterparts. Nor was Western society any more tolerant of merchants than Muslim or Indian societies. But Western commercial endeavors were clearly gaining in dynamism. Because Western governments were weak, with few economic functions, merchants had a freer hand than in many other civilizations. Many of the growing cities, in particular, were ruled by commercial leagues. Monarchs liked to encourage the cities as a counterbalance to the power of the landed aristocracy, and in the later Middle Ages and beyond, traders and kings were typically allied. But aside from taxing merchants and using them as sources of loans, royal governments did not interfere extensively with trading activities. Merchants even developed their own codes of commercial law, administered by city courts. Thus, the rising merchant class, although not unusual in strength or its adventurous spirit, was staking out an unusually powerful and independent role in European society. Christian concerns about profitmaking began to decline.

However, capitalism was not yet typical of the Western economy. Most peasants and landlords had not become enmeshed in a market system. In the cities, the dominant economic ethic stressed group protection, not unlimited profit-seeking. The characteristic institution was not the international trading firm but the merchant or artisan guild. These organizations, new in western Europe but similar to guilds in various parts of Asia, stressed security and mutual control. Merchant guilds thus sought to ensure all members a share in any endeavor. If a ship docked with a cargo of wool, the clothiers' guild of the city insisted that all members participate in the purchase of that commodity, so no one member monopolized the ensuing profits. Artisan guilds were composed of the people in the cities who actually made cloth, bread, jewelry, or furniture. These guilds tried to limit membership, so that all members were assured of work. They regulated apprenticeships to guarantee good training, but also to make sure that no member employed too many apprentices and thus garnered undue wealth. They discouraged new methods, again because security and general equality, not maximum individual profit, was the goal. Guilds also tried to guarantee good workmanship, so that consumers would not have to worry about shoddy quality on the part of some unscrupulous profit seeker. Guilds played an important political and social role in the cities, ensuring their members of recognized status and, often, a voice in city government. Their statutes were, in turn, upheld by municipal law and often backed by the royal government as well.

Despite the traditionalism and security-mindedness of the guilds, manufacturing as well as commercial methods did improve in medieval Europe. Western Europe was not yet as advanced as Asia in ironmaking or textile manufacture, but it was beginning to catch up. In a few areas, such as clock making—which reflected both sophisticated technology and an interest in precise time—

and heavy metallurgical casting for monumental church bells, European artisans had, in fact, forged a world lead. Furthermore, some manufacturing spilled beyond the bounds of guild control. Particularly in the Low Countries and parts of Italy, groups of workers were employed by capitalists to produce for a wide market, working with simple equipment in their homes.

The plain fact was that, by the later Middle Ages, western Europe's economy and society embraced a number of contradictory groups and principles. Commercial and capitalist elements coexisted alongside the slower pace of economic life in the countryside and even the dominant group protectionism of most urban guilds. Most people remained peasants, but a minority had escaped to the cities, where they found more excitement, although also increased danger and higher rates of disease. A few prosperous capitalists flourished, but most people operated according to quite different economic values. At the same time, the conditions of serfdom were easing for many in rural life. This was not, in sum, either a static society or an early model of a modern commercial society. It simply had its own flavor and its own tensions—the fruit of several centuries of economic and social change.

WOMEN AND FAMILY LIFE

The increasing complexity of medieval social and economic life may have had one final effect that is familiar from patterns in other agricultural societies: setting new limits on the conditions of women. Women's work remained, of course, vital in most families. Christian emphasis on the equality of all souls and the practical importance of monastic groups organized for women, offering some an alternative to marriage, continued to lend distinctive features to women's lives in Western society. The popular veneration of Mary and other female religious figures gave women real cultural prestige, counterbalancing the biblical emphasis on Eve as the source of human sin. In some respects, women in the West had higher status than their sisters under Islam: they were less segregated at religious services (although they could not lead them) and less confined to the household. Still, women's effective voice in the family may have declined during the Middle Ages. Urban women often played important roles in local commerce and even operated some craft guilds, but they found themselves increasingly constrained by male-dominated organizations. By the late Middle Ages, a literature arose that stressed women's subordinate role to men, listing supplemental household tasks and extolling docile behaviors as women's distinct destiny. Patriarchal structures seemed to be taking deeper root.

TENSIONS IN THE LATER MIDDLE AGES

Medieval society reached its apogee in the 12th and 13th centuries. Beginning about 1300 and continuing for about 150 years, it exhibited a number of symptoms of stagnation and decline. This was not a collapse of Western civilization or even a deterioration of the long-term sort that began to affect Muslim civilization during the same period. Rather, western Europe encountered a number of short-term difficulties. These, in turn, prompted the society to shed part of its medieval skin, snakelike, only to emerge with renewed dynamism in somewhat different garb toward the middle of the 15th century.

Item. By the early 1300s, medieval population had clearly surpassed the limits that the existing economy could sustain. Growing food crises caused widespread starvation through severe periodic famines. Then, massive plague, sweeping through city and countryside alike, took its deadly toll. The Black Death, the bubonic plague, killed more than a quarter of the population during the late 14th century. Population loss of this sort both reflected and caused economic dislocation.

Item. During the 14th century, the ruling class of medieval society, the landowning aristocracy, began to show signs of confusion about its function. It had long staked its claim to power on its control of much of the land and also on its military prowess. However, its skill in warfare was now open to question. The growth of professional armies and particularly the new weaponry of crossbow and cannon made traditional fighting methods increasingly irrelevant. The aristocracy did not, as a result, simply disappear. Rather, the nobility chose to emphasize a rich ceremonial lifestyle, featuring tournaments in which military expertise could be employed in competitive games. The spread of courtly love poems signaled another new focus, an interest in a more refined culture. The idea of chivalry—carefully controlled, polite behavior, especially toward women—gained ground. This was a potentially fruitful development in indicating increased cultivation among the upper class. We have seen similar transformations in considering earlier changes in the Chinese and Muslim aristocracy. But at the time of transition in the West, some of the elaborate ceremonies of chivalry seemed rather shallow, even a bit silly—a sign that medieval values were losing hold without being replaced by a new set of beliefs.

Item. The balance between church and state, which had characterized medieval life, began to shift decisively after 1300. For several decades, French kings controlled the papacy, which they relocated from Rome to a town in France; then rival claimants to the papacy confused the issue further. Ultimately, a single pope was returned to Rome, but the church was clearly weakened. Moreover, the church began to lose some of its grip over Western religious life. Church leaders were so preoccupied with their political quarrels that they tended to neglect the spiritual side of their faith. Religion did not decline as a result. Indeed, signs of intense popular piety blossomed, along with the formation of new religious groups. But devotion became partially separate from the institution of the church. One result, again starting in the 14th century, was a series of popular heresies, with leaders in places such as

England and Bohemia preaching against the hierarchical structure of the church in favor of a more direct experience of God.

Item. The medieval intellectual and even artistic movements started to falter. After the work of Aquinas, later rationalists engaged in petty debates over such topics as how many angels could dance on the head of a pin. Church officials became less tolerant of intellectual pursuit, as they even declared some of Aquinas's writings heretical. In art, a growing interest in realistic portrayals of nature suggested the beginnings of a shift away from medieval artistic standards. Some medieval artistic styles became trite; gothic design, for example, soon exhibited great detail, in a style called *flamboyant gothic*—a symptom of waning creativity.

Item. Social unrest increased in the 14th and 15th centuries, spurred in part by the new economic problems and popular religious heresies. Many peasants and townspeople joined in egalitarian protests against the control of guild masters or landlords. Sometimes, they spoke out for greater equality. As an English rioter put it, "When Adam delved and Eve span, Who was then a gentleman?" In the Italian city of Florence, a democratic government was briefly installed after an artisan revolt in 1378. These revolts had little lasting success, although they did set in motion a new current of protest that, in certain respects, lasted for several centuries. Peasants were beginning to seek greater freedom from what was left of serfdom, and lower-level artisans wondered if the guild system was working equitably. At times, these groups revolted in a violent manner. One English observer wrote of peasant attacks on manorial lords and records:

> These myschevous people thus assembled without capitayne or armoure, robbed, brent and slewe all gentylmen that they coude lay handes one, and forced and ravysshed ladyes and dawmosels and dyd such shameful dedes that no hymayne creature ought to think on any such.

Elements of this protest tradition lasted well beyond the period of medieval decline and ultimately help reshape political and social relationships in the West. At the time, popular uprisings served as one final indication that the medieval version of a social and economic structure was losing its validity.

PATHS TO THE PRESENT

The postclassical period established several enduring features of western European civilization, adding to elements revived from the classical Mediterranean. Many historians believe, in fact, that the core of Western civilization took shape during this period.

The civilization was defined in part by a shared version of Christianity, including the important separation between the institutional church and the state. Even though Christianity has changed and, in many cases, declined in western Europe since that time, the common intellectual legacy remains. The sense of religious limits on the state later helped generate distinctive statements about political power.

The European version of feudalism, with its emphasis on contract and consultation, also helped shape the region's political tradition. The emergence of parliaments during this era, though not yet modern in form, suggests the emerging notion of legislative checks on executive power. This balance was not always preserved in later Western political history, but it has always recurred.

Western society, from its postclassical roots, was also warlike and open to technologies that could aid in the art of war. Many argue that this characteristic persists in Western civilization, helping to define its later approach to the wider world.

The postclassical period also saw the rise of merchant activity in the west. This was not in itself distinctive: Islamic, Indian, Chinese, and African merchants rivaled or surpassed western levels of trade. But merchants in the west faced fewer political controls than those in some other regions, because of the weakness of the feudal state. This provided a backdrop for later interest in relatively unregulated merchant activity.

Many aspects of the postclassical west were confined to the period: religious art, for example, though still treasured in museums, is not an active force in Western art today. But in at least four respects—and further analysis might suggest more—important precedents were created for Western society later on, not only in Europe, but also in areas unusually open to Western influence.

SUGGESTED WEB SITES

For more on the Middle Ages, see http://www.byu.edu/ipt/projects/middleages/; visit the Arador Amour Library at http://www.arador.com/main/index.html; on Medieval European history, see http://www.medieval-life.net/history_main.htm; visit the Early Middle Ages Museum at http://www.roma2000.it/zmumedio.html.

SUGGESTED READINGS

Recent work includes Peter N. Stearns, *Western Civilization in World History* (2003); Richard Landes, ed., *The Apocalyptic Year 1000* (2003); Richard F. Gyug, *Medieval Cultures in Contact* (2003); Charles Freeman, *The Closing of the Western Mind: The Rise of Faith and the Fall of Reason* (2003); Christopher Dyer, *An Age of Transition? Economy and Society in England in the Later Middle Ages* (2005); John H. Arnold, *Belief and Unbelief in Medieval Europe* (2005); Paul Maurice Clogan, ed., *Studies in Medieval and Renaissance Culture: Reengaging History* (2005); Roger French, *Medicine Before Science: The Rational and Learned Doctor from the Middle Ages to the Enlightenment* (2003); Lawrence Besser-

man, ed., *Sacred and Secular in Medieval and Early Modern Cultures: New Essays* (2006); Chiara Frugoni, *A Day in a Medieval City* (2005); Rosalynn Voaden and Diane Wolfthal, *Framing the Family: Narrative and Representation in the Medieval and Early Modern Periods* (2005). See also Georges Duby's *Art and Society in the Middle Ages* (2000) and Tom Chippey, ed., *Appropriating the Middle Ages: Scholarship, Politics, Fraud* (2001). B. Tierney's *The Middle Ages* (1978) provides useful source material. See also Michael D. Bailey's *Battling Demons: Witchcraft, Heresy, and Reform in the Late Middle Ages* (2003). For unusual insight into medieval society, also with considerable source material, see the highly readable E. Leroy-Ladurie's *Montaillou: The Promised Land of Error* (1979). Excellent studies on more specialized topics include J. R. Strayer, *On the Medieval Origins of the Modern State* (1972); C. Brooke, *The 12th Century Renaissance* (1970); H. Rashdall, *The Universities of Europe in the Middle Ages* (1936); H. Berman, *Law and Revolution: The Formation of the Western Legal Tradition* (1983); R. Bridenthal and C. Koonz, *Becoming Visible: Women in European History* (1977); and N. Pevsner, *An Outline of European Architecture* (1963).

On the medieval economy, consult J. Gimpel, *The Medieval Machine: The Industrial Revolution of the Middle Ages* (1977), and David Landes, *Revolution in Time: Clocks and the Making of the Modern World* (1985). Social history has dominated much recent research on the period; see P. Ariès and G. Duby, eds., *A History of Private Life*, Vol. 2 (1984), and Barbara Hanawalt, *The Ties That Bound: Peasant Families in Medieval England* (1986), for important findings in this area. David Herlihy's *Medieval Households* (1985) is a vital contribution, as is J. Chapelot and R. Fossier's *The Village and House in the Middle Ages* (1985). J. Kirshner and S. F. Wemple, eds., *Women of the Medieval World* (1985), is a good collection. On tensions in popular religion, see C. Bynum, *Jesus as Mother: Studies in the Spirituality of the High Middle Ages* (1982), and L. Little, *Religious Poverty and the Profit Economy in Medieval Europe* (1978).

13

The Spread of East Asian Civilization

This chapter returns to the subject of the world network and deals with a second set of connections within it: those radiating from China. These connections were partially separated from the Islam-generated network and operated within a decidedly smaller orbit than the one Islam had forged. They primarily affected east Asia and to some extent southeast Asia. Trade and some technology exchange linked China to the rest of Asia and, through it, to Europe and Africa.

Although the Islam network was much larger than the connective web generated by China, developments in east Asia during this period were crucial in their own right. Japan, for example, formed some of its key characteristics during this period. Several specific innovations, for instance, advances in Chinese and Korean technology, gained worldwide importance. And, despite the massive changes in religious affiliations and trading patterns that erupted throughout the Middle East and southern Asia after 600 C.E., these cultural currents had little impact on China and its east Asian neighbors. The Chinese briefly encountered Arab soldiers on their western borders and had some interaction with Turkish converts to Islam, but, although the western Chinese population at times included an Islamic minority, China did not become Islamic. Similarly, trade in Chinese goods, toward points west, passed increasingly into Arab hands. But these developments were peripheral to Chinese history in the period. After the year 500, however, the Chinese did react to the one serious outside influence that had reached deeply into their population: Buddhism. Apart from this interchange, however, the Chinese proceeded, as they long had done, as if there was little to learn from beyond their borders.

Despite China's relative isolation, the postclassical centuries between 600 and 1400 C.E. were a vigorous and important period in Chinese history and in China's relations with other parts of east Asia. China introduced innovations in bureaucracy, art, foreign policy, and technology. Indeed, during this time, the Chinese were responsible for more fundamental improvements in technology than any other civilization.

Any student of world history, after mastering an understanding of the basic patterns of individual civilizations, is tempted to look for larger themes or lessons. Do civilizations, for example, follow some general law of rise and fall? There certainly seems to be a common scenario in which a culture starts to grow with unusual vigor—such as the Arabs in the 7th century—and then, some centuries later, begins to wane. But one should not make too much of this rise-and-fall pattern. For, while some civilizations decline or stagnate, others go through temporary periods of readjustment only to reemerge with equal or greater strength. China clearly illustrates this latter process and may still be exemplifying it in our own day as the nation revives after more than a century of partial eclipse.

Furthermore, China radiated a vigorous regional influence during this period, serving as a model to many other societies in east Asia. Vietnam, Korea, and Japan did not become smaller versions of China; each had distinctive features that long differentiated it from its giant neighbor. But important elements of Chinese society were exported to these cultures, and a larger east Asian zone of civilization took shape. The spread of civilization in east Asia on the basis of a significant Chinese example forms one of the key illustrations of the general phenomenon of civilization's extension and the new process of borrowing during the postclassical centuries.

The period opens soon after the year 500, when the sequence of China's ruling dynasties was renewed, ending the long period of disruption that followed the collapse of the Han dynasty. Also around 500, Japan began to import techniques from China, including writing, enabling it to become a clear domain of east Asian civilization—although during this entire period, Japan played a far less commanding part in Asian civilization than China.

The era did not end smoothly, reflecting the fact that east Asian patterns of civilization remained somewhat separate from those in other parts of the Eurasian world. In 1278, Mongol invaders toppled the reigning Chinese dynasty; the invaders were expelled 90 years later. These decades serve as something of a transition in Chinese history. During the 1330s, Japan entered a new period of political instability. Thus, there was a sense of change in Japan and China, although for different reasons, during the 14th and early 15th centuries.

KEY QUESTIONS *The China that emerged in the postclassical period revived many basic features of classical China. Two questions emerge: Why was there so much continuity? And what did, nevertheless, change? ("How did postclassical China differ from China during the Han dynasty?" is another way to ask the second question.) The next question involves the larger east Asian region, including Korea and Japan: were these societies, given their partial imitation of China, part of a common east Asian civilization?*

POLITICAL AND CULTURAL DEVELOPMENTS IN CHINA

Because Chinese civilization was not new, or even reformulated during the centuries after 500, there is no need to describe its most familiar features. Following China's recovery from the nomadic invasions, during the 6th century, the dynastic cycle resumed and served to express and organize much of the nation's political structure. The first postclassical dynasty, the Sui, formed in 589 and was short-lived, although it reestablished a centralized state and repaired the Great Wall. The Sui dynasty also undertook a series of new conquests, pressing into Vietnam and the island of Taiwan and also extending westward, into Turkish lands of central Asia. A period of popular unrest against high taxes brought an end to the Sui ruling family, however, and the Tang dynasty emerged in its place. The reign of this dynasty, along with the earlier Han, is regarded as one of the two golden eras of Chinese history.

The Tang dynasty continued the policy of expansion. Its conquest of Turkish areas in central Asia helped push the Turks westward, thus setting in motion their advance toward the Middle East. The Tang regime also formed protectorates over Tibet, Vietnam, and Korea, which helped spread Chinese institutions without directly annexing these areas to the empire. Japan paid tribute to the Tang. In effect, the Chinese now controlled the entire world, as they knew it. The Tang did lose a key battle with the Arabs, at Talas in 754, which reduced their influence in central Asia, where conversions to Islam increased. But the results did not show immediately.

Under rulers such as the Empress Wu (690–705), one of the few women to reign over China, the Tang reestablished the power of the central government. Like earlier dynasties, notably the Qin and Han, the Tang government reduced the power of independent landlords. Their taxing power was abolished, in favor of direct payment by peasants to the state. The government required the free peasants to submit to military training, which greatly increased the power of the state and its role in individual lives. Finally, the government established comprehensive, accurate censuses of people and property, as the means for imposing fair but also reliable taxation. A growing bureaucracy accompanied these new measures, and the civil service examinations, based on political knowledge but also Chinese philosophy and literature, were revived. As before, this examination system provided relatively able bureaucrats, although drawn mainly from the upper classes, and also promoted cultural unity within the empire. Indeed, the bureaucratic system was greatly elaborated under the Tang. Examinations became stricter, and education counted far more than birthright as the aristocratic role faded in favor of a scholar-bureaucrat ideal. Bureaucrats even amassed the authority to

correct the emperor by citing relevant Confucian wisdom or historical examples.

The Tang dynasty resumed the tradition of extensive government functions, regulating trade, building roads and canals, and organizing justice and defense. A new agency, the Board of Censors, was created to supervise the bureaucracy and guard against misconduct.

The Tang program ultimately included a vigorous attack on Buddhism as a potentially subversive element. Although early Tang emperors had favored Buddhism, the religion was finally officially rejected, as alien and subversive. Thousands of shrines and monasteries were destroyed. Buddhism remained an important minority religion in China, but its period of growth was forcibly brought to a halt. The Tang, even more than their Han predecessors, clearly felt that they had both the right and the duty to regulate the beliefs of their subjects in the interests of political loyalty.

The dynastic decline of the Tang began in the late 700s. Government became less effective. Earlier population growth, the result of Tang prosperity, had increased poverty; there was not enough land to go around. The Tang policy of direct taxation on peasants drove the latter to seek landlord protection and spurred a series of major popular protests. Attacks by nomads from central Asia increased. The Tang dynasty was finally displaced by civil war in 906. However, this time chaos did not last long, for the traditions of centralized rule were too powerful to lapse. The dynasty might fade, but the bureaucratic state was virtually indestructible.

A new dynasty, the Song, came into power in 960. Again, it broke the power of local military leaders, encouraging them to enter civilian life. The Song dynasty did not regain all the territory the Tang had held; indeed, northern China, along the Huanghe River, remained in the hands of nomadic invaders, including some Mongol groups. The founder of the Song dynasty, a northern general named Zhao Kuangyin, realized that he could not take on all

WORLD PROFILES

TAIZONG
(626–649 C.E.)

The Tang emperor Taizong was a brilliant general and an astute administrator. He set the stage for one of China's major dynasties by restoring the imperialist bureaucratic system of the Han and increasing the emphasis on education. He was a tolerant and cosmopolitan emperor as well, unperturbed by the continued spread of Buddhism. Finally, Taizong masterminded Chinese military gains in Vietnam, Tibet, Mongolia, and Korea, where Chinese influence combined with continued political autonomy. Through his immense personal abilities, Taizong was responsible for the revival and dissemination of basic trends in Chinese political history. How does his role as an individual compare to that of his near contemporary in the Middle East—Muhammad?

This image of Tang emperor Taizong was created by a Song dynasty court painter several centuries after the emperor's death.

enemies simultaneously, so he was willing to allow the continued presence of the nomadic warriors in the north. But he developed an excellent strategy for assuming control of the prosperous southern states, and he extended his influence into Indochina. Despite sporadic warfare, the Song dynasty was economically dynamic, with abundant tax revenues and a tight central administration. Commercial and urban life expanded notably, including heightened consumerism. Population growth and the expansion of cities followed from improved agricultural productivity and advances in the output of coal and iron. The use of commodities such as tea, previously an upper-class luxury, spread more widely. Trade within China increased, and although mainly in the hands of foreign merchants, exports to India and the Middle East grew as well. Song taxation

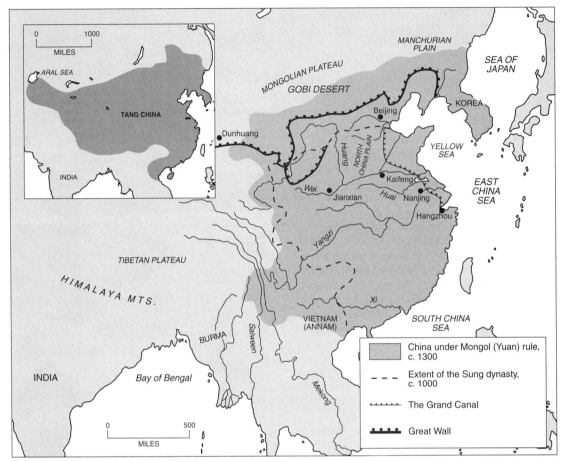

The Political Divisions of China

relieved the peasantry by focusing on merchants instead, and peasant revolts subsided for centuries.

Nonetheless, the Song, too, ultimately faded, in part because they never definitively resolved the problem of nomadic warriors in the north. Although the economy remained prosperous, including the large manufacturing sector, administrative inefficiency reduced tax revenues. One Song emperor tried to introduce reforms to relieve the hard-pressed peasantry, but he was undermined by the powerful, conservative bureaucracy. Invasions by nomadic peoples, particularly the Mongols, became harder to contain.

Finally by 1278, under brilliant new generalship, the Mongols conquered the entire Song empire.

During the Sui, Tang, and Song dynasties, Chinese culture enjoyed a brilliant period. Confucianism remained the dominant philosophy. The challenge of Buddhism led Confucian thinkers to expand their range of philosophical concerns. The philosopher Zhu Xi (1120–1200) played a major role in drawing together some Buddhist themes and orthodox Confucianism, to discuss the nature of the universe and its basic patterns as well as the more familiar issues of ethics and political loyalty. Zhu Xi emphasized family rule, under the benevolence of the father, and the state as a family system applied to the whole empire. He demonstrated how Confucian traditions could be confirmed but also taken in new directions. Giving Confucianism a scope it previously lacked, he also opened a dialogue on basic philosophical issues that had been monopolized earlier by Buddhist thinkers and urged meditation. Such was Zhu Xi's creativity that his own work became part of the Chinese classics, read and relied on for centuries along with the Confucian *Analects* and the Five Classics. While confirming basic features of the Confucian ethic, with emphasis on moral teaching and self-restraint, Zhu Xi added depth to the Chinese philosophical tradition, extending it to areas that Buddhist beliefs, urging meditative union with some basic essence, had opened to new consideration. However, Zhu Xi's success had some drawbacks. Its breathtaking range, from philosophy through history, encouraged the perception that a final synthesis had been achieved; further

speculation was discouraged. In the long run, this promoted a growing sterility in Chinese intellectual life, but the accomplishments of Zhu Xi himself illustrate the creativity of the Tang and Song periods of Chinese history.

Daoism and Buddhism continued to be important popular religions. Also, the Chinese introduced several variants of the Mahayana Buddhist faith. The most famous of these, known now as Zen, its later Japanese name, stressed meditation and spiritual growth. Chinese Buddhism continued, however, to be less otherworldly than its southeast Asian counterpart. Chinese Buddhists stressed the value of hard work and a love of nature, and not simply contemplation. For its part, Daoism continued its development as a religion, integrating popular beliefs in magical healing as it spread more widely.

The incorporation of Buddhism in popular culture, particularly before the Tang persecutions, led to new developments in literature and especially art. Chinese sculptors copied some Indian

Guo Xi (Chinese, ca. 1020–1075). *Old Trees, Level Distance*, 11th century, Northern/Song dynasty (960–1127). Handscroll, ink and color on silk.

styles of statuary. The pagoda was introduced as a new architectural form and spread from China to other parts of Asia, including Japan and Thailand. Buddhist artists painted religious scenes and also acquired a new interest in nature. Even after Buddhism declined as a cultural force in China, the reliance on natural subjects remained. Chinese artists stressed simple statements of nature, carefully arranged and with muted colors. An emperor issued a guide to painters: "Depict objects as they exist. Simplicity and nobility of line is to be the aim." A small object from nature, such as a spray of bamboo, was held to represent the whole universe.

Other arts flourished under the Tang and the Song, and many artists became well known by name, not simply as anonymous craftworkers. Pottery took on a more sophisticated style. The emperors built elaborate palaces, including pagodas with glazed roofs and upturned eaves at the end, designed to withstand windstorms. Urban architecture became something of an art itself. Cities were planned rationally, in a checkerboard pattern. The Tang capital of Zhangan was a rectangular city, contained by walls, which held a population of almost 2 million people. Neighborhoods were laid out in blocks, and a central boulevard led to the government headquarters.

In sum, Chinese art combined growing sophistication in technology and orderly planning with a love of nature inspired by Daoist and Buddhist thought. Chinese art showed the diversity of a civilization that, although traditionalist, remained creative.

In literature, the traditional pursuits of compiling the classics and writing histories combined with new styles. In poetry, a five-syllable meter, called the *shi*, became increasingly popular. Both Daoist and Confucian poets flourished. Li Bo (701–762) was a Daoist who wrote of his love of wine; legend has it that he drowned while reaching out in drunken ecstasy for the reflection of the moon in the water. The popularity of poetry as an art for educated gentlemen led to the composition of hundreds of thousands of poems during this period, with themes ranging from

Confucian morality to the beauties of nature. Many verses had a slightly melancholy ring, such as these lines from the Song poet Meng Zhao:

> Man's life is like morning dew,
> A flame eating up the oil night by night.
> Why should I strain my ears
> Listening to the squeaks of this autumn
>   insect?
> Better lay aside the book
> And drink my cup of jade-white wine.

During the Song period, finally, more urban literary forms appeared, particularly through the rise of popular romantic stories and an active theater.

Chinese science retained its vitality. The government sponsored mapmaking and astronomical observation. Chemistry advanced, and biologists accumulated new information on the pharmaceutical uses of plants and minerals. Texts were written on forensic medicine; in fact, the Chinese were the first to develop a science of crime detection. Hosts of encyclopedias summed up available scientific knowledge ranging from mathematics to the principles of magnetism. As before, the Chinese did not emphasize sweeping scientific theories but, rather, placed value on precise and practical observations. Their scientists knew a great deal about the actual working of the physical universe, and their grasp increased steadily through research and compilation.

Science, in this Chinese tradition, was linked closely to technology, and here the mastery of this civilization remained unmatched. Experiments led to new procedures in insect control. Engineers developed the first suspension bridges, the first locks on canals, the first gear systems to be applied to the milling of grain. The invention of the magnetic compass served as a great aid to navigation. The abacus came into use in calculating commercial transactions. Even the invention of the simple wheelbarrow, not known in other societies for many centuries, was a great boost to agriculture and construction. Porcelain manufacture arose under the Tang, creating a new artistic and production specialty.

The most significant inventions of the Tang–Song period were explosive powder and the printing press. Explosive powder, first used for fireworks, was applied to weaponry by the Song dynasty, which developed land mines, hand grenades, and other projectiles. Printing (first introduced in Korea) resulted from the desire to circulate authentic versions of important books, such as the Buddhist sutras. By the 7th century, the Chinese could rub paper over inked, carved stone in a primitive form of the block press. Woodblocks were soon in use. By the middle of the 10th century, every classic was in print, and books of all types became common under the Song. Paper currency and playing cards were other resulting uses of print. The technology of printing, like explosive powder, spread to the West by the 15th century, via central Asia and the Middle East.

ECONOMY AND SOCIETY IN CHINA

Chinese politics and culture depended on a flourishing economy, and many of the new inventions directly spurred agricultural production and manufacturing. The state continued to encourage economic development, particularly by extending the transportation network. The Chinese genius for practical organization led to standardized measurements for grain, silk, and other goods, an innovation that facilitated both taxation and commerce.

In the vigorous periods of the Tang and Song dynasties, China became the most prosperous agricultural society in the world. As a result of prosperity, the empire's population tripled, passing the 100 million mark even in the restricted territory of the Song dynasty.

Chinese agriculture benefited from the introduction of quick-growing strains of rice and an increasing use of fertilizers. Production of commercial crops such as tea and cotton expanded. In the manufacturing sector, such enterprises as food processing, ceramic making, shipbuilding, and papermaking all improved in technique. A major iron and steel industry developed, with coal heated to make coke, which was then used to fire blast furnaces for iron smelting. Iron was used mainly for weapons but also for farming and construction tools.

An expanding commerce followed from the growth of agriculture and manufacturing. China underwent something of a commercial revolution between 700 and 1200. Marketplaces and shops cropped up throughout the cities, and commercial cities, rather than urban areas serving primarily as political centers, came into being for the first time. Canal building encouraged trade, particularly between the rice-growing regions and the north. Private merchants proliferated, and merchant associations, called *hang*, coordinated their efforts and aided in banking and long-distance transactions. The use of money spread rapidly, with paper currency making its debut in 811.

Foreign trade flourished, although overseas operations remained mainly in the hands of Muslim merchants who exported Chinese goods as far as east Africa. Koreans dominated China's trade with Japan. But under the Song, Chinese merchants took a more active role in oceangoing trade. Overall, China was the most commercial society in the world by 1300, with the most highly developed manufacturing sector. Clear evidence of China's economic power lay in its ability to export finished manufactured goods and import mainly cheaper raw materials, including horses, leather, and precious stones.

Despite all its accomplishments, China did not break the basic mold of an agricultural economy. Some scholars have speculated that it could have done so in this period by parlaying its extensive natural resources, excellent technology, and sheer wealth into an industrial revolution. The advancement of Chinese society was restricted by at least three factors. First, population growth often outstripped available resources, making it difficult for the economy to keep up, much less

Yan Ciyu, *Hostelry in the Mountains,* late 12th century, Southern Song Dynasty.

to evolve into radically new forms. Periods of stability encouraged population increases, which put pressure on the available land, making subsistence, not change, the main goal. Second, the government bureaucracy remained conservative, eager for abundant tax revenues but not interested in pioneering commercial ventures. Government taxation and regulation, indeed, often interfered with economic growth. Finally, Chinese society retained its adherence to values that stressed the importance of scholarship and bureaucratic achievement. Merchants, for all their gains, were still frowned upon, and many traders used their wealth not to establish the basis for further economic gains but to seek entry into the educated, bureaucratic, landowning elite. So China did not fundamentally alter its course, and indeed, by the later Song period, the pace of economic growth began to slow.

Nevertheless, China remained a world economic leader, particularly in manufacturing. Many women were involved in production, especially in silks. Under the Song, new encouragement promoted oceangoing trade, from which the dynasty hoped for further tax revenues. A maritime trade commission in nine coastal cities pushed for more commerce while improving harbors. By 1150, China had the most sophisticated ships in the world, guided by compasses and sailing regularly along southeast Asia and in the Indian Ocean to the Persian Gulf.

Economic change also produced social change. Cities did spring up, and an important urban culture developed. Urban entertainments, including houses of prostitution, and theaters and gambling establishments, proliferated for a wealthy minority. But the landlord-bureaucratic class continued to command peak prestige. Many in this group, in fact, resided in the growing cities and scorned the backwardness of rural ways. Upper-class society increasingly turned away from military pursuits, devoting itself instead to a life of ceremony and cultivated amusements.

Some interest in what we today call consumerism developed in the urban upper classes. New luxuries in food and clothing spread among the rich. Previously, drinks such as tea had not been available, and even though China produced silk, most wealthy people in north China wore coarse hemp cloth. Under the Tang dynasty (618–907), however, things changed. Tea and sugar (this last imported from southeast Asia), and rituals and objects associated with their use, gained great attention among the wealthy. Wu Tzu-mu noted that "the things that people cannot do without every day are firewood, rice, oil, salt, soybean sauce and tea." The idea of fashion—clear but also changing standards of dress—appeared at the imperial court. One royal consort, Yang Kue-fei, exerted particular influence through a taste for exotic fads and fancies. Tang fashions spread elsewhere. A tall lady's hat made its way to Europe, where it was called the *bennin* in the French court. Wealthy merchants in China also picked up a taste for fashion, and sections of cities such as Hangzhou mixed stores selling novelty items with new kinds of entertainments. Marco Polo

described Hangzhou as a pleasure city, with just a bit of overgeneralization:

> For the people of this city think of nothing else, once they have done the work of their craft and their trade, but to spend a part of the day with their womenfolk, or with hired women, in enjoying themselves either in their barges or in riding about the city in carriages. . . . For their minds and thoughts are intent upon nothing but bodily pleasure and the delights of society.

A full consumer society, devoted to acquisition and new styles, did not develop, however. These interests clashed with Confucian emphases on devotion to the public good and to clear social hierarchy. Confucianism, not hostile to wealth, was hostile to excessive display and novelty. Later Tang emperors passed laws confirming established fashions in clothing and banning innovations. A few style leaders were put to death, a clear warning to others not to press new values too far.

The masses of people in China did not find the rhythms of their life greatly interrupted, even when new crops and tools were introduced. Village life did not change significantly for most peasants. The growth of cities did create a burgeoning class of urban poor, who were aided, inadequately, by private and government charity efforts.

The position of women deteriorated somewhat during the Tang dynasty, ironically as a result of rising prosperity. Chinese family life had long been strictly patriarchal. In upper-class life, women had fewer functions than they had maintained before, particularly in the cities. As a result, they were increasingly treated as mere ornaments. Officials and some merchants often took more than one wife. The upper class introduced the custom of binding women's feet: While still young, girls had their feet tightly wrapped until the arch was broken and the toes bent under. The practice resulted in permanent crippling but produced small, delicate feet and a shuffling walk that were considered to be the marks of great beauty. The custom of footbinding gradually spread to

Going Up the River at the Spring Festival: Life in the city of Kaifeng. This painting illustrates China's development of a larger urban culture.

the masses mainly between 1500 and 1900, except in a few parts of south China, and it persisted among wealthier groups into the 20th century. Women's conditions improved somewhat during the Song. Some conducted businesses; others gained education. But public opportunities remained limited for respectable women, and the patriarchal system persisted.

Developments in Chinese society, although significant, displayed on the whole less vitality

than parallel alterations in economic and cultural life. Basic values did not shift, and stability was cherished. To most Chinese, or at least to the civilization's leaders, it seemed that a satisfying balance had been achieved, in which prosperity and cultivated diversions were compatible with continuities in political and intellectual life. Increasingly, China's upper class began to think in terms of protecting this rich tradition from outside forces. The 90 years of Mongol rule enhanced the perception that the world outside China was a hostile, dangerous, but inferior place from which China was wise to isolate itself. This adherence to tradition and suspicion of outside forces persisted into modern times, providing the Chinese with great and understandable pride in their own culture but compromising their ability to respond to changes in other parts of the world.

CIVILIZATION IN KOREA, VIETNAM, AND JAPAN

China's power and prestige during the Tang and Song dynasties guided the spread of civilization to other parts of east Asia. Korea and Vietnam adapted Chinese ideographs to their local languages, resulting in the first writing in these languages. Chinese artistic styles, the bureaucratic examination system, and Confucian learning were assimilated in these areas as well, along with the Buddhist religion as it had passed through China. Chinese influence in Korea peaked between the 7th and 9th centuries, during which time Korean rulers imitated Chinese city planning, imported Confucianism, and copied Chinese artistic styles. The Korean economy was less advanced than China's, however, and depended on virtual slave labor for work in the mines to produce raw materials for export. The aristocracy oppressed the Korean masses, although for several centuries Buddhism was shared across class lines. A social revolt in the 14th century resulted in a new dynasty, the Yi, who ruled until the 20th century and quickly restored aristocratic rule. This dynasty also enforced a rigorous Confucianism, emphasizing the gap between elites and commoners and attacking Buddhism. Confucian ceremonies around the royal court replaced religious ones, particularly within the new capital of Seoul.

Chinese influence in Vietnam also affected the upper classes more than the common people, whose culture, including the enjoyment of cockfights, was more like that of other parts of southeast Asia. Vietnamese rulers, after periods of Chinese occupation, realized they needed to emulate Chinese strengths simply to protect their region, and Chinese bureaucracy and agricultural technology were widely imitated. After the fall of the Tang dynasty in China, Vietnamese rulers gained their independence and began a process of expansion southward. Unlike in Korea, political unity was rare, and internal warfare frequently consumed Vietnamese energies.

Japan was the third geographic area to enter the Chinese orbit. Even more than Korea and Vietnam, however, Japan remained distinct in important respects, in part because, as an island network, the Chinese never conquered it. Thus, the Japanese produced a unique variant of east Asian civilization, akin to Chinese but sufficiently different as to make Japan, ultimately, a major separate force in the world.

As Japan became aware of Chinese achievements, by about the year 400, it developed the habit of selective borrowing—a practice the Chinese had never seen fit to adopt. The custom remained in Japan's collective memory, promoting, much later, a response to Western influences that bore some resemblance to Japan's acceptance of Chinese ways. In the centuries after the year 500, the Japanese proved willing to learn from a superior culture—the Chinese—while retaining a vigorous sense of their own traditions. Particularly in social and political structure, however, the Japanese ultimately did not imitate the Chinese model.

Before Chinese influences happened upon the scene, the Japanese had already developed strong regional political units; the Shinto religion, which worshiped the spirits of nature in local shrines and regarded the emperor as divine; and a prosperous agriculture based on the cultivation of rice. The fragmentation of politics was fostered by the mountains that divide the major islands of Japan, making communication difficult. Shintoism provided a simple, satisfying ritual in which priests led ceremonies and offerings to the gods. The religion also emphasized rituals of cleanliness and discouraged popular festivals featuring games and drinking. Shintoism, like the regional political pattern, long survived influences from the outside, indeed coexisting with them; thus, Japanese Confucianists, Buddhists, and, more recently, dynamic business leaders combine newer values with older Shinto practices.

Japan began copying China in earnest around the year 600. Students and envoys traveled to China and were impressed with the economic and political achievements there. In 604, the Japanese ruler, Prince Shotoku, issued a constitution establishing a centralized government and bureaucracy and urging reverence for Buddhism and Confucian virtues. Chinese-style architecture and urban planning were introduced, along with Chinese ideographs. Regular exchanges with China, organized by the Japanese government, brought back increasing knowledge, as well as the artistic products of the neighboring giant. Under Chinese influence, a new calendar was adopted. A significant result of Japan's assimilation of Chinese culture was that the position of Japanese women deteriorated. Japanese families had long been tightly knit, but with important public and workplace roles for women. Confucian values led to women being considered inferior, and although the Japanese never went as far as their Chinese mentors did in proscribing women's roles, they did confine women's authority to household and child-rearing. In the arts, too, Japan mirrored its neighbor. Chinese dance and musical forms were introduced to court ceremonies and remain the basis for traditional Japanese culture in these areas even today.

As noted, however, complete imitation did not take place, in part because the Japanese economy remained more backward and less commercial than China's. The centralized Japanese bureaucracy did not succeed in displacing local landowning aristocrats. In politics, particularly, the Chinese model soon began to pall. The Japanese aristocracy was quite comfortable with numerous aspects of Chinese culture, but it did not hesitate to diverge from China in terms of political style. In any event, the decline of the Tang dynasty made the Chinese model less attractive for a time. The short-lived Japanese experiment with centralized government soon faded. The emperor remained, but chiefly as a religious figure, rather than an effective political ruler. Real government lay in the hands of regional military leaders.

Japanese rule was, by the year 800, a full-blown feudal system, quite similar to that which developed separately in western Europe during roughly the same period. Powerful regional aristocrats grouped local landowners under their banners, providing protection and courts of law in return for economic aid and military service. The result was a pyramid, with the peasant masses at the bottom of this power structure. The great lords, called *daimyo,* or "great names," used their revenues to hire professional soldiers, called *samurai.* This feudal system was, obviously, a step backward from centralized rule. It brought frequent periods of warfare to the islands and a considerably greater emphasis on military virtues than prevailed in China. Major wars occurred between 1051 and 1088, and again in the following centuries. Nonetheless, the feudal system blended with Confucian values learned from China. Samurai soldiers had a powerful code of honor and bravery and were expected to commit ritual suicide if they dishonored this code. At the same time, the samurai valued literary accomplishments, such as the writing of poetry, and important ceremonies, such as the tea ceremony. In this respect, Japanese feudal lords were different from their rougher-hewn European counterparts. Other distinctions existed between Eastern and Western feudalism. Because Confucianism encouraged the Japanese lords to believe that good government required absolute loyalty, Japanese feudalism did not give way to institutions designed to check the power of the greater lords, like the parliaments that arose from European feudalism. According to the Japanese, admirable personal conduct, the loyalty of the lesser lords, and the mutual devotion of the

Scroll with Depictions of the Night Attack on the Sanjo Palace (Sanjo-den youchi no emaki). Illustrated scrolls on the events of the Heiji Era, Japan, second half of the 13th century, Kamakura period. Handscroll; ink and colors on paper (11.4000).

daimyo to their servants produced proper government. Japanese feudalism involved tight group cohesion, whereas the western European version was characterized by a greater sense of contract between individuals. These differences between Japanese and Western society, translated today into business organizations, are a key example of how successful features of a civilization survive and adapt.

Japanese feudalism was used to build a somewhat stronger government structure after 1185. A single aristocratic family, the Minamoto, gained military dominance over the whole of Japan, establishing a central office called the *shogunate.* Each shogun served officially as chief officer to the emperor, but in fact the shogun was the real ruler of the country and commanded the fidelity of the regional lords. Faithful generals were rewarded with estates scattered throughout the country, which helped convert feudal loyalties into effective national politics. The new shogunate took its name from its capital city of Kamakura. Under the

Kamakura shogunate, which lasted until 1333, Japan experienced greater peace than ever before. The new government was strong enough, among other things, to resist two attempts by Mongol invaders from China to conquer their country. In the second invasion effort, the Mongols massed the largest overseas expedition the world had ever known, with 140,000 men. However, a typhoon destroyed the fleet, and this "divine wind" was long remembered by the Japanese, who believed that their country was uniquely blessed by the gods.

Japanese politics, as it had developed by the end of the Kamakura period, provided a unique mix of Chinese and local ingredients. Confucian loyalty and ceremony blended with military skills, including elaborate exercises in horsemanship, archery, and fencing, and with intense devotion to one's lord. The bureaucratic element of Chinese culture played little role as yet. The feudal code, imposing mutual bonds between leaders and followers, served instead as the principal

HISTORY DEBATE

EAST ASIAN CIVILIZATION?

The spread of civilizations in the postclassical world increased the number of existing civilizations. It also raised questions about how to define particular societies—whether to subsume them under larger civilization headings or to treat them as separate entities.

Japan's pattern of imitating China produced binding connections between the two countries (Vietnam and particularly Korea also were linked to these two cultures). Many historians, as a result, have talked of a larger east Asian civilization, strongly based in Chinese power and precedent. This civilization used Chinese characters, even when other writing systems were introduced. It shared the Chinese version of Buddhism, though some of the smaller countries did so with greater intensity than China itself. It developed common artistic forms, for example, in painting and gardening. It shared social and family ideas, though did not directly copy specific Chinese forms such as footbinding. It was strongly influenced by Confucianism beginning in the postclassical period, and even more so later. It emphasized intricate social etiquette and careful manners. These shared features took on and were compatible with local variations and innovations, but they arguably provided a framework for a larger common culture.

But Japan was not China, even aside from variations and incomplete imitations. The very fact of imitation created potential differences, for China lacked Japan's experience with borrowing from outsiders. Most obviously, Japanese feudalism created a significantly different set of political and military traditions from China's, which permanently shaped Japanese history.

The question of whether the differences among China and its smaller, imitative neighbors outweighed their similarities affects analysis of the region's history, not least because of the sheer number of civilizations that must be considered. This issue is not merely academic. China's economy is joining Japan's as one of the modern world's leading forces, and Korea has begun to participate more on the world stage. Thus, it is important to consider whether a distinctive set of east Asian political and economic approaches is defining the world's future—or whether the differences among the region's countries will modify or dilute this impact.

political link. Even today, the feudal heritage of Japan manifests itself in the close connection between government, business managers, and workers. The Kamakura shoguns translated the dominant sense of group loyalty into a series of committees to oversee their administration. The tradition of collective rule, rather than individual or purely bureaucratic control, also maintains a strong hold on Japanese society; it is, in part, responsible for the unusual skill of the Japanese in group leadership and for the economic surge of their nation in the contemporary world.

CULTURE, SOCIETY, AND ECONOMY IN JAPAN

The Japanese economy developed steadily under the feudal system and the Kamakura shogunate. Even periods of internal warfare did not permanently retard economic growth. Farming became increasingly productive. The aristocracy was conscious of the importance of good agricultural administration, and village leaders instilled the same goals among ordinary peasants. Japanese agriculture, supported by careful systems of irrigation for the rice crop, sustained a far larger population than most areas of comparable size elsewhere in the world.

Commercial ties spread among the islands. By the 12th century, trading cities dotted the nation; manufacturing increased, with a focus on metallurgy, paper, and pottery as well as textiles. Japan still depended on China for most luxury products, including silks, but it offered some manufactured goods in exchange. Moreover, trade and manufacturing produced a growing group of townspeople and merchants. Japanese society, like Chinese society, was originally centered on divisions between aristocratic landlords and peasants, and of course the feudal system tended to reinforce this hierarchy. A small number of slaves also existed, confined to menial occupations. The rise of an aggressive merchant group, skilled in seafaring and navigation through the use of instruments invented in China, jostled the foundations of an agricultural society. Japan did not officially value the merchant middle class highly, but it never developed the intense prejudice against moneymaking characteristic of Chinese elites.

The Japanese borrowed more heavily from China in culture than in politics or social structure. A Japanese system of writing developed, after an initial attempt to use Chinese characters to express the quite different spoken language of Japan; the new system was still based on Chinese ideographs. As in China, poetry was the preferred literary form, although some novels and adventure stories were also produced during the Kamakura period. A collection of some 4500 poems appeared around the year 700. Japanese poetry emphasized form, particularly short poems written in a careful sequence of syllables. For example, the *tanka* form required 31 syllables written in 5 lines, in a 5–7–5–7–7 syllable sequence. Japanese poetry often involved the use of words with multiple meanings. The phrase *Senkata naku* means "there is nothing to be done," with the word *naku* making the sentence nega-

tive, but the same word also means "to cry," allowing a poet to suggest futility and sorrow in the same phrase. Like Chinese poetry, although with different specific forms, Japanese poetry stressed elegance, technical virtuosity, and a pervasive melancholy.

Thus, one poet expressed his sorrow over the death of his wife:

> Suddenly there came a messenger
> Who told me she was dead—
> Was gone like a yellow leaf of autumn,
> Dead as the day dies with the setting sun,
> Lost as the bright moon is lost behind the
>   clouds,
> Alas, she is no more, whose soul
> Was bent to mine like bending seaweed.

As in China, finally, the growth of cities added new literary interests to the Japanese repertoire, particularly through the development of theater. The *No* plays, dramatic poems enacted by dancers, became an especially popular and symbolic form, alternating ritualistic gestures and slapstick comedy.

Japanese literature was, even apart from specific differences in form, no mere imitation of Chinese styles. A delight in war stories provided a distinctive element. But the strong similarities between Japanese and Chinese literary styles brought complexity to Japanese life. The warlords and samurai differed greatly from their Chinese counterparts in political relationships and military ardor, but they shared an interest in appreciating and even writing poetry and drama.

Japanese art derived much from China as well. Buddhist temples, often using the pagoda form, were sometimes built by Chinese architects. Buddhist statuary developed widely. Many Buddhist painters and sculptors created both frightening images to ward off hell and temple decorations representing spiritual joys. Japanese painters featured landscape scenes as well as religious subjects, using bold strokes to capture mountains, waterfalls, and forests. Gardening and

WORLD PROFILES

MUGAI NYODAI

On the surface, and in many ways in fact, patriarchalism deepened in Japan because of Chinese influence. Women's property and inheritance rights declined, for example, though Japan never pressed women's inferiority as far as China did with footbinding. There were two ways, however, in which certain upper-class women found new opportunities in postclassical Japan. The first was writing. Precisely because Chinese models were so prestigious, educated women who wrote in Japanese had a relatively free hand. It was a woman, Murasaki Shikibu, 978–c. 1016, who wrote the world's first novel, *The Tale of Genji*.

Buddhism was another channel. Mugai Nyodai, in the 13th century, served as director of more than 15 temples and Zen convents. Born to an aristocratic family, she had been trained by a Chinese Buddhist priest invited to Japan by a regional leader. Mugai became the priest's successor. Buddhism was ambivalent about women, sometimes holding them to be impure. But they did acknowledge women's spirituality and provided convent life as an alternative to marriage. Mugai was a leading beneficiary of this kind of interest. And some male Zen leaders provided remarkable statements of principle along the same lines. The leader Dogen thus noted, "When we talk of noble persons, these surely include women. Learning the Law of Buddha and achieving release from illusion have nothing to do with whether one happens to be a man or a woman. . . . The four elements of the human body are the same for a man as for a woman. . . . You should not waste your time in futile discussions of the superiority of one sex over the other."

Mugai Nyodai.

flower arrangement, or *ikebana,* became an important art form in Japan as well as in China. Emphasis was placed on small, carefully constructed courtyard gardens, often with one or two artificial hills and a pond with an island and bridge.

Japanese culture during this period did not involve elaborate philosophical speculations or significant scientific work. In this respect, Japan simply omitted some important aspects of Chinese intellectual life. Confucian ethics, as well as a sense of ceremony, did spread widely. Many Japanese combined Buddhism with Shintoism, seeing Shintoism as a set of comforting rituals and Buddhist ceremonies as an avenue to salvation. Buddhist scholars provided detailed descriptions of the horrors of hell and the bliss of paradise. Adherents of the Buddhist faith ranged from the emperor down to many common people, whose religious fervor tended to strengthen in times of political strife. This religious mix was considerably different from that in China and included not only a greater Buddhist element, but also an emphasis on popular congregations and the doctrines of salvation that made Japanese Buddhism increasingly distinctive.

Japanese society was still in the process of development when the Kamakura shogunate fell in 1333, bringing a new period of internal warfare. Further developments in Japanese culture evolved only in later centuries. Yet the Japanese had already created a distinctive variant of east Asian civilization, combining Chinese forms with local religious, political, and social traditions. The result was a society with more contradictory ingredients than in China—which may have been a source of creativity in the long run.

Despite their burgeoning culture, the Japanese did not do what many other newly civilized people have done: embark on an effort of conquest. There was an exception to this: during the 16th century, they tried to capture Korea, but failed. Logically, the Japanese, increasingly skilled in seafaring, might have moved toward the Philippines, or even North America. But at this point, the Japanese orbit was so firmly set by China that expansion made little sense. Like the Chinese, the Japanese considered real civilization to exist only in their world, so they were not tempted to stray widely from its path. And, although Japanese sea trade expanded, it was not yet a match for Muslim fleets or for the navies from Christian Europe that followed later.

Russia and Japan as Imitators

The fact of widespread, reasonably explicit imitation during the postclassical period raises obvious comparisons of various world civilizations. Japan and Russia, for instance, developed in ways so unlike each other because they were in contact with very different models—China and the Byzantine Empire, respectively. Further, Japan was much more imitative than Russia was.

Yet, interesting commonalities existed between Japan and Russia. Both strongly emphasized important cultural forms and cultural apparatus, including writing systems and religion. Both were interested in the political achievements of their "mentors" but were unable to import more sophisticated and centralized political forms at this point. Why cultural imitation seemed more significant and feasible than political imitation is worth pondering: is the same thing true in imitation situations today?

Despite these similarities, differences between the two cultures loomed large again at the end of the postclassical period. With the decline of the Byzantine Empire and a myriad of internal problems, Russia found itself on the cusp of a difficult time that was capped by the Mongol invasion. Japan was spared invasion and, proud of its new Chinese-augmented culture, began to believe that it had surpassed its model, especially when China fell to the Mongols. Its experience, like Russia's, was about to change, but in vastly different ways.

EAST ASIAN SELF-CONFIDENCE

The Japanese, like the Chinese, concentrated mainly on their own development. They even came to believe in their own peculiar destiny. When China was overrun by the Mongols, Japan found itself—by its own standards—the only real civilization it knew about. Thus, the Japanese became accustomed to thinking in terms of their superiority. This confidence remained part of Japanese culture, characterizing the Japanese even during the past century as they have freely imitated Western society. It also served, ironically, to limit Japanese influence in the wider world for many centuries, for the Japanese, like the Chinese, were accustomed to the isolation of their civilization and not eager to participate in exchanges with other cultures. And so, east Asian civilization entered the next period of world history in many ways the best developed of any of the major world cultures, but among the least eager to investigate what was happening outside its own orbit. Thus, without intending to, the civilization left the door open for expansionary forces from other areas, regions in many ways less developed than east Asia itself.

PATHS TO THE PRESENT

The postclassical period was important in shaping China. More active international trade provided connections and precedents that later Chinese commerce built upon. The creation of significant urban traditions, even some definable consumerism, generated dynamics that, arguably, are still influence China today. The further establishment of traditions of bureaucracy and bureaucratic education resurfaced in contemporary China, though with different specific forms.

This period was more obviously formative for Japan. Many cultural elements borrowed by Japan from China, including painting techniques and styles, still partially define Japanese culture. Japan's ability to successfully imitate its giant neighbor without losing its identity, undoubtedly encouraged the country's active interest in similarly selective cultural borrowing in modern times. (This precedent helps explain some differ-

ences between Chine and Japanese reactions to outside influence during the past century or so.) Japanese feudalism, with its special emphasis on group loyalty, generated features that show up in Japanese politics and business even now, differentiating the specifics of Japanese economic success from those of the West. Here, quite clearly, experiences accumulated many centuries ago echo in the contemporary world. Some commentators even find strong traces of samurai self-discipline and team loyalty in the success of current Japanese baseball players—the past can reach far beyond itself.

SUGGESTED WEB SITES

For more information on Asia during the Middle Ages, see http://www.medieval-life.net/asia.htm; on the dynasties of classical imperial China, see http://www.mnsu.edu/emuseum/prehistory/china/classical_imperial_china/fivedynasties.html; on Chinese studies, see http://www.chinaknowledge.de/index.html.

SUGGESTED READINGS

Recent work includes Wang Ping, *Aching for Beauty: Footbinding in China* (2002); William E. Deal, *Handbook to Life in Medieval and Early Modern Japan* (2006); David R. Knechtges and Eugene Vance, eds., *Rhetoric and the Discourses of Power in Court Culture: China, Europe, and Japan* (2005); Charles D. Benn, *Daily Life in Traditional China: The Tang Dynasty* (2002); Tonia Eckfeld, *Imperial Tombs in Tang China, 618–907: The Politics of Paradise* (2005); Linda Walton, *Academics and Society in Southern Sung China* (1999); Heng Chye Kiang, *Cities of Aristocrats and Bureaucrats: The Development of Medieval Chinese Cityscapes* (1999); and Tansen Sen, *Buddhism, Diplomacy and Trade: The Realignment of Sino-Indian Relations, 600–1400* (2003).

Several studies deal with special features of Chinese history during this period (but see also the general surveys mentioned in Chapter 2): Arthur Wright and Denis Twitchett, eds., *Perspectives on the T'ang*

(1973); Mark Elvin, *The Pattern of the Chinese Past* (1973); Jacques Gernet, *Daily Life in China on the Eve of the Mongol Invasion, 1250–1276* (1962); Patricia Ebrey, *The Inner Question: The Lives of Chinese Women in the Sung Period* (1993); and J. Dardess, *Conquerors and Confucians: Aspects of Political Change in Late Yüan China* (1973). On Chinese consumerism (and consumerism's later history), see Peter N. Stearns, *Consumerism in World History* (2002). On Korea, see William Henthorn, *History of Korea* (1971). On Vietnam, see Alexander Woodside, *Vietnam and the Chinese Model* (1971). On Japan, G. Sansom's *A History of Japan to 1334* (1958) provides an excellent survey. Fine specialized studies include P. Duus, *Feudalism in Japan* (1969); G. Sansom, *Japan: A Short Cultural History,* rev. ed. (1943); J. W. Hall, *Government and Local Power in Japan: 500–1700: A Study Based in Bizen Province* (1966); J. W. Hall, *Japan from Prehistory to Modern Times* (1970); H. Paul Varley, *Japanese Culture: A Short History* (1973); and J. M. Kitagawa, *Religion in Japanese History* (1966).

14 Centers of Civilization in the Americas

Far from the world trading network and the missionary religions, two centers in the Western Hemisphere experienced a significant expansion of civilization in the postclassical period and slightly beyond: Central America and the Andes region. Civilization was not, of course, new to either of these areas. The Olmecs and others had already established a basis for solid political organization, an elaborate religion whose followers worshipped at massive monuments, and extensive agriculture and trade.

The centers of civilization in the Americas had no link with the international network taking shape in Asia, Africa, and Europe. At most, they serve, by negative example, to highlight how important that network was. The Americas formed a separate system in the history of world civilizations, although the two major American centers of civilization had no regular contact even with each other. For this reason, as well as the paucity of domesticated animals, American Indian civilizations, though impressive in many ways, lagged behind other societies in the level of technology available. While groups in the Andes used the llama for carrying light cargo, Central Americans had no animals to use for transport or for plowing. Furthermore, American Indian civilizations did not utilize the wheel, save for children's toys, and ironworking was not practiced. Nevertheless, these civilizations developed a complex agriculture, capable of sustaining large populations. The leading Aztec city was far bigger than European cities of the time and awed the first Spanish invaders.

In some respects, the flourishing of impressive civilizations in the Americas resembled a somewhat earlier stage in civilization's rise elsewhere. The growth of civilization in the Americas is more similar to that in Egypt and Mesopotamia than in classical China or the Islamic Middle East and north Africa. The resulting differences in religion and technology between the Americas and the European–Asian axis guaranteed massive problems in later

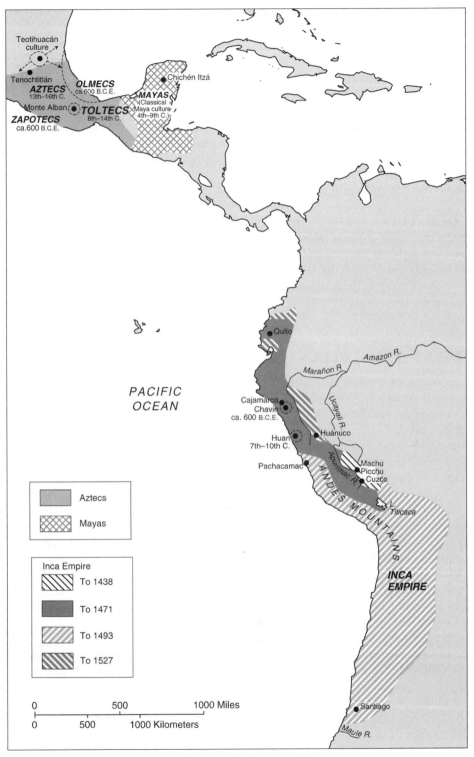

Teotihuacán
culture

Tenochtitlán

AZTECS
13th–16th C.

OLMECS
ca.600 B.C.E.

Monte Alban

TOLTECS
8th–14th C.

ZAPOTECS
ca.600 B.C.E.

Chichén Itzá

MAYAS
(Classical
Maya culture
4th–9th C.)

**PACIFIC
OCEAN**

Quito

Amazon R.

Marañon R.

Cajamarca
Chavin
ca. 600 B.C.E.

Ucayali R.

Huánuco

Huan
7th–10th C.

Pachacamac

Machu
Picchu
Cuzco

Apurímac R.

L.
Titicaca

A N D E S   M O U N T A I N S

**INCA
EMPIRE**

| | Aztecs |
| | Mayas |

Inca Empire

	To 1438
	To 1471
	To 1493
	To 1527

Santiago

Maule R.

| 0 | | 500 | | 1000 Miles |
| 0 | 500 | | 1000 Kilometers | |

The Americas Before the Spanish Conquest

encounters, when the Americas were drawn into worldwide contacts for the first time.

Note that, because American patterns developed separately, Afro-Eurasian chronology does not fit them tidily: key developments in the Americas began before the postclassical period, while Aztec and Inca achievements crested between 1450 and the early 16th century; 1500, not 1450, was the key break in American history.

■ **KEY QUESTIONS** *Central American and Andes centers were quite different. What comparisons best highlight the values and institutions of each center? How did both manage to flourish without many of the standard features of civilizations in Afro-Eurasia?*

THE MAYAS AND AZTECS

The disappearance of the first agricultural societies in Central America, those of the Olmecs and their immediate successors, is shrouded in considerable mystery. Direct traces of these civilizations, except for the monumental ruins that still remain, vanished by the 7th century. Probably one factor in their decline involved invasion by peoples farther north, in the valley that runs through present-day central Mexico. Several of these peoples, in turn, were able to build on the earlier civilizations, creating still more elaborate cultures of their own. The most important of these societies were the Mayas, who established their initial civilization by about 100 C.E. and emerged as the dominant group in the middle region of Central America by the year 600. From this point, Maya history divided into three stages: the first phase of particular creativity, from 600 to about 900, centered in the northern portion of present-day Guatemala; then a decline and move northward to the Yucatán peninsula in Mexico, where the Mayas intermingled with other American Indian groups from the north, notably the Toltecs; and then the definitive collapse of this mixed culture, from about 1200 on, culminating in the virtual destruction of formal Maya society, including its written language, during the Spanish conquest of the 16th century.

Maya civilization sprang from a tropical rain forest, in areas of great fertility that required immense efforts to maintain. The difficulty of preserving agricultural land from animals, insects, and lush vegetation helps explain the intensity of Maya polytheistic religion, bent on placating a host of savage gods. Central American civilization practiced blood-letting through self-mutilation and human sacrifice, which Mayas believed kept the universe going. Body piercing was also common.

It was religion that gave the clearest structure to Maya society. Huge temples and pyramids were erected to honor the gods. The Mayas did not construct cities in the usual sense, where a variety of activities could take place; they instead built enormous ceremonial complexes, such as Chichén Itzá. Here, priests conducted rituals to honor the gods. Religious festivals in these centers stimulated intense involvement among ordinary men and women, who produced richly decorated costumes and performed elaborate dances. Games were conducted in the religious centers as well, again to honor the gods. In one game, played in a rectangular courtyard, opposing teams tried to throw a ball through a small circular hoop attached to the side wall; the team that lost was killed as a sacrifice—although it is important to note that scoring was so difficult that most games ended in a tie. Political organization, too, seems to have been dominated by the priestly caste, which organized secret societies to preserve their aura of power and mystery.

Science was also oriented toward the service of religion. Along with the massive monuments the Mayas constructed, the development of a detailed calendar, based on careful astronomical studies made from observatories in the religious centers, rates as their highest achievement. More than any other people at this point, the Mayas had an extraordinary sense of time. The calendar was used particularly to regulate the cycle of religious

Maya ruins: Temple of Inscriptions, Palenque, Mexico. Priests ruled the tops of these pyramids, which contained rooms for secret meetings and places to lead prayer and sacrifice.

celebrations and coordinate them with the cycle of the agricultural year. However, the Mayas also used their calendar to calculate back by hundreds of thousands of years, perhaps realizing that time had no beginning. Maya culture also predicted future upheavals based on calendar formulas. Associated with calendar development came unusually accurate measurements of the length of the year (which Mayas figured out to within two hours) and sophisticated mathematics; the Mayas were one of only three civilizations to independently devise the concept of zero.

Religion dominated art. The great pyramids, normally uninhabited except for priests, were designed to impress observers with the remoteness of the gods and the power of those who climbed the steps to commune with them. Statues portrayed gods, often in semi-animal form, with emphasis on the feline grace and ferocity of the jaguar; other statues, particularly in female form, celebrated more benign deities of fertility.

Finally, the Mayas developed a hieroglyphic writing, which they used for decorating temples, composing books, and establishing markers for the passage of time.

Maya society was hierarchical. Upper-class families set themselves apart visually. They used a kind of press to distort the skulls of their children, before the skulls hardened. This gave the heads an elongated appearance and was presumably regarded with respect.

Several features of Maya civilization remain unknown. The jungle now claims many religious centers. Few books have survived, for the Spanish tried zealously to destroy all traces of Maya culture in their thirst to Christianize the heathen. Somewhat more extensive evidence of the Maya-Toltec culture exists on the Yucatán peninsula than for classical Maya achievements. Through the Toltecs, the Mayas added to their religion some human sacrifice, chiefly involving prisoners of war. Secular rulers seem to have gained

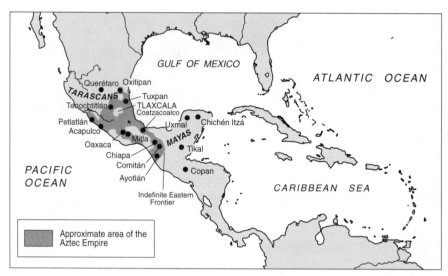

Aztec and Maya Civilizations

increasing prominence. Invasions by other American Indian groups proved to be a growing problem; in the 13th century, the great center of Chichén Itzá was sacked by invaders. The Mayas then constructed another capital defended by five miles of walls. This too was conquered, apparently by an uprising of Maya peasants, in about 1460. By this point, Maya civilization was virtually extinguished, although the last Maya stronghold surrendered to the Spanish only in 1699.

Because of technological limitations, particularly the absence of extensive ironworking and the lack of a usable wheel, but also because of the failure to develop arches as a means of support for their buildings, Maya culture depended on immense human labor. At the same time, the extensive religious activity, especially in the ceremonial complexes, required a great deal of human effort. Perhaps it was for this reason that the Mayas proved so vulnerable to invasion and that their art and political skills deteriorated relatively quickly after the high point of the civilization—in some contrast to the more complex ebb and flow of most civilizations in Asia and the Mediterranean. A related explanation of the dramatic declines of American civilizations such as the Maya emphasizes the problems of maintaining adequate agriculture. With no metal tools and few fertilizers, it was hard to maintain the land, keep weeds at bay, and expand acreage. Periods of Maya decline remain hard to interpret. A recent theory suggests that Maya political structure may have permitted families to simply move away when the ruling class became too oppressive.

The Aztec Empire

The Aztecs entered the central valley of Mexico from the north, prior to 1350. They displaced the Toltecs, who had already dispersed, and extended the Aztec empire into other parts of Central America. Their capital was a new city constructed on the marshes around Lake Texcoco, where they built an elaborate network of bridges and causeways to support their great center, Tenochtitlán. The Aztec empire was a military establishment, controlled by a warrior people who allowed subordinate groups, including the Mayas, to run their own regions so long as they paid regular, high tribute in the form of gold and slaves. Aztec religion, featuring gods of war as

HISTORY DEBATE

WHAT HAPPENED TO THE MAYAS?

Figuring out why a people fade from power after centuries of creative achievement is always fascinating. In the case of the Mayas, debate is heightened by the absence of abundant sources. We have no records of anyone musing about what was going wrong. Among historians, warfare was an early favorite as an explanation because of what we know of its destructive power. But on the whole, archeological evidence does not support this, and in fact wars, by themselves, seldom have ended a civilization outright. Soil exhaustion or degradation of the land is another possibility. Some experts now argue that changes in the water supply—or what is called the "Great Maya Drought"—played a major role. The problem with this theory is that declines occurred in different times and places, and while there is evidence of water shortage, the dates do not correlate perfectly with the Maya withdrawal. So far, in other words, no one explanation is perfect. This may mean that a more complex combination of factors was in play. Would this correspond to the causes of decline in other world history cases?

Despite decline, elements of Maya culture survived, combining with that of later peoples such as the Toltecs. Maya villages remain to this day in the Yucatán peninsula of Mexico and in Guatemala. And Maya people may still go to church to pray to a saint who is also one of the old gods. But the apparatus of the civilization unquestionably disintegrated.

well as gods of nature, blended fairly readily with the religions already current in the region, and the Aztecs devoted considerable attention to works of art and pyramidal monuments in honor of the gods.

The Aztec empire displayed great magnificence. Tenochtitlán, which was the forerunner to the Spanish capital Mexico City, contained about 100,000 inhabitants and featured ornate palaces, statuary, and temples. The most intensive agriculture in the world developed to support a population of perhaps 20 million. Extensive regional trade included vibrant markets, and the Aztecs used merchants as spies. Central America traded widely with Indian societies in what is now the United States southwest. Culturally, Aztecs relied on the earlier stylistic achievements of the Mayas and Toltecs. More important, they depended on extensive slave labor and, as noted, exacted tributes to maintain their luxury. Thus, although their wealth and engineering accomplishments

awed the first Spanish settlers, who claimed that the Aztecs' cities surpassed the glories of Rome or Constantinople, they failed to create any basis other than force for their political regime. Government was centralized, under a king who claimed divine authority, and the level of violence was high.

To glorify their gods, the Aztecs extended earlier practices of human sacrifice, killing no less than 20,000 people at the dedication of one of the great pyramids. The Aztecs believed that the gods themselves had been sacrificed in order to create the sun, which needed human blood as food, and their worship reenacted this drama. As a result, not only the economy but also the religion required a steady flow of victims, mainly drawn from persistent warfare. This was an inherently fragile period in Central American history, for the subjects of Aztec rule had no reason to revere their masters. In fact, many American Indian groups initially welcomed the arrival of the Spanish explorers as liberators from their harsh tyranny. Ironically, the Aztecs were hampered in their response to Spanish incursions, not only by their inferior weaponry—for they lacked guns or iron weapons of any sort—but also by their own uncertainty about the future of their rule. Their empire, built on the greater creativity of earlier civilizations in the region, proved to have scant impact beyond its own time.

The Inca Empire

A second and quite separate center of American Indian civilization developed, during the centuries of Maya and Aztec ascendancy, in the Andes mountains of present-day Peru and Bolivia. Here, building on the earlier culture that had extended carefully terraced agriculture in the region and constructed substantial monuments to the gods, an Inca empire arose from the 12th century on.

The American Indian civilization in Central America, particularly before the final Aztec period, in certain features resembled the earlier river valley civilization of Mesopotamia. The emphasis on regional states, the creativity in science, the interest in art and active trade in luxury goods, even the pessimistic tone of the religion—all offer vague echoes of Sumer and its successors. In contrast, the Inca empire reflects, again in very general terms, the styles of ancient Egypt, especially in its focus on the sun god and the establishment of a highly centralized state led by a ruler regarded as divine.

The Incas, centered initially in a small area in what is now Peru, began expanding their authority over other civilized peoples in the region, learning more elaborate political and artistic forms as they went. By the late 1400s, their empire extended from Ecuador to central Chile, constituting the largest governmental unit ever created up until that time in the Americas. The empire included a network of roads over 10,000 miles of mountain terrain. On these roads, runners regularly carried messages, both carefully

Lady of the Serpent Skirt: carving of the Aztec goddess Coatlicue. Coatlicue was also mother of the war god and goddess of the earth and death.

memorized oral communications—for the Incas never developed writing—and records coded by knots in colored ropes (a system called *quipu*). The Inca people themselves served as a ruling caste in their empire. They were led by a man called *Sapa Inca,* or "only Inca." This ruler governed despotically, regulating marriage and movement and officially controlling all produce. The government, in other words, monitored the labor force closely. Exchanges, carried by llama transport, provided food for craftsworkers and cloth for the farmers. There was no trade in the sense of a money economy, and local self-sufficiency was emphasized.

Many areas traded mainly among various levels in the same region, from mountain to valley, each producing what was best suited and exchanging for the rest. Copper tools were manufactured, and gold and silver were used for luxurious ornamentation in the royal palaces. The government regulated the education of local elites among the conquered peoples to ensure their allegiance. Protest was dealt with by military force, followed by the resettlement of disaffected peoples to reduce the potential for further trouble.

The Inca system, far less brutal than that of the Aztecs, was extremely tolerant of local beliefs and religion, although the Incas themselves worshipped a sun deity from whom the royal family was presumably descended. The Incan religion highlighted separate lines of gods and goddesses. Like the ancient Egyptians, the Incas mummified their dead to preserve them for an afterlife.

By the 1400s, the Incas had probably overextended their territory. Without writing, their recordkeeping ability was limited, which meant substantial dependence on local leadership. Conquered peoples were not always content, and technology lagged, which further limited the economic and political links that could be sustained. Thus, the Inca empire was already receding somewhat even before the Spanish conquest, and in any event the methods and weapons of war the Incas had developed were no match for the guns of the Spaniards.

THE ISSUE OF ISOLATION

The achievements of the American civilizations were impressive by any standard, but particularly when viewed within the context of unusually stark isolation from any other civilized areas. All societies in Asia, Africa, Europe, and even China had benefited from ideas and techniques they borrowed from others, and as we have seen in previous chapters, the importance of borrowing increased during the postclassical period for several areas of new civilization. The Americas had no part in this or in the shared disease pool that resulted from international contacts.

Several other major areas sponsored important new developments in isolation during the postclassical centuries. Polynesian contacts with Hawaii became more extensive, and the settlement of New Zealand began. Polynesians adapted an essentially Neolithic technology in their new settings, utilizing local resources for foods while importing certain animals. As in Central America, a rigid social structure helped compensate for technological limitations; it included an important priestly caste and was geared for frequent warfare. Polynesian society was able to maintain its isolated development until the 18th century, when European contacts brought many of the same results, in terms of conquest and disease, that the Americas had earlier experienced. Here, too, isolation became a historical issue—and a very grave one—when it was ended.

PATHS
TO THE PRESENT

The high cultures of the Mayas and Incas left few traces for later civilization in the Americas to build on, in part because of their internal limitations but especially because of their conquest by Europeans, beginning in the 16th century. Tragically, the Europeans brought with them not only greater firepower but also a host of diseases against which the original Americans had not developed immunity; 80 percent of the Indian population was stricken, without the benefit of available treatment. The civilizations that did arise in the Americas after European conquest owed little to previous indigenous patterns at the level of formal religion or politics. Had the Europeans not come, with their superior technology, civilization might well have spread or diversified.

Even as the Incas declined, new centers of advanced culture developed in places such as present-day Colombia. In North America, although many Indian groups followed a hunting-and-gathering economy combined with seasonal farming, settled agriculture had spread not only to the southwest, from the more advanced centers in Mexico, but also along the Atlantic coast. Pueblo Indians reflected Central American civilization, whereas slash-and-burn farming enhanced Indian societies in the Mississippi and New England regions. Loose political alliances had formed among certain peoples, such as the five Iroquois tribes around the eastern Great Lakes, which might ultimately have developed into a tighter form of administration. This future was undone, however, by European control and the spread of certain diseases.

However, in important respects, the history of American Indian civilizations did reverberate in later periods, even aside from the fact that surviving Indian groups in both North and South America preserved an important sense of language and heritage. There were two clear links to the present. First, the crops so creatively developed during centuries of agriculture, particularly in Central America and the Andes, were a vital contribution to the nutrition of peoples worldwide when they were more widely disseminated. European settlers in the Americas, as well as Africans, Asians, and Europeans, found their diets and thus their lives substantially altered by corn, squash, and the potato, whose cultivation had been developed by the Incas and Mayas and their ancestors. The spread of important new foods from the Americas from the 16th and 17th centuries on was a major factor in world history.

Second, beneath the surface, where American Indian civilizations had taken deepest root, significant traces of their societies remained long after official European conquest. Thus, in Central America and the Andes, American Indians long preserved elements of older religious beliefs, even under a facade of Christianity. Communal festivals as well as some secret rituals allowed tra-

ditional dances, games, and other recreations to survive. More important still, many American Indian groups preserved certain artistic patterns in their geometrically designed pottery and jewelry and their brightly colored clothing that became characteristic of the new civilization formed by a merger between Spanish and American Indian heritages. Finally, American Indians in these areas maintained distinctive local customs and economic and political styles into the 21st century. The very appearance of Indian villages, notably in Central America, resembled that of traditional communities, with a Christian church and perhaps an official government building merely supplementing earlier housing patterns and a characteristic market square.

Many villages also preserved a communal system of agriculture that had supported the larger American Indian civilization. In the Andes, villagers frequently held land in common, rather than through individual ownership, and stressed the production of most goods essential to village life. Elaborate market systems and a profitmaking motive long remained foreign to this village tradition. Important segments of the indigenous population thus long resisted fully embracing the habits and institutions of the conquering Europeans. This fact encouraged a distinctive, sometimes uncomfortable fusion of European and American Indian ways, beneath the levels of official government and religion, toward forming a Latin American culture that was neither purely American Indian nor purely European in nature. The surviving traditions also ensured future conflicts when, as in recent decades, customary economic values encountered much more direct challenges than initial Spanish conquest and administration had compelled. It is overly simplistic to claim that popular culture in the areas of Latin America where American Indian populations remained largest—notably, those areas that had previously been civilized and so possessed a vigorous agricultural base—merely combined European and American Indian customs to produce a new culture. Such a statement ignores the

UNDERSTANDING CULTURES

THE QUESTION OF LEGACIES

One of the central tasks of historical interpretation is to see what beliefs and values we entertain as a result of legacies from the past. Cultural heritage from great periods of civilization includes such things as major religions or venerated literary and artistic models. It also includes ways to approach science. In this book, we trace connections of this sort between China, India, Islam, and the classical Mediterranean.

Heritage from the American Indian civilizations that flourished during the postclassical period is much harder to assess. When the Spanish arrived, from the early 16th century on, they resolutely attacked Maya, Aztec, and Inca high culture in favor of Christianity. Even Maya writings were largely destroyed, so it is only now that scholars are regaining the ability to decipher remnants of the Maya alphabet.

Nonetheless, it is difficult to uproot a culture entirely. Popular beliefs and rituals are harder to dis-

lodge than a more formal intellectual life, for popular systems do not depend mainly on writing. Spanish conquerors, furthermore, had to tolerate some popular holdovers as part of persuading ordinary people to accept the trappings of Christianity. Thus, Maya colors and designs were used to decorate Christian statues. Older indigenous holidays were combined with Christian festivals, and features of older gods were preserved in American Indian versions of Christian saints. Here was another case of syncretism. Elements of polytheism and traditional celebrations were combined with Christianity, from Central America to the Andes. The American Indian component of Latin American culture remained a serious factor even as European and African elements were introduced following the postclassical period. Prayer to saints who are also Maya gods continues for some people even today.

fact that the governing institutions of American Indian civilization really were destroyed; therefore, there were great differences in the bargaining power of the conqueror and the conquered. But important popular forms did persist alongside new or imported patterns brought by the Spaniards and their heirs, and they continue to influence the lives of Latin Americans in Mexico, Peru, Bolivia (where an Indian was elected President for the first time in 2006), and other countries of these regions even in the present day.

SUGGESTED WEB SITES

On the ancient Maya history, see http://www.digitalmeesh.com/maya/history.htm and http://www.mnh.si.edu/anthro/maya/; on Inca civi-

lization, see http://www.crystalinks.com/incan.html; on the Ancient Aztecs, see http://library.thinkquest.org/27981/; on the culture and history of the Americas, see http://www.loc.gov/exhibits/kislak/.

SUGGESTED READINGS

Recent work includes Robert Sharer, *The Ancient Maya* (2006); Adam Herring, *Art and Writing in the Maya Cities* (2005); Michael D. Coe, *The Maya* (2005); Peter G. Tsouras, *Montezuma: Warlord of the Aztecs* (2005); Karen Vieira Powers, *Women in the Crucible of Conquest: The Gendered Genesis of Spanish American Society, 1500–1600* (2005); Frances F. Berdan, *The Aztecs of Central Mexico: An Imperial Society* (2005); David Carrasco et al., *Montezuma's Mexico: Visions of the Aztec World* (2003); Michael E. Moseley, *The Incas and Their Ancestors: The Archaeology of Peru* (2001); Rosemary A. Joyce, *Gender and Power in Prehispanic Mesoamerica* (2000); Michael E. Smith and Marilyn A. Masson, *The Ancient Civilizations of Mesoamerica: A Reader* (2000); Stuart Stirling, *The Last Conquistador* (1999); Catherine Julien, *Reading Inca History* (2000); Hugh Thomson, *The White Rock: An Exploration of the Inca Heartland* (2003); and Ian Graham, *Alfred Maudslay and the Maya: A Biography* (2002).

On Indian civilization in the Americas, see also Ignacio Bernard, *Mexico Before Cortez: Art, History, Legend* (1975); M. D. Coe, *Mexico* (1984); Frances Berdan, *The Aztecs of Central Mexico: An Imperial Society* (1982);

M. P. Weaver, *The Aztec, Maya and Their Predecessors* (1981); and Eric R. Wolf, ed., *The Valley of Mexico: Studies in Pre-Hispanic Ecology and Society* (1976). Inga Clendinnen's *The Aztecs* (1991) is splendid.

On the Incas, consult J. A. Mason, *The Ancient Civilizations of Peru* (1973); Richard W. Keatinge, ed., *Peruvian Prehistory* (1988); Alfred Metraux, *The History of the Incas* (1970); John Murra, *The Economic Organization of the Inca State* (1980); Irene Silverblatt, *Moon, Sun, and Witches: Gender Ideologies and Class in Inca and Colonial Peru* (1987); and John V. Murra, Nathan Wachtel, and Jacques Revel, eds., *Anthropological History of Andean Politics* (1986).

15

The Mongol Interlude and the End of the Postclassical Period

This chapter focuses on the huge changes that occurred between 1250 and 1450, including the decline of Arab leadership and the rise of new frameworks for global interactions in Afro-Eurasia. Contacts among cultures increased. Both east Asia and western Europe became more involved in the world network of interactions. Africa, partly because it worked through the Middle East as an intermediary, was less affected. In addition to these societal shifts, key technologies also changed, establishing the groundwork for further developments. The result was a different world balance by 1450 from that which prevailed two centuries before.

Not surprisingly, cultural trends among major societies varied greatly as the postclassical period drew to a close. Peasants in western Europe gained some freedom from serfdom, while their counterparts in the Middle East encountered new landlord demands. Russia began to lose vitality, even before the Mongol invasions, as Japan and western Europe gained momentum. A few trends, however, were generally similar across diverse cultures, in much of Asia, Africa, and Europe. For example, many aristocracies shifted from their emphasis on warfare to focus on gaining greater cultural sophistication. Conditions for women deteriorated as agricultural economies yielded larger surpluses, permitting families to treat women as mere ornaments. And, the great world religions continued to gain ground. There is no question, however, that societies in the postclassical world remained widely separated and, for the most part, followed quite different patterns—some of which, such as the formation of regional kingdoms in Africa, persisted into the next period of world history.

Nevertheless, because the international network had intensified during the postclassical period, several major developments caused changes that brought the period itself to a close while setting the stage for the initial dynamics of the period to come. Isolated civilizations were not affected by these changes, however, and

Africa was less touched by them than were Asia and Europe.

The first of these developments was the decline of Arab political strength and the narrowing of Middle-Eastern culture and economy. The Arabs had played such a strong leadership role in forming the international network that their problems inevitably reverberated beyond their borders. African trading, although still vigorous, was constrained by the shifts in Arab society, with which African merchants most closely interacted. Western Europe, although heartened by Arab decline, grew anxious as the second of these developments took place: the Turks' vigorous invasions of the Middle East and their establishment of a new Muslim empire. The Turks succeeded in capturing Constantinople in 1453 and assumed control of Byzantine holdings in the Balkans, as well as in much of the Arab Middle East, acts that reconfigured this region. They also provoked major reactions, particularly on the part of nervous Europeans, who redoubled their efforts to find trade routes that would allow them to bypass the Muslim heartland.

The ramifications of Arab decline and Turkish invasion were amplified by an even greater event—the Mongol conquests in Asia and eastern Europe.

■ **KEY QUESTIONS** *Mongols were often regarded as fierce, brutal invaders; most world historians now emphasize constructive features of their rule, including the new connections they promoted. Which is the correct judgment, and why do such polarized views exist? What happened when the Mongol emperors declined? How was the world different in 1400 from what it had been in 1200, as a result of the Mongol era?*

MONGOL EMPIRES

The Mongol conquests in this period—the last of their kind, in which nomadic warriors overturned the governments of agricultural societies—contributed to important changes in east Asia, southern Asia, the Middle East, and Russia. Even more, they enhanced the international network, facilitating new exchanges and whetting appetites for greater international involvements.

Mongol herders had been pressing at the northern frontiers of China for some time. They were superb equestrians and archers, using an iron stirrup that allowed them to fire their bows while riding; peasant foot soldiers could not compete with such military prowess. Organized in family clans by leaders who advanced because of their military abilities, the Mongols formed a tightly knit fighting unit, highly trained and able to ride in close formation. Europeans called this fighting force a "horde." The Mongol cavalry ultimately included between 50,000 and 70,000 horsemen, all adept at avoiding head-on clashes with larger forces and skilled at organizing ambushes and cutting off supply routes.

The great Mongol conqueror Chinggis (or Genghis) Khan was born about 1147. His first task was to unify the tribal groups of Mongols; his name, which meant "universal ruler," was adopted at the end of this process, in 1206. Chinggis was a superb general and also an able administrator who used Turkish writing or script to facilitate his bureaucracy. Chinggis Khan invaded China early in the 13th century; he also conquered a Turkish kingdom in south central Asia. Each conquest fed Mongol wealth and increased the size of the armies. Successors to Chinggis Khan swept through the Middle East, toppling the Abbasid caliphate. An Egyptian army pushed the Mongols back to Persia in 1260 with a victory in present-day Israel, but a Mongol-controlled Persia persisted for decades. The Mongols' impact on the eastern Islamic lands, including the terror they generated, long reverberated. They also seized all of Russia and pressed into the smaller kingdoms of eastern Europe. They might have continued farther west, but they were called back by a domestic political crisis.

Mongol forces completed the conquest of China, unseating the Song dynasty in 1279. From the Chinese base, the greatest Mongol emperor,

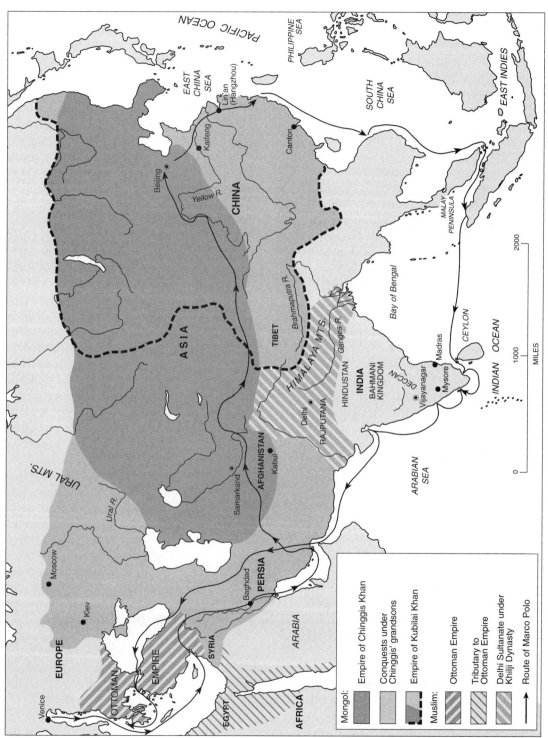

Mongol and Muslim Empires, c. 1000–1500 C.E.

Mongol:
- Empire of Chinggis Khan
- Conquests under Chinggis' grandsons
- Empire of Kubilai Khan

Muslim:
- Ottoman Empire
- Tributary to Ottoman Empire
- Delhi Sultanate under Khilji Dynasty
- → Route of Marco Polo

MILES
0   1000   2000

Chinggis Khan's grandson Kubilai Khan, organized invasions into southeast Asia and India. He also attempted seaborne attacks on Indonesia and Japan, although these ended in failure. The first effort against Japan was undone by a typhoon. The Japanese, seeing this as a "divine wind," thought they were specially protected by the gods. Despite these setbacks, by 1300 the Mongols ruled or influenced most of the Eurasian civilized world. Their own territories stretched 6000 miles.

The Mongol period produced fascinating interactions between personalities and history. Various Mongol rulers converted to Buddhism or Islam. Kubilai Khan himself ruled China in grand style. Of necessity, he preserved the Chinese bureaucratic system but used foreigners—Turks and other Muslims and even a handful of Europeans— as his chief ministers because he distrusted the Chinese Mandarins, who were assigned to lower bureaucratic ranks. Repressive laws that prevented the Chinese from assembling or traveling by night bred resentment. But for some decades, Kubilai Khan ruled as few Chinese dynasts had ever done before him, operating a splendid court that was completely open to foreign visitors. Among these were members of an Italian family—Marco Polo and his father and uncle—who had traveled across Asia to serve at the Great Khan's court. Encouraged by the Khan's friendly curiosity, Marco Polo was able to learn a great deal about China. Some items he could not understand, given his European background, including the use of coal to smelt iron. However, his travel account was widely read; at first regarded as fantasy, it contributed greatly to acquainting Europeans with the East.

But the Mongol empire was short-lived. It was weakened by protests and banditry in places such as China. Disputes over leadership succession also plagued the Mongols. China withdrew from Mongol control later in the 14th century, and the main Mongol legacy in China was an enhanced distaste for foreigners, for the Mongols had been bitterly resented as barbarians. Mongol impact in the Middle East was also short-lived, for the Turks increasingly held power in this region. Direct

Mongol influence in India was also slight, although a later Mongol-Turkish force, pressing into India early in the 1500s, established another great Muslim empire in much of the subcontinent. Only in Russia did Mongol control leave an enduring legacy, perhaps setting back economic and cultural levels but also stimulating an intense desire, on the part of the Russians, to imitate Mongol conquests. Russia gained full freedom from Mongol domination in 1480 and began a pattern of expansion of great importance in world history.

The Mongols' impact on world history, however brief, was significant in several respects. Mongols provided safe passage for travelers over land routes, and they were tolerant, interested in learning from newcomers. So the vast stretch of territory under Mongol control made possible the interchange of knowledge and products among the various civilizations of Europe and Asia. In particular, Chinese discoveries—gunpowder, paper money, printing, porcelain, and medical techniques, even playing cards—began to make their way westward. Mongol-facilitated diffusion was of special benefit to western Europe, previously backward, and helps explain this region's subsequent rise, as Asian technology was combined with a territorially ambitious, aggressive spirit. The Mongol presence was also significant in keeping western Europe, albeit accidentally, out of the hands of foreign powers. For a century (and more than that in Russia), most major civilizations in eastern Europe and Asia were preoccupied with invasion, the threat of invasion, or foreign control. Western society enjoyed the fruits of new contacts with Asia without the attendant hardships and distractions. This, too, helps us understand why Western nations displayed such surprising vigor on the world scene by the late 15th century.

The Mongols also affected the conduct of war. They helped teach both the Turks and Europeans the effective use of explosive powder. By the early 15th century, both groups were utilizing the cannon in warfare, to great effect.

New international contacts also promoted new contagions, an unhappy by-product of the

WORLD PROFILES

CHABI KHAN

Chabi, wife of the great Mongol emperor Kubilai Khan (who ruled from 1260 to 1294), was an important historical personage in her own right. Obviously, in patriarchal societies, a woman most commonly gained access to power (even on a very local level) through the position of her husband. Chabi advised Kubilai actively, guiding counterstrategies against his ambitious brothers and promoting Buddhist interests in the highest government circles. Chabi also urged tolerance for the defeated Chinese rulers, arguing that leniency would best reconcile the Chinese to Mongol rule; she influenced her husband to abandon a plan to turn farmland near the capital into pastures for the Mongols' horses. At the same time, Chabi and other Mongol women resisted integration with Chinese customs concerning women, from Confucian doctrines to footbinding. They moved freely in public, and they hunted on horseback with their husbands and in parties of their own. These women had no enduring impact on Chinese gender patterns, however. Does this suggest some distinctive limitations on the historical role of even great women in the postclassical era? Or do great people in general have limited power to change the directions of a society?

Chabi, wife of Kubilai Khan, the 13th-century Mongol ruler of China.

increased level of Eurasian commerce by the end of the postclassical period. Bubonic plague broke out in western China early in the 14th century. Carried probably by fleas on pack animals, it reached the Middle East by the mid-14th century, hitting north African ports by the 1360s. From there, it spread quickly to Italian ports and then to the rest of western Europe. The overall result was one of the most deadly world epidemics in all of human history, with mortality rates more than 25 percent in parts of the Middle East and Europe. Only the plagues of the late classical period and the later European-borne diseases in the Americas and Pacific island areas rival this international plague in known consequences.

The Mongol period was finite, of course. By the 14th century, China had expelled the great Khans, and soon after Russia would do the same. With the revival of separate civilizations, some barriers to international exchange were restored.

European contacts with China, for example, were reduced for some time. Overland travel became more difficult, placing a new premium on sea routes. Nevertheless, the knowledge of new techniques, products, and trade routes could not be reversed. The international network was poised for further definition.

Although the Mongols disappeared from the world stage, they continued to hold significant territory for several centuries. A Mongol, or Tatar, khanate ruled the Crimea (now part of Ukraine) under Turkish patronage until Russian conquest in the late 18th century. Though Muslims, they tolerated their Christian subjects. Taxes were low, as the Khans raised money by selling salt and other services. Tatar Khans regularly conducted council meetings, and council approval was necessary for any decisions by the Khan. Here is a reminder that legislated traditions existed outside the West. Several older women from the harem sat with the council, for the Tatars preserved Mongol respect for women's opinion. The Crimean Khan also periodically raided Russia, once, in 1550, reaching as far as Moscow.

Bubonic Plague

As Mongol power began to loosen, Asian and European history was rocked by the rapid spread of contagious disease, the plague that would be known in Europe as the Black Death. Epidemics that crossed regions were not new in world history; they had played a major role in the late classical centuries, for example. But bubonic plague spread unusually rapidly, a sign of the acceleration of interregional contacts, including shipping, because ships bore infected rats from port to port.

The plague developed in China's Gobi desert early in the 14th century. By mid-century it reached the Middle East and North Africa, where it killed up to a quarter of the population and spurred an increase in Muslim piety. Plague hit western Europe by 1365, leading to a population reduction of more than 25 percent and stimulating heightened social protest by peasants and craftsworkers.

The impact of plague was concrete, and, indeed, recurrent epidemics affected Europe for several centuries. But, somewhat surprisingly, disease did not prevent new economic initiatives from both China and Europe. These initiatives, subsequent to the Mongol decline, developed novel frameworks for interregional trade and made clear the growing importance of sea trade, given the new political divisions that complicated the overland routes between Asia and Europe. But they did not, obviously, depend on population pressure.

CHINA AND THE WEST AS NEW WORLD POWERS

The revived Chinese empire, under its new Ming dynasty, provided the first response. The Ming dynasty marked a period of unusual stability in Chinese history, but it began with an unaccustomed display of expansionist behavior. It was as if a release from Mongol control awakened a desire to push outward—as happened later, with more durable results, in Russia. The first Ming emperor rather naturally expanded China's land boundaries by pushing the Mongols to the north. The Ming also reestablished influence over neighboring governments, as in the earlier Tang period, winning tribute from states in Korea, Vietnam, and Tibet. What was more unusual was a new policy, adopted in the early 1400s, of mounting huge, state-sponsored trading expeditions to southern Asia. A first fleet, under a Muslim Chinese admiral, Zheng He, sailed in 1405 to India, with 62 ships carrying 28,000 men. Later voyages reached the Middle East and the eastern coast of Africa, bringing chinaware and copper coins in exchange for local goods. Chinese shipping at its height consisted of 2700 coast guard vessels, 400 armed naval ships, and at least as many long-distance ships. Nine great "treasure ships" were the biggest in the world, capable of carrying a year's supply of grain and equipped with tubs to grow garden vegetables. Ships of this sort, the most sophisticated in the world at the time in their

HISTORY DEBATE

CAUSES OF GLOBAL CHANGE BY 1450

It is easy to see that world conditions were changing rapidly by the 15th century. Western Europe, although still backward in many respects, was beginning to extend its reach toward new power—a long process that lasted into the 19th century. What were the key causes of such global change? Here is where the debate lies.

Several explanations focus on various features of Europe. Christianity provided a missionary spirit. Feudal wars accustomed Europeans to fighting and schooled them in the importance of gaining an advantage over rivals. The new Renaissance, a cultural movement, gave Europeans greater confidence in the powers of individual effort and generated more interest in secular, rather than purely religious, goals (see Chapter 16).

These explanations may be supplemented by focusing on the traditionalism of societies outside Europe. Carlo Cipolla, writing about European expansion, notes that the Chinese, for example, simply refused to follow Europe's technological gains, because innovation would threaten the established social structure, with scholar-gentry on top, and anticommercial Confucian values. Again, Europe can be seen as unique.

A different argument focuses on changes in world conditions that almost accidentally gave western Europe an advantage. The Mongol era provided western Europe with a chance to imitate Chinese technology without actually experiencing invasion (an obvious contrast with eastern Europe or even the Middle East). After the Mongol era, new barriers to overland international trade shifted attention to ocean routes—another boon for western Europe. Europe was motivated to seek change not necessarily because of a distinctive culture, but rather because of certain acute economic liabilities. It simply did not have the goods to exchange for the spices and other Asian products it had come to cherish, so it needed to find sources of gold. It also feared dependence on Muslim merchants, particularly as Ottoman power showed a revival of Muslim political strength, so it looked for alternative sea routes. According to this worldview, changing world forces, not special European qualities or strange Asian blind spots, were the primary reason for increasing European power.

Which historical approach seems most plausible? Are there ways to combine them?

size and provisions and also in the improved compasses they used for navigation, explored not only the Indian Ocean but also the Persian Gulf and Red Sea, establishing regular trade with all parts of southern Asia and the Middle East.

Historians have debated the reasons for the expeditions. There was no desire to conquer, though Chinese forces engaged in some battles in southeast Asia. Trade was probably an indirect motive. What the Chinese emperors probably intended was an expanded system of tribute, as already occurred with neighboring states such as Vietnam and Japan. Certainly many of the gifts brought back, for example giraffes from Africa (which created a sensation), intrigued the Chinese

elite. The expeditions also built on the trade patterns that the earlier Song dynasty had established.

There is no question that, had the Chinese thrust continued, the course of world history would have been immeasurably altered, for the tiny European expeditions that began to venture down the western coast of Africa at about the same time would have been no match for China's combination of merchant and military organization. But the emperors called the expeditions to a halt in 1433. The costs seemed unacceptable, given the continuing expenses of the campaigns against the Mongols and the desire to build a luxurious new capital city in Beijing. The government was rebuilding the Great Wall, at huge expense. Confucian suspicion concerning merchants surfaced as well. This decision left the door open for a new west European surge, which began to take clear shape by the mid-15th century.

West Europeans had several bases for this unprecedented advance, despite their backwardness during the postclassical period. They had merchant skills and a vigorous iron industry. They had a missionary Christian religion, an active military tradition, and a host of internal rivalries that could propel traders and kings alike to seek advantageous gains by successful ventures abroad. They also had some problems. They feared the new Turkish Empire. Their upper classes had a taste for Asian luxuries and spices that the European economy could not easily afford. During the postclassical period, this trade lay largely in Muslim hands, with Europeans transporting the goods only in the Mediterranean. Now it seemed desirable to find more direct access, without the Muslim intermediary. Europe's economy, furthermore, generated few goods that Asians wanted. They supplied some tin, wool, and salt, but the balance had to be paid for in gold. Europe had no real gold supply; this was another reason to push into new territories, in the hope of finding rich holdings. Finally, Europeans by the 15th century were able to assimilate some of the technologies that had passed their way thanks to the Mongol empire and even to improve on them. They had cannons and gunpowder; they possessed the compass; they were advancing in the design of sailing ships.

Initial European attempts to find routes to Asia and gold began earlier in the postclassical period. As early as 1291, an expedition from the Italian port city of Genoa sailed into the Atlantic seeking a westward route to the Indies, but the expedition was never heard from again. During the 14th century, Italian sailors reached islands in the Atlantic—the Canaries, the Madeiras, and possibly the Azores. There they established sugar plantations, importing African slaves to do the work—a sign of the system Europeans soon developed into worldwide traffic of human beings.

Spanish expeditions also ventured as far as the northwest Atlantic coast of Africa. However, such voyages were limited by the small, oar-propelled ships used in Mediterranean trade, for they could not press far into the oceans. During the 15th century, however, round-hulled ships were developed for the Atlantic, and the Europeans also began to use a compass for navigation—an instrument that they copied from the Arabs, who in turn had learned of it from the Chinese. Map-making and other navigational devices improved as well. Western Europe was ready for its big push.

THE END OF TRANSITION: POSTCLASSICAL TO EARLY MODERN

By 1450, the world had changed in many ways from just three centuries before. The Arabs, who had provided the first global civilization, were in partial eclipse. Major empires in the Americas were tottering. The reverberations of Mongol conquests continued, particularly in central Asia, Russia, and India, although the Mongols themselves were in retreat. New players in the game of international influence were beginning to emerge. The powerful influence of world religions continued, but this theme was no longer center stage. The clearest constant, aside from regional continuities in China and elsewhere, was the importance of international contacts. The greatest contribution of the postclassical period to world history was the creation of a regular international network affecting most of Asia, Africa, and Europe. The definition of the network changed, as Arabs yielded to Mongols and Mongols to Chinese as effective chief administrators of the network. However, its importance steadily intensified. What was about to happen, after the postclassical period closed, was a reformulation of the network, which broadened to include the entire world for the first time in history.

The Mongol period generated different effects in various parts of the world network. Even direct Mongol control, for example, affected Russia differently from China. Japan, spared invasion, gained in self-confidence in relation to the rest of the world. Mongol incursions added to instability in the Middle East. Western Europe benefited from new contacts, as learning opportunities, without facing a direct threat. Sub-Saharan Africa continued its international interactions—Mongol leaders wore headdresses made from monkey skins imported from east Africa—but was not directly affected by the Mongols, in terms of new contacts or new threats. Its stability contrasted with other regions in the network. These variations had obvious impact in the next stages of international contact, after the Mongol era passed.

The Mongol conquests, and the even briefer flurry of Chinese expeditions, are anchored in the past. China's decision to end its expeditions, opening the way for other international traders, may seem more important than the ventures themselves. The modern nation of Mongolia, meanwhile, has been under Soviet Russian control since 1991. In an attempt to reclaim some of its postclassical glory, it has renewed its celebration of heroes such as Chinggis Khan, but it remains on the benches, rather than being a world player.

PATHS TO THE PRESENT

The most obvious legacy of the postclassical transition period is the world's heightened realization of the importance of interregional trade and exchange. At the end of this period, China decided to reduce its involvement in this network—though not to end it, for its role in world trade remained vital. This did not slow the pace of global commerce, however, which accelerated due to others' efforts. New European access to Asian technologies, another result of the Mongol period, helps explain Europe's increasingly active role in a world network that was about to be redefined.

SUGGESTED WEB SITES

On the Mongols in world history, see http://afe.easia.columbia.edu/mongols/ and http://www.coldsiberia.org/; for more information on Chinggis Khan and the Mongols, see http://www.fsmitha.com/h3/h11mon.htm and http://www.lacma.org/khan/index_flash.htm.

SUGGESTED READINGS

Recent work includes Lynn A. Struve, ed., *Time, Temporality, and Imperial Transition: East Asia from Ming to Qing* (2005); Gerard Chaliand, *Nomadic Empires: From Mongolia to the Danube* (2004); Jean-Paul Roux, *Genghis Khan and the Mongol Empire* (2003); Stephen Turnbull, *Genghis Khan & the Mongol Conquests, 1190–1400* (2004); Paul D. Buell, *Historical Dictionary of the Mongol World Empire* (2003); Sarah Schneewind, *Community Schools and the State in Ming China* (2006); Frances Wood, *The Silk Road: Two Thousand Years in the Heart of Asia* (2002); Peter C. Perdue, *China Marches West: The Qing Conquest of Central Eurasia* (2005); Jack Weatherford, *Genghis Khan and the Making of the Modern World* (2004); David Wang Der-wei and Shang Wei, eds., *Dynastic Crisis and Cultural Innovation: From the Late Ming to the Late Qing and Beyond* (2005); Thomas Allsen, *Culture and Conquest in Mongol Eurasia* (2001); Linda Komaroff, *The Legacy of Genghis Khan: Courtly Art and Culture in Western Asia* (2002); Bat-Orchid Bold, *Mongol Nomadic Society: A Reconstruction of the Medieval History of Mongolia* (2001); and Uradyn E. Bulag, *Mongols at China's Edge: History and the Politics of National Unity* (2002).

The fullest and most accessible summary of the links between Mongol expansion and the spread of the Black Death can be found in William H. McNeill's *Plagues and Peoples* (1976). On international contacts, see Jerry H. Bentley, *Old World Encounters: Cross-Cultural Contacts and Exchanges in Pre-Modern Times* (1993), and J. L. Abu-Lughod, *Before European Hegemony: The World System A.D. 1250–1350* (1989). Also see Frances Wood, *Did Marco Polo Go to China?* (1996).

The Postclassical Period, 500–1450 C.E.

CONTACTS AND IDENTITIES

The growing importance of interregional contacts raised vital issues of regional identity during the postclassical period. More and more societies modified their previously separate patterns of development through mutual influence and even outright imitation. The postclassical period was a crucial turning point in the balance between localized and global perspectives.

Not all contacts had huge impacts on identity, of course. Europe's growing taste for Asian spices, for example, was fairly neutral in terms of its affect on European identity—though it did signal a softening of the military aristocracy in favor of greater consumerism.

But the new level of tension among world societies at the end of this period was real and measurable. The spread of the world religions shifted identities in favor of outside influences. While great ethnic and linguistic diversity persisted in the Middle East and North Africa, more and more people in these regions modified their identities not only to become Muslim, but also to become assimilated into an Arab identity. Of course, distinctions persisted even amid religious conversions. Persians became Muslim in the main, and Zoroastrianism faded, but they maintained a separate language and a more representational artistic tradition despite Muslim precepts. Similarly, Arab travelers to west Africa noted how the local elites had become truly pious Muslims while also, however, retaining local customs concerning the dress and behavior of women. Even today, Muslims in some of the mountainous regions of central Asia continue to combine Islam with the worship of nature spirits. Scandinavians converted to Christianity but also retained traditions such as burning large pine trees during summer solstice ceremonies to honor the sun and keep it in the heavens. All of these were compromises that allowed citizens of a given region to retain a sense of local identity amid growing cultural convergence.

Explicit efforts at imitation obviously challenged identity. In the 7th century, many Japanese leaders wanted Japan to become as Chinese as possible. This goal misfired, as we have seen in previous chapters: even as the Japanese became more like the Chinese, the Japanese identity persisted, especially in high culture and in politics. This convergence, however, involved a different and more subtle balance of cultures than the ones mentioned above.

Identity issues also showed clearly in Europeans' love-hate relationship with the Middle East. Middle Eastern goods and ideas were greatly valued by Europeans, and they deliberately and extensively borrowed these entities from Arab culture. But Christians' hostility to Islam as a false religion maintained clearly separate identities between Europeans and Arabs. Many Europeans, in fact, downplayed the extent of their imitation of the Middle East in favor of claiming an assertive Christianity.

The tension between identity and interaction became steadily more complex during the postclassical period. One result was an unpredictable intersection between abrupt insistence on identity and considerable intercultural tolerance. China's Tang dynasty thus moved from acceptance of Buddhism to an assertion of a separate Chinese identity against Buddhist influence. Christians and Muslims interacted creatively and peacefully in Muslim Spain, but the Christian crusading spirit, which included "reconquering" Spain, defined Christian identity as being quite different from that of Muslims.

Credits

Chapter 1
2: Douglas Mazonowicz/Art Resource, NY; 3: Des and Jen Bartlett/Bruce Coleman; 9: Museo Prehistorico, Florence/Art Resource, NY; 16: Robert Harding Picture Library

Chapter 2
22 (left): Courtesy Phoebe Apperson Hearst Museum of Anthropology and Research, University of California, Berkeley; 22 (right): Werner Forman/Art Resource, NY; 23: Iraq Museum, Baghdad, Iraq/Scala/Art Resource, NY; 25: Neema Frederic/Corbis Sygma; 26: Erich Lessing/Art Resource, NY; 27: Borromeo/Art Resource, NY; 30: Musee Cernuschi, Musee des Arts de l'Asie de la Ville de Paris; 34: Kunsthistorisches Museum, Vienna, Austria/Erich Lessing/Art Resource, NY

Chapter 3
38: F. A. O. Photos/United Nations; 40: Bibliotheque Nationale, Paris; 41: Bibliotheque Nationale, Paris

Chapter 4
56: Nancy McKenna/Photo Researchers, Inc.; 62: The Granger Collection, NY; 65: Freer Gallery of Art, Smithsonian Institution, Washington, D. C., Early Chinese Art, 15.103; 66: AP/Wide World Photos; 68: Courtesy of the Trustees of the British Museum; 69: Wango-Weng Archives

Chapter 5
78: Borromeo/Art Resource, NY; 83: Punjab Government Museum, Simla/Werner Forman/Art Resource, NY; 85: The British Museum; 87: Cleveland Museum of Art. Purchase from the J. H. Wade Fund, 30.331

Chapter 6
95: Giraudon/Art Resource, NY; 102: Alinari/Art Resource, NY; 104: National Archaeological Museum, Athens, Greece/Borromeo/Art Resource, NY; 106: Giraudon/Art Resource, NY; 107: AP/Wide World Photos; 108: Scala/Art Resource, NY

Chapter 7
123: Alinari/Art Resource, NY; 129: The Granger Collection, NY; 132: Basilica San Giusto, Trieste/Dagli Orti/The Art Archive; 133: Alinari/Art Resource, NY

Chapter 8
150: Spencer Collection, New York Pubic Library; 158: Sandro Vannini/Corbis; 159: Kazuyoshi Nomachi/Corbis; 161: Freer Gallery of Art, Smithsonian Institution, Washington, D. C. 30.60; 162: Bettmann/Corbis

Chapter 9
173: Ric Ergenbright Photography; 175: Indian Museum, Calcutta; 178: Corbis

Chapter 10
183: The Granger Collection NY; 186: Peter Adams/Zefa/Corbis; 187: Fogg Art Museum, Harvard University

Chapter 11
194: Erich Lessing/Art Resource, NY; 197: The Granger Collection, NY; 198: Robert Frerck/Odyssey; 199: Archivo Iconografico, S. A./Corbis; 203: Adam Woolfitt/Corbis

Chapter 12
216: The Granger Collection, NY; 217: Jochen Helle/Bildarchiv Monheim Fotofinder/IPN; 219: Giraudon/Art Resource, NY

Chapter 13
229: National Palace Museum, Taipei; 231: Metropolitan Museum of Art, New York. Gift of John M. Crawford Jr., in honor of Douglas Dillon, 1981. 1981.276; 234: Freer Gallery of Art, Smithsonian Institution, Washington, D. C. 1935.10; 236: Werner Forman Archive/Peking Palace Museum/Art Resource, NY; 239: Courtesy Museum of Fine Arts, Boston/Fenollosa-Weld Collection (41.33699.7); 242: Kawanbe Kyosai Memorial Museum, Japan

Chapter 14
249: Peter Menzel Photography; 252: National Museum of Anthropology, Mexico City/Lee Boltin/The Bridgeman Art Library

Chapter 15
261: The Granger Collection, NY

Index